"DEEP PLAY"—
JOHN GAY
AND
THE INVENTION OF MODERNITY

Fig. 1. "A New Deceptio Visûs," engraving by George Bickham after William Aikman (1729). Courtesy of the National Portrait Gallery, London.

"DEEP PLAY"— JOHN GAY AND THE INVENTION OF MODERNITY

Dianne Dugaw

DELAWARE

Newark: University of Delaware Press
London: Associated University Presses

Associated University Presses
440 Forsgate Drive
Cranbury, NJ 08512

Associated University Presses
16 Barter Street
London WC1A 2AH, England

Associated University Presses
P.O. Box 338, Port Credit
Mississauga, Ontario
Canada L5G 4L8

The paper used in this publication meets the requirements of the American National Standard for Permanence of Paper for Printed Library Materials Z39.48-1984.

Library of Congress Cataloging-in-Publication Data

Dugaw, Dianne.
    Deep Play—John Gay and the invention of modernity / Dianne Dugaw.
        p.   cm.
    Includes bibliographical references and index.
    ISBN 0-87413-731-4 (alk. paper)
    1. Gay, John, 1685–1732—Criticism and interpretation. 2. Modernism (Literature)—England—History—18th century. 3. Literature and society—England—History—18th century. 4. Satire, English—History and criticism. I. Title.

PR3474 .D84   2001
821'.5—dc21   00-031518

For Amanda

"Love is by long enjoying."
—John Gay

Contents

Illustrations

Musical Examples

Dance Diagrams

Acknowledgments

It is with great pleasure and appreciation that I acknowledge those whose support has made this book possible. I thank the libraries and archives from whose collections I have gleaned this story: the Huntington and William Andrews Clark Libraries in Los Angeles; the Houghton and Widener Libraries at Harvard University; the Bodleian Library at Oxford University; the National Portrait Gallery, and the British Museum and British Library in London.

Generous research grants supported my work. A Mellon Faculty Fellowship at Harvard enabled me to begin this project. I am grateful to the National Endowment for the Humanities for a Summer Research Fellowship, to the Huntington Library for a Research Fellowship, and especially to the William Andrews Clark Memorial Library and UCLA Center for Seventeenth- and Eighteenth-century Studies, which sponsored my research at the beginning and my writing at the final stage. I am indebted especially to the knowledgeable archivists who made available to me countless boxes, books, and broadsides and contributed to my thinking about them. At the University of Oregon, research funding was provided by the Oregon Humanities Center, the Office of Research and Faculty Development, and the Center for the Study of Women in Society, especially the Feminist Humanities Project. Without such assistance to my research and writing, this book would not have been possible.

Many individuals have contributed to this project. To Morris Brownell, Doug Canfield, Margaret Doody, Max Novak, Calhoun Winton, Yvonne Noble, and especially Ruth Perry, I owe many thanks for scholarly help and guidance over the years. This book, I hope, reflects something of what I have learned from their impeccable scholarship and kind support. Friends and colleagues who will recognize their much appreciated insights and contributions in my notes and text include Lowell Bowditch, Ian Duncan, Michael Heaney, Roy Palmer, and Neil Rosenberg. The performance of Galatea's arias with my sister Anne Dugaw prompted my first analysis of

Acis and Galatea. My thanks to those people whose reading of all or part of the manuscript shaped its course, especially Henry Alley and Jayne Lewis, whose insight, expertise, and heartening were invaluable to my writing and thinking. Christine Retz and her staff at Associated University Presses have helped me to make a book of a complicated and multifaceted manuscript. Leslie Sullivan aided with the graphic design. Dorothy Attneave's expertise and collaboration have been indispensable to the presentation of the dances. My special thanks to her and to numerous students, colleagues, friends, and unsuspecting conference audiences who gamely tried out with me the dances and catches. Through the kind patronage of Ken Allan the manuscript for *"Deep Play"* was finished in a hospitable orange and brown caravan high on the Yorkshire moors. From my dear friend and long-standing mentor Geneva Phillips I have received many years of editorial consultation, generous hospitality, and loving encouragement. My parents, Bill and Donna Dugaw, have offered ongoing support; I especially appreciate the music and thinking, books and animals, that they made part of our lives from the beginning. Mary T. Whitney gave years of tutelage as she helped me show up day by day and not take it all too seriously. And finally to my beloved Amanda Powell I owe my deepest thanks. Without her loving support, astute editing, and always welcome participation in every phase of my thinking and writing, *"Deep Play"* would be a much diminished book. To all of you, I extend my heartfelt gratitude.

"DEEP PLAY"—
JOHN GAY
AND
THE INVENTION OF MODERNITY

Prologue

> *Macheath.* There will be deep play tonight at Marybone, and conse-
> quently money may be picked up upon the road. Meet me there,
> and I'll give you the hint who is worth setting.
>> —*The Beggar's Opera*

As *The Beggar's Opera* (1728) reaches a dramatic turning point, the swash-buckling highwayman Macheath apprises his gang of the opportunity afforded by "deep play" (i.e., high-stakes gambling) "tonight at Mary[le]bone." This scene of gamblers—their money changing hands in a flurry of play, their assets turning to cash at the tables of moneylenders nearby, and the booty both of players and of lenders subject to forays on the highway by the likes of Macheath—gathers individuals into a mercurial interplay of anticipation, negotiation, risk, self-interested exchange, and transmutations of value. An image of transformative private interaction, Macheath's "deep play" captures the dynamic at the heart of the new capitalist order of markets, money, and trade on which *The Beggar's Opera* fixes our attention. It suggests as well the varied "depths," from high to low, of that order, whose popular forms from different social levels mirror and mock each other throughout this ragtag opera.

In current parlance, the term "deep play" resonates with anthropologist Clifford Geertz's application of it—borrowed from Jeremy Bentham—to "read" the larger sociocultural meaning of cockfights that entail high-stakes gambling on the island of Bali.[1] For Geertz, the term becomes a pun, for the "play" of these fights is "deep" beyond the individual risks of the betting. They function polysemously, rendering for their human players "a cultural figure against a social ground . . . an expressive form . . . [that] provides a metasocial commentary upon the whole matter of assorting human beings into fixed hierarchical ranks" (23). As a figure to be "read," the cockfight discloses the governing structures and values of Balinese society. For Geertz it reveals as well a motivation rooted in the social, wherein individuals put themselves at risk in passionate displays that form artful,

19

metaphorical parts of a community dynamic. Such risk-taking was found by the rationalist, profit-minded Bentham (1748–1832) to be indefensibly irrational, and hence, immoral.[2] As Geertz suggests, these risks may be—and of necessity likely are—part of the system. The image of gambling for high stakes, as Gay posed it in his time and as Geertz does in ours, supplies an apt emblem for the individualized moral and political dilemmas at the center of Gay's satire, and also for its method of profound and fluid handling of the meanings and referents that contextualize this moral universe.

"*Deep Play*" explores the correspondence of forms of culture with a market-driven, class-shuffling society. The satires of John Gay both use and reveal an emerging fixation on cultural markers of social rank. In order to study these satires and their vivid place in eighteenth-century arts, this book examines a range of popular forms—ballads and songs, country dances, catches, mumming plays, beliefs and sayings, fables, stories, and legends—especially as these plebeian materials are brought by Gay to comment on "polite" opera, drama, and literature. Such works as *The Beggar's Opera*, *The Shepherd's Week*, and *Achilles* employ complex strategies of allusion and parody that are best understood in and illuminate this context of "under-" and "upper-" class expression. Here Gay created moments of "deep play" to be read, in the Geertzian fashion, for what they disclose of the moral and aesthetic workings of a world in which people of the middle and lower sort voice the tensions of this historical moment of social shuffling.

Early-eighteenth-century satires by various authors include songs, images, stories, dances, and sayings from identifiable social registers. Gay stands out foɾ the ways he fashions materials identified with one social level so as ironically to mirror those from another, posing satiric readings from these juxtaposed similarities and differences. In this interplay, we can trace the emerging cultural and class politics of a "modern" world-in-the-making. Indeed, Gay's works themselves take a role in the subsequent formulation of the terms "culture" and "class."

Gay's satires, which remained popular for generations across social levels, display rank as corresponding to modes of what we have come to call cultural expression. Further, Gay positions the poet as a self-aware, self-implicating onlooker in an ethnographer-like relation to what he observes and represents. The "Beggar" of *The Beggar's Opera*, the "Bowzybean" poet of *The Shepherd's Week*, the wry glossaries and footnotes of *The Shepherd's Week*, *The What-d'Ye-Call-It*, and *Trivia*—each authorial framing comes with a facetious apparatus that reminds us of the onlooking creator. Gay's works reveal today, as they did for the eighteenth and early nineteenth centuries, an important early phase in the shift to a complex understanding of "culture" as the outlook and way of life of a group, manifested through customary arts, behaviors, expression, and beliefs.[3] He identified shared means by which individuals from varied contexts—ranks or locales—voice their points of view in relation to and distinction from those of others.

Hierarchical differences of social status were hardly new in the 1700s, nor was the interdependency of people of differing ranks. At the same time, social "class" in the modern, industrial-era sense did not exist in Georgian England.[4] Yet Gay's burlesque renderings presage a modern conception of class. He shows aristocratic, bourgeois, and subaltern individuals against backdrops conspicuous in their attention to social demarcation. Rendered as matters of cultural expression, these images delineate a dialectics of social rank in the post-Enlightenment modern world. The mirroring oppositions in Gay's works—indeed, the opposition intrinsic to burlesque as a strategy—pose the dialectical premises by which social class has subsequently been understood in the Marxist tradition.

It is not that Gay's works show us "real life" for eighteenth-century highwaymen or prime ministers. Rather, a modern understanding of social class emerged in no small part from the images and lessons engendered by Gay's satirical burlesques, which drew to the attention of generations of audiences the conflicts and predation among socially differentiated individuals in the not-so-brave new world of Hanoverian Britain. This rapidly capitalizing society of shifting and decentralizing institutions was premised on principles that required a notably relational and socially attuned morality. Gay's work supplies a lens onto this popular realm that helps us perceive the ingredients, articulation, and historical formation that such analysts as E. P. Thompson sought for the emergence of class "identity."[5]

Gay's satire also opens to view a nascent conception of "culture" in the burgeoning eighteenth-century commerce in popular arts and pastimes. In Gay we see the simultaneous processes of cultural construction and cultural critique, with a level of (self-) consciousness unsurpassed even in our own day. His exposure of the artifice of expression pinpoints how "culture" as a concept emerges from a class-stratifying context. As part of his anatomizing of a sociopolitical world becoming unhinged from earlier traditional institutions, Gay recognized in expressive forms and customary behaviors the overlooked artistry of the "low" as well as the customariness of the "high." As he saw, what we call "cultural forms" came to express and mark stratifying categories in a socioeconomic system of striving individuals. These forms include not only what is now designated as class identity, but also race, gender, and sexual orientation. The generations immediately after Gay took up as industries both the production of popular forms as well as their study.

Despite an all-too-explicable neglect by critics and historians, John Gay is a major writer of Augustan England. Recent works of scholarship, especially a full-length study by Calhoun Winton, a collection of essays edited by Peter Lewis and Nigel Wood, and a new biography by David Nokes, acknowledge Gay's significance and offer insightful analysis.[6] Tremendously influential in his own time, Gay's works continued to sell throughout the eighteenth century to readers and theatergoers at every social level. *The Beggar's Opera*, his ballad opera invention of 1728, was continuously staged in the English-speaking world over the next century and remains a frequently produced play. From its opening, this satire spawned nearly two hundred offspring within a few years and can be considered the progenitor of modern musical comedy. A cavalcade of imitations entertained audiences at Lincoln's Inn Fields, Covent Garden, the Haymarket, and other theaters. Gay's farcical *What-d'Ye-Call-It* of 1715 was one of the era's most popular afterpieces, staged regularly from 1715 until the end of the eighteenth century. *The Shepherd's Week*, a comical collection of Theocritan pastorals, was issued in more than a dozen editions by the 1760s and served as a model for the new vogue for "realistic" pastoral writing. Gay's *Fables* appeared and reappeared in a staggering number of versions. Perhaps the most widely printed text of the century, the *Fables* circulated at all social levels well into the Victorian era. Given the popularity and pertinence of his works, it is remarkable that Gay's writing has been studied in depth by so few scholars of literature and culture.

Gay's satire also looms large as a shaping force for modern and postmodern theater. In *The Beggar's Opera* and its sequel *Polly*, Gay critiqued the moral and political dynamics of an emerging world order driven by acquisition and expansion of capital. While full of specific reference to public policy and personalities of his time, his reading of individuals propelled by profit in a society organized around the possession and exchange of property avails to our present day. The play mapped for his own generation and the following three centuries what is at play and at stake in the jostling worldview, material systems, and social and institutional relations that make up the modern nation state. *The Beggar's Opera* has exerted an eye-opening influence on the sensibility of key modern authors. Still revived as a period piece, it has also been retranslated at pivotal political moments in the twentieth century: by Bertolt Brecht in the looming shadow of Nazi Germany, by Václav Havel at the height of Soviet domination of eastern Europe, and by Alan Ayckbourn in Margaret Thatcher's privatizing Britain of the 1980s. Eighteenth-century England was a watershed moment and place. Gay's satire offers a durable look at the governing principles, the predilections, and the sociocultural underpinnings of the European and North American empires of the past four centuries.

Popular materials gave Gay's satires meaning in a broad social context and ensured them enduring favor for generations. For us, these materials supply a necessary key to Gay's work. His burlesque method sets out that notion of people's felt experience which, for E. P. Thompson and other historians and critics, culminates in social consciousness and class identity.[7] However, as Joan Scott has noted of Thompson:

> Class is finally an identity rooted in structural relations that preexist politics. What this obscures is the contradictory and contested process by which class itself was conceptualized and by which diverse kinds of subject positions were assigned, felt, contested, and embraced. As a result, Thompson's brilliant history of the English working class, which set out to historicize the category of class, ends up essentializing it.[8]

The satiric handling of social hierarchies and cultural materials in Gay's works—cognizant as these works are of a metaphorical "deep play" (in Geertz's sense) among representational forms—gives us a way of historicizing the category of class.

Gay reassigns subject positions in parodic and exposing ways that precisely inscribe literary modes of expression in terms of relational power. When England was forging the first modern, capitalist nation-state and empire, Gay's poems, plays, and songs supplied markers for those social registers of expression that would make categories of social class culturally identifiable and identifying. The parodic method, the highlighted "deep play" in these satires hinges on that literary relativizing of history that, for Gayatri Spivak, "make[s] visible the assignment of subject positions."[9] Gay's commoners speak not as characters in the subplots to the "high" plot, but as protagonists of *the* central plot.

The mixing of plebeian, bourgeois, and aristocratic traditions in Gay's works is pivotal to their success: audiences see the laughable yet sympathetic familiarity of their ordinary, sociocultural selves. Even three centuries later, Gay's works spring into a revealing dimensionality when we bring to bear on them the popular realm of creative arts, customs, beliefs, and behaviors that they incorporate and to which they refer. Against a backdrop of culture and custom, Gay delineated the dynamics of social difference and, with particular emphasis on gender, the introspective politics of social and personal relations that characterize the modern sensibility. Gay's literary landscape is not ours. At the same time, his burlesques signal a break with the literature of the past and probe new subjects and subject positions.

An ongoing ambivalence, or, in most cases, polyvalence, characterizes Gay's vision. This viewing and voicing of contraries is a "double capacity," to quote from *The Beggar's Opera* (I.i.10)—being "both against rogues and for 'em." Gay's satire itself cherishes even as it ridicules. This ambivalence results from a strategy of reversal which in its parodic relocation of point of view shifts the identification of the audience. In empathizing with the usually overlooked and objectified victim in a power relationship, we recognize innocence and suffering and feel sympathy, while taking risible pleasure in the burlesque wit of the formal topsy-turviness. Gay is always at pains to lever our sympathy for his parodically relocated subjects and to direct our ridicule to deeper and larger targets. Pity joins with laughter in a delicately balanced, unresolving, and paradoxical tension of sentiments. Amidst this ambivalence, Gay reaches beyond the ridiculing of characters within his works, not only to satirize literary and political targets of the time, but to interrogate as well deep structures of power and thought. Time and again he exposes bullies and people with real or imagined power who want to "have it both ways" and assert their innocence while operating with guile. At the same time, he exposes the artifice and figuration of our cultural meanings, reminding us that we think through language which is itself symbolic. This "deep play" puts at humorous yet solemn stake, as it were, serious matters of justice and rule in the figurative play of textual surfaces and references.

How can we "get at" a satire that is by turns evasively glancing and evocatively encompassing? Gay bids us attend to the parodic configurings and reconfigurings of cultural materials that structure his ballad operas and other satiric works. Like the simultaneous cross-referencing of computer hypertext, Gay's "deep play" rereads a line or image by evoking refractory, often subversive allusions that reframe the figure's initial orientation— moral, social, conceptual. This move of allusive, parodic imitation has yet to be fully explored as a web of analogy that renders one situation by means of another. Naïveté and innocence exist vis-à-vis cunning and knowledge; people of differing ranks relationally define each other in counterpoint; the postures of an individual in the private sphere implicate and expose matters in public. Unmooring analogy and moral critique from fixed and stable systems, such a dynamic and unstinting relativity as Gay's remains a notably contemporary outlook.

This analogic and imitative process typically renders parody as Linda Hutcheon has analyzed it with regard to postmodern art, that is, as resemblance and difference working together, creating laughably ironic underminings and contradictions that apply in several directions and levels at once.[10] Also helpful for understanding the intricately allusive Gay is the rhetorical trope of metalepsis or transumption, defined by John Hollander and Angus Fletcher as "a moment or turn of revisionary, reinterpretive allusiveness," used in both poetic and narrative works.[11] Gay structures his texts with references that contextualize and reinterpret the "present here" of the poem or play in a matrix of allusion to decisions, articulations, events, and accidents of past times, other places, and other textual and social spheres.

Such analogies create correspondences that, for a knowing audience, call the elements of comparison to mind, yet make a one-to-one or reductively determinate identification impossible, because of the interjection of difference—for example, the variant of social class in burlesque, or gender in the parody of cross-dressing, or species difference in an animal fable.

Gay highlights the artifice and constructedness of utterance and image. His self-awareness inevitably has a social dimension as it takes up issues of power and justice revealed in the intertextual genealogies of association and parody. The result: a critical and moral repositioning of ourselves. This "deep play," however laughable or ironic, diagnoses power in a political way and recommends justice in an ethical mode. Actions and relationships evoke by analogy other actions and relationships. As allusions accrue, a play of meanings alerts a cognizant audience to the moral risks and perplexities confronting characters caught in situations that function as analogy and history. The politics of these resonant situations thus becomes familiar and decipherable in ways that are closed off by such determinate tropes as metaphor and metonymy. As allusions, they pose more individualized and questioning representations than the more rational mode of allegory.

Gay's satires interrogate injustice, exploitation, conflict, and value in burlesques set up to expose the dynamic between those wielding power and taking action, and those deprived of power and acted upon. In other words, they articulate the *politics* of relational individualism that stands at the core of the capitalist modern world, particularly as expression itself always remains inscribed within this politics. With our new-millennial sensibility of reflexivity, indeterminacy, and virtual spaces, we can appreciate Gay's art perhaps more than any audience since his time; we too inhabit a world of (sometimes alarmingly) contingent, rather than absolute, forms and values.

Gay's attention to and further popularizing of widely known materials set the stage for the intellectual delineation of a socially and ethnographically determined and determining category called "culture." In this, he certainly forecasts the modern world and retains appeal for the postmodern. The identification of Gay with the middle and lower rungs of the social ladder ensured his practical influence, relevance, and popularity in his own century. Conversely, it contributes to the theoretical neglect of his work by critics since that time, trained to study a belles lettres defined as apposite to this popular realm.[12] Ironically, in identifying correspondent modes of art and culture across social ranks, Gay's satire itself contributed the terms for this distinction.

Part I of *"Deep Play"* outlines the book's material and methodological points of departure, examining Gay's importance and history together with the matrix of popular forms that is both revealed by his work and gives it meaning. Chapter 1 looks at "translations" of *The Beggar's Opera* by Brecht, Havel, and Ayckbourn as these underscore preoccupations of the modern and postmodern world traceable to and made visible by Gay's ballad operas. Chapter 2 examines Gay's reputation historiographically, showing that a current of depreciation through the Victorian age can be linked to a literary politics of class, gender, and sexuality. Chapter 3 examines Gay's use of and relation to oral and written popular culture. Chapter 4 analyzes Gay's treatment of Virgilian tradition in mock pastorals, uncovering strategies of parody and metalepsis at the heart of his satirical "deep play."

Part II looks more closely at the popular materials—songs, dances, customs, fables—that appear in particular works, with emphasis on the social formations of culture, class, gender, sexuality, and nature. Chapter 5, "Village Mumming on an Urban Stage" takes up the social and aesthetic politics of folk mumming plays and Gay's use of them to articulate this politics and demarcate parameters of a kind of class identification in the dynamics of burlesque oppositions. Chapter 6 analyzes the music and text of Gay and Handel's operatic *Acis and Galatea* to show its articulation of social identification through cultural reference on the one hand, and on the other, an articulation in Galatea of the individual interiority of the modern sensibility. Chapter 7 examines the use of popular songs in the ballad operas, revealing the intersections of political and economic power, social level, gender, and race. Chapter 8 takes up popular dance forms as they marked different social spheres and supplied Gay with analogues from the culture of private life for the dynamics and expansionist culture of the public sphere. Chapter 9 shows how Gay's use of popular diversions—the pastimes of the bourgeois family—presages "camp" ironies, revealing not only new identifications of social place and structure, but the categorization of sexual desire into personal identity based on hetero- or homoeroticism. Chapter 10 looks at Gay's animal fables as they mediate the social and cultural realms of localized, interpersonal relations, positing at once a satire of an acquisitive world of appetite and a morality of individual application. Tracing the popularity of the fables through the eighteenth century, this chapter analyzes Gay's message and significance by means of illustrations of the fables by Thomas Bewick and William Blake.

Gay made use of his mercantile upbringing in the west of England, especially in his late works, to expose and undercut the ironies of the new political and social order of bourgeois capitalism which locates value in ownership, markets, and profit.[13] His preoccupation with these themes is true to his era, as development of them in George Lillo's *The London Merchant* (1731) or the novels of Daniel Defoe attests. Nonetheless, Gay's vibrant netting of the materials of his time from every level and his presentation of the politics of culture and the cultures of politics was, and remains, new. Gay identified human beings—at all levels—as culture-bearing creatures. "Culture" becomes in his satires a category of expression, behavior, and belief identifying who we are and where we come from.

In revealing cultural mirroring, however ironic, Gay poses the modern position: we are humans; we are equals. This message was powerful in its time, as the ongoing popularity of his works with eighteenth-century readers and audiences, especially at the lower ranks, attests. Gay's genre-confounding satire is markedly modern in representing us to ourselves as individuals derived from social and cultural matrices. Paradoxically and ironically we are connected to each other, for better and worse, simultaneously comic, satiric, pathetic—and noticeably *not* heroic: we live neither tragedy, romance, nor epic. It is my hope that *"Deep Play"—John Gay and the Invention of Modernity* will speak to a wide range of readers who are interested in the vibrant culture and history of the early modern era, particularly as that era and Gay's sense of it supply the intellectual, artistic, and sociopolitical grounding for our own.

Part I
Metaleptic Methods

1

The Beggar's Opera in the Twentieth Century: Brecht, Havel, and Ayckbourn Rewrite Macheath

Notable twentieth-century authors have reworked *The Beggar's Opera*, Gay's acknowledged masterpiece, at three pivotal moments of modern European history. These strategically situated modern and postmodern writers found in Gay's critique of incipient modernity a resonant subtext against which to update elements of a familiar plot and engaging characters. For their own satiric readings, *The Beggar's Opera* provided both the general outline and specific ingredients for critiquing the particular recipe for poverty and corruption offered by recent history. These revisionary "translations" bring to the fore what was so new and so lasting in 1728: Gay's recognition of the changed dynamics of corrosive abuse in the new collusion between a determining economic order of trade and consumption and the forces of social control. More than any other early modern writer, Gay interrogated the essential dynamics of the world still in place in ways so pointedly and, perhaps, unsettlingly applicable that they seem to be over-. looked except in their redeployment by like-minded satirists.[1]

In 1928, Bertolt Brecht and Kurt Weill brought *Die Dreigroschenoper* (The threepenny opera) to a Berlin about to succumb to the seductions of Nazi control. In the 1970s, Václav Havel's *Žebrácká Opera* (The beggar's opera) reimagined Gay's play in Gustáv Husák's repressive Czechoslovakia after the brief popular uprising and subsequent Soviet invasion of 1968. In 1984, Alan Ayckbourn's *A Chorus of Disapproval* resituated *The Beggar's Opera* in Margaret Thatcher's Tory England, amidst the 1980s rush of privatizing and globalization that signaled the onset of the postmodern capitalist era. All three plays explore, reconfigure, and expand on the moral terrain that *The Beggar's Opera* had already mapped: an internalized self-awareness in a demythologized world of increasingly secular and bureaucratic cast. Evil in this context becomes the individual locus and reach of a predatory appetite that prompts corrupting alliances, deceptions, and cruelties that in turn victimize others. Good, for its part, is the small heroism of a generous survival: an honest laugh, fleeting beauty, freedom from the systematic predation and personal deception that govern at all levels. Certainly neither predation nor deception were new problems for Gay's generation. Prescient, however, was his fingering of these as key to the moral dilemmas of people who live amidst the web of institutions—governments, schools, armies and navies, banks, insurance companies, unions of workers, corporations of owners, certifying agencies, and so on—that structure post-Enlightenment societies.

Havel and Ayckbourn take up especially that "double-capacity" in *The Beggar's Opera* that Ian Donaldson so aptly applies to the drama itself. I would extend the phrase to the ironic sensibility of the modern onlooker that Gay's satire identifies more generally.[2] In the opening remarks of *The Beggar's Opera*, the criminal organizer Peachum, who operates simultaneously outside the law and within it, identifies this "act[ing] in a double capacity, both against rogues and for 'em." As he says, " 'Tis fitting that we should protect and encourage cheats, since we live by them" (I.i.9–12). This flexible appreciation at the heart of *The Beggar's Opera* stands as well at the heart of its postmodern reincarnations from both sides of the Cold War divide. In each, centralized power renders darkly ironic the heroic pretensions to glory and love of increasingly powerless Macheaths and Pollys, whose pathetically limited deceits and failures, like our own, we simultaneously lament and appreciate. The mock-heroic was nothing new in 1728. What was new was to render its diminishments in a universal aesthetic that at one and the same time humanized the lower orders even as it outlined the mutually obliging networks of a predatory system that ensures suffering even as it makes heroism—which requires agency—impossible.

Gay's *Beggar's Opera* is a play intent on undermining the generic expectations of tragedy and comedy while it calls attention to itself as a new art form composed of very common and familiar elements not considered the stuff of "art." Thus, Gay poses the socially resonant opposition between "art" and "non-art" which will, with the study of the very underclass materials he cites, become the modern world's reciprocal delineations of "fine art" or "belles lettres" and "popular culture." Gay frames the plot of the drama within a structural conceit that depicts ragged street people putting on an "opera." Thus, a "beggar" author who specializes in catches and jingles presents the "opera" he has written to celebrate the marriage of "two most excellent ballad-singers." The play, as he remarks, has been "frequently represented" in St. Giles's parish—a notorious eighteenth-century slum—and is now being brought before a fancy London audience.[3] Following this introduction, the "opera" begins with the "beggar" actors bringing onto the stage rakish highwaymen, competing damsels, conniving and interfering fathers, and betraying doxies in a plot that unfolds in spoken dialogue, punctuated by songs set to the tunes of popular street ballads of the day. This playful meditation on the artifice of one "beggar's" aesthetic expression as contextualized by a shared expressive milieu exactly poses the workings of "culture" in the modern sense. At the same time, Gay situates both art and culture within a world whose satire is economically premised on an uncomfortable division between rich and poor, while aligning dramatic point of view in a new way with the latter.

The play centers on the earnest Polly Peachum and the rakish highwayman Macheath, who has won her heart and secretly married her. The plot develops two lines of complication: First, Polly's roguish parents oppose the match and, with complicated double-dealing, strive to have Macheath "peached"—that is, prosecuted—so that their daughter (and they) may profitably enjoy "the comfortable estate of widowhood" (I.x.21). "Hang your husband, and be dutiful," her mother (comically) enjoins the resistant Polly. Then, as the Peachums betray and Polly protects her "Captain," his own double-dealing in love comes to light: "I love the sex," he declares, "And a man who loves money might as well be contented with one guinea as I with one woman" (II.iii.2–3). Calling for a host of his familiar whores, Macheath is betrayed by Jenny Diver to the jailer Lockit. His daughter Lucy, we discover, has succumbed to the "Captain's" charms as well, for she comes—pregnant and angry—to the jail cell to confront her captured despoiler.

The play reaches a rollicking climax as the two "wives," the devoted Polly and the ruined Lucy, competitively flank the shackled and condemned Macheath to bid him farewell. Nearing its "tragic" conclusion, with Macheath poised to be hanged, the play returns to its frame. An outraged "Player" demands a reprieve, insisting that "an opera must end happily . . . to comply with the taste of the town" (III.xvi.8–15). The "Beggar" poet acquiesces: "Let the prisoner be brought back to his wives in triumph" (III.xvi.13–14). The now comic ending resolves in a dance as a final ironic comment from the "Beggar" hovers in the air, presenting the mirrorings of rich and poor that in a single complex stroke propose a satire that is at base social:

Through the whole piece you may observe such a similitude of manners in high and low life, that it is difficult to determine whether (in the fashionable

vices) the fine gentlemen imitate the gentlemen of the road, or the gentlemen of the road the fine gentlemen. Had the play remained as I at first
intended, it would have carried a most excellent moral. 'Twould have shown
that the lower sort of people have their vices in a degree as well as the rich,
and that they are punished for them.

(III.xvi.16–24)

But of course, the poor are punished with hanging and transportation, only
one of a range of discomfiting ironies Gay's reverberating moral/mock moral
contains. Twentieth-century satirists took up this glancing, mercurial play
of figures and counterfigures to consider in Gay's manner the modern cruelties for ordinary people committed by "fine gentlemen" in Nazi-domi-
nated Berlin, Soviet-controlled Prague, and increasingly corporate Britain.

The Beggar's Opera makes burlesquing sport with the ideal of the hero,
as Macheath stands poised between two pivotal figures in self-interested
alliance with each other: Peachum, the market-minded father of Macheath's
naive and devoted Polly; and the turnkey Lockit, accomplice in Peachum's
elaborate schemes and father of the pregnant Lucy. Systematically, Peachum
and Lockit trade for profit in the capture of thieves (who are sometimes
punished, sometimes "freed" to continue their "service") and in their stolen goods (which are sometimes restored and sometimes resold). Allusive
of the 1720s government of Whig prime minister Robert Walpole, Gay's play
exposed key features of the sensibility and the mechanisms of power that
have determined Western governance and social life since the eighteenth
century.

Romantic and moral heroism fails laughably in a mercantile world where
promiscuous, self-interested Macheaths accommodate themselves to self-
interested shopkeeping Peachums. Audiences of 1728 had no difficulty
applying the satire to the legendary corruption of Robert Walpole, England's
first ruling politician. With remarkable single-handedness Walpole dominated England, including the titular Hanoverian monarchs, George I and
George II, for some twenty years. He was a towering figure, despised for
the influence he levered and maintained for himself and for the tactics of
ministerial and parliamentary strong-arming by which he wrested from a
compromised monarchy a program of ministerial rule. People at the time,
especially the literati, realized that, beyond the famed ruthlessness and corruption of his governing, Walpole's pragmatic brokering of alliances and
consolidation of power through buy offs, bluffs, profiteering, deal-making,
opportunism, manipulation of public opinion, and other notably political
tactics signaled a new kind of rule. Historian Paul Langford, who views
Walpole's rule favorably as a harbinger to parliamentary democracy, observes: "It was the way in which he came to stand for an entire system of
finance and government which made him so unpopular."[4] Opponents saw a

minister who became "prime" through a base and businesslike corruption. Gay winningly identified and critiqued the profit-driven politics and systemic vice of this new order in a satiric comedy whose ironies and biting jokes still find ready targets.

Robert Walpole came to power against the backdrop of a disputed monarchy installed in 1714 and a financial crisis that culminated in 1720. The German George I of Hanover had a contested claim to the throne of England; even more tenuous was his capacity or commitment to rule a burgeoning empire based in a land whose language he never bothered to learn. With the Hanoverian succession, stock investment both at home and abroad expanded unchecked until the crisis of 1720. The South Sea Bubble stock scandal left England reeling, with financial loss and uncertainty in the business sphere, corruption and fraud in high places, and rumors and threats of political disorder. Walpole managed during this crisis to solidify his position by distancing himself from the center of the scandal and by calibrating accusations against some players, and cover-ups on behalf of others, so as to keep the ruling monarchy and business structures of the nation intact. Averting civil disorder and political overthrow by accommodation and instrumental pragmatism, he enjoyed a rule famously driven by self-interest and profit.[5]

Gay had Walpole in mind in his "beggar's" depiction of an organized underworld of stolen goods and traders and alternately protected and accused thieves. In 1725, amidst much popular notoriety and comment, one Jonathan Wild was executed in London after years of official protection. Wild had operated, very much like Gay's Peachum, in a double capacity both as a government-sponsored thief-taker and as an underworld "fence," kingpin of an elaborate network for trading in stolen goods. As everyone suspected, Wild's payoffs and protections extended to the very top of Walpole's ministry. These were the corrupt "double capacities" that Gay most immediately targeted for laughter and satire.[6] At the same time, the mercurial allusions are capable of multiple referents, moving at once among generalizations and particularities. Thus, the metaleptic figure may conjure at one moment the general type—the Wild- or Walpole-like character and system—at another, a particular circumstance involving Wild and/or Walpole.[7] The rebounding placement of referents in "this-world" is key. Gay's parodic use of allusion disengages figuration from the metahistorical symbol systems that govern and stabilize the tenor-vehicle relations of metaphor and especially of allegory. However complex and multiply reverberating, however "deep" the "play" of figures in Gay's allusive mirroring, this world is notably an historical, not a mythic one.

Plots of both love and war play out for Macheath and his "wives" within a world of self-interested profit and trade moralized in terms of bourgeois family life and values. Polly and Macheath's dramatic plots of love and war take place in the mercantile terms of a newly capitalizing order. The trade-minded fathers Peachum and Lockit are in charge. As partner-antagonists, they are mutually double-dealing with each other and everyone else, a "peacher" on the one hand—that is, one who trades in stolen goods derived from "accus[ing] and prosecut[ing] for Felony and Treason," and a jailer on the other, who enforces and profits from this trade in accusation and prosecution.[8] Brecht equalizes the two. In turn, Havel and Ayckbourn accentuate the tandem poles of this system of trade in goods and people on the one hand, and in accusation and confinement on the other. Gay's *Beggar's Opera*, with its comic send-up of the England of Walpole's ministry and its thematic attention to family life, mercantile trading, new institutional arrangements, and transvaluations and relational values, supplies a blueprint for moral dilemmas and aesthetic impulses that continue to hold sway nearly three hundred years later.

DIE DREIGROSCHENOPER (1928)

With sardonic sweep, Bertolt Brecht and Kurt Weill worked from Elisabeth Hauptmann's German translation of *The Beggar's Opera* to reimagine Gay in a post-Victorian, postcolonizing twentieth-century world. Brecht probably based his drama on both of Gay's *Beggar's Opera* plays, which Nigel Playfair had revived with considerable fanfare and success in London in the early 1920s.[9] *Die Dreigroschenoper* (The threepenny opera) weaves Gay's insistent social criticism into a grim indictment of a bourgeois society now two hundred years older and, as we see in hindsight, on the verge of assuming fascist governance. Striking a familiar chord for its first audiences, *The Threepenny Opera* was a runaway hit in Weimar Germany and has continued to be revived in many languages. Brecht and Weill's play influenced virtually all musical theater since its New York revival in the 1950s, recently numbered among the "50 works that shaped the century."[10]

Like Gay's original, *The Threepenny Opera* touched a political nerve. A 1931 film adaptation of the play directed by G. W. Pabst leveled its satire at Hitler and the imminent Nazi takeover even more explicitly than the earlier stageplay.[11] Once in power, the Nazis set out—at first, it was thought, successfully—to destroy all copies of the film.[12] This 1930s suppression has its eighteenth-century precedent. *Polly*, Gay's sequel to *The Beggar's Opera*, takes Macheath and Polly to the West Indies with harsher, more politically direct satire than the first play. *Polly* was suppressed in rehearsal and prevented from being staged by Walpole, who, to quote a contemporary, "rather than suffer himself to be produced for thirty nights together upon the stage in the person of a highwayman . . . put a stop to the representation of it."[13] Two centuries later, a similarly fearful government banned Brecht's threatening adaptation of Gay. Clearly, the plays were onto something.

Gay's social and political vision had a timely applicability in Brecht and Weill's reworking, supplying for it an aptly metaleptic starting point that, as Theodor Adorno said of the 1920s play, "captures the little ghosts of the bourgeois world."[14] The rousing success of *The Threepenny Opera* attests to the relevance of its skeptical portrayal, as does the later film's even more emphatic alarm against Hitler and then rapid suppression by him. As Brecht observed in 1929:

> Under the title *The Beggar's Opera, The Threepenny Opera* has been performed for the past two hundred years in the theaters throughout England. . . . We still have the same *sociological* situation. Just like two hundred years ago we have a social order in which virtually all levels, even if in a wide variety of ways, pay respect to moral principles not by leading a moral life but by living off morality.[15]

The Threepenny Opera underscores Gay's disclosure of key features of the "*sociological* situation" of the then new world order of capital, trade, and colonialism: the problem of predation and betrayal among individuals in a secularized world governed by opportunism and profit. Gay critiqued a new kind of exploitative self-interest. The choice of subject and form followed intrinsically—albeit ingeniously—from his earlier writing, especially those works poised between and freely mirroring both high art and low. The punning language, self-conscious generic contradictions, and mimicking intertextualities, especially in *The Beggar's Opera* and *Polly*, expose the extent to which "currency" and "interest" define this world, whose corrupt public policies and institutions troublingly intersect with and parody the affectional relationships and forms of private life.

Sexual acts, especially for women, signify entrepreneurial expediency in a moneyed economy of trade and colonial conquest. Gay's ballad operas introduce revealing depictions of gender politics and sexuality: Polly in trousers, Achilles in petticoats. Amidst a language of squeamishness and sentimentality which Gay renders comical and ironic, sexual desire is an obsessive taboo at the same time that it is a market necessity.[16] Heroic and romantic values tilt and totter, absurdly touted while pragmatically undermined by mercantilist policies and values. As Gay suggests, this incompatibility is masked by an insistent mouthing of idealism by an industry of retrospective nostalgia for heroism and romance—what Brecht satirically develops as "living off morality." Moreover, as the later "Beggar's Operas" of

Václav Havel and Alan Ayckbourn make even clearer, this system of trade and conquest is maintained through habits and institutions carefully built upon betrayal, thieving, and fraud on a grand scale.

The discrepancies between words and deeds which Brecht finds fully treacherous, Gay treats with comic irony, as sympathetic if problematic individuals maneuver in flawed and sometimes treacherous ways amidst the larger, self-interested usurpations of rulers and their institutions. Moreover, failure is not solely of individual morality but of the very capacities of language, culture, and art, which are contingent upon, implicated in, and constituted by the material and political advantages that confer and structure power. Brecht and Gay touched a nerve. Our own time, replete with righteous bannings and cleansings and sexually preoccupied persecutions, seems again suited to the angry dissuasion of Brecht, the unsettling laughter of Gay.

In *The Threepenny Opera* Gay's mock-heroic becomes a grim anti-heroism that condemns bourgeois values and rule without qualification. Brecht's Mackie Messer (Mack the Knife) is a businessman, kin to the sleazy, shopkeeping Peachum of Gay's play: his business is illicit goods; his pleasure is illicit women.[17] Brecht's Peachum indicts a post-Victorian, postindustrialized bourgeois morality considerably more developed and institutionalized than the first gestures of civic-minded benevolence of Gay's time. The corruption of the 1920s Peachum—gained through unscrupulous, entrepreneurial manipulation of ethical and religious rhetoric and thereby of the proletarian masses—is for the Marxist Brecht a key piece in his updating of Gay. In this portrait of Polly's *papa* as a profiteering organizer of street beggars, Brecht develops the moralizing tendencies of Gay's smug Peachum that had already received the notice of some eighteenth-century readers. (For example, Sarah Fielding's *The Governess: or, Little Female Academy* of 1749 identifies the starched governess of her girls academy "in the Northern Parts" as "Mrs. Teachum.")[18]

From the Georgian era's sly wink at the duplicitous antics of individuals amidst a shifting world order, Brecht draws a sardonic and foreboding vision of systemic decay in the self-serving alignments of oppressive institutions: Mackie's traffic in stolen goods, Peachum's marketed "charity," the double-dealing police state presided over by Tiger Brown, Brecht's Lockit. In Pabst's film of 1931, *Hausfrau,* Polly's brisk and steely transformation of Mackie's gang of hoodlums to respectable bankers who finance and control this collusion of the three spheres seems, in retrospect, a disturbing prophecy of the Nazi takeover of a willing 1930s Germany.

The Threepenny Opera opens—on both stage and film—as a tattered street singer intones the poignant melody and metamorphosing chromatic harmonies that Weill weaves hauntingly through the play.

> See the shark with teeth like razors,
> All can read his open face.
> And Macheath has got a knife, but
> Not in such an obvious place.[19]

From beginning to end, Brecht decries the cruel as well as absurd hypocrisy of respectability, especially its institutional and ideological support. As *The Threepenny Opera* draws to its first, "tragic" close with the hanging of the fastidiously treacherous Macheath, the prosecuting tradesman, Peachum, up to now the chief proponent of this end to things, declares:

> But as we want to keep our fingers clean
> And you are people we can't risk offending
> We thought we'd better do without this scene
> And substitute a different ending.
>
> (scene 9)

The bourgeois Mackie Messer is then rescued by a royal official who arrives on horseback with a pardon from the Queen (scene 9).

The movie *Threepenny Opera* extends even further than the play the theme of the collusion between corrupt and treacherous forces beneath the veneer of respectability. After both Polly and Jenny—businesswoman wife and streetwise whore—rescue Mackie from jail, he takes his place on the board of "Citibank, Piccadilly," Polly's transformation of his gang. As the film ends with a pathetically surly rabble taking to the streets, Mackie and his gang, now respectable hoodlums under Polly's tutelage, are joined by her moralizing tradesman father, Peachum, and the police chief, Tiger Brown: "Over luncheon, reunited, / See them clear the poor man's plate."[20] Peppered with parodic mimings of Hitler's mannerisms among the principals, the movie's depiction of this business-as-usual trade and respectability among thieves takes on an ominous hue.

Brecht honed Gay's preoccupation with treachery made legitimate and systematic by the strong arm of institutional power and the cloak of social respectability. The antihero gangster, Mackie Messer—his womanizing more cruel and manipulative than that of Macheath, his thieving and murdering both more heinous and more businesslike—cuts a more sinister figure than Gay's mock-heroic highwayman. However, Gay's conception did include a stolid and essentially bourgeois fastidiousness in Macheath's predatory habits and turn of mind, as the portraits of him in Hogarth's famous series on *The Beggar's Opera* attest. His shackled feet planted solidly on the planks of the stage and his arms businesslike across his chest, Hogarth's Macheath stands prosaically evaluating his predicament as his weeping paramours, Lucy and Polly, beseech their respective fathers to release him.[21]

Fig. 2. Scene from *The Beggar's Opera* by William Hogarth (c. 1729). Courtesy of the Tate Gallery, London.

Taking this image of respectability from Gay, Brecht elaborates on its function as a false cover for such cloaked and rapacious sharks as Mack the Knife. An abusive pimp to Jenny, Mackie traffics with his whores compulsively and indulgently. With smug self-interest, he couples with Polly in a marriage characterized by a flurry of commodities and mockingly lifeless echoes of romance and sentiment (recalling Adorno's "little ghosts of the bourgeois world"). A dangerous if pathetic antihero, Brecht's Macheath, even more than Gay's, indicts what he represents.

With a sardonic nod to heroic tradition, Brecht has Mackie and Brown remember their days as foot soldiers in Victoria's imperial wars: "Ah, Jackie, do you remember how we served in India together?" asks Mackie (scene 2, p. 167). Lustily intoning "The Cannon Song," the two old comrades invoke the glories of their combat days "When confronting some heathen commotion." As they remember their colleagues "under the cannon's thunder" amid Brecht's uneasy homoerotic innuendo, the song conveys the alienation of common foot soldiers in this colonial enterprise: "Not that the army gave a bugger who they were." With a grisly cacophony worthy of Swift, Brecht and Weill reiterate with each chorus the visceral racism and appetitiveness of this colonial rampage, a theme already present in Gay's *Polly:*

> The troops live under
> The cannon's thunder
> From Sind to Cooch Behar.
> Moving from place to place
> When they come face to face
> With men of a different color
> With darker skins or duller
> They quick as winking chop them into
>   beefsteak tartare.

(scene 2, p. 168)

Ominously foreshadowing the Nazi obsession with race, Pabst's film brings the final collaboration of Mackie, Jackie (Brown), Peachum, and Polly to a close with this satiric recipe for racial conquest. While the darkness of this vision seems a far distance from the laughter and fun we expect of Gay, Brecht read the original with attention. Though we find Gay genial and cherishing, he is not wholly so, as his own era recognized. *The Threepenny Opera* drew from *The Beggar's Opera* and *Polly*, works by Gay originally suspect and suppressed.

HAVEL, GAY, AND THE POSTMODERN: COMMUNISM IN THE 1970s

Brecht's play takes on eerie resonance as we look back to it through the intervening lens of German fascism. More recent plays by Havel and Ayckbourn apply Gay's critique to the later twentieth-century's sociopolitical structures and zeitgeist. The prism of *The Beggar's Opera* recasts contesting yet mutually implicating socioeconomic systems of the Cold War to disclose areas of surprising kinship between communist collectivism and privatizing capitalism. Despite inimical ideologies, these societies share the Peachum-Lockit dynamic with regard to market profiteering in goods and mechanisms of social control—which are carried out with abstract centralization in both systems. As these late-twentieth-century adaptations show, the betrayals and fraudulence outlined by Gay in 1728 continue to serve purportedly opposing systems. Havel and Ayckbourn demonstrate that *The Beggar's Opera* prefigures the terms of political and cultural discourse for a modern world whose gendered individuals live in nation-states centralized—whether through government or market forces—as capital- and trade-driven economies.

Havel's *Beggar's Opera* reimagines Gay's play in a 1970s Czechoslovakia that is thinly disguised as London in "the second half of the 18th century." The Soviet invasion of 1968 abruptly ended liberalizing trends of the 1960s, replacing Alexander Dubcek's reform government with the repressive, pro-Soviet regime of Gustav Husák. Havel satirizes a web of spying and betrayal among his characters against the backdrop of black-market, goods-trading "organizations." Dominating this world of competing syndicates and secret-police surveillance is a system of social control ruled by Bill Lockit. The emphasis shifts to Macheath's marriage to Lockit's daughter, Lucy (rather than to Polly Peachum, as in Gay's play), and to Macheath's betrayal by the whore, Jenny Diver, a pivotal representative of the plebeian underclass in Brecht's play. Calhoun Winton notes that, as in the case of *Threepenny Opera*, both of Gay's 1728 plays, *Polly* and *The Beggar's Opera*, underpin Havel's play.[22] Here, Macheath's relations with all three women—his wives Polly and Lucy; and Jenny, his dalliance—show that the realm of love is for women the sole preoccupation, a private and domestic sphere of heterosexual relationship in which women betray and rescue—by turns—the men they love and desire. This gendered and intrigue-laden dynamic of private life occurs within the larger masculinized context of balanced and colluding economic systems. These are ultimately controlled—with ambiguity, compromise, and duplicity on all sides—by the same policing central authority that requires and oversees individual participation in surveillance of and informing on family members and mates. Here, the psychology of the individual and of interpersonal relations gives Havel a ready new lexicon with which to update the private delusions and deceiving ironies in Gay's original.

The play opens with insistence on Peachum's "middle-class solidity" and his "puritanical stodginess," to quote the madam, Diana Trapes, who arrives to consult with him about upgrading the furnishings of her brothel.[23] Peachum, dressed "in a housecoat," sits in his home with his ledger books. His apron-clad wife, emblem of twentieth-century domesticity, stands at a stove, cooking dinner. At play's end, the final scene exactly mirrors this scene of "Will" Peachum's respectable household except that it shows the

cozy kitchen of the housecoat-robed "Bill" Lockit and *his* apron-clad wife—
an image worthy to open a television comedy.

Havel's Peachum and Macheath are competitors, leaders of vying underworld syndicates that traffic competitively in officially prohibited goods
and services. Peachum's daughter Polly has been "sleeping with Macheath"
(3) as her father had instructed, so as to spy on him. However, Mrs.
Peachum—like her prototype in Gay's play—fears that Polly may not be
revealing the extent of her liaison. "Don't forget," she reminds her husband, "Macheath has a way with girls" (7). Of course she is right.

Scene 2 finds Macheath in "a pub frequented by thieves" instructing
his followers Jim and Jack in the "modern dynamic" of living a "truly
fulfilling human life": "vitality, imagination, and style." He is no "dried up
stick-in-the mud like Peachum" (8). Jim marvels: "You even find time for
babes." Macheath responds with romantic recommendations (rather like
Ovid's *Ars amatoria*) that the seducer feign "the pretence of an inferiority
complex; because women absolutely love to help someone, to save someone" (9).[24] Macheath has two wives; and "in one case" (that is, with Polly),
he discloses in a modest boast, he is "actually a newlywed" (12).

By scene 3 the theme of spying and betrayal that governs the play is
apparent in all the characters. Peachum wants Polly "to obtain sufficient
evidence about [her husband's] activities to have him convicted and put
away for life!" (15) Polly goes to Macheath, declares her love, warns him
of his danger, and is directed to "go home, ask Papa's forgiveness, say that
[she'd] come to [her] senses" (19), and begin counterspying on her father.
In turn, the prostitute Jenny arrives to avenge her previous seduction by
Macheath, embraces him, and signals to the police who take him away.
When the scene shifts to Lockit's jail, where selected prisoners serve as
deputies, this world of informing, betrayal, and side-switching is exposed
as an institutionalized system.

In this Havelian setting, the entrepreneurial "Willy" Peachum answers
to the prison master "Bill" Lockit, a reversal of the dynamics between the
two in Gay's play. Indeed, Lockit has set Peachum up in business for the
purpose of spying: "to gain and maintain . . . the confidence of the underworld" (29). An anxious Peachum, worried that things are not going as
planned, protests: "But I did my best, Bill. I even sacrificed my own daughter
just to get as much evidence as possible" (29). To which Lockit replies:
"I'm sorry to say this, Willy, but the results could have been expected: you
know how good Mac is with women!" (29) Lockit's own benightedness is
made apparent: the next scene brings his daughter Lucy to Macheath's cell
as the discontented *other* wife.

"Where were you," Lucy demands of her husband, "since the wedding
. . . more than a year ago?" (31). Macheath placates her with the *leitmotiv*

of bourgeois domestic life with which Havel began. "You've got to believe me, Lucy," Macheath protests, "It's all just a series of unfortunate misunderstandings. . . . Every day I would dream about a smallish country chateau built of red bricks, covered with ivy, set amidst green meadows and elm groves, and the two of us, keeping house together" (32). Like Polly, Lucy succumbs: "Oh, Mackie! What can I do to make it happen?" "Bring me a hacksaw," he replies (33). She does; he escapes.

Women cannot resist this sentimental dream of domesticity, particularly when it accompanies the confession of "inferiority" and the suffering that constitute a hero's recommended arts of wooing. Gay's Mrs. Peachum noted in 1728: "Women indeed are bitter bad judges . . . for they are so partial to the brave that they think every man handsome who is going to the camp or the gallows" (*Beggar's Opera*, I.iv.9–11). With Havel's Macheath in prison, betrayed yet again by Jenny, all three women will irresistibly fall for the smooth-talking condemned man. First, the furious Lucy and Polly descend upon Macheath, slapping him by turns.

> *Polly.* We gave you all that we had to give; our loyalty, our love—
> *Lucy.* Our bodies—
> *Polly.* Our honour!
> *Lucy.* And how did you repay us? You deceived us despicably!
> *Polly.* All your speeches about love were dirty lies—
> *Lucy.* Because, in fact, all you wanted was to gain control of Mr. Peachum's organization by using Polly—
> *Polly.* And to gain influence over Mr. Lockit by using Lucy!
>
> (52)

Macheath pauses, "contemplatively paces around the cell, then solemnly turns to Polly and Lucy" (53). He delivers a long defense of his love for both and of the rightness of his marrying them both, so that neither would suffer the disadvantages and inequities in his having one for wife and the other as mistress. With delicious allusive verve, Havel's text echoes the 1970s fashion for psychological fulfillment and attention to gender equality, revealing in Macheath's desperately mollifying self-justification the susceptibility of both to ironic manipulation.

> Do you see how this solution [a man's having a wife and a mistress] is callous towards both women? Was this the route I should have taken? No, girls! If I were to best fulfill my responsibilities towards both of you, I could not follow other men, but had to create my own path—maybe untrodden—but decidedly more honourable—that is, the path which gives both of you an equal measure of legitimacy and dignity. Such then is the true basis on which you must judge me!
>
> (53)

Having justified the situation in terms of their "psychological" and "political" interest, Macheath reminds them of his impending execution—after which "all that will be left of [him] will be a memory" (54). Both women begin to weep. Macheath pleads for understanding and forgiveness, as Havel continues this wonderfully pop-psychologizing rendering of Gay's famous prison scene of the hero between his two wives.

> I therefore beg of you to put yourselves in my place, understand the logic and morality of my actions and, by doing so, recognize that—within the limits of available possibilities—I conducted myself honourably!"
>
> (p. 54)

Of course it works. Polly and Lucy "begin to sob loudly; they both throw themselves at Macheath, embrace him passionately, kiss him wildly, and cry hysterically" (54). As Gay's Lucy observed in *The Beggar's Opera* of 1728: "There is nothing moves one so much as a great man in distress" (III.xv.8–9).

With the execution nigh, Peachum brings an offer for Macheath: the two will merge their respective organizations into a single syndicate; Macheath will publicly wed and set up house with Polly (the latter presumably enlisted by her father to spy on the son-in-law/partner); and Peachum will intercede on behalf of Macheath with Lockit. Macheath at first resists, suspecting the scheme to originate with the more powerful Lockit, but finally agrees. The arrangement, he decides, is balanced delicately by the capacity of every player to double-cross every other. As Peachum declares: "I pursue my goals and cover up my ass at the same time." To which Macheath replies: "What you actually want is to double-cross Lockit?" (64). They agree to embark, as if initiating an official five-year plan, "on a period of solid and constructive cooperation" (65).

As the play draws to a close, Jenny returns. Here the gender dynamic of pathos and forgiveness contextualized by a sentimentalized dream of domestic life is most clearly interwoven with the interpersonal spying, betrayal, and double-dealing that permeate the play. In a mock-courtship scene reminiscent of the relationship of the two in Gay's *Polly*—updated to a post-Freudian era—Macheath identifies in Jenny an "inner need" to betray him. "Jenny, your treachery excited me because it was suppressing your love," he tells her. Then he reaches for her help: "Your love suppressing your treachery will excite me even more!" "You're so horrible, Mackie!" Jenny responds, "I was so sure that I'd win, but now I see that unless I betray you again right away, it will be the end of me." Macheath, once more a captive, again hopes for rescue and fashions the irresistible dream of domestic felicity. His words end the scene. Hanging in the air without response, they continue to hold sway: "On the contrary, Jenny. This is the moment of our beginning. Today I'll be released from here and the two of us will immediately run off somewhere, far away where no one will ever find us; no one, that is, except for the birds and stars!" (69).

The play ends with an indulgent crescendo of double-crossing in Lockit's kitchen, a scene of respectable domesticity identical to that in Peachum's kitchen where the play began. Havel's target: a world of hidden but ineluctable central control in which spying and betrayal set the terms for relations. Lockit, at the table, studies his ledger; his wife is busy at the stove. When the handcuffed Macheath is brought in, Lockit quotes verbatim from the jail-cell conversation with Peachum, which he has obviously heard, and accuses his prisoner of refusing to "buy the scam" of the merger (72). Macheath voices surprise:

> *Macheath.* Why do you say I didn't buy it? After all, didn't I accept Peachum's offer?
> *Lockit.* Yes, you did! but only to get out, to acquire the assets of both organizations within the framework of the faked merger and then, before I could finally catch you together with all your boys, run off with a certain lady somewhere far away where no one would ever find you—no one, that is, except for the birds and stars—*(Macheath jumps up, excitedly.)* In other words, when you realized that Peachum was, in fact double-crossing you while pretending to double-cross me, you decided to double-cross him. However—luckily for us, and unluckily for you— you yourself were immediately double-crossed. Now do you get it? *(The bewildered Macheath stares ahead, then he sighs.)*
> (72)

Initially Macheath expresses outrage and resistance, then settles into the "modern dynamic" he espoused at the play's beginning. With Macheath sipping a cordial bestowed by the Missus, Lockit makes him a proposal: that he merge as agreed with Peachum and spy on him to Lockit. In another long self-justifying speech, Macheath rationalizes his way to agreement— and to articulating Havel's ironic sociopolitical commentary: "If, as seems to be the case, I'm being double-crossed by everyone, it can only mean that they expect me to do the same. In fact, by doing so they're extending an offer of a certain kind of basis for our mutual interaction" (74). Declaring it more courageous to accommodate than to die "a typically useless death," Macheath whips the conclusion of his speech into a laughably elongated pudding of mixed banalities:

> In other words, the only correct, dignified, and truly manly solution to my situation is to face life head-on, to courageously plunge into its stormy waters, not to fear its dirt and all its hidden traps along the way, to devote

all my strength and my know-how to the struggle to make life easier in the future than it is now!

(74)

"Spoken like a real man, Mac!" Lockit enthuses, "I'm deeply moved." Then, with movements as contorted, forced, and ironically undermined as his metaphors, the shackled Macheath closes the deal with a clumsy handshake and an even clumsier signing of Lockit's contract.[25] With these images of coerced accommodation in memory, we hear Lockit echo Peachum's remarks of the scene before: "I trust that the two of us have just embarked on a period of solid and constructive cooperation!" (75). As she proceeds with dinner, Mrs. Lockit sets the terms for Macheath in love: "I trust that now, since everything turned out so well, you'll stop your hanky-panky and will at last settle down with your Lucy. She loves you so much." "You can count on me, Mom!" Macheath replies just before he rushes off to leave the couple to their dinner and the *"Bon appétit!"* which ends the play. From the vantage of the communist bloc's version of the modern nation, Havel's satirized web of intrigues and betrayals centers on the balancing of power relations by the spying and counterspying endemic to a system dominated by imprisonment and a hypocritically corrupt "collectivity."

AYCKBOURN, GAY, AND GLOBAL CAPITALISM

Alan Ayckbourn's *A Chorus of Disapproval*, first staged in 1984 and remade as a film in 1989, situates *The Beggar's Opera* vis-à-vis Tory prime minister Margaret Thatcher's 1980s Britain, a setting of frenetic competition, privatization, and speculative corporate buyouts.[26] In Ayckbourn the relations, intrigues, and betrayals of all the characters smack of the acquisitive, self-aggrandizing Peachum. A competitive trafficking in goods figures as the quintessential late-twentieth century capitalist preoccupation: the private buying and selling of land in profit-making real estate ventures comically echoed in the central character's "trading up" through successive roles, from bit player to star, in a production of none other than *The Beggar's Opera*. Ayckbourn revisits Gay's play in *A Chorus of Disapproval*'s presentation of modest British "Everyman" and "Everywoman" characters, who are themselves portraying Gay's memorable highwaymen and whores, mothers and wives, daughters and fathers.

As Ayckbourn's plot unfolds, "The Pendon Amateur Light Opera Company" prepares to stage Gay's *Beggar's Opera*: "First produced when was it—? 1728," exclaims the director, the combustible Welsh Dafydd, "it's as entertaining and as vital and as relevant as it was then . . . Suky Tawdry . . .

Dolly Trull . . . Mrs. Vixen . . . Those are the whores and pimps of the town
. . . almost see their faces in their names, can't you? Polly Peachum. That
tells you all you need to know about her, doesn't it? What an age, eh? What
an age. Well, compared to our own" (41). While as a cast the townspeople
rehearse Gay's play-within-the-play, in the framing drama they mirror and
echo Gay's satire in an intricate web of sexual and business betrayals, most
of them centered on a plot of land adjoining the local branch of "BLM," a
faceless and powerful multinational corporation. Ayckbourn's players, as
hapless as Havel's, scramble to outswindle each other against the backdrop
of an increasingly enormous, remote, and sinister centralized control of the
properties and decisions that matter.

   The unassuming Guy Jones, recently widowed and transferred to the
town as an employee of BLM, answers a newspaper ad and auditions for a
part in the upcoming *Beggar's Opera*. Over the course of rehearsals, Guy
finds himself in increasingly important roles: from the one-line "Crook-
Fingered Jack," he moves to the supporting role of "Matt of the Mint" and
then "Filch," and finally takes the lead as Macheath. This progress takes
place as Guy makes a Macheath-like sexual progress among his actress
colleagues, beginning with Hannah, the play's "Polly" and wife of Dafydd.

   In related intrigues, various cast members scheme to enlist Guy in helping them outmaneuver each other to buy a small piece of land "slap bang
adjoining" Guy's plant, as Dafydd puts it, and thought to be suddenly valuable because of BLM's rumored plans to expand. The sexual and real estate intrigues loop around the naive and obliging Guy as the play discloses
the small-town cast as a tightly knit company of not unlikable, if pathetic,
Peachums who strive to dupe and double-cross each other.

   The last laugh showers everyone. With the opening night curtain about
to rise, word spreads: rather than expanding, BLM is to relocate with a loss
of five hundred jobs. All betrayals have been for nought. As tempers flare,
treacheries come to light, and *The Beggar's Opera* goes on. The small town's
inner and outer plays end with John Gay. Guy, raised to Macheath, but now
rendered jobless and friendless, "with his Doxies around," wins his stage
reprieve and sings Gay's final chorus: "But think of this Maxim, and Put
off your Sorrow, / The Wretch of To-day, may be happy To-morrow" (125–
26).

   Guy stands at the center of *A Chorus of Disapproval*, a naive and pli-
able Macheath even more luckless than Havel's. Indeed, Ayckbourn has
reworked in his abashed rake the complicitous diffidence that so endear-
ingly characterized Gay's original Polly Peachum to her eighteenth-century audiences.[27] Early in *A Chorus of Disapproval*, Guy articulates, with
the comically abstract language of contemporary corporate management,
his uncomprehending view of BLM and his own insignificance at the com-

pany. At his first meeting with Dafydd's wife Hannah, who will soon play "Polly" to Guy's "Macheath" in more ways than one, she asks about the company: "I mean what do they do?" she asks, "Do they make anything?"

> *Dafydd* (laughing). Vast profits mostly . . . Right? . . .
> *Guy.* We're a multi-national company that's become extremely diversified.
> . . . And so it's a bit difficult to pin down. Certainly it is from my limited viewpoint. In a rather small local branch in a rather obscure department called Alternative Forward Costing. In which I am a very small cog indeed.
> *Hannah.* I'm impressed anyway.
>
> (46–47)

"It's interesting you should be in BLM," Dafydd interjects, in the first of many probes for inside information on the company and the land. As the play continues, Guy's self-confessed insignificance as a "small cog" becomes increasingly ironic. Inquiry by inquiry, his stature in *The Beggar's Opera* grows as cast members surreptitiously angle and bribe in Peachum-like maneuverings with regard to the coveted piece of land.

A Chorus of Disapproval ends on the inner play's opening night when Guy's actual insignificance in the company becomes clear indeed. As *The Beggar's Opera* is about to begin, word circulates: the corporation's "big boys" have announced the closure of this "small local branch," abandoning the town and its halfpenny Peachums to a future of hard times. Some employees will be relocated; Guy is not among them. His naive obstruction of various of the "dirty tricks" has earned retaliation.[28] "If it makes you feel any better," he declares to cast members who stare at the headlines, "I don't happen to have been included in the one hundred and twenty-eight [whose jobs will relocate]." "I'm hardly surprised," says the ever-tipsy Rebecca, wife of the crooked city councillor who maneuvered most Peachum-like in the plot (25).

Fifteen excerpts from *The Beggar's Opera*, most of them featuring Gay's pungent songs, weave through *A Chorus of Disapproval*, punctuating the outer plot that develops as the inner play moves to production. Unfolding sequentially in their order of appearance in Gay's play, these excerpts provide a skeletal subtext that parallels events in the "real world" of the outer drama. In counterpoint, the two plots parodically echo and cite one another by turns, undermining the stability of figure and ground with a lively, parodic resonance worthy of Gay. *The Beggar's Opera* is altogether relevant to Ayckbourn's provincial Everytown, the suggestively named, dependent "Pendon."

Gay brought to his early eighteenth-century moment a sharp-sighted analysis of the quintessentially capitalist and modern predicament: an on-going system of transvaluation makes relational power the crux of mean-ing and worth. Such instability can only be shown parodically in a metaleptic strategy that shifts point of view so as to look from below or from the side with the ironic vantage of the disempowered. Powerful and powerless, agents and acted-upon alike all become implicated in ruling systems in which economic gain and social interrelations are utterly imbricated.

Through his developing analysis of class, gender, and culture in the capitalizing Britain of his early Georgian era, Gay brought into being a pointed and playful critique of this dynamic that is arrestingly relevant today. The collusions of his Peachum and Lockit provide a blueprint for the ideologically opposed state systems of the modern age, which similarly consolidate and enforce a centralized control that is as increasingly sweep-ing as it is remote. At the ground level of these systems are the basely or naively ineffectual Pollys and Macheaths who muddle along to small hero-isms and more likely betrayals amidst the colluding double capacities of the Peachums and Lockits who hold the keys—figurative and literal—to institutional life.

All three twentieth-century revisitings of Gay present an increasing abstraction and consolidation of social control. With Ayckbourn's play the real dynamic of Peachum and Lockit has moved entirely offstage, far from the petty thieves and highwaymen rehearsing their *Beggar's Opera*. Gay continues to supply a relevant structural and thematic model for under-standing the institutional world and social and individualized sensibility that have come into being since the Enlightenment. *A Chorus of Disap-proval* transposes *The Beggar's Opera* onto the postmodern, transnational "globalization" of the 1980s and 1990s. Ayckbourn renders his Macheath as earnestly gullible as Gay's Polly. Like her, he can be read ambiguously with regard to how disingenuous his role in shifting relations, including amatory relations, really is. Yet this very ambiguity resides, as with Polly, in his essentially victimized or acted-upon status. Agreeably passive in "love," he is equally docile in "war," amiably struggling to please and serve everyone as each player schemes to outcheat the others. With delicious irony, Guy unwittingly foils the attempts of each of the swindlers to out-swindle the others even as all significant dealings are decided well beyond the ken of these underlings. Both Havel and Ayckbourn present a satiric world of players too small and hapless to earn their desires, match their dreams, or deserve their failures. With parodic wit, they revisit Gay's satiric laugh-ter amidst the still prevalent "double capacities" of modern experience, taking up as they do the self-consciously gendered and psychologized sen-sibilities of women and men of the late twentieth century.

The Beggar's Opera amused its first audiences with satiric reference—

sometimes pointed, sometimes glancing—to specific events and circumstances in Gay's 1720s England. Modern and postmodern "translations" of the play attest that its satire has lasting application. Indeed, *The Beggar's Opera* acquires deeper significance both within a wider view of eighteenth-century cultural materials across class lines, and within a longer, more historicized consideration of the enduring aspects of that mercantile order and sensibility which Gay opens to scrutiny.

2

Dangerous Sissy:
The Life of John Gay and the
Making of a "Manly" Canon

Gay's own era judged him a prominent figure sparking controversy and emulation. By the last quarter of the eighteenth century this prominence declined, even as literary criticism metamorphosed from a descriptive project to a determinant of taste and values. By the nineteenth century, a discredited Gay became something of a cautionary tale. Successive renderings of his biography and character served this process. Historiographically viewed, these open a window onto ideological imperatives that have, over time, shaped the valuing of authors and texts. Concerns about a proper authorial identity with regard to gender and social class—in themselves, ideological focal points of Gay's probing of the emerging new order—came to shape the canon of English literary history, dictating patterns of exclusion as well as of excellence.[1] As an increasing number of editors worried over the irreverent subversiveness in Gay's writing, they supposed even more dangers in his character, presented as a negative admonition with regard to manliness and social position.

Gay's often controversial poems and plays were subject to critique in his own time, that Georgian heyday of deprecation. Nonetheless, his success was indisputable. The initial acclaim and polemical responses that met *The Beggar's Opera* on its own terms gave way in the latter part of his century as the aesthetic tenor of Gay's era shifted. The richly discordant sensibility of an age of satire—inherited from Dryden and present in the works of Swift, Delarivière Manley, Gay, and others—yielded to a more unifying view of art as bodying forth expressive, original (and relatively stable) signifiers. Works achieved prominence as the creation of striving individuals—increasingly understood as gendered—within the context of a society that valued private virtues: self-motivation, assiduousness, an orderly and rational independence, gainful employment, personal and financial acquisition, social and personal responsibility, domestic order, and so on. The English-language literary canon we have inherited emerges from a reimagining, over the course of the eighteenth century, of the function and nature of literature in connection with these values and the project of establishing art's "seriousness" as the product and shaper of persons of lofty mind.[2]

Samuel Johnson played a pivotal role with regard to Gay's reputation. Moralist of his age, Johnson brought to his retrospective survey of English authors an ideal of a private, personal heroism that informed his biographical sketches. Johnson, as we shall see, found in Gay a negative lesson: a man womanishly trivial, childishly dependent, a "poet of a lower order." Especially after Johnson, commentators enlisted these valences of gender and class (intersecting with what we currently term "sexual orientation") in the presentation of authors as biographical subjects. This chapter examines the downward trajectory of Gay's reputation, as seen through a sampling of "Lives" of the poet published from his own Georgian era to the twentieth century. In them, a didactic resistance shifts attention from the poet's works to his biography with a fictionalizing attention fixed on his life, his character, and finally his body. The pattern of these accounts shows how biographical and personal assessments can serve the dismissal of unsuitably "unmanly" writers (a category that of course includes all women).

JOHN GAY (1685–1732)

Gay's origins[3] in the West Country and his somewhat problematic economic background and social rank inform the authorial stance typical of his writing: he voices the ironically self-aware, yet evasive and vulnerable position of the onlooking outsider. He was born in 1685 into a less affluent branch of a large and long-prominent trading family in the Devonshire market town of Barnstaple, on the Irish Sea. Orphaned at the age of ten, Gay lived in the home of an uncle and was schooled at the local Barnstaple grammar school where the thorough, basic education of the day included training in Latin and elements of English verse.[4] However, he did not go on to university experience or schooling. In 1704 the nineteen-year-old Gay went to London, apprenticed to a draper. Apparently the arrangement did not work out, for he returned to Devon in 1706, breaking off his apprenticeship well before the usual term. By 1707 he was again in London, a member of the circle of the ambitious and rising young literary man, Aaron Hill, a childhood classmate also from Barnstaple. From 1708 to 1711, Gay collaborated with other young wits on Hill's *The British Apollo*, a journal catering to a readership of "the middling sort." By 1714 he had published several poems, pamphlets, and plays and was moving in a circle of urbane courtiers and such writer-friends as Alexander Pope and Jonathan Swift.

Gay sought aristocratic patronage at the court of the Stuart Queen Anne to stabilize his finances. However, the political climate shifted with the succession of the Hanoverian George I to the throne in 1714, and Gay's ties to the out-of-favor Tory party worked against his hopes for a court appointment. His poetry and drama made him some financial gains, particularly by 1720, when he published a well-subscribed collection of his works. However, the money he accrued from this publication was almost immediately lost in investments in the South Sea Company stocks, which "bubbled" and "crashed" in the summer of 1720.

It was in the wake of this stock-market venture and the related consolidation of Walpole's ministerial power that Gay created, in 1728, *The Beggar's Opera* and the ballad opera form with its mixing of drama and popular songs. Gay achieved financial security from the success of *The Beggar's Opera* and its sequel, *Polly*, published the following year. Although the latter was banned, the notoriety that resulted made the published play a runaway bestseller. However, because of his disfavor with the government, Gay was ejected from his lodgings in Whitehall. In poor health, he was supported and housed by his friends, the duke and duchess of Queensberry, with whom he lived until his death in 1732 at the age of forty-seven.

John Gay emerges as a considerate, comical, and on balance eminently likeable man. His correspondence reveals a sensitive, sometimes melancholy and uncertain speaker whose observations and comments can, in a moment, take flight in a rollicking turn of humor. Ironic and self-deprecating about himself, his remarks to his friends—several of them women—are generous and affectionate. Gay's epistolary style, when not in business mode, is often casual, even careless-seeming. Routinely entertaining and sometimes ingeniously ironic and witty, Gay's letters convey an artful, genial voice that is notably forthcoming and unstaged.[5]

In the last five years of his life Gay wrote for the theater—including two ballad operas—and composed two sets of animal fables modeled on those of La Fontaine and such classical writers as the Roman Phaedrus. These fables were enormously popular into the nineteenth century, becoming an oft-cited repository of proverbial wit and wisdom for English readers at every social level. When he died, Gay was, as one writer put it, the "envy of the playwrights." He was buried in ceremony in Westminster Abbey, his grave originally marked by a handsome monument erected by his friends and admirers. Adorned with a sculpture by John Michael Rysbrack (1693–1770), one of the most prominent sculptors of the age, this lavish marker was removed in 1939 when medieval paintings were discovered behind the wall in Poet's Corner where Gay lies buried. In recent years, champions of Gay have campaigned for restoration of this monument, now stowed away in an inaccessible triforium, to greater prominence. So far, their efforts have failed, and John Gay's monument still remains hidden, his grave unmarked.[6]

"ENVY OF THE PLAYWRIGHTS": GAY'S INITIAL PREEMINENCE

Eighteenth-century commentators assumed the importance of Gay's writing. Early in the century his works drew extensive comment, while his life—as was typical in such accounts—received little or none. John Mottley (1692–1750) is the supposed author of "A Compleat List of all the English Dramatic Poets, and of All the Plays ever printed in the English Language to the Present Year 1747"; his account of Gay is complimentary and respectful.[7] The "Compleat List" presents dramas not as literature to be read but as staged works forming a public and ongoing theatrical tradition. Plays appear with brief remarks about their character and performance history. Notably, the "Compleat List" focuses entirely on the works, allotting almost no space to the lives or even the characteristic sensibilities of particular authors. Nevertheless, Mottley's comments and especially the length of his entries reveal a weighting of authors. Of the ninety playwrights from Mottley's own era—the reigns of Anne, George I, and George II—only the still living Colley Cibber (1671–1757), Henry Fielding (1707–54), and Mottley himself are accorded longer entries than Gay (who died early in the reign of George II). For the 184 writers from the era immediately preceding Gay's (the reigns of Charles II, James II, and William and Mary), only the discussions of John Dryden and Aphra Behn extend beyond the three pages allotted to Gay. For the period before Cromwell's closing of the theaters, only William Shakespeare and Ben Jonson occupy more attention. In Mottley's history of the "English Dramatic Poets," Gay was a major figure.

Other critics at midcentury and after remark on the excellence and popularity of Gay's work. In 1745 William Ayre finds Gay unexcelled, and indeed superior to Pope, in the pastoral.[8] In *Lives of the Poets of Great Britain and Ireland* (1753), Theophilus Cibber conveys the prevailing admiration. With a sweep, his discussion of Gay proclaims: "As to his genius it would be superfluous to say any thing here, his works are in the hands of every reader of taste, and speak for themselves."[9] Oliver Goldsmith praises Gay with the commonplace apogee that "he more resembles Theocritus than any other English pastoral writer whatsoever."[10] The editor of a 1772 edition describes *The Beggar's Opera* as "an unrivalled master piece" and accords *The Fables* "the same rank of estimation."[11] *Biographia Dramatica* (1782) states that *The What-d'Ye-Call-It*, almost forgotten today, "became so popular that it excited the envy of the playwrights."[12] In his *History of England* (1790), Tobias Smollett praises Gay's "genius for pastoral" and his fables which "vie with those of La Fontaine, in native humour, ease, and simplicity."[13] Gay's work here finds a place among that of influential authors ancient and modern.

Not all was praise. Throughout the eighteenth century, Gay's satire along with that of Swift and Pope sparked heated discussion. A moral outcry at the mock-heroic underworld of highwaymen and whores in *The Beggar's Opera* followed the play's first run.[14] Indeed, the social tenor of Gay's satirical critiques and his delineation of the emerging politics of rank caught the attention of decriers from the start. Furthermore, Gay's consistent targeting of the ministry and court was not lost on his contemporaries, and at least one later commentator remarked on its panache. A Dublin editor in 1770 condemns Gay's audaciousness precisely because of his "undistinguished" background:

> There is scarcely, if at all, to be found in history an example, where a private subject, undistinguished either by birth or fortune, had it in his power, to feast his resentment so richly at the expense of his sovereign.[15]

The attention to social order in Gay's burlesques with their irreverent mirrorings of high and low steadily provoked uneasiness as well as laughter. Already in 1746 Eliza Haywood located a troubling politics readable in Gay's *Beggar's Opera*: "a constant Strain runs through it, of putting the whole Species pretty much upon a Level." Haywood goes on to express her own (anxious) sentiments: "The late witty and ingenious Mr. *Gay* . . . tells us, I very well remember, '*Your little Villains must submit to Fate, / That great Ones may enjoy the World in State.*' I *should* be extremely sorry indeed to be assured that this Piece of Satire were as *just* as it is *severe.*"[16]

As stated earlier, the preoccupation with exertions of power in personal and social relationships in Gay's works is rooted in an awareness and exposure of those arrangements of hierarchical placement that since the nineteenth century have been understood as socioeconomic "class." The newly emerging features—and conceptualization—of these arrangements came increasingly to the fore through the course of the eighteenth century as people of the middling sort continued to gain in power and cultural influence and as people of the lower ranks began to find a voice and have a felt presence.[17] At the same time, commentators on Gay expressed increasing concern over what we might call the social politics in his works.

In 1756, clergyman Joseph Warton disclosed his own ambivalence toward the poet in remarks that foreshadow later disapproval. While placing

Gay in then-accepted fashion among poetry's elite ("such as possessed the true poetical genius"), Warton's comments evince a discomfort similar to, if less assured than, Haywood's at a destabilizing of the social order. Despite his deferential ranking of the poet, Warton finds little to commend when he turns to specific works. His response is a moral one, but is cast in terms of the actual street-level "pickpockets, strumpets, and highwaymen" peopling Gay's works as "little Villains" who, as burlesque figures, expose "great Ones." Admitting that he "could never percieve [*sic*] that fine vein of concealed satire supposed to run through [*The Beggar's Opera*]," Warton says:

> [T]hough I should not join with a bench of Westminster Justices in forbidding it to be represented on the stage, yet I think pickpockets, strumpets, and highwaymen, may be hardened in their vices by this piece; and that *Pope* and *Swift* talked too highly of its moral good effects.[18]

Uncertain how to negotiate the metaleptic complexity of Gay's "deep play," Warton fears its unhealthy influence for a class of people indelicate as well as threatening. He misses, or assumes that "lesser" readers may miss, the ironic social reversals: pickpockets, strumpets, and highwaymen stand in for prime ministers and politicians, tradesmen and kings. Eliding satire and sincerity, he responds uneasily—and tellingly—to the slippage of social categories that such reversals make imaginable. Gay's works could be seen by the wrong eyes as dangerous examples.

Through the course of the eighteenth century, literary commentary began to focus on the lives and characters of authors quite as much as on their works. Thus Gay's life assumed greater importance; his own social background became a highlighted problem. Early literary historians—discussing the works rather than the life—gloss over or elevate the poet's ambiguous social rank. As the orphaned younger son of a younger son from a West Country trading family, Gay possessed financial prospects that were only precarious at best, and his formal education, if solid, was acquired only at a provincial grammar school. Almost the only records we have from his early years are inauspicious: these document his unfinished tenure as apprentice to a draper.[19] The few independently verifiable facts are readily summoned. As a teenager, Gay went from his hometown to London, apprenticed to one Willet, a silk mercer in the Strand. In the summer of 1706 he was released, and he returned to Devon. Nothing else is certain. This episode—itself an emblem of rank and social context—accrued an importance in the presentation of Gay's life and works that extends to this day.

David Nokes finds in the apprenticeship and other elements in the poet's biography evidence suggesting that Gay was (as we now say) gay: "During his early years in London, Gay had been employed as a draper's apprentice at Willet's shop in the New Exchange, an area notorious as a favourite haunt of sodomites."[20] Nokes suggests that much later Gay's friends, Pope in particular, closeted this information about his early life, their "guilty secret" as he (perhaps squeamishly) terms it. "When Pope was approached by Richard Savage in 1736 for biographical information about Gay's early life," Nokes observes, "he was keen to draw a veil over this period. 'As to his being apprenticed to one Willet, etc.,' Pope protested, 'what are such things to the public? Authors are to be remembered by the works and merits, not accidents of their lives.'"[21] Pope here might appropriately be taken primarily at his word, as valuing literary output over life circumstance, in keeping with period assessments.

Nokes's interpretation here, leading to this biographical "outing" of Gay, is part of a long-standing trend of critical attention to the poet's personal life. From the eighteenth to the nineteenth century, the language of this attention is increasingly valenced by preoccupations and terminology for what we would call social class and gender. Wary and ever more negative readings of Gay's character began to accumulate, with the apprenticeship episode gaining new shape and importance. Indeed, in addition to supplying a measure by which to assess the growing importance of Gay's "life" to his reputation, the episode demonstrates a shift in the values enlisted to interpret that "life": the author's proper orientation with regard to a defining manliness.

Nokes's reading of Gay's character places the 1995 biography in this tradition. With a somewhat anachronistic psychologizing, he draws from Gay's life—beginning with the apprenticeship episode—evidence for "secret homosexual tendencies," which for Nokes are problematic handicaps to a proper manliness. Applying to his eighteenth-century subject a later psychology based upon gendered traits, Nokes thus finds in his (negatively) queered Gay a "painful sense of inferiority" (364) and "anxieties about his own sexuality" (329). According to Nokes, these stem from the poet's failure as a (normal) "predatory male" and from his "basic psychological" discomfort at being an "emasculated one," an "honorary female" (340). However mid- to late-twentieth-century Nokes's terminology in this instance may be, such a reading of Gay's character is not new. Analysis of the tradition of such readings illuminates those emerging categories of class and gender as applied to individual character that Gay's satiric art itself investigates and interrogates.

An erosion in Gay's stature becomes apparent if we examine biographical representations over time. The first commentators on Gay's life invariably see his youthful engagement and subsequent failure as a silk mercer's apprentice as a mark of superiority, strength, and genius. They move quickly over the provinciality and apparent financial need in Gay's background, and justify his leave-taking from commercial employment. The Ayre account of 1745 is quick to see Gay's gentlemanly love of books beneath his failure at the "Slavery" of trade:

> [H]e grew so fond of Reading and Study, that he frequently neglected to exert himself in putting off Silks and Velvets to the Ladies. . . . Not being able to go thro' this Slavery, and doing what he did in the Shop with a mind quite bent another Way, his Master seldom put him forward to serve, but some other, who had the Business more at Heart: By Degrees Mr. *Gay* became entirely to absent himself from the Shop, and at last, by Agreement with his Master, to withdraw from it, and retire into the Country.[22]

The 1760 preface to the *Plays* published by the Tonsons describes Gay's apprenticeship as a "station not suiting his liberal spirit," likewise approving his departure:

> Having thus honourably got free from all restraint, he followed the bent of his genius, and soon gave the public some admirable proofs of the character for which he was formed by nature.[23]

A 1770 Dublin edition of his works depicts his termination from the mercer's shop in similar terms. Characterizing Gay as "an original poetic genius," the biographer says:

> [H]aving thus purchased the ease of his mind, he indulged himself freely and fully in that course of life, to which he was irresistibly drawn by nature. Genius concurred with inclination; poetry was at once his delight and his talent.[24]

This version of the curtailed apprenticeship serves a portrait of the poet's innately genteel genius. However, new attitudes applied to the same facts soon produced a different tale.

"POET OF A LOWER ORDER": AN UNHEROIC GAY

Samuel Johnson's late-eighteenth-century treatment of poets' works and lives created criticism of a new kind. *The Lives of the English Poets* (1779) confers on certain writers a celebration of individual accomplishment that has undergirded the literary canon to our own time and has helped to define heroism in general in the post-Enlightenment world.[25] Johnson took up with keen if sometimes perplexed attention the interplay of a writer's works and *his* life (the masculine pronoun is definitional). Geared to readers at the middle ranks, such a moral heroism became, as it has remained, a matter of right thinking and behavior in the context, not of kingly politics or the battles of knight-warriors, but of the individual, private histories of ordinary (male) persons. The poet became exemplar on the one hand, or caveat on the other. Johnson articulated, through his survey of English men of letters, an ideal of autonomous, forceful, rational, and prevailing manliness. Necessarily excluding women from serious discussion of such heroism, the new criterion introduced considerations of character framed by the question: How properly "manly" are the poet's conduct and works?[26]

Johnson's apotheosis of the writer ennobled private life and thus fit the late-Georgian sensibility of an increasingly business- and civic-minded nation oriented toward and shaped by the "middling sort." This evaluation stands at odds with the parodic and relational ethos that underpins the satire of John Gay. Moreover, this late-century criticism served a new cultural function: where earlier commentary had articulated a reflection of prevailing performance practice (and the public taste it implied), Johnson's opinions formed and led assessments of aesthetic merit and inferiority designed to instruct an audience of readers. His declarations about Gay in *The Lives* seem to have been particularly influential, echoing time and again through the remarks of subsequent writers of prefaces, biographical dictionaries, and works of literary commentary.[27]

Johnson begins his discussion of Gay with a qualified and chary discussion of his poetry and drama. Although the sixteen-page account is not Johnson's most damning portrait, his disaffection emerges—with a suggestive hint of inferior rank as well as an explicit association with the lesser gender. "As a poet he cannot be rated very high," Johnson declares, "He was, as I once heard a female critick remark, 'of a lower order.' He had not in any great degree the *mens divinior*, the dignity of genius."[28] Early in the discussion, Gay's "life," as Johnson gives it, becomes a charged and determining presence which structures the reading of the writer's works. Moral faults dominate. A charge of failed personal heroism permeates the account.

Johnson and Gay held not only different but *competing* moral agendas. Gay, the satirist, limned a world that human beings negotiate relationally and politically at every turn. By contrast, Johnson was a moralist of the individual—of an ostensibly depoliticized individual at that. As Jeffrey Plank observes, literature in Johnson is, at least overtly, "separated from politics."[29] For Johnson, right thinking and behaving are matters of the rational conscience, transcending the dynamics of the social and the political; although from our vantage point, Johnson's individual seems altogether political, and the morality of personal striving and reason fittingly reflects and serves the socioeconomic currents and nationalist ideology of Hanoverian England.

Plank identifies Johnson's method in the *Lives* as a "recombination" of the poetic device of inserting an "inset narrative as a moral tale in descriptive poetry" (335). The "poets" (as represented in emblematic life stories) and their works equally serve a didactic purpose.[30] The "moral" in Gay's "life" emerges as Johnson shapes the poet's biography. The first ten paragraphs take up the known facts: Gay's parentage; his early schooling and apprenticeship; his service to the Duchess of Monmouth; his writing of *The Shepherd's Week* and other early "trifles"; the poet's failure to gain court patronage. Tellingly, Johnson imaginatively embroiders on the apprenticeship story:

> How long he continued behind the counter, or with what degree of softness and dexterity he received and accommodated the Ladies, as he probably took no delight in telling it, is not known. The report is that he was soon weary of either the restraint or servility of his occupation, and easily persuaded his master to discharge him.[31]

Johnson, in contrast to earlier writers, uses the possessive pronoun—"his occupation"—thus identifying rather than distancing the young man and future poet with the "servility" of working as an apprentice in such shop. Johnson's language suggests a "pliant" Gay, whose hypothesized characteristics of "softness and dexterity" seem to align him in this sentence, with the presumed "softness and dexterity" of the "Ladies" he was "accommodating." Similarly, gendered and feminizing associations characterize subsequent accounts.

In Johnson's treatment, Gay's "life" next supplies an "unheroic" admonition: pliancy, awkwardness, eagerness to please, and success through luck alone cannot produce great literary accomplishment. From this point, Johnson's fictionalizing of the account increases noticeably as he infers from known events the imagined "hopes," thoughts, and feelings that create for the poet a character to serve the intended lesson. He finds in Gay

> a man easily incited to hope and deeply depressed when his hopes were disappointed. This is not the character of a hero; but it may naturally imply something more generally welcome, a soft and civil companion. Whoever is apt to hope good from others is diligent to please them; but he that believes his powers strong enough to force their own way, commonly tries only to please himself. (2:272)

Johnson scoffs that Gay "had been simple enough to imagine that those who laughed at the *What d'Ye Call It* would raise the fortune of its author" (2:272). Later he retells a "class-conscious" anecdote about Gay's awkwardness at court, describing how the poet, "advancing with reverence, too great for any other attention, stumbled at a stool" (2:274). A subsequent paragraph ends accusingly: "[Gay] is said to have been promised a reward, which he had doubtless magnified with all the wild expectations of indigence and vanity" (2:274). Projecting into the mind of his subject "magnifications" and "expectations," Johnson castigates his protagonist's projected lack of diligence and humility: "This is not the character of a hero."

Johnson descried nothing principled in Gay's work. *The Beggar's Opera* he describes as "without any moral purpose" (2:278). Of the fables he says:

> For a Fable he gives now and then a Tale or an abstracted Allegory; and from some, by whatever name they may be called, it will be difficult to extract any moral principle. (2:283)

Johnson's distaste is not surprising; his pronouncements would offer an easy target to the very fables he fails to appreciate. Gay's satires, especially the fables, insistently interrogate the configurations and delusions of varieties of human power, not the least of these being moral expression.[32] With conscious self-implication, Gay often moralizes about moralizing per se. Exposing the inherent self-deception in pontification, he targets the combined grandiosity and impossibility of imagining morality in absolute terms removed from the specifics governed by social relation, context, and either self-serving or subjecting power. Gay's metaleptic strategies of glancing allusion and provocative mirrorings create a satire that at once insists that morality is relational and sets a standard for alert, subversive literary lessons of a public and social character, as twentieth-century reawakenings in Brecht, Havel, and Ayckbourn attest.

Johnson likewise dismisses the pastoral, unable to see the mode with its long tradition of political comment as a linchpin for the allusive and figurative method of Gay's critique.[33] At its conclusion, the "Life of Gay" discloses Johnson's blindness to both the politics of the pastoral and the politics embedded in his own viewpoint.

> There is something in the poetical Arcadia so remote from known reality and speculative possibility, that we can never support its representation through a long work. A Pastoral of an hundred lines may be endured; but who will hear of sheep and goats, and myrtle bowers and purling rivulets, through five acts? Such scenes please barbarians in the dawn of literature, and children in the dawn of life; but will be for the most part thrown away as men grow wise, and nations grow learned. (2:285)

This closing scene of "wise men" and "learned nations" looking with superior self-satisfaction on "barbarians" and "children" resonates like a parodic image from one of Gay's fables. It is little surprise to find Samuel Johnson an unsympathetic reader of John Gay. How could this moralist not rebuke the fabulist who playfully imagines the absurdity of didactic assurance like Johnson's own? In one fable a monkey moralizes after "seeing the world":

> Hear and improve, he pertly crys,
> I come to make a nation wise.
>
> (XIV.35–36)

Were Gay asked to comment on Johnson as a model, one easily imagines him fabling of monkeys "come to make a nation wise."

The "portrait" that accompanied Johnson's "Life" corresponds visually to this new trivializing and feminizing biographical portrait of a John Gay no longer read as satirical. An engraved image by William Smith, after a now lost portrait in enamel by C. F. Zincke, first appeared in 1775. Adapted by J. Hall, this portrait accompanies Johnson's biography of Gay in various printings and editions of *The Works of the English Poets* from 1779 on.[34] In a pose of coy—not to say girlish—youthfulness, Gay meets us in a visual rendering of the unlearned softness, indirection, and pliancy that led in Johnson's account to a castigated "indolence" and "vanity." This late-century portrait, which quickly found wider circulation, marks a notable departure—rather like Johnson's text, which it routinely accompanied—from earlier visual images of the poet. It contrasts with all previous depictions both in its physical rendering and especially in its representation of Gay's character and cultural stature. The mature, determined man in a conventionally authoritative pose is replaced by a youthful gamine. (See fig. 3.)

The iconographic history of John Gay presents a complicated mosaic.[35] The only portrait for which he is known to have sat dates from the 1720s, a painting by William Aikman for Henrietta Howard, countess of Suffolk. This touchstone portrait has not been discovered (although as documents in the archives of the National Portrait Gallery in London attest, paintings said to be the "lost Aikman" have surfaced now and again since the nineteenth century). With the success of *The Beggar's Opera*, this Aikman portrait was reproduced in a mezzotint by Francis Kyte in the summer of 1728 and in an engraving by George Bickham, "The New Deceptio Visûs" of 1729. (See fig. 1). "My portrait mezzotint is published from Mrs. Howard's painting," Gay wrote in July 1728.[36] (See fig. 4.)

Two early sculptures also resemble the image of Gay taken from Aikman. A carved bust of the poet adorns the wooden frame of Hogarth's oil painting of the climactic scene in *The Beggar's Opera* (discussed in chapter 1) and is believed to be an original frame that dates, like the painting, to the years immediately following the play when Gay was still living. His visage recalling the engravings from Aikman, the poet is flanked on

Fig. 3. Mezzotint portrait of John Gay by William Smith after C. F. Zincke (1775). Courtesy of the National Portrait Gallery, London.

Fig. 4. Mezzotint portrait of John Gay by Francis Kyte after William Aikman (1729).
© Copyright The British Museum.

Fig. 5. Sculpted marble portrait of John Gay by John Michael Rysbrack (1736) in Westminster Abbey, London. Courtesy of Westminster Abbey; photograph by Amanda Powell.

the frame by the contextualizing masks of comedy and tragedy (see fig. 2). A posthumous relief by Michael Rysbrack on Gay's burial monument in Westminster Abbey (1736), like the carving with the Hogarth painting, resembles the prints derived from the Aikman image. (See fig. 5.)

Another portrait said to be of Gay and attributed to Michael Dahl (1659?–1743) was purchased by John Frederick, third duke of Dorset in the 1770s for his gallery of literary portraits. Its subject bears a likeness to the man in the earlier images, especially in the less literally realistic terms of period portraiture, and the painting probably dates well before the 1770s (possibly to Gay's lifetime). (See fig. 6.) Only these depictions of Gay, together with the Zincke image of 1775 that was reproduced in Johnson's *Lives*, are traceable to the eighteenth century. The engravings taken from the missing Aikman and possibly the small carving on the frame of the Hogarth painting are the only images that appear before the poet's death in 1732.

The early portraits, those few dateable to before midcentury, represent the poet as a mature man evoked in a steadfast and authoritative pose. In several instances the man is contextualized with reference to his works and to his stature as a satirist. A sharp contrast to these images is the later, fanciful depiction of the boy-Gay who, with his softened, androgynous features, looks over his shoulder coquettishly from *The Lives of the Poets*. This noticeable distinction bears out, in visual terms, the course of Gay's representation as a literary figure in textual sources, from early to late century.

"THE LITTLE FAT POET": A TRIVIALIZING TRADITION

Johnson's negative and trivializing assessment of Gay in *The Lives of the English Poets* tremendously influenced subsequent criticism and biography. Eventually, disapproving editors enlisted didactic readings to counter the widespread popularity of Gay's poems and plays among readers of the lower ranks whose behavior became the concern of educators. Johnson's admonitions about character, particularly as he expressed these in language suggestive of proper behavior and attitudes with regard to rank and gender, were taken up and elaborated in later accounts. Moreover, in an increasingly earnest and sentimentally moral nineteenth century, Gay's writing and character came to represent for commentators the decadent sensibility of his satiric age.

Commentators after the 1780s almost invariably contend with Johnson's verdicts, engaging his assessment even to counter it. Thus, Gay's admirers testify to the sway of Johnson's taste by objecting to it. In 1790 the flippant

Fig. 6. Portrait of John Gay by Michael Dahl (17–?), in a private collection.

author of *The Bystander; or, Universal Weekly Expositor by a Literary Association* questions Johnson's own character, inferring that the dismissal of Gay stems from a dour envy:

> [T]hough *Oliver* [Johnson], in compliance to a lady, will not allow him to have been more than of the *lower order*—which expression one would think the *world* has imitated—yet I will venture to say if he himself could

have boasted half his lyric merits, he would have maintained a much higher rank in poetic fame.[37]

In a 1796 edition of the *Fables*, William Coxe complains:

> Johnson certainly did not sufficiently estimate the poetical works of Gay. . . . Though Gay cannot be classed among the highest ranks in the Temple of Fame, yet he certainly does not deserve to be placed in the lower order.[38]

The "Life of the Author" appended to a 1794 *Poetical Works of John Gay* counters Johnson using the latter's terms: "[Gay's] compositions, though original in some parts, are not of the highest kind." The anonymous editor then goes on to complain that "The estimate of his poetical character, as given by Dr. Johnson, is, in some instances, too severe to be approved by readers uncorrupted by literary prejudices."[39] This objection to a tainting by "literary prejudice" comments suggestively on the formation of a national literary history and canon (then in process), and on Johnson's role in this emerging cultural project.

Subsequent critics and historians extended Johnson's moral agenda. As Gay's works entered the stream of literature especially printed for the instruction of youth of various classes, the poet's early biography took on a fresh homiletic significance. In new editions of Gay's "life" and works, the anecdotal history of his apprenticeship metamorphoses further, with pointed application to the burgeoning market for children and people of the lower order.[40]

In tracing Gay's reputation, the issue of social rank plays an interesting role, both as early to later critics reacted to the topic in the works, where reversals of low and high structure the burlesque strategies, and as commentators regarded the poet's own background. Curiously, Gay's reputation suffered diminishment as critics took up a feminizing and infantilizing language to describe his character, while at the same time, his friend Pope— whose deformities and ill health certainly made him an apt candidate for such treatment—rose, to an extent, above his infirmities.[41] Two factors seem to contribute to the construction of Gay's lesser stature, especially with regard to his Scriblerian colleagues. One of these is social rank. However marginalizing Pope's health and his Roman Catholicism, the social, educational, and financial circumstances of his upbringing near London gave him a considerably more auspicious beginning than Gay's. In his prosperity, Pope was positioned to exemplify the new morality discussed above. Self-reliant as well as prosperous, Pope forged a career in letters that at once bespoke his independence of mind and successfully provided him a comfortable, self-generated income. He supplied a model for the new private heroism of the age. Moreover, as commentators have long observed, Pope shrewdly cultivated his own reputation.

The second factor that bears importantly on the legacy of Gay's subordination in literary history is the fact that his reputation, from the beginning, was shaped by his colleagues, friends, and survivors Swift and Pope—and not always to Gay's advantage. Gay died in 1732, at the age of forty-seven, well before his elder, Swift (1667–1745) and his junior, Pope (1688–1744). As already noted regarding epistolary style, Gay was casual, even careless about the management of his image. His career ended just after he had acquired the kind of celebrity that encourages public self-promotion. In addition, the cult of literary personality at which Pope especially was later to excel had not yet become so prevalent in the marketing of literature.

Gay's reticence in this arena sharply contrasts with the forwardness of Pope and even Swift, who, especially in their later years, lavished considerable attention on their reputations, overseeing such retrospective publications as editions of their correspondence.[42] In the 1740s, a virtual industry of anecdote began to accrue around Pope (as it was to surround Johnson in the next generation). The events and conversations captured therein invariably serve to enhance Pope's reputation. From these retrospective traditions connected to Swift, and especially Pope, surfaces much of the biographical detail that we have about Gay. Typically, Gay appears as a lesser figure who functions in the anecdotes to enhance the stature of his friends.[43] A kind of social subordination in Gay's position among the Scriblerians can be read into the information that survives.[44] On the other hand, Gay's status there may simply reflect the nature and purpose of the records. In any case, Gay emerges as secondary in these accounts even as social subordination continues to be developed as a moral thread in biographical treatments of him that continued to be published after Johnson's.

Popular editions of Gay's works from the end of the century onward take up and elaborate Johnson's warnings. There, the apprenticeship episode takes an illuminating turn as, far from giving evidence of Gay's genius, it begins to teach a lesson about a morally remiss individual of a particular social class. Like Johnson, the anonymous editor-biographers identify the young Gay with the job of apprentice; for such persons, poetry is no excuse for shirking one's duties. In a rhetorical maneuver that tellingly renders literary gifts subservient to the work ethic and hierarchy of shop-keeping, some accounts of the incident shift the reader's perception of the event from Gay's point of view to that of the unnamed silk mercer. A "Life of the Author" of 1793, for example, describes the young future poet's leave-taking thus: "Of an occupation ill suited to his talents he soon became weary, and easily procured a discharge from his master, *to whom he was like to be of little service*" (emphasis mine).[45] An 1801 version supplies the feelings of apprentice and master, sympathy clearly residing with the latter:

[T]he accommodating nature of moving behind a counter became disgust-
ing. His consequent want of attendance and assiduity gave much dissatisfaction to his master, which procured his release on easy conditions, long
before the expiration of his term of servitude.[46]

Purposing to instruct an audience of people from the lowest ranks by means
of school editions and cheap popular prints, this rendering of the story
carefully outlines with some elaboration the expected behavior for an apprentice.

Gay came to represent not only a failure of personal character but of
the moral and aesthetic sensibility taken to be characteristic of his time.
His works continued to be enjoyed, especially *The Beggar's Opera*, *The
Fables*, *Trivia*, and *The What-d'Ye-Call-It*. However, by the late eighteenth
century expurgated versions appeared, trimmed of "savage," "heathen,"
and "indelicate" elements.[47] The Library of Standard Music published *The
Beggar's Opera* in the 1830s with "the objectionable poetry altered."[48] James
Plumptre's remarks of 1823 capture the tone of this trimming. In his preface to a school edition, Plumptre declares to "the Special and Sub-commit-
tees of the Society for promoting Christian Knowledge" that he has re-
lieved the fables of "a very considerable portion of alloy" so that "nothing
should appear inconsistent with the faith, the conversation, and the practice of a Christian."[49] In an unpublished manuscript, Plumptre makes the
point even more bluntly: "[Gay] was promoted into a walk, which rendered his talents a snare to himself, and in general a nuisance to his fellow
creatures. . . . Let his example prove a warning to others, and it will not
have been in vain."[50]

In his 1849 edition of *Select Works of the British Poets*, John Aikin
identifies Gay as an epitome of indelicate Augustan times. Aikin passes
over Gay's poetry and drama with dispatch to focus on the character of
both poet and era. Despite a "sweetness of disposition," Gay "was indolent
and improvident;"[51] the success of *The Beggar's Opera* indicates "a coarse-
ness in the national taste which could be delighted with the repetition of
popular ballad-tunes, as well as a fondness for the delineation of scenes of
vice and vulgarity" (283). Gay's works, full of singable songs and plebeian
characters, presented a more unsettling (because more accessible) satire
than other Augustan works, the intricately ironic mock-treatises of Swift
for instance, or the finely finished high burlesques of Pope.

As the nineteenth century continued, the attention in commentary about
Gay began to focus ever more insistently on his faulty character. Offering a
sampling of Addison, Gay, and Somerville, Charles Cowden Clarke critiques Gay in his 1875 introduction with scarcely a mention of the works.[52]
Focusing his "reading" on the poet himself, Clarke declares briskly: "Gay's

works lie in a narrow compass, and hardly require minute criticism" (158). The fables Clarke understands entirely in terms of Gay's character: "He understands animals, because he has more than an ordinary share of the animal in his own constitution" (159).

Gay's most influential Victorian critic was William Thackeray, whose lecture in "The English Humourists" (1853) at once attends to and trivializes the poet's person.[53] With a breezy tone Thackeray reads Gay as Johnson's "playfellow of the wits," apparently alluding to the image from Zincke that was duplicated in Johnson's *Lives:*

> In the portraits of the literary worthies of the early part of the last century, Gay's face is the pleasantest perhaps of all. It appears adorned with neither periwig nor nightcap . . . and he laughs at you over his shoulder with an honest boyish glee—an artless sweet humour. He was so kind, so gentle, so jocular, so delightfully brisk at times, so dismally woebegone at others, such a natural good creature that the Giants loved him. (587)

As Thackeray continues, Gay becomes, in the Johnsonian manner, an object of personal critique and admonition. His habits and his body itself receive the critic's curious fixation:

> But we have Gay here before us, in these letters—lazy, kindly, uncommonly idle; rather slovenly, I'm afraid; forever eating and saying good things; a little, round, French abbé of a man, sleek, soft-handed, and soft-hearted. (590)

Thackeray's discussion passes over the works in favor of a critique of his subject's presumably "lazy," "idle," "slovenly" character. With insistent gaze upon the poet's person, Thackeray constructs a caricature of the kind often found in criticism of women writers; his comments recur to the physical plane in a language that is notably sensual. His Gay is suggestively "sleek, soft-handed, and soft-hearted."

In turn, Thackeray dismisses the "morality" of Gay's *Fables*, arguing not from the texts themselves, but from their imagined failure to improve the infant prince to whom Gay dedicated them in 1727 (grown to manhood to be "The Butcher of Culloden" in 1745):

> Mr. Gay's *Fables*, which were written to benefit that amiable prince, the Duke of Cumberland, the warrior of Dettingen and Culloden, I have not, I own, been able to peruse since a period of very early youth; and it must be confessed that they did not effect much benefit upon the illustrious young prince, whose manners they were intended to mollify, and whose natural ferocity our gentle-hearted Satirist perhaps proposed to restrain. (591)

The contrast between the naturally ferocious warrior prince and the soft, "gentle-hearted Satirist" continues the feminizing of Gay, once more bringing together in a single image the issues of gender and rank as the poet is cast, unflatteringly, in the role of ineffectively nurturing or instructive servant to the prince.

Thackeray adds to his novelistic portrait a further projection of otherness of class and ethnicity as he imagines the poet in a figurative circus. His text continues the fixation on rank, the association with the "ladies," and the trivializing use of diminutive adjectives that had become something of a tradition in such commentary on Gay.

> But the quality of this true humourist was to laugh and make laugh, though always with a secret kindness and tenderness, to perform the drollest little antics and capers, but always with a certain grace, and to sweet music—as you may have seen a Savoyard boy abroad, with a hurdy-gurdy and a monkey, turning over head and heels, or clattering and piroueting in a pair of wooden shoes, yet always with a look of love and appeal in his bright eyes, and a smile that asks and wins affection and protection. Happy they who have that sweet gift of nature! It was this which made the great folks and Court ladies free and friendly with John Gay—which made Pope and Arbuthnot love him—which melted the savage heart of Swift when he thought of him—and drove away, for a moment or two, the dark frenzies which obscured the lonely tyrant's brain, as he heard Gay's voice with its simple melody and artless ringing laughter. (591–92)

Thackeray's discussion has little connection with the satirist or his work. This simile of the dancing dark-skinned boy hoping for "affection and protection" from such (men) as are "lonely tyrants" proceeds from the same aesthetic and moral promontory from which Johnson looked out over "barbarians" and "children." In his trivializing fiction of Gay, Thackeray speaks from the position of Johnson's wise and manly writer. The sexualized effeminacy and racial inferiority of his "Gay" make explicit larger, troubling implications in Johnson's view.

Late-nineteenth-century commentators turned biographical description into stridently personal attack. Austin Dobson in 1899 recast a now familiar anecdote with added emphasis on Gay's supposed passivity:

> In his boyhood . . . it must be assumed that Gay's indolence was more strongly developed than his application, for his friends could find no better opening for him than that of apprentice to a London silk mercer.[54]

Dobson reiterates the images of women and children:

> He was thoroughly kindly and affectionate, with just that touch of clinging
> in his character, and of helplessness in his nature, which, when it does not
> inspire contempt . . . makes a man the spoiled child of men and the playfellow
> of women. (271)

Duncan Tovey's essay of 1897 dismisses Gay with a striking preoccupation. Tied to the material, Gay is "unsuited for high themes": "This plump Artaeus had no strength but when he touched earth."[55] Gay's works are entirely bypassed as the poet, become an objectified body, exists only in the company of others to whom he owes whatever work he has:

> "Let us lend friend Gay a hand," we can fancy these greater gods [Swift,
> Pope, etc.] saying, bursting in upon the little fat poet who is racking his
> brains in that most painful of all tasks, the quest of things sprightly or
> naive. (117)

With the overdetermined bodily imagery of "the little fat poet . . . racking his brains," Tovey fully trivializes Gay's "quest" with the adjectives "sprightly" and "naive," words customarily reserved for the (denigrated) elderly, women, and children. Character and works conflate completely when Tovey proposes that: "We may . . . treat [Gay's] memory with the good-humoured indulgence which his friends extended to his life" (137). This sweeping dismissal contrasts sharply with the prestige accorded Gay by such Georgian writers as Cibber, Mottley, and even the wary Warton. Tovey's portrait stands in a long line of highly inferential—indeed, fictionalized—treatments of Gay's life and person.[56]

While a tradition of ethical controversy has followed Gay's work from the beginning, a tradition of dismissal shaped his literary reputation from the eighteenth century. Troubling and curious at first view, this derogation becomes legible and revealing when seen against the developing standards of literary historiography. Gay's character became feminized, an "unheroic" and dangerous model. His works required censure, alteration, and careful sifting. Certainly this tradition of dismissal supplies an important context for our received ideas about Gay today. Moreover, the interbraiding of concerns about gender and social rank that are used to diminish Gay's stature supply an ironic validation for the aptness of his own examinations of these hierarchies. In his satires, people of the lower ranks, women, and animals supply the pivotal categories that structure Gay's burlesques.

3

Apollo, Bowzybeus, and Molly Mog:
Popular Culture, Print Markets,
and Oral Traditions

The eighteenth century saw a shuffling of social strata as mercantile capitalism relocated economic power from a landed aristocracy to a new elite based on capital, trade, and individualized ownership of goods and services. In this world of shifting social identity, cultural codes marking class—arts, education, pastimes, and manners—took on new importance as such old indicators as feudal sumptuary laws and the stable roles of manorial and village life gave way. "Taste" (which can be acquired) replaced "breeding" as the mark of status.[1] John Gay's satire critiques power relations within these shifts of authority and values. In plays and poems teeming with figures, sayings, and concepts drawn from folklore, Gay identifies and makes use of the customary and expressive forms that increasingly marked relative positions of dominance and place. His burlesques thus sketched conceptual outlines of the relationship between culture and social structures that would survive, gain currency, and shape study and art into the twenty-first century.

In their highlighted delineations of how it looked and sounded to be "popular" on the one hand and "polite" on the other, Gay's burlesques set the stage for the formulation of the category "culture."[2] The lineaments of culture as an idea in the modern sense are recognizable in the late eighteenth-century interest in ballads and folk songs—exactly the materials identified as "low" in Gay, and already recognized by him as forms that function as part of social contexts that individuals identify as "their own" or as "other." As satires, Gay's works mark as well the relational exploitation of the economically "low" by the "high," a conceptual design that eventually came to be articulated as the political dynamics of social class.

With increasing social and economic mobility, culture at every level—

that is, performed and expressive arts and manners—took on a new function: it served to distinguish relational access to or exclusion from social and political authority. Gay manipulates taste to indicate rank precisely because cultural forms—songs, texts, images, sartorial fashions, dances—were accruing new representational importance. Without parodic self-awareness, Addison and Steele in *The Spectator* purpose to identify those ways of behaving, thinking, consuming, and appearing that would mark a "polite" social order. When "high" birth no longer provided the sole route to dominion, people striving for influence acquired or imitated, as best they could, commodities or behaviors that signified their own advantageous identity in class and power relationships.

As Britain stood poised to dominate the world, Gay wrote in appreciation and critique of its hierarchical mix of peoples, highlighting with a thoroughness that was entirely new the strivings and viewpoints of those at the lower ranks. His satires—popular, eclectic, genre-defying, parodic, and polyvalent—gather up, like a country fair, the sights and sounds, flavors and smells, tensions and merrymakings of the community's yearlong strivings. Analysis of this world of belief and expression not only clarifies Gay's complex and enduring vision, but allows us to examine the pivotal historical moment it mirrors.

POPULAR CULTURE IN GAY

Gay's comic satire enlists what we now call cultural forms, that is, representations of amusement and taste connected to community identity and social context. These references open to view the new relationship between culture and power that was being forged as England took the lead in transforming the early modern world into the modern.[3] Gay represents and satirizes this shift as he links cultural pastimes and representations to social division and power.

The profusion of traditional lore in Gay's work has gone largely unexamined by scholars.[4] Critical attention to *The Beggar's Opera* has omitted the genuinely popular nature of its musical underlayer—its referentiality to the traditional and significantly oral culture of people of the lowest ranks. Moreover, the pristine division that folklorists themselves at one time imagined between "pure" oral and "corrupt" printed songs likewise masked the popular and genuinely folkloric character of Gay's subtexts.[5] The songs in *The Beggar's Opera* flourished interchangeably in oral traditions and in print as well: on cheap broadsides sold on the streets and in collections like Thomas D'Urfey's best-selling *Pills to Purge Melancholy*.[6]

Complex traditional borrowings elsewhere in Gay's work make clear that these songs represent an ongoing preoccupation with and anatomizing of social rank in terms of cultural materials.

Other popular materials texture Gay's works. His dramatic and poetic portraits—of common people especially—always include traditional speech forms and beliefs: proverbs, riddles, and superstitions of all kinds. In the eighteenth century proverbs came to be associated with the underclass. In a letter from 25 July 1741, Lord Chesterfield recommends that his son avoid "old sayings" and "common proverbs" which were "proofs of having kept bad and low company . . . that you had never kept company with anybody above footmen and housemaids."[7] The voicing of long-standing conventions of wisdom, custom, and belief marks Gay's commoners. In *The Shepherd's Week* (1714), the love-smitten Lobbin declares: "True speaks that ancient Proverb, *Love is blind*." ("Monday," l. 99)[8] Similarly, the Quaker Tabitha in *The Espousal* (1720) declares proverbially: "The only present love demands is love"(l. 55).[9] In *The Wife of Bath* (1713; 1730), the characters Alison and Franklyn carry on an exuberant flyting of proverbs current even today in oral tradition:

> *Alison.* One Wedding, the proverb says, begets another: What think you, old Heart of Oak, shall Experience supply the want of Youth?—come, let you and I for once verifie the old Saying—give me thy Hand, Old Boy.
> *Franklyn.* Hold, hold, Dame, Marry in haste and repent in leisure—There is a Proverb for your Proverb. . . .
> *Alison.* Slidikins!—Old, old!—pray do not measure my Corn with your Bushel, old dry Bones. . . .
> *Franklyn.* A very pretty Excuse!—Old Birds are not caught with Chaff, Friend . . .
>
> (I,i,293-304)[10]

The pastoral shepherds and milkmaids of *The Shepherd's Week* (1714) supply a virtual catalogue of still-reported seasonal customs of courtship and love divination: securing a lock of a sweetheart's hair ("Thursday," ll. 21–24)[11]; scattering a "Bag of Hemp-seed" at Midsummer's Eve to prompt the sight of a "True-Love" (ll. 27–34);[12] setting a snail in ashes overnight to "write" the initials of one's sweetheart's name (ll. 49–59);[13] tossing apple parings (ll. 91–96) which similarly fall into the shape of initials.[14] Other love portents include the marriage-foretelling first encounter on Valentine's morning (ll. 39–44); prognosticating treatments of hazelnuts (ll. 61–66), peascods (ll. 69–72), and apple seeds (ll. 99–105); and the still-remembered love rhyme about the kindly Lady Bug: "Fly, Lady-Bird, North, South,

East or West. / Fly where the Man is found that I love best" (ll. 86–87).[15]
Other traditional forms in Gay's works include games and folk drama, as
well as such deeper structures as themes and motifs.[16] These elements of
customary speech and belief—some of them enduringly part of traditional
lore—bring to life the uncourtly, "sub-bourgeois" speakers in Gay's satires
and the cultural levels they delineate.

Especially with the invention of ballad opera, such plebeian materials
became standard ingredients in the art and eventually the scholarship of a
class-conscious society. Mapping increasingly unstable and scrutinized
stratifications of rank in 1720s England, Gay's parodies articulated the new
mode of classificatory thinking, in Mary Poovey's term, that in turn informed the next century's development of modern "class" categories.[17]
Through a parodic play of representational forms across social boundaries,
Gay's works not only confound high and low literary genres and values
through burlesque, but do so as "deep play" to create a satire of the new
power terms of a market economy. The strategy of metalepsis enacts, through
figurative allusions, the dynamics of transmutation of the known into wildly
surprising new values by the ongoing play of risky exchange and reappearance. But the figure of allusion is always constructing the new appearance
against a backdrop whose valences, by definition, are historical and social.
An allusion is, by definition, a cultural inheritance.

Gay appropriates elements of popular discourse in three modes: (1) as
references and subtexts that set up ironic backdrops for his own compositions—for example, using the tune of a bawdy popular song as the air for a
text of his own; (2) as ways of characterizing and bringing into tangible
life common people and their world, evoking their voices and mannerisms;
and (3) as thematic and structural templates that shape both the message of
his satire and its method. These three uses of popular materials together create
in Gay's satire a parodic questioning of social stratification that is remarkably
forward-looking in its assumption of the system as dynamic and as an artifice. Typically, a popular form—a custom, belief, ballad, or motif—serves
as a site for Gay, whose own discourse then develops with greater complexity and satiric purpose, issues and attitudes raised by the form itself.

Gay's attitude toward the "low" material in his works has continued to
perplex critics. Commentators often see the satire as deriding commoners.
Hoyt Trowbridge, for example, declares:

> Like Shakespeare's artisans, shepherds, and squires, Gay's rustics have a
> certain naive charm, but from the sophisticated urban point of view which
> Gay (like Shakespeare) expected in his readers, these dairymaids and swine-
> herds are ludicrous—delightful but absurd.[18]

However, as Trowbridge himself demonstrates, *The Shepherd's Week* targets not the rustics so much as "the sophisticated urban point of view" enacted in such intellectual debates as the pastoral controversy swirling among the London literati of 1714. This dispute, which centered on a personal quarrel between Ambrose Philips and Alexander Pope, replayed some of the general issues of the long-standing "Moderns" versus "Ancients" argument and had political implications as well. Philips and his Whig cohorts in the modern or rationalist camp championed the writing of pastorals with reference to English settings and rural people, imitating colloquial speech and manners. Pope and his Tory circle promoted the writing of neoclassical pastorals modeled on those of Greece and Rome and set in a Golden Age of harmony and poetic artistry.[19]

A friend and supporter of Pope, Gay certainly took his side and on more than one occasion satirized Philips and others in his party. At the same time, it is a misreading to reduce Gay's pastoral strategies to this localized quarrel. Often, as in *The Shepherd's Week*, Gay facetiously undercuts his rustics and his own disingenuously naive voice as rustic bard. Nonetheless, he simultaneously validates both in his more thoroughgoing dismantling of "the urban point of view" from that marginal rural perspective. In fact, Gay's satire engineers a decentering that not only conveys the tangible actualities of underclass life and people, but looks on critically from that vantage point. These pastorals add to the literary and philosophical controversy a dimension of sociopolitical comment.[20]

Popular traditions also supplied Gay with organizing patterns. Some works owe their very framework to popular forms. His first produced play, *The Wife of Bath* (1713), pivots on a long-standing courtship custom. *The What-d'Ye- Call-It* (a two-act playlet of 1715 that critics have called many things) is a genre-confounding piece: satire, farce, melodrama, parody. Gay himself subtitled it "A Tragi-Comi-Pastoral Farce."[21] In fact, as we shall see, *The What-d'Ye-Call-It* cleverly reworks folk mumming patterns to expose the abuses found not only in polite theater and literature, but (more seriously) in the fabric of political and social life as well. In a similar fashion, Gay based *Polly*, his sequel to *The Beggar's Opera*, on the conventional Female Warrior motif of popular balladry. The venturing heroine wakes up to find herself inhabiting a Female Warrior narrative, her story unfolding along the lines of the conventional ballads. *Polly* undermines the gendering of the heroic ideal upon which the motif, the popular ballads, and the whole European ideology of heroism depend.[22] The interrogation of organizing patterns, of the interworking of the artistic and cultural together with the sociopolitical, is precisely the design that the three modern satirists—Brecht, Havel, and Ayckbourn—modeled on Gay.

The British Apollo

Gay's first literary effort was his anonymous and collaborative author-ship of *The British Apollo*, a popularly marketed subscription periodical begun by his fellow Devonian, Aaron Hill (1685–1750). The ironic yet exuberant presentation of quotidian popular materials in *The British Apollo* supplies background for later uses of popular materials and customary be-lief, speech, and behavior in Gay's poetry and drama. Published from 1708 to 1711, *The British Apollo*, modeled on *The Athenian Gazette* of John Dunton from the 1690s, joined a handful of reports of foreign and domes-tic news with a lively "question and answer" dialogic with subscribers. The authors included Gay and a whole circle of friends and acquaintances of Hill.[23]

Gay himself facetiously describes the paper in terms of social class, saying in 1711 that, "having of late Retreated out of this end of the Town [Westminster] into the City," it "still recommends its self by deciding Wa-gers at Cards, and giving good Advice to the Shop-keepers, and their Ap-prentices."[24] Something of an Augustan "Dear Abby," the collaborative "Apollo" took up myriad questions—probably many of them formulated by the authors themselves—on theology, courtship, geography and natural history, health, science, mythology, and all kinds of antiquarian and pro-verbial lore. Sometimes serious and factual, but often facetious in tone, the journal contains a plethora of popularly held beliefs, customs, and rhymes, as its authors responded to queries about the existence of fairies, move-ments of celestial bodies, the blackness of Africans, causes and cures of ailments, the origins and meanings of proverbial sayings, solutions to math-ematical problems, recommended courtship strategies, the interpretation of scriptural passages, and so on. Throughout, *Apollo* draws our attention—along with our laughter—to the links between customary belief and behav-ior on the one hand and identity on the other. In addition, however face-tious, "his" responses assume the onlooking rhetorical stance of modern ethnographic observation and comment.

Apollo carefully answered questions in the format in which they were posed. "*Why do the* Ancient Britains (*viz.* Welch men) *wear Leaks in their Hats on the first of March, and how long it has been a Custom among them?*" queries a (supposed) reader in Number 10 (from Friday, 12 March, to Wednesday, 17 March 1708). The cheeky oracle replies, citing a well-known chapbook history:

A. This Ceremony is observ'd on the first of *March*, in Commemoration of a signal Victory obtain'd by the *Britains* under the Command of a famous

General, known vulgarly by the Name of St. *David*. The *Britains* wore a Leak in their Hats to distinguish their Friends from their Enemies in the heat of the Battle. But *Apollo* somewhat fatigu'd by the number of his Addressers, begs leave to refer the Querist (for further Particulars) to the celebrated History of the *Seven Champions of Christendom.*[25]

Waggishly juxtaposing the proverbial and the pedantic, *British Apollo* Number 36 (From Friday, 11 June, to Wednesday, 16 June 1708) contains the following exchange:

Q. An your Godship pleases an humble Suitor Adresses you in the most obsequious manner, and Superlative Degree, acknowledging at the same time, your superabundant and excessive share of Wit, in the Solving of all intricate obstruse and mystical Questions, which Nature had concealed in her Womb of Oblivion, had not there arose such an infallible, supernatural, miraculous, and never-failing Society, to Pardigmatize and Rhetorically to explain all obstupifying Quiddities, to the Surprize and Astonishment of Mirriads of South Britains at your mighty Acatalepsie. After this, the humble Offering of one of your greatest Admirers, I beg a Solution of the following Question, and you'l infinitely Oblige Your most humble, most obliged and most Obedient Servant Q.X.

Why Men this Miracle believe,
And dream this mighty wonder,
That Mares do by the Wind conceive,
And Swans are hatch'd by Thunder?

A. Since our Querist, the more to engage our Beneplacity, has exhausted his Scaturiginous Brains, to explore Epithets demonstrative of his sublime Conceptions of our ineffable Perspicuity, in solving Ænigmatical Positions and confirming the Desultorious: And also (avoiding all Verbosity and Petulancy, Horrisonant to our Harmonious Entity) has selected all the choicest Flowers of Eloquence, within the Verge of his Comprehensibility, even to the Danger of an Eternal Future Sterility, thereby to render his Lines more worthy of our Cognisance; in Consideration whereof, we will Condescend to dissipate those impending Clouds of Perplexity he labours under, and resolve his Problem.

The Spanish Gennets, swift as Wind,
Some thought they thence Conceiv'd;
And frighted Swans their Nests more Mind,
Thence Thunder-hatch'd, believ'd.

Such self-reflexive mixing of rhetorical registers, with the ironic undermining and social coding it creates, outlines a key move in the parodic method of Gay's later satire. Moreover, the vivid and relational rendering of these registers marked an important new attention to them as systems of communal "cultivation"—that is, as "cultures."

Mock Pastorals

Gay does not sentimentalize folk traditions or their adherents, as antiquarians in search of "cultural survivals" would do a century or so later. Obviously steeped in traditional lore and eager to use it, Gay is at the same time detached, ironic, sometimes even scoffing in his references. The "Walker" in the mock-georgic *Trivia* (1717) determinedly sets himself apart from the superstitious realm of "cred'lous Boys" and "prattling Nurses," admonishing his readers sternly: "All Superstition from thy Breast repel." (ll. 175–86) But such momentary interdictions barely belie a manifest fascination with popular lore of all kinds, particularly as such customary discourse characterized people's social placement and made possible a parodic satire of a world dividing into stratified ranks that, untethered by the old symbolic order, are marked only by money and custom.

In the last eclogue of his mock-pastoral collection, *The Shepherd's Week* (1714), the rustic balladeer, Bowzybeus is "giddy" with drink and sings to the "Lads and Lasses" about him "with a Note so shrilling sweet and loud" (l. 48). His subjects are the stuff of popular discourse: on the one hand, the natural world of "Owles" and "Glow-worms," "Turnips" and "Will-a-Wisps," and on the other, the realm of rural, lower-class culture with its "Fairs and shows," "Lott'ries," "Thimbles," "Rings of Gold," "Balsoms," "Ague spells," and long-popular stories, psalms, and ballads.[26] The singing and fiddling Bowzybeus speaks from the experience and perspective of the lower orders of rural eighteenth-century England.

Gay identifies Bowzybeus as an ironically constructed alter ego. The poem's "Prologue" says self-deprecatingly to his dedicatee, the aristocratic Henry St. John, 1st Viscount Bolingbroke:

> Lo here, thou hast mine Eclogues fair,
> But let not these detain thine Ear.
> Let not th' Affairs of States and Kings
> Wait, while our *Bowzybeus* sings.
>
> (ll. 87–90)[27]

In this vein, the first-person narrator of the "Prologue" recounts a journey to court from the backcountry—for which Gay's west Devon origins would certainly qualify:

> Lo, I who erst beneath a Tree
> Sung *Bumkinet* and *Bowzybee* . . .
> Now write my Sonnets in a Book,
> For my good Lord of *Bolingbroke*.
>
> (ll. 1–6)

At the same time that he identifies with the songster Bowzybeus (albeit with a measure of irony), the writing author who supervises the publishing of his pastorals for such reading patrons as Bolingbroke separates himself from that realm of oral custom and tradition, noting with self-awareness the interposing mediation of the culture and experience of writing and reading. The engraved scene of the frontispiece to *The Shepherd's Week* illustrates this relation of the mediating poet-onlooker to the customary "real world" pastoral of a rural England: pen-in-hand, the poet sits in the corner writing as he watches the traditional village dance before him. The modern ethnographic stance of Gay's onlooker seems, in its self-awareness, more postmodern. As mentioned earlier, this self-reflexive attention to the authorial framing of written utterance and the moral and political dynamics contingent on any speaker's point of view remained a preoccupation for Gay. (See fig. 7.)

Like the drunken Silenus of Virgil's sixth eclogue, for whom (as we shall see) he is a simultaneously comic and appreciative parody, Bowzybeus is a custodian of culture and worldview. Thus, he "sooths th' attentive Ear" (1. 50) with "Carrols" of "Nature's Laws": "Why the grave Owl can never face the Sun" (1. 52); "How Turnips hide their swelling Heads below" (1. 55); and "How *Will-a-Wisp* mis-leads Night-faring Clowns" (1. 57). This catalogue takes up just such popular concerns as the young John Gay, fresh from the rustic West, answered for *The British Apollo*.[28]

The cavalcade of Bowzybeus's old songs generally fits the category that Addison in his famous *Spectator* essays on ballads called "the Darling Songs of the Common People."[29] As scholars have noted, Bowzybeus's "stamm'ring Speech" (1. 42) identifies him with the popular songsmith and playwright Thomas D'Urfey, who surfaces as an allusion several times in *The Shepherd's Week*.[30] However, most of the dozen or so ballads that Bowzybeus sings are old, anonymous broadside songs which do not appear in D'Urfey's anthologies. The single stage song in his repertoire—facetiously footnoted—is "A Soldier and a Sailor," a ribald ditty sung by Ben Sampson, the raucous sailor in Congreve's *Love for Love* (1695) (III.iv). The other of Bowzybeus's songs from the aristocratic level is "All in the Land of Essex," a similarly randy Restoration-era satire on buggering Quakers who "turn Gallants" with "sleek Mares." This unseemly song, too, is treated to elaborate scholarly comment.[31] The rest of the songs, however, are old ballads, most going back a century, that circulated on cheaply printed broadsides among working people in both the cities and the countryside. These songs would also have been recognizable to aristocratic singers because they supplied tunes for political lampoons.

Like the secrets of "Nature" cited by Bowzybeus with their suggestion of the topics of discussion in *The British Apollo*, this invocation of ballads

Frontispiece.   Lud.Du Guernier inv.et Scul.

Fig. 7. Engraving by du Guernier from the frontispiece to John Gay's *The Shepherd's Week* (1714). Courtesy of the William Andrews Clark Memorial Library, University of California, Los Angeles.

was, already at this early date, self-implicating. Gay had penned a half-dozen song lyrics for his plays, the unproduced *Mohocks* (1712) and *The Wife of Bath* (1713).[32] Within a few years he would prove himself not only one of the finest songwriters, but one of the earliest students, of British song culture.

GAY'S POPULAR BALLADS

Popular songs are vivid and evocative cultural markers. Eighteenth-century people at all levels were making diverse musics, and those musics, as Gay noted, came to code differences that signaled rank. Ballads and songs are at the center of Gay's satire, and the winning articulation of conventional form in his own song compositions lived on. After their immediate relevance waned, their lively and plebeian character made some of Gay's ballads popular for generations. His "Sweet William's Farewell" continues in oral tradition to our own day. Other songs by him circulated in print into the nineteenth century.

With an awareness of the traditionality of songs, Gay is significant both to the development of Anglo-American song traditions and to the study of them. A vibrant medium of popular taste and a marker of social class, balladry provides a key to Gay's satire; conversely, Gay's situating of ballads amidst other socially coded art forms reveals key features of early modern song traditions and their links to class structures and identity. His ballad operas, together with the nearly two hundred plays of the 1730s and 1740s that others wrote in imitation of them, have left an invaluable collection of printed tunes to popular ballads and dances of the seventeenth and eighteenth centuries. Moreover, the interest in these songs that followed their theatrical popularity prepared the way for the "ballad revival" of the mid-eighteenth century which demarcated popular songs as a field of inquiry and, with antiquarianism, launched the whole endeavor of cultural studies.[33]

Gay participated in popular song culture throughout his career, contributing ballads and songs within the broadside tradition as well as parodies commenting on that tradition. True ballad narratives in the broadside style like "Sweet William's Farewell" and "The Newgate Garland" reveal an easy familiarity with popular forms, as do the lyric songs "Molly Mog" and "A New Song of New Similes." In addition, Gay wrote pieces, often in dramas, that self-consciously position themselves as parodies vis-à-vis balladry and its social context. Gay thus calls attention to ballad traditions: the keepers and singers of ballads are characters in a burlesqued cultural context that divides into "high" art and "low." Gay's songs critique that context as we identify with the songs and their singers, sympathetic players in a politics of social rank.

Two of Gay's songs conform stylistically to "popular ballad" conventions of narrative, theme, language, and music and persisted with continuity and variation over time in people's song traditions. These are "ballads" in the folkloristic meaning of the term: sung narratives set to rounded tunes.[34] Gay wrote "Sweet William's Farewell to Black-eyed Susan" (also titled "Dark-eyed Susan") sometime before 1720, for it appears in his *Works* of that date as well as in song collections from the 1720s.[35] "The Newgate Garland" (also titled "Blueskin's Ballad") was probably written originally for John Thurmond's *Harlequin Sheppard*, a satirical pantomime of 1724. Immediately, this ballad too circulated in songbook and broadside versions.[36] These two ballads—one sentimental and the other satiric—fall into two of the principal story types that governed popular ballads on printed broadsides: the parting of a sailor and his lover and the murder of an underworld ruffian.[37] They show the accomplishment and self-consciousness of Gay's writing directed to a sophisticated audience of songbook purchasers and playgoers.

Both ballads evoke the street-ballad milieu, while their literary artfulness directs them to an audience aware of that milieu as an "other" (i.e., lower) social and economic level.[38] In this context, Gay positions himself as he does in the illustration to *The Shepherd's Week* noted above, as the onlooker at the margin, pen in hand. Songs like "Sweet William's Farewell" and especially the parodic ballads and songs contributed to the fashion for balladry together with the social interpretation of it that, in turn, prepared the way for the invention of ballad opera in 1728 and laid the groundwork for the next generation's "ballad revival" at both the "polite" and the popular levels.[39]

"Sweet William's Farewell" was surely Gay's most popular ballad. The text appears in songbooks and on broadsides of the 1720s with tunes by Richard Leveridge, Henry Carey, Pietro Sandoni, and George Hayden.[40] With regard to Gay's songs, Albert Friedman's claim that for Gay "the choice of the ballad style" to make a "joke" of that style and the people it served does not fit.[41] Balladry and ballad singers are generally not targets of Gay's ridicule. Rather, he identified the social coding that ballads afforded, using it to critique those in power and the world they kept in place. Gay's relationship to balladry is complex, nuanced, and participatory.

"Sweet William's Farewell" first appears on the more expensive engraved broadsides bearing musical notation that were directed to a musically literate audience of well-to-do concertgoers. Immediately the ballad became a stock item on cheaper woodcut broadsides and chapbooks without tunes, and continued to be sold as such on the streets well into the nineteenth century. G. Malcolm Laws summarizes the narrative:

Susan comes on board a ship seeking William. Hearing her voice, he slides
down a rope to the deck, kisses away her tears, and promises to be faithful
to her wherever he goes. The ship prepares to leave, and Susan waves a sad
farewell from her boat.[42]

The song, with the tune by Richard Leveridge that has persisted in tradition, begins as follows:

> All in the Downs the fleet was moor'd,
> The streamers waving in the wind,
> When black-ey'd Susan came aboard.
> Oh! where shall I my true love find!
> Tell me, ye jovial sailors, tell me true,
> If my sweet William sails among the crew.

Black-Eyed Susan   [B]

Sung by Mr. Thomas Young, West Petpeswick.

Ex. 1. Traditional version of Gay's "Sweet William's Farewell."[43]

The thematic context for Gay's song in tradition is the cluster of ballads depicting lovers' farewells, for example those in Laws's category "Ballads of Faithful Lovers" from O–27 through O–33. ("Sweet William" is
number O–28.)[44] Gay's ballad calls up the pattern and the kindred Annies
and Jimmys, Mollys and Johnnys who enact similar good-byes. At the same

time, "Sweet William's Farewell" stands out from tradition, invoking yet simultaneously deviating from the pattern. The verse has the deftness of a practiced poet: When William comes from "high upon the yard" on hearing Susan's voice, "The cord slides swiftly through his glowing hands, / And, (quick as lightning,) on the deck he stands." The imagery harkens back to polite verse; alongside such clichés as "quick as lightning" are elaborate metaphors that echo such poets as Dryden and Donne: "so the sweet lark . . . if, chance, his mate's shrill call he hear"; "my heart shall be / The faithful compass that still points to thee"; "The sails their swelling bosom spread."[45]

Despite its heightened "vocabulary," Gay's ballad has persisted among traditional singers, encouraged over the years, no doubt, by frequent printing on both sides of the Atlantic. A recent folklorist has remarked on the poetic self-consciousness of the text. Neil Rosenberg reports that collector Anita Best of Newfoundland, a singer herself, "always found ['Dark-eyed Susan'] too flowery but her mother and others of her mother's generation in the Placentia Bay area sang it."[46] Presumably the song continues to be sung by people who, like Best's mother, favor a "flowery" style.

Gay's "Newgate's Garland" or "Blue-Skin's Ballad" eschews the effusive language of "Sweet William's Farewell." Its tale of "How Mr. Jonathan Wild's Throat was cut, from Ear to Ear, with a Penknife" is taken up well within the stylistic patterns and diction of broadside murder ballads. The ballad refers to an unsuccessful knifing of the notorious Wild (whose position between the criminal underworld and official circles was discussed in chapter 1). Set to "Packington's Pound," a staple of broadsides going back to Elizabethan times, Gay's text conforms to conventions of imagery, diction, and narrative. It opens with the standard "come-all-ye" *incipit* and fills its listeners' ears with balladry's stock of "rogues", "news", "penknives", "wives", "widows", and "orphans". At the same time, like "Sweet William's Farewell," it takes up street-ballad forms with exceptional artfulness. In this case, the glance to so-called high culture is not aesthetic or stylistic, like the "flowery" glance in "Sweet William's Farewell", but rather political. The entire ballad can be read—rather as a precursor to *The Beggar's Opera*—as an almost allegorically applicable satire on Robert Walpole's Whig government of the 1720s.[47] Each stanza resounds: "And every Man round me may rob, if he please," a tag that invites analogy to contexts loftier than the "Old-Bailey" setting of the ballad. The final stanzas make this application inevitable as they refer to those who "cheat in the Customs," "rob the Excise," "steal from a Charity" or "publick Revenues," and set government monetary policies.[48] In this metaleptic swirl of allusions, the phrases ricochet off the surface meaning to a bounding, glancing, gathering play of meanings at the level of political and social comment.

Two popular love songs by Gay *were* jokes focused on the comical distortions of language itself. "Molly Mog: or, the Fair Maid of the Inn" and "A New Song of New Similies" reveal Gay's comic artistry as well as his attention to conventions of popular song and speech. "Molly Mog," which first appeared in *Mist's Weekly Journal* for 20 August 1726, is a "crambo" poem, that is, a text designed to exhaust all the rhymes possible on a name.[49] The song was popular enough through the eighteenth century to earn an obituary notice some forty years later for its celebrated namesake, a Wokingham landlord's daughter.[50] Alfred Williams found it still being sung in 1914 in Gloucestershire.[51] In its fifteen stanzas, the song—rather in the mode of *The British Apollo*—relishes such lines comically rhyming with "Mog" as "That women at best are a clog"; "The schoolmaster's joy is to flog"; "Thro' ditch, and thro' quagmire and bog"; "It here and there leaps like a frog"; "I wish I were hang'd like a dog"; "And writing another Eclogue." Again, an appreciative paean to the artifice of cultural convention.

Similarly focused on laughable contortions of language, "A New Song of New Similies" opens with "My Passion is as Mustard strong" and then continues for eighty lines that lament the indifference of the speaker's beloved "Molly" in a comical cavalcade of proverbial similes: "like a *March-Hare* mad," "Cool as a Cucumber," "Lean as a Rake," "Plump as a Partridge," "soft as Silk," "busy as a Bee," "dead as a Door-Nail," "lighter than a Feather," "Brown as a Berry," "black as Jet," "as the Turtle kind," "like the Gospel true," "tender as a Chick," "dull as any Post," "Flat as a Flounder," and so on. The joke hinges upon Gay's attention not just to language utterances, but to deeply shared and ritualized speech traditions that signify and create communities of meaning and *praxis*. A variant title for the song was "A New Song of *Old* Similies."[52]

Gay's songs shimmer with citations of, allusions to, and semantic interconnections among the mobile and increasingly self-conscious levels of eighteenth-century social and economic rank. In several instances popular forms are recast not just as jokes *within* popular tradition like "Molly Mog" and "A New Song of Similies," but as parodies that expose differences of social rank and concomitant power valences. Two collaborations with George Friedrich Handel combine elements of street ballad form and style on the one hand, and aristocratic arts on the other. "'Twas When the Seas Were Roaring" from *The What-d'Ye-Call-It* (1715) and "O Ruddier than the Cherry" from *Acis and Galatea* (1718) parody ballad tradition. Both songs, which will be looked at in more detail in later chapters, took on lives of their own as independent pieces sold to eighteenth-century broadside and songbook buyers of the middle ranks. "'Twas When the Seas" enacts stylistically the incongruous braiding of "flowery" text and music with conventional ballad references, the crisscrossing of cultural markers for social strata that, as we shall see, is the play's message. Yet " 'Twas When the Seas Were Roaring" emerges from its parodic context to become a perfectly singable ballad on its own, as its independent popularity attests. "A Damsel" on the shore awaits the return of "her Dear," spies his "floating Corpse" in conventional fashion, and just as conventionally "bow'[s] her Head, and dy'[s]" (II.viii.22–61).

Acis and Galatea is an operatic masque that similarly plays forms of high and low culture off each other. The first aria of the rustic Cyclops, Polyphemus, identifies him as a devotee of popular songs. Rendering love's similes in the Bowzybean terms of English "country" song, Polyphemus lumbers over his angular bass line, singing the excellencies of his beloved: "O ruddier than the Cherry, O sweeter than the Berry!" (II.17–18). His text abounds with homely comparisons like those in the "Song of Similies." Polyphemus beautifully exudes the lowbrow culture of English pub and countryside; like most of Gay's songs, "O Ruddier than the Cherry" continued to flourish as an individually published popular piece in the eighteenth century.

Key to his critique of a world that found its social divisions increasingly coded by taste and culture, popular materials mark for Gay boundaries of power and identify communities of traditional expression. In his vibrant contributions to popular song traditions and particularly in his cognizance of the ballad as a vital form, Gay set the stage for the ballad revival of the mid-eighteenth century and the history of popular songs in the modern era that derives from it. In such hybrids as " 'Twas When the Seas Were Roaring" and "O Ruddier than the Cherry," Gay posed the outlines of balladry *as a cultural tradition* in a way that has both exposed the social divisions and cultural configurations of power and guided our study of popular songs for the past two and a half centuries. Gay's use of popular materials directs his notably lasting social critique of the modern system taking shape around him, while it provides a key to understanding the ways that cultural materials have come to function as commodities and signifiers in that system.

Studying the sensibility of another jesting satirist of the eighteenth century, Gretchen Wheelock observes Joseph Haydn's ongoing citations of familiar musical topoi that signaled association with court, urban, and country life: dance gestures, meters, and patterns; ceremonious military fanfares and marches; horn signals for the hunt; the rustic drones of bagpipes; *seria* and *buffa* styles of operatic genres; the studious counterpoint of the church style; and the repetitions, archaisms, and surprises of folk music. As she notes, these supplied Haydn "musical frames of affective and social reference" as well as "a ready lexicon of the familiar." Present as citations, this wealth of reference in Haydn "provided opportunities for the subversion of traditional categories and hierarchies when used in incongruous combinations and contexts."[53] Such subversion works richly throughout the writing of John Gay.

4

Virgil Upended:
Literary Tradition, Mock Pastoral,
and Social Rank

A steady beam of political and artistic self-consciousness shines through Gay's work. Structured by a foreshadowing class awareness, his satires undertake a social criticism that remains—as Brecht, Havel, and Ayckbourn show—viable to the present era. The disapproving Johnson recognized that Gay constructed most of his works in relation to the ideology and traditions of Virgilian pastoral. Its themes, forms, and expectations he turned upside down, reformulated, decentered, and reconfigured in every conceivable way. The resulting parodies call attention both to literary expectations and to "real life" conditions that existed in the rural and urban contexts of an economically transforming Britain.

With regard to the latter, Gay's depictions, in their attention to work and working people as individuals and as a group, not only convey a new sympathy, but also articulate a subjectivity and identity available to both onlooker and looked-upon. The enclosure of the English countryside hovers behind the often anxious and threatened animals, swains, and milkmaids that populate Gay's mock pastorals. This privatizing of traditionally public lands swept away an old order, especially for the common people, and gave the pastoral in Gay's time a political resonance.[1] Several early poems—*Rural Sports* (1713), *The Shepherd's Week* (1714), *Trivia* (1717), and *The Birth of the Squire* (1720)—reveal Gay's fascination with the pastoral tradition and show as well his systematic recasting of its conventions and expectations with allusive and metaleptic play.

Gay takes up the pastoral in both senses of the term: that is, he writes works that (1) explicitly refer or conform to the literary genres connected to Virgilian rural poetry, the eclogue and the georgic and (2) express a more general preoccupation with the countryside and the ideology of its superiority as a site for critique. Gay's own provincial background supplied him with the outlook of an outlander and a keen awareness of the rural-urban opposition. His west Devonshire upbringing, limited grammar-school education, and financially straitened background prepared him for a demystifying perspective on pastoral forms and politics, particularly as these could be used to render the dynamics of insiders and outsiders, those with power and those without. In short, he had just such an experience of "the pastoral" in real life as would prepare him both to gravitate toward and to question the constructs of the literary tradition. A politics of stratification emerges from Gay's pastoral satire which, from the beginning, presents voices speaking from the margins. He continued to speak as a disruptive Theocritus to the too-easy harmonies of Virgilian tradition, a "Divine Bucoliast" as Pope playfully christened him in a letter of 1714.[2]

Gay's early works unfold with referential vitality that makes use of the rhetorical trope of metalepsis or transumption. John Hollander and Angus Fletcher define the trope as "a moment or turn of revisionary, reinterpretive allusiveness" and find it applicable to poetics and narratology.[3] Most useful to the reading of John Gay is the potentially subversive (literally "overturning") potential of this strategy and its basis in the historical and cultural legacies of this world. Relying as they do on recognized texts, authors, conventions, events, utterances, and so on, metaleptic tropes frequently set up tenor-vehicle dynamics that imply and play on issues of rank and value. As Hollander elaborates, metalepsis entails a figural evocation of precedent, an enlistment of history:

> We deal with diachronic trope all the time, and yet we have no name for it as a class. An echo of the kind we have been considering may occur in a figure in a poem, and it may echo the language of a figure in a previous one. But the echoing itself makes a figure, and the interpretive or revisionary power which raises the echo even louder than the original voice is that of a trope of diachrony. I propose that we apply the name of the classical rhetoricians' trope of *transumption* (or *metalepsis*, in its Greek form) to these diachronic, allusive figures.[4]

This concept of "a diachronic semantics" thus yields to analysis those panchronic moments in particular texts that cast back onto a cultural matrix of prior meanings. Strategies of metalepsis are notably rich and dynamic in an ironist such as Gay. As we shall see, his polyvalent references range across social registers as his satire builds upon multileveled mirrorings and complicated reversals. With skewering vision that amounts to prescience, Gay's satires, organized as they are around the cultural registers of rank, supply literary articulation of the classificatory and historical thinking that would come to characterize the post-Enlightenment worldview.

The mock pastorals of Gay hold complex conversations not only with key progenitors but also with peers—Dryden and Virgil in the former camp, and Pope and such adversaries as Ambrose Philips and John Dennis in the latter. The parodic complexity of Gay's sensibility stands aware of and contributes to pastoral tradition as he poses a comic and questioning Theocritus (the Sicilian progenitor of the tradition, who wrote in Greek) to Dryden and Pope's monumentalizing of Virgil (who later polished, in the Latin poetry of Rome, what Theocritus had begun). He does so while decentering the classical view to take up the less-than-ideal experience of the "rustic" and underling as subject rather than object. Thus, Gay's burlesquing of the pastoral dream probes beneath daunting social and ethical problems of his particular era to the deeper new politics of power itself as a nearby relational dynamic among petty individuals. This deeper politics reappears in Brecht, Havel, and especially Ayckbourn, whose Macheaths and Pollys play their plays against the dwarfing and sinister backdrops of late-twentieth-century politics.

Parody for Gay is a profound stance, a design more far-reaching and complex than a simple critical targeting of a particular author or form. It is "deep play" of the sort that Linda Hutcheon analyzes in her discussion of postmodern art, in which she identifies parody as "imitation with a difference":

> Parody, therefore, is a form of imitation, but imitation characterized by ironic inversion, not always at the expense of the parodied text. . . . Parody is, in another formulation, repetition with critical distance, which marks difference rather than similarity. . . . [The] ironic playing with multiple conventions, [the] extended repetition with critical difference . . . a stylistic confrontation . . . a modern recoding which establishes difference at the heart of similarity.[5]

Works by Gay like the early poems *Rural Sports* and *The Shepherd's Week* as well as the late ballad operas hinge on this "imitation with a difference," which shifts our vantage to that of the usually unvoiced, disempowered figure in whatever scene is depicted: from high to low, magistrate to beggar, man to woman, human to animal, animate to inanimate, and so on. Gay's parodic move is thus inevitably social, imitation with a *politically charged* difference.

As Annabel Patterson demonstrates, the early modern pastoral was an inherently political arena:

> [I]ntellectuals continued to do through pastoral, and especially through their attitudes to Virgil's *Eclogues*, what they had done throughout the Renaissance and the earlier seventeenth century: to denote their ideological stance

as writers in relation to their sociopolitical environment; and while some of them accepted and supported the premises of Neo-classicism, others, who were equally neoclassicist in their strategies, positioned themselves through irony, anxiety, or anger against the status quo. If Neoclassicism as a cultural formation was a stabilizing force, pastoral with its supporting and *competing* theories, was potentially destabilizing.[6]

Gay's mock pastorals, playfully self-aware and pointedly referential, take up the intellectual debates then surrounding pastoral poetry, notably the controversy regarding ancient and modern poetry. This entailed a range of philosophical, literary, and political issues: national identities, vernacular learning and cultural expression, literal versus figurative language, sociopolitical mobility and identification.[7] Gay's early poetry fits into this contemporary context; at the same time, the sometimes facetious "realism" of its characterizations ensured the enduring and widespread popularity of some poems—*The Shepherd's Week* and *Trivia* in particular.

RURAL SPORTS

Gay's first significant poem, and one which demonstrates his commentary on the pastoral, appears in print in 1713 under the title *Rural Sports. A Poem. Inscribed To Mr. Pope.*[8] As a letter from Gay's friend, Maurice Johnson attests, the poem was initially identified as a pastoral; Johnson writes on 13 January 1713 of a "Letter from my dear Friend Mr. JOHN GAY, with *Rural Sports*, a Pastoral Poem."[9] Some years later Gay revised *Rural Sports*, making it *"A Georgic,"* publishing the new version in 1720 in his *Poems on Several Occasions.*[10] Commentators invariably discuss this second text, conflating the two versions. Though related, the two poems are revealingly discrepant. The 1720 version transforms the allusive and ingenious—if sometimes awkward—1713 parody of pastoral themes and conventions into a tamer, more homogeneous georgic that retreats from the satiric reversals of the original. The revision of 1720 retracts as well the original poem's metaleptic engagement with Pope's pastorals and the Virgilian tradition.

The original *Rural Sports* of 1713, with its parodic hybridity, undoes both pastoral and georgic conventions and poses the pivotal preoccupation of all Gay's satire: the dynamics of power, usually in a pastoral context (both literary and geographical), that are rendered parodic by reversals that engineer pathos and a sociopolitical critique because of their seeing, from the legitimized subject position of the victim, the victimizing, and thus delegitimized cruelties of privilege. *Rural Sports* exemplifies Hutcheon's parodic mode: "an integrated structural modeling process of revising, replaying, inverting, and 'trans-contextualizing' previous works of art. . . . a dialogue with the past."[11] The poem contrasts a harried, part-time pastoral poet with his graciously leisured addressee, Alexander Pope, who, "'Midst *Windsor Groves*" his "easie Hours employ[s]" in the placid writing of pastorals.[12] The speaker of *Rural Sports* relates that he only visits the countryside of his poem for a brief "*Asylum*" from "the Town and Care" where he has "Respir'd it's Smoak, and all it's Toils endur'd" (1). *Rural Sports* thus suggests Gay's West Country background and subsequent employment in the city. Linking the monumental figure of Virgil to that of Pope, the poem expands the referential matrix for this tilted contribution of Gay's part-time pastoralist to the revered tradition:

> My Muse shall rove through flow'ry Meads and Plains,
> And Rural Sports adorn these homely Strains,
> And the same Road ambitiously pursue,
> Frequented by the *Mantuan* Swain, and You.
>
> (2)

The epigraph for the original *Rural Sports* of 1713 explicitly announces the parody in its metaleptic appropriation of the Virgilian tradition: "*Agrestem tenui Musam meditabor Avena.* Virg." ("I will rehearse the rural Muse on my slight Reed"), an ambivalent reference to Virgilian eclogues 1 and 6, blending lines from the two poems.[13] Modern commentators Dearing and Beckwith miss the impact of this reference, imagining it only a lapse in memory, and thus making *Rural Sports* a paean to country life, "a West-Country poem, redolent of Gay's native Devonshire."[14] In fact, the hybrid epigraph evokes the two most politically charged and satirically self-conscious of Virgil's eclogues—a reference certainly not lost on Gay's contemporaries. The allusion frames and accentuates the ironic reversals that Gay's own *Rural Sports* "ambitiously pursue[s]."

The epigraph owes most to the sixth eclogue, its wording being almost identical to the poem's eighth line. This well-known locus classicus supplies a resonant backdrop. Virgil tells the story of Silenus, tricked into singing of the "Formation of the Universe and the Original of Animals," as Dryden's translation of 1697 says.[15] This invocation of the animal realm directs our attention to the point of Gay's poem: a complex tilting of sympathy in "rural sporting" from predator to prey.

Gay's irony, that disingenuous simplicity that often masks for modern readers the ambition in his writing, has its prototype in Virgil's eclogue, which contains a polyvalenced self-consciousness hardly lost on Gay.

> *cum canerem reges et proelia, Cinthius aurem*
> *vellit et admonuit: "pastorem, Tityre, pinguis*

pascere oportet ovis, deductem dicere carmen."
nunc ego (namque super tibi erunt, qui dicere laudes,
Vare, tuas cupiant et tristia condere bella)
agrestem tenui meditabor harundine Musam.

(ll. 3–8)

[When I would have sung about kings and battles,
Apollo pulled my ear and admonished: "A shepherd,
Tityrus, ought to feed fat sheep and sing a soft song."
Now—for certainly there will be plenty who sing
your praises, Varus, and want to write of grim war—
I will declaim a rustic poetry on my slight reed.][16]

The passage contrasts the "innocent" pastoral and the more "serious" poetry that flatters rulers and sings of war. This self-deprecatingly posed opposition, with its veiled references to what is *not* being said, propels the satire inherent in the pastoral tradition from Virgil on. Virgil/Tityrus refrains from writing of "grim war" in favor of a "soft song," a "rustic poetry on his slight reed." The claim is delicately disingenuous. Indeed, the expansive and philosophical Eclogue 6 is hardly a "soft song," nor does it shirk the subject of "grim war" except in the most literal sense. Such an ironic "rustic poetry" serves aptly as Gay's model, for his countryside, as we shall see, is far from "soft" and peaceful.

The epigraph's simultaneous evocation of Eclogue 1 suggestively frames the opening apostrophe to Pope with a shift of point of view from Virgil's Tityrus to the city-bound Meliboeus. In Eclogue 1 the departing Meliboeus complains that Tityrus, whose lands remain in his possession due to imperial favor, can recline beneath the spreading beech singing his rural songs.[17] By contrast, the outcast Meliboeus must take to the road, deprived of his "sweet plowed fields," exiled from his homeland, his *"patriam."* Gay's speaker, "immur'd . . . in the noisie Town" with no "Plough-shares" or "Paternal Land" (1) speaks from this Virgilian framework, echoing the politically charged beginning of the first Eclogue: the exiled Meliboeus (Gay) addresses the reclining Tityrus (Pope), emblem of the pastoral poet.

Gay's Meliboeus will sing a countering "Sylvan Song" of his own. *Rural Sports* recasts Virgilian tradition to imagine a Meliboean pastoral: the *"Agrestem Musam"* of the exile returned to the country after innocence has been lost—in the city. Throughout, *Rural Sports* undercuts its pastoral and georgic themes even as it invokes them. Virgil's Eclogues 1 and 6 themselves suggest that the pastoral "Age" was only "Golden" for some. Gay depicts a countryside whose "innocence" and "peace" clearly depend upon whose experience is sung.

Pope identified pastoral poetry with an idyllic Golden Age and set rules by which such poetry might maintain this "tranquillity of a country life."[18] His "Tityran" pastorals follow the four seasons with emphasis on harmony in nature and the innocence of rural life. Gay's poem counters with a Meliboean view of rural seasons marked by grim wars of human intervention which render disingenuous the epigraph's protestation of pastoral innocence evoked on a "slight reed."

Gay sets the conventions of pastoral poetry to the task of depicting an unidyllic world, seen from the usually unsung perspective of its prey. He parodically reimagines the artificialities of the pastoral with its idly happy creatures, animal and human; its typically harmonious and personified landscapes; its elaborate expressions of carefree relations by singing birds and piping shepherds; and so on. In the process, Gay reconfigures the conventional morality of this poetry—that such purity and innocence is superior to a corrupt urbanity. Highlighting the artifice of the form itself, he reveals a rural England at odds with such poetic landscapes. An insistent thematic focus on the politics of power relations renders a world of subaltern subjects who experience both individual subjectivity as speakers and subjectedness to those who exert over them power and exploitation.

A lavish pastoral scene—complete with the "gladsome Birds," "chearful Plains" and "jocund Fields" that result when an eclogue's "Spring" "throws" her "verdant Mantle" (2–3)—follows the opening address to Pope. The scene culminates in an image of "sporting Fish" that

> . . . range with frequent Leaps the shallow Streams,
> And their bright Scales reflect the daz'ling Beams.

Punning play on the word "sport" begins to darken the idyll with issues of risk and survival as the point of view shifts. The poem pivots from rural "sports"—promising a conventional georgic—to "sporting" fish. Innocently "sporting," they will to their detriment become engaged as "sport" to a markedly uninnocent mock-georgic Fisherman who

> . . . does now his Toils prepare,
> And Arms himself with ev'ry watry Snare,
> He meditates new Methods to betray,
> Threat'ning Destruction to the finny Prey.

Even as the fish becomes personalized, the fisherman recedes into the abstracted "Toils," "Arms," and "Methods" by which he engineers the ensuing "Destruction." With tactile imagery and intentional ambiguity, the language slides from fisherman to fish and back as if tracking the pull of the line to its final painful point. The ambiguity of pronouns makes it impossible not to be carried by the text to the personified fish's experience of the "sport."

> The trembling Rod the joyful Angler eyes,
> And the strait Line assures him of the Prize;
> With a quick Hand the nibbled Hook he draws,
> And strikes the barbed Steel within his Jaws;
> The Fish now flounces with the startling Pain,
> And, plunging, strives to free himself, in vain:
> Into the thinner Element he's cast,
> And on the verdant Margin gasps his Last.

Almost imperceptibly, the passage moves from angler to trout by means of the pronoun "he," whose referent shifts in a couplet which elides the two sides of the relationship. "Sport" to one "he" is death to the other—"deep play" indeed:

> With a quick Hand the nibbled Hook *he* draws,
> And strikes the barbed Steel within *his* Jaws;

Losing the linguistic distinction between predator and prey, the poem slides with ironic resonance into the ambiguous line:

> *He* must not ev'ry Worm promiscuous use,
> Judgment will tell him proper Bait to chuse;

Matter-of-fact advice to the angler, this line resonates with a mocking irony for the trout.

The poem moves to the subject of fly-fishing, similarly pivoting on an indeterminate personal pronoun that masks the identities of predator and prey. Thus, for the reader, the capture and markedly cruel death of "an huge scaly Salmon" becomes a subjective experience as the reference shifts back and forth without signal, establishing the tandem relation of predator and prey.

> Each Motion humours with his steady Hands,
> And a slight Hair the mighty bulk commands;
> Till tir'd at last, despoil'd of all his Strength,
> The fish athwart the Streams unfolds his Length.
> He now, with Pleasure, views the gasping Prize
> Gnash his sharp Teeth, and roll his Blood-shot Eyes,
> Then draws him t'wards the Shore, with gentle Care,
> And holds his Nostrils in the sick'ning Air:

(8–9)

Confounding easy recognition of pronoun referents, the passage displays the scene by oxymoronic images: "slight Hair" linked with "mighty bulk"; "Pleasure" with "gasping Prize," "Gnash[ing] . . . sharp Teeth," and "roll[ing] Blood-shot Eyes"; and "gentle Care" with "hold[ing] his Nostrils in the sick'ning Air." In the countryside of his ironic "Agrestem Musam," Gay discloses startlingly physical images of "grim war."

As the day heats up and "Swains with fainting Hand their Labour ply," the strolling Meliboeus-identified speaker retreats to his own "secret Covert" where the "tall Oak . . . with the Beech a mutual Shade combines" (12). Tityrus for a day, he reads his Virgil.[19] Foreshadowing the disruption of this naive bower, the speaker calls to mind the betrayal of "fair *Calisto*" in just "such a Shade" (12). The allusion underscores the classical literariness of the scene. At the same time, it nervously alludes to Calisto's betrayal and heralds the preoccupation of the following pages with the hunted prey of this "peaceful" countryside. Calisto, huntress with Diana, was raped by Jupiter in "such a Shade," then turned by the jealous Juno into a bear, herself subject to the hunt.[20] Again, there is a history to such bowers.

Gay's Meliboeus reclines in the shade to read his *Virgil* before taking "an indulgent Walk" to the seashore to watch the sunset. Here, as "Night in silent State begins to rise," the poem salutes the recently negotiated peace of Utrecht (1713): "Oh happy Plains! remote from War's Alarms, / And all the Rages of Hostile Arms."[21] A negative catalogue pointedly summons— with ironic innuendo—the images of war that are missing: "no rude Soldier," "No trampling Steed," "Nor crackling Flames," "No flaming Beacons," "No Trumpet's Clangor" (15–16). Juxtaposed to the mock-militaristic hunting scenes that follow, this is an extravagant send-up of political peace as an unsettled absence.

Mock-epic elaborations of hunting sports—shooting pheasants and chasing rabbits—disturb the countryside with images of "Tyrant War."[22] "The Spaniel . . . bids his watchful Lord prepare to Arms" as the "Pheasant" eyes "his noisie Foe," then flies, a "pale Coward from the Battel . . . 'Till Fate behind aims a disgraceful Wound, / And throws his gasping Carcass to the Ground" (18–19). A greyhound's chase of a "tim'rous Hare" quickly reaches a grisly end, capped by an ironically urban commodifying of such "unbought Dainties" (19–20).

Rural Sports ends with a long (48 lines) and notably "unwholesome" description of hounds chasing a "skulking" and "frighted" hare. The subject is broached ironically: "But still the Chase, a pleasing Task, remains." Following the dogs' "Nostril[s]" into "the thorny Brake" as they "trace the Game along the tainted Dew" (20), the scene stands at odds with the elevated artifice of the Golden Age pastoral and epic (21). As "scow'r[ing]" hounds plunder the woods, the poem takes the vantage of "the list'ning Hare":

Th'advancing Dogs still haunt his list'ning Ear,
And ev'ry Breeze augments his growing Fear:
'Till tir'd at last, he pants, and heaves for Breath
Then lays him down, and waits approaching Death.

(21–22)

A disjunctive glee at the ending underscores the deep and troubling irony in the poem's reversals—by turns playful, grim, dazzling—of pastoral and epic fantasy: "Oh happy Fields, unknown to Noise and Strife" (22). "Farewel.—Now business calls me from the Plains," declares Gay's speaker (22), hastily exiting this unsettling generic hybrid.

The revision of 1720 attempts to transform the *Rural Sports* of 1713— sprawling, referential, hybrid, parodic, and polyvalent—into a more straight-forward georgic. Removing the Virgilian epigraph, the revision suppresses the Meliboean framework of the first poem, putting the speaker in alliance with Pope and Virgil. The charged opposition between country and city that permeates the 1713 version, which characteristically pushes the pasto-ral in a political direction, is toned down in the revision. In the same vein, when depicting the animal world of trout, partridge, and hare, the 1720 poem removes those similes to humans—courtiers, coquets, boys, squires, soldiers—which turned the earlier "pastoral" scenes to parody by drawing attention to classes of beings. Simple weariness prompts the less-troubled later poet to the countryside: "Fatigu'd at last; a calm retreat I chose" (l. 23).

The 1720 *Rural Sports* never quite frees itself from the hybridity of the original, but the revision curbs the self-conscious intertextuality and ongo-ing play with pastoral tradition. The reference to Calisto disappears en-tirely as does the speaker's reading of Virgil in the bower. The highly figured descriptions are cut along with the counterpointing mock-heroic images. The new poem shifts the vantages of the original: from fish to angler, from pheasant to hunter, from hare to dog, from prey to predator, from animal to human. Throughout, the language leavens—not altogether convincingly, as critics note—the disjunctions and ironies of the first version. Gay be-calmed his Meliboean pastoral as the revision strives for the very harmony its risky prototype questioned.

The rewriting of *Rural Sports* may reflect Gay's changed circumstances as well as his desire to smooth out an ambitious but uneven early poem. By 1720 he had achieved considerable success and some notoriety on the stage and was intent on obtaining court patronage. The georgic version appeared in the 1720 collection, *Poems on Several Occasions*, an expensive publica-tion whose list of subscribers was a virtual "Who's Who" of London aristo-crats.[23] The outsider pose of the original poem may have seemed to Gay open to revision. Likewise Pope was by 1720 a close friend and ally of Gay as well as a formidable authorial presence. Gay may have removed the

Meliboean countering of Pope's pastorals in the original *Rural Sports* in the context of his solidarity with and admiration for Pope.

THE SHEPHERD'S WEEK

The Shepherd's Week consists of six mock-pastoral poems, one for each of the workdays of the week from Monday to Saturday, presented with a self-consciously metaleptic invocation of Edmund Spenser's *Shepherd's Calendar* of 1579. Gay's eclogues depict rural swains and doxies as comical speakers from a world of detailed and quotidian rural labor and custom. Full of facetious glosses and references to the long and much-discussed tradition of pastoral poetry, *The Shepherd's Week* manipulates its Virgilian, Spenserian, and Augustan models with a wit that is at once intertextual and appreciatively satiric.

Gay continues in *The Shepherd's Week* the presentation of himself as an ironic onlooker poised between country and city. Both "The Prologue" and the last eclogue, "The Flights" suggest the pose that Gay assumes as Bowzybeus, the pastoral songsmith and his own comic alter ego. The poems recreate the song contests and love plaints conventional to pastoral. "Monday" depicts a song competition between the country swains, Lobbin Clout and Cuddy. In "Tuesday" the hardworking Marian laments the unfaithfulness of her Colin. In "Wednesday," Sparabella likewise bemoans her abandonment by Bumkinet and contemplates, then pragmatically defers her suicide. Hobnelia similarly recounts a "piteous Tale" of abandonment in "Thursday." Fearing the loss of Lubberkin's affection to a faux-medieval-cum-Spenserian "Maiden fine bedight" from the town, Hobnelia spins a catalog of traditional love spells to win him back in an echoing of eclogues by Virgil and Theocritus. In "Friday" Bumkinet and Grubbinol lament the death of Blouzelinda—until, espying her sister, "In Ale and Kisses they forget their Cares, / And Susan Blouzelinda's Loss repairs" (ll. 163–64). In "Saturday" the host of "Reapers"—"Lads" and "Damsels"— come upon the sleeping Bowzybeus and prompt his song in a parodic reflection of pastoral precedents in Virgil and Dryden.

A popular and influential work in the period, Gay's *Shepherd's Week* is considerably more than the clever defense of Pope that modern criticism has found it.[24] In *The Life of Alexander Pope, Esq.*, one of the early sources linking Gay's poem and the Ancients vs. Moderns dispute between Pope and Ambrose Philips, Owen Ruffhead acknowledges the complexity of Gay's burlesque:

> Mr. Philips's mean injustice on this head, raised the indignation of some of
> Mr. Pope's friends, and particularly occasioned the SHEPHERD's WEEK of

Gay, in the proem of which, that *simplicity*, for which Mr. Philips so much valued himself, in his pastorals, is pleasantly ridiculed; as is the naivete of the incidents of these pastorals in the SHEPHERD'S WEEK itself. Yet, this is remarkable, that they who were not in the secret, mistook Gay's pastorals for a burlesque on Virgil's. How far this goes towards a vindication of Philips's manner in the construction of his poem, let others judge.[25]

Ruffhead supplies an early description of that "double-capacity" of Gay, both "against rogues, and for 'em." As the witty and complicated textual references throughout attest, Gay's pastorals are "a burlesque on Virgil's," or more accurately, a parodically interrogating commentary—with both aesthetic and especially social effects—on the whole tradition of pastoral poetry. As Nigel Wood remarks, the irony in *The Shepherd's Week* "is a weapon . . . and its target the Courteous reader, not a blundering Grubbinol or Sparabella" (97). Gay's larger concerns are the workings and limitations of literary artifice, particularly when "read" against the relational politics of a human subjectivity experienced by people of lower rank as well as higher.

Gay's satire in *The Shepherd's Week* moves out in concentric circles from a center point that is the most localized and immediate target of his gaze, the speakers and events that the poems depict. Parodic moves and allusions to other texts give each subpoem's rural speakers and events further meaning, in turn giving the text ever-widening targets as we see "through" these characters to other ranges of satire and parody. Thus, at allusive moments, the poems engage enlarging circles of reference that move outward: (1) the imaginative scenes of each poem, peopled with comic swains and milkmaids drawn from a rural Britain familiar to the Devonian Gay; (2) references to authors and texts—in a first circle, a satiric invocation of such contemporary authors of his own time as the pastoral-writing Ambrose Philips and the song-writing Thomas D'Urfey, and in a wider-reaching circle, more respectfully playful allusions to and imitations of texts by Theocritus, Virgil, Spenser, Chaucer, Shakespeare, and others; (3) sociopolitical relationships—for example, squires and tenants, townsmen and farmworkers, and so on—within which literary texts exist as cultural representations of a world that in Gay's time was being increasingly organized by work, money, and rank; and finally, (4) the largest, contextualizing circle of satiric questioning, which frames the workings of literature, language, and expressive representation itself in a world vacated of God, King, and feudal allegory. *The Shepherd's Week* creates moments that engage us in recognizing—sometimes with contradictory sentiments—points of meaning for all four of these ever-widening circles of allusive "reading."

The Shepherd's Week conveys a knowledge of and comic sympathy for both its speakers and the material, expressive, rustic culture they inhabit.

Gay's steady and innovative look at rural people, working women in particular, has not gone unnoticed.[26] Few commentators, however, recognize the intricacy of Gay's ironies and the complex strategies that direct our empathy especially to the women in *The Shepherd's Week*. Their perspective, like that of the preyed-upon animals in *Rural Sports*, accrues increasing sympathy against a backdrop of exploitation and disempowerment. Three of Gay's six pastorals—the second, third, and fourth at the center of the collection—have women as speakers, a change in the gender of the male subjects of cited pastorals by Virgil and others. For all the laughter they inspire, the voices of these speakers (Marian, Sparabella, and Hobnelia) elicit as well a notable comprehension and compassion for their predicaments and sentiments. The lovesick Marian of "Tuesday," for example, becomes sympathetic as her complaint details a catalog of kindnesses and gifts to a loutish, unfaithful, and unappreciative Colin. The joke is not on Marian. "My Sheep were silly, but more silly I" (l. 28), she declares with a self-awareness and resilience that make Gay's rural "damsels" typically humorous and, at the same time, admirable.

While it creates vivid portraits of English shepherds and milkmaids, *The Shepherd's Week* opens out an historical matrix of authors and texts that constitute its literary references. "The Prologue" wittily frames this ongoing dimension with Spenserian archaisms ("yclept," "hye with Glee," "eke a Knot") and a mock-scholarly framework of pedantic commentary, references, definitions, and etymologies that, its facetiousness notwithstanding, marks such materials as "cultural" in the modern, ethnographic sense. Rollicking rhymes and earthy images contrast with the somber extravagancies of conventional pastoral song contests and complaints in Philips's pastorals—and those in Pope's, Spenser's, and Virgil's, for that matter.

Gay's eclogues fairly bubble with direct and indirect citations and mirrorings of familiar poems and authors: Theocritus, Virgil, Chaucer, Spenser, Shakespeare, Dryden, Pope, Philips, D'Urfey, and so on. Well-known pastorals, especially Virgil's, supply obvious parallels, as Ruffhead observes. But the mélange of allusions creates the kind of textual counter-pointing that typifies Gay's dense cultural referencing. An interplay of direct mirrorings, paradoxical reversals, and sidelong glances positions the present textual moment in an echo chamber of resonating textual history. Marian's plaint in "Tuesday" takes off from Pope and Gay's spoof of Ambrose Philips's pastorals which appeared in *Guardian*, Number 40.[27] "Wednesday" invokes popular songsmith and playwright, Thomas D'Urfey (l.9). "Friday" cites Virgil's Eclogue 5 and Philips's close (and somber) imitation of it in his Third Pastoral, with no systematic imitation of either.[28] At home with her cat, "Tuesday's" Marian notes that "No troublous Thoughts the Cat or *Colin* move, / While I alone am kept awake by Love"

(91–92). Her sturdy matter-of-factness recalls Chaucer's Wife of Bath, a figure Gay had studied just before *The Shepherd's Week* occupied his imagination.[29]

In "Saturday," Bowzybeus exemplifies the complexity and indeterminacy of the parody in *The Shepherd's Week*. This final eclogue echoes "The Pollio," Virgil's fourth eclogue—to which we shall return—then comically retells Virgil's sixth eclogue, on the ineffable sublimity of poetry and song. Virgil's poem tells how the drunken Silenus, bound and tricked by two shepherd boys, sings of the "Formation of the Universe, and the Original of Animals," to quote Dryden, as he memorializes ancient story traditions of gods and titans.[30] Virgil's poem on Silenus's songs does indeed reach for the sublime, a fact Gay brings to mind by the opening nod to Eclogue 4— "Sublimer Strains, O rustick Muse, prepare" (l. 1).

Virgil is not the only sublimely immortalized poet Bowzybeus calls to mind; Dryden is alluded to as well. The engraving of the drunkenly sleeping Bowzybeus in Gay's collection parodies the corresponding illustration of the supine Silenus of eclogue 6 from Dryden's 1697 translation of Virgil's *Works,* one of the most lavishly monumentalizing tributes in publication history.[31] Dryden's *Virgil* presented a recognized political polemic against the Whig settlement of 1688 and in support of the Jacobite claim to the throne. With this parody of Dryden, Gay once again highlights the historicity of art as well as its cultural character which comes into view in the paralleling of low and high. It is another of the Meliboean moves by which Gay reconfigured recognized elements of European pastoral tradition in satiric or at least revealingly discrepant relation both to each other and to features of his own sociopolitical moment. (See figs. 8 and 9.)

Bowzybeus, like other figures, alludes in more than one direction. Along with such lofty precursors for Bowzybeus as Virgil and Dryden, Gay invokes the songsmith-playwright Thomas D'Urfey, a staunch supporter of the Whig ascendancy, drawing attention to his legendary stuttering in lines which move into a direct mimicry of Virgil:

> [Bowzybeus] rubs his Nostril, and in wonted Joke
> The sneering Swains with stamm'ring Speech bespoke.
> To you, my Lads, I'll sing my Carrols o'er,
> As for the Maids,—I've something else in store.
>
> (ll. 41–44)[32]

Bowzybeus thus resonates with metaleptic echoes on several levels. As a figure, he is a parodic echo of Virgil's Silenus, especially as the latter reappears in Dryden. Then, with a notable reversal of political affiliation, Bowzybeus becomes, momentarily, the stuttering D'Urfey, readable as a Whiggish,

the Flights.   Lud. Du Guernier inv et sculp

Fig. 8. Engraving by du Guernier from eclogue 6 of *The Shepherd's Week* (1714). Courtesy of the William Andrews Clark Memorial Library, University of California, Los Angeles.

To the Right Hon.ble Hugh Lord Viscount Cholmondely of Kelles in the Kingdom of Jreland and Baron of Wichmalbank in the Kingdom of England.

Part. 6.

Fig. 9. Engraving from eclogue 6 of John Dryden's *Works of Virgil* (1697). Courtesy of the William Andrews Clark Memorial Library, University of California, Los Angeles.

lowbrow burlesque of Dryden's Jacobite, highbrow Silenus. Yet no one allusion occludes the others, as referential reinterpretations rise incarnationally from one allusive context after another. In sum, Bowzybeus signals Gay himself—in the sound parody of his name and in his presence as a frame at the beginning and end of *The Shepherd's Week*—as mock-pastoral Meliboeus.

The Shepherd's Week interjects into its literary parody the bite of economic sociopolitics. Gay's pastoral "clowns," far from the "Court Clowns, or Clown Courtiers" to which he addresses his prefatory "Proeme," are working "Tenants"—and serve just such landowners as his "Courteous READERS." "It is my Purpose, gentle Reader," he announces, "to set before thee, as it were a Picture, or rather lively Landscape of thy own Country, just as thou mightest see it, didest thou take a Walk into the Fields at the proper Season" (ll. 34–35). Then, the "Proeme" cites a sinister parallel for this country walk: the lines from *Paradise Lost* in which Satan, in the position of the aristocratic gazers, observes the innocent Eve in her rural paradise. The mordant allusion, like so many in Gay, critiques the gazers—identified with Satan—by turning their view onto themselves through the representation. Nor are we, to be sure, free from predatory implications of the allusion as we "Courteous READERS" gaze.

Parodic juxtapositions of polite and popular traditions in *The Shepherd's Week* set up intersections of art and the social world that make visible otherwise occluded points of view. Calling up Virgil's eighth eclogue and its polite scholarly and literary audience, "Wednesday" comically intertwines with this highbrow textual tradition vivid elements of oral folk culture: D'Urfey's ballads "that swell in every Voice" (l. 16); decorative ribbons won in contests by "val'rous Cudgels" (l. 29); traditional proverbs—"Eyes *(but love, they say, has none)*" (l. 31); the tools of rural work life—spades, rakes, and churns; the ducking stool and other traditional customs.[33] As the courtly "Damon" of Virgil's eclogue becomes in parody the laboring "Sparabella," the poem views the world from two lowering categories: gender and rank. Moreover, with regard to the latter, Gay's depictions of commoners consistently show them laboring, often with complaint and meager reward. "Alike with yearning Love and Labour worn"(l. 23), thus Sparabella sings her "Plaint." The fatigue of her "Labour" injects a pitiable discomfort into the idyllic literary pastoral.

As it unfolds, the story sets up as a background to her "plaint" a predatory system in which some must work for others' leisure, subjected to exploitation. Sparabella develops reference to her social subordination with a dramatic irony that enhances both her vulnerability and our sympathy. Describing her own loyalty to the faithless Bumkinet, she recounts being accosted by and resisting "the *Squire* in yonder Wood," despite his proffer of money and a purchased wedding to "keep [her] from Disgrace" (ll. 75–86). Gay parodies the conventional pastoral topos of the pursued nymph with a poignantly nonidyllic reference to the social categories that mark individuals. Sparabella becomes a sympathetic agent as the conventions of the literary pastoral are turned upside down, rendered from the nymph's point of view in the nonliterary countryside of preyed-upon, working-class maidens.

The Shepherd's Week reflects onto the literary pastoral the economic, social, and political features of the "real life" counterpart to the form. Celebrating the Treaty of Utrecht, Gay's "Prologue" marks the effects of policy for his Lobbins and Cuddys, freed from impressment:

> So forth I far'd to Court with speed,
> Of Soldier's Drum withouten Dreed;
> For Peace allays the Shepherd's Fear
> Of wearing Cap of Granadier.

(ll. 45–48)

Throughout Gay's satire, pastoral forms and themes dominate as the social structure of the countryside is seen from the point of view of people of the lower ranks.

The seams and forms of language itself ultimately reflect those same sociopolitical relationships which literature may pretend to escape, but cannot. Gay shows this to be the joke for all readers, particularly those of us who may be "Clown Courtiers" collecting rents as we tour the country. Facetiously, he says:

That principally, courteous Reader, whereof I would have thee to be advertised . . . is touching the Language of my Shepherds; which is, soothly to say, such as is neither spoken by the country Maiden nor the courtly Dame; nay, not only such as in the present Times is not uttered, but was never uttered in Times past; and, if I judge aright, will never be uttered in Times future. It having too much of the country to be fit for the Court; too much of the court to be fit for the country, too much of the Language of old Times to be fit for the Present, too much of the Present to have been fit for the Old, and too much of both to be fit for any time to come. (ll. 67–75)

Thus, like the magic spells of "Thursday's" Hobnelia, these pastorals of Bowzybeus—together with those of his echoing precursors—are but the spinning art of language: "such as is neither spoken by the country Maiden nor the courtly Dame." Yet these poems wend their allusive way from figure to figure, story to story, drawing us into the spell of the pleasures and desires of language until we, like Hobnelia, hear Light-Foot bark as the looked-for Lubberkin appears before us, climbing his way "o'er yonder Stile" (l. 132).

With the final complex image of Gay's singing, alter ego Bowzybeus, *The Shepherd's Week* completes a circle of inquiry begun with the mock criticism of "The Proeme," ending with those issues of authorial voice, poetic language, and social context that frame his eclogues from the start. Attentive to media and preoccupied with the interplay of oral and written, especially as customary forms are transformed by the gaze of writing, Gay's satires inevitably raise for consideration the modes, conventions, ironies, and limits of language itself.

TRIVIA

Patricia Spacks has remarked that *Trivia* (1716) did for the town what *The Shepherd's Week* had done for the country.[34] Taken together, the two poems reveal both the preoccupations of Gay's social commentary about rank and power and his parodic and self-implicating poetics, summoning the cultural reflexivity of literature and language. Two features of *Trivia* govern its complexity: (1) the manipulation of oppositions—cultural forms in particular—which resonate with the emerging urban proletariat (to use a later term); and (2) the ironic and parodic treatment of the narrative voice of the "Walker" who wends his perilous way through London streets. However sympathetically comic *Trivia*'s Walker is, his reliability is nonetheless artfully undone throughout the poem, in terms that continually raise issues of work, art, and social place. Indeed, the Walker's voice takes Gay's comic identification with Bowzybeus and his rural colleagues into town, as an ironic narrator constructed with satire as well as enjoyment in a complex and purposeful ambiguity. He becomes a rather modern-seeming man-in-the-street: vulnerable, middling, beset.

As the Virgilian references make clear, the narrator arrives on the scene of this urban mock georgic straight from the pastoral tradition. He is a Meliboeus or Moeris (even a Bowzybeus perhaps?) with the wryness and ambition, one supposes, of a John Gay from Barnstaple. The speaker laughably protests the benefits of his pedestrianism for our instruction, in the georgic tradition, while at the same time delineating—in elaborately mock-heroic terms—the threatening forces and circumstances that put him in constant jeopardy. The voice of the Walker elaborates the comic yet sympathetic vulnerability of a Hobnelia or a Marian. The Walker presents perceptions and sentiments of vincibility—all too identifiable for anyone thwarted by modern urban discomfort. Detailed recommendations for surviving a walk in Gay's London prompt our laughter at the Walker's insignificance in the face of the epic scenes he imagines, with a fop's sensibility, on all sides.

Who would of *Watling-street* the Dangers share,
When the broad Pavement of *Cheap-side* is near?
Or who that rugged Street would traverse o'er,
That stretches, O *Fleet-ditch*, from thy black Shore
To the *Tow'r*'s moated Walls? Here Streams ascend
That, in mix'd Fumes, the wrinkled Nose offend.

(243–48)

Hyperbolically imagined "Dangers" tumble down the verse until we find
ourselves offended like the synecdochic "wrinkled Nose." With characteristically ambivalent poise, Gay alludes at the same time to legendary historical realities of suffering behind such specificities as "the *Tow'r*'s moated
Walls."

With greater nuance than in his mock eclogues, Gay develops the irony
that surrounds the speaker in *Trivia* and the ambivalence this creates for
the poem. As we appreciate and identify with the predicament, position,
and opinions of the Walker, we also see his silliness: the risible delusion in
his self-importance; the dandyism in his preoccupation with his fashion-
wear; the ridiculous rendering in heroic terms of his struggle to keep
unspattered and unjostled. The writer's tongue is in his cheek; in the walker
we find a comically fallible perspective. Yet, like the milkmaids in *the
Shepherd's Week*, he is simultaneously sympathetic and silly.[35]

Trivia, like *The Shepherd's Week*, is a playful polyphony of textual
reference. Throughout, the poem echoes Virgil's epic, pastoral, and georgic
poetry as well as English poems modeled on Virgilian prototypes. The opening parodies the *Aeneid:*

Through Winter Streets to steer your Course aright,
How to walk clean by Day, and safe by Night,
How jostling Crouds, with Prudence, to decline,
When to assert the Wall, and when resign,
I sing . . .

(ll. 1–5)[36]

The original edition of the poem appeared, like *The Shepherd's Week,* encased in a mock-scholarly framework of solemn side notes, footnotes, and
a semialphabetized index.[37] Again, literary tradition and the forms and values of poetry itself are a primary point of focus.

Trivia's Walker is an ironically naive observer, an outlander whose
perspective is at once undercut, yet Socratic in its capacity to expose even
greater foolishness. The poem questions those larger heroic assumptions
that underlie not just the georgic, but the entire ethos and aesthetic of heroic
pastoral ideology, what Maynard Mack has called the "cluster of attitudes

and feelings [at whose] center beats a sophisticated longing for something that is experienced as 'missing'; a way of life, a power of seeing, a desired condition of things now viewed as lost (though possibly recoverable), even though it may never actually have existed or been in fact enjoyed."[38] With regard to Gay's sensibility, I would expand this nostalgia to include the heroic and the tragic, and note as well this loss as a preoccupation of the modern era.

Quoting from Virgil's Eclogue 3, the "Advertisement" preceding *Trivia* links the poet, once again, with the realm of popular music. "I beg you to oblige me in accepting the following *Motto. —Non tu, in* Triviis, *Indocte, solebas / Stridenti, miserum, stipula, disperdere Carmen?*" The quoted taunt playfully conjures a rude music: "Was it not you, Master Dunce, who at the cross-roads used to murder a sorry tune on a scrannel straw?"[39] With playful self-mockery, the implied affirmative identifies this mocking "*Carmen in* Triviis" (song at the crossroads) with Bowzybeus, who "Sings with a Note so shrilling sweet and loud" (l. 48). With elaborate, if facetious, evocation of Virgilian texts, concerns, and traditions, Gay includes himself within the circle of his literary mockery.

Trivia contains an ongoing flurry of "I's" on the one hand and "you's" and "thy's on the other, creating in the poem a dynamic of personal intimacy between speaker and reader. The Walker and his poem are situated with great self-consciousness *between* his reader and the bustling, mock-heroic urban amble he describes. Second-person admonitions, instructions, and advice begin with recommendations on apparel: "Let firm, well-hammer'd Soles protect thy Feet" (I.33); "Be [thy coat] of *Kersey* firm, though small the Cost" (I.59); "If the strong Cane support thy walking Hand, / Chairmen no longer shall the Wall command" (I.61–62); "Let thy worst Wig, long us'd to Storms, be worn" (I.126). We receive instruction on belief and behavior: "All Superstition from thy Breast repel" (I.175); "Let due Civilities be strictly paid" (II.45). The poem offers advice on directions and safety: "Let the sworn Porter point thee through the Town" (II.66); "Though Expedition bids, yet never stray, / Where no rang'd Posts defend the rugged Way" (II.227–28); "Guard well thy Pocket" (III.79). Any number of burlesque jokes reside in admonition: "The thoughtless Wits shall frequent Forfeits pay, / Who 'gainst the Centry's Box discharge their Tea. / Do thou some Court, or secret Corner seek . . ." (II.297–99). These mingle mockingly with appeals to high morality: "O! may thy Virtue Guard thee through the Roads / Of *Drury's* mazy Courts, and dark Abodes" (III, 259–60).

Trivia is premised on a comic reversal of the basis for giving advice, for it is a naive countryman's georgic about how to do things in the city. The opening epigraph from Virgil's Eclogue 9, similar to that for *Rural*

Sports, establishes this mock-Virgilian point of departure. *"Quo te Moeri pedes? An, quo via ducit, in Urbem?"* ("Whither afoot, Moeris? Is it, as the path leads, to town?")[40] As Gay's audience certainly recalled, this sentence opens a pensive and politically suggestive eclogue. The lamenting Moeris goes to town homeless, like Meliboeus, his land given as political spoils to another.[41] This reference to the displaced Moeris, like that in *Rural Sports*, opens *Trivia* with a less than sunny invocation of those "other" of Virgil's shepherds whose displaced and forcibly unpastoral point of view Gay develops in his mock pastorals. At a certain level the comic *Trivia* is not a joke, as it shows literary form and tradition engaged with the placements and displacements of social power.

As in *The Shepherd's Week*, *Trivia* identifies people of the lower ranks as working bootblacks, barbers, footmen, oystermongers, coachmen, booksellers, milkmaids, perfumers, bakers, chimney sweepers, chandlers, butchers, porters, apprentices, brewers, prostitutes, and servants and peddlers of all sorts. Again, these working people of the lower sort serve an empowered group, which is portrayed not within the tenant-landlord opposition, but rather as a leisured class, self-protectively encased in their clothes and coaches. Between these two classes strolls the clever, silly, and vulnerable Walker.

While working people fill the streets of *Trivia*, georgic parody does not ridicule such hawking, driving, peddling, cleaning, building workers as the milkmaid or watchman. Rather, the depictions shift between extravagant mock-heroic vignettes or pathetic juxtapositions of flesh-and-blood people on the street with mythic parallels. In either case, the discrepancies expose a world organized in classificatory terms. The georgic joke is a class-conscious satire of the foppish Walker's travail of getting down the street unbesmirched in the costume marking his station and stylishness, amidst conspicuously hard at work people of the lower sort, displaced shepherds and milkmaids. As usual, the ridicule is mitigated by sympathy. The Walker's wit and perceptions are winning; his marginality with regard to rank and power make him sympathetic. This liminal figure stands conspicuously vulnerable between the bustling, sweating, struggling workers and those "Proud Coaches" (II.451) and "Beaus" in "gilded Chariot[s]" (II.523–25).

The 1720 revision of *Trivia* accentuates the poem's consciousness of social stratification and sympathetic attention to the lower ranks in the city's economy of services and servitude. Here Gay added a mock-mythical digression on the origins of shoeshine boys.[42] The story of the bootblack and his goddess mother of the sewers, Cloacina, signals that complex literary and social satire at which Gay excelled, and whose point continues to elude critics.[43] Cloacina is herself a parodic figure both as a visual burlesque with her outfit of turnip tops and eels, and in her gender-reversing mimicry of

Jove: her mating with a mortal scavenger supplies for her the boy's sire. Thus, the episode constructs a world turned upside down. With allusive echo, this evocation of London's sewers evokes the grandly excremental dystopia of Dryden's *Macflecknoe* and looks ahead to Pope's *Dunciad*.[44]

Through this parodic tilt we learn not only how it looks, but how it feels to be on the underside. The pathetic voice of the orphan shoeshine boy foreshadows *The Songs of Innocence* by William Blake, a poet much influenced by Gay:

> At length he sighing cry'd; That Boy was blest,
> Whose Infant Lips have drain'd a Mother's Breast;
> But happier far are those, (if such be known)
> Whom both a Father and a Mother own:
> But I, alas! hard Fortune's utmost Scorn,
> Who ne'er knew Parent, was an Orphan born!
> Some Boys are rich by Birth beyond all Wants,
> Belov'd by Uncles, and kind good old Aunts;
> When Time comes round, a Christmas-box they bear,
> And one Day makes them rich for all the Year.
> Had I the Precepts of a Father learn'd,
> Perhaps I then the Coachman's Fare had earn'd,
> For lesser Boys can drive; I thirsty stand
> And see the double Flaggon charge their Hand,
> See them puff off the Froth, and gulp amain,
> While with dry Tongue I lick my Lips in vain.
>
> (II.177–92)

Against the comic backdrop of the turnip-topped Cloacina, the rippling sewers of Dryden's "Augusta," and the unreliability of the poem's narrator who confesses to this narrative digression as frivolous as a street ballad (II.217), the boy speaks, like Sparabella, from a place of sympathetic vulnerability. Once again, Gay gives voice and subjectivity to categories—children, women, laborers—that have come to constitute defining identity groups in the social organization of the post-eighteenth-century world.

Such moments of pathos serve as touchstones for Gay's satire. The sympathy we feel for the destitute orphan makes his parodic mother's solution of making him a shoeshine boy less than satisfying. The image with which *Trivia* closes the Walker's "amusing Lay" reinscribes those differences of upbringing the boy laments:

> His treble Voice resounds along the *Meuse*,
> And *White-hall* echoes—*Clean your Honour's Shoes*.
>
> (II.215–16)

This couplet underscores the attention to the discrepancies of rank which pepper the observed streets of *Trivia*. Haunting in their familiarity, the lines capture a moment of class awareness remarkable in its modernity. We need barely translate here to movies of the 1940s and 1950s: "Shoeshine, Mister?"

THE BIRTH OF THE SQUIRE

Gay's work after *Trivia* took on a greater seriousness of tone. His *Poems on Several Occasions* of 1720 displays this shift, including the less parodic, georgic version of *Rural Sports*, his sexuality-exploring pastoral tragedy *Dione*, and his sardonic mock eclogue *The Birth of the Squire*.[45] This last, an uncharacteristically unambiguous satire entirely imagined within what a later age would call a politics of class, illuminates a window onto the critique of the later ballad operas because of its relatively direct and unambivalent identification of villainy and its victims. Here Gay's reworkings of the pastoral continued as his view deepened and darkened, and in turn led to the complex texturing of comedy, irony, and satire in *The Beggar's Opera* and its sequels, *Polly* and *Achilles*. The grimly parodic *Birth of the Squire* reveals key aspects of the power and purpose of the later, more ambiguous "Newgate pastorals."

This mock eclogue plays off Virgil's fourth eclogue, "The Pollio." The poem reveals both Gay's systematic method and his satiric seriousness of purpose. *The Birth of the Squire* jars critics convinced of Gay's frivolity and lightness. James Sutherland remarks:

> Gay's tone [in *The Birth of the Squire*] is, for him, oddly uncompromising; it comes near to disgust. We may perhaps suspect that he had some particularly unfavourable specimen of the squirearchy in mind, some arrogant lout remembered from his boyhood years in Devon.[46]

Sutherland sees the poem in somewhat trivializing biographical terms as an eccentric portrait. But *The Birth of the Squire* supplies an instructive blueprint for Gay's ongoing satiric enterprise with regard to social stratification. As Marcus Walsh notes, in this poem "the satire is more direct, Gay dispensing here, unusually, with a *persona*."[47] Uncomplicated by the self-implicating irony that typifies Gay's prevalent comic turn, *The Birth of the Squire* provides a direct view of his targets and method.

The Birth of the Squire sees and hears from those spaces where the less empowered figures in a context stand. "Hark! the bells ring," the poem announces after the literary- and rank-conscious reminder that "Not all in shades, and humble cotts delight" (ll. 3–4) A working "swain leans upon his fork" (ll. 5–6) to listen. What prompts the bells? "A hopeful heir is born" to the ruling squire. The poem shifts to an even more vulnerable class of creatures, intoning an ominous warning of destruction: "Mourn, mourn, ye stags; and all ye beasts of chase" (l. 9).

As the newborn son comes into view, the imagery heightens the critique. "Beagles and spaniels round his cradle stand" (l. 15) in an emblem of courtly flattery and corruption. The pastoral landscape itself offers resonant debasement as the "paternal acres," redolent with decay, yield for this debauched ruling son only the barley, metheglin, and hops for his intoxicating "bowles" (ll. 19–24). The land itself is left to rot. In this troubled and far-from-innocent pastoral, Gay unstintingly identifies corrupt, appetitive governance as the problem.

Instead of enjoying bucolic characters in a comic mode, *The Birth of the Squire* rivets our attention on the manor house as we look from the position of the humble subjects affected by its rule. The poem considers this burlesque newborn savior in the mocking terms of a base and abusive predator. Recklessly he hunts the countryside for "horny spoils" to "grace the walls." Meanwhile, "monstrous" hunting stories "which descend from son to son" "indulge his greedy ears" (ll. 25–40), a sardonic twist on the image of heroic tales. For "stolen love" he preys on "the milk-maid (thoughtless of her future shame)" until, nine months later, she becomes a milk-maid indeed, "the white drops bath[ing her] swelling breast" (ll. 50–59). "Prodigal of life" and "with bloody heel" he prods his horse and "headlong falls . . . to crack the collar bone" (ll. 61–72). Surviving this mocking parody of heroism, he takes his place "to snore away Debates in Parliament." "A Justice with grave Justices," he devotes himself—with grimly laughable irony—to poaching laws, a reference to those game laws which marked a key political shift in the rule of rural England. The poem closes with a bleary vision of this drunken misruler sinking to an ignominious end. Gay's booby squire "expires" in a grotesque scene reminiscent of, though much less playful than, the fall of Dryden's fatuous Flecknoe:

> Triumphant, o'er the prostrate brutes he stands,
> The mighty bumper trembles in his hands;
> Boldly he drinks, and like his glorious Sires,
> In copious gulps of potent ale expires.
>
> (ll. 105–8)

Unlike the eclogues of *The Shepherd's Week* or the laughing *Trivia*, *The Birth of the Squire* does not look about *in* the marginal space of the lower ranks, but rather looks *on* from that space in a dark and damning portrait of the ruling center. *The Birth of the Squire* not only indicts such overlords, but necessarily subverts its revered Virgilian model, implicating it in the corruption of the system that produces its polished discourse. Gay's is a rather modern-seeming skepticism with regard to rulers and their sustaining culture. Repositioned, we look on from the standpoint of the squire's victims—the tenants, the wild game, his horses, the ruined milkmaid.

The Virgilian referencing is oblique rather than slavish. *The Birth of the Squire* burlesques not a single poem, but rather the entire Virgilian tradition, enlisting it to critique, with ironic bite, cruelties that it has been enlisted to support. The parody serves an unswervingly serious point; this mock "Pollio" is not funny. It spins off a Virgilian prototype which was not only serious, but also bore the extensive weight of a long, subsequent tradition of Christian appropriation of this lavish image of a newborn son of promise. The Virgilian reference skeptically questions this model of literary endeavor directed in support of rule, the appropriation of literature in support of rulers.

The Birth of the Squire thus places us on a margin looking on at the structures of power and the literary forms enlisted to perpetuate them. Just as Brecht's Mackie Messer exposes what is not comic about the rake, this menacing satire turns another familiar comic figure, the booby squire, into a sinister emblem of misrule. Skirting Gay's familiar comic vision, *The Birth of the Squire* gives no cherishing and ambivalently laughable focus on sympathetic underclass characters and no reassuringly self-implicating references to the community of popular forms. The satiric message here is unambiguous and relentless, Brecht-like in its dark, didactic satire.

Part II
Mapping the New Order: Rank and Mobility, Gender and Sexuality, Culture and Nature

5

Village Mumming on an Urban Stage:
The What-d'Ye-Call-It and
Three Hours After Marriage

Gay composed two of his early satires, *The What-d'Ye-Call-It* (1715) and *Three Hours After Marriage* (1717) along the lines of traditional mumming plays. These popular seasonal folk customs feature disguised figures who entertain their hosts with speeches, songs, dances, and a short drama.[1] Drawing attention to hierarchies of rank in their use of this plebeian matrix as a reference, both of Gay's plays position themselves in a parodically reflexive space between "high" art and "low." These satires comment pointedly on "high" forms by finding parallels in common customs and expressions. The plays employ a Theocritan burlesquing like that of *The Shepherd's Week* to reveal the interlocking dynamics of rank that were in the process of the shift from feudal patterns to a modern class structure and consciousness. Both plays bring into parodic interplay the sportive forms of popular drama and song and the "refined" (whether decorous or scabrous) genres of the London theater world. In Gay we find a significant shift from earlier depictions of commoners and their entertainments; he identifies them as sympathetic subjects even as he underscores their subjectedness. Their stories are not entertaining subplots of the sort that occurs, say, in *Midsummer Night's Dream*; their stories are the plot.

THE WHAT-D'YE-CALL-IT

Drury Lane staged *The What-d'Ye-Call-It* in February 1715.[2] Sharing methods and message with *The Shepherd's Week*, this burlesque entertains with a laughter prompted by incongruity and reversal at the same time that it exposes, underneath its laughable incongruities, problems of corruption and injustice. The play creates more than a simple topsy-turvydom, for the

121

allusions and parody look at high art and low, at traditions both above stairs and below, with ethical questions in mind. Rife with references to well-known literary works from the revered tradition, *The What-d'Ye-Call-It* uses as well the structural and thematic elements of underclass forms—mumming and ballads—with careful presentation of the social context of their provenance and its routinely exploited relation to the "polite" world. As Peter Lewis observes:

> Laughter is a right response to the play, but at times the laughter is close to tears. . . . [L]owering an elevated idiom by applying it to those at the bottom of the social scale has the effect of raising the humble characters themselves to a more serious status. . . . The transformation operates in two ways, and if burlesque is one side of Gay's mock heroic, social satire is the other. Gay establishes the hardships and sufferings of a rural peasantry, largely at the mercy of their social superiors and a ruthless legal system, both of which are frequently characterized by corruption, officiousness, and inhumanity.[3]

Like *The Shepherd's Week*, *The What-d'Ye-Call-It* gives voice to subalterns. Celebrated authors and works are echoed in the words and forms of the ploughboys and milkmaids of the English countryside. Here, however, the construction of the play itself depends more fundamentally upon popular forms and traditions; with keen bite, the play looks out from the context of lower-class discourse, the culture below stairs. Viewing its topics and themes from the vantage of common people at the lower rungs, it inaugurates a modern preoccupation with popular culture, both as offering a market and as exposing social stratification at all levels.

The What-d'Ye-Call-It is constructed tightly and wittily as a play-within-a-play, evoking such well-known ancestors as *A Midsummer Night's Dream* and *Hamlet*. The piece opens at Christmastime in the manor of Sir Roger, a country squire. In the big house a cast of his tenants prepares to present to him and two jurist cronies a holiday drama under the direction of his chief steward.[4] This pastoral scene is far from innocent. The steward-playwright undertakes his revels with two themes in mind, both of them concerns fit for social-action committees: (1) impressment and the treatment of common soldiers; and (2) the predicament of a pregnant, unmarried servant girl. Gay's steward designs his play to resolve an immediate instance of the second of these themes:

> My Daughter debauched! and by that Booby Squire! Well, perhaps the Conduct of this Play may retrieve her Folly, and preserve her Reputation. Poor Girl! I cannot forget thy Tears.
>
> (Introductory Scene, ll. 44–46)

With his mumming play, the steward—with a literalness that will get the last laugh—schemes to avert tragedy with comedy: to upend the (junior) squire's seduction and desertion of Katherine with a marriage ending.

Gay's play sets up a scheme for pondering art and context: the inner play is in rhyme, the outer framing play in prose. At a telling point, the two will intersect. The steward assigns "Kitty Carrot," the heroine's role in his Christmas gambol, to his unfortunate "debauched" daughter, Katherine. "Thomas Filbert," the hero of his play, is to be played by Squire Thomas, the debauching son. As Peter Lewis observes: "By transforming some actors into their roles and other roles back into their actors, Gay tantalizingly touches on the dichotomies between art and nature and between illusion and reality."[5] The plot of the inner play renders those polestars of heroic tragedy—wooing and warring—from a parodying underclass vantage, much like the vantage of the trout or pheasant of *Rural Sports* on the fishing and hunting pleasures of the georgic. Brimming with allusions to polite literature, the satire of the inner play is literary; intersecting with the outer, it is social.

The steward playwright's plot takes up the matter of Christmas mumming plays, which also (to Gay's evident delight) traditionally render wooing and war, here parodically tilted by bastardy and forced recruitment. The truehearted "Filbert" (played by the falsehearted Thomas) will leave his truehearted "Kitty" (played by the pregnant Katherine) and go to war because he refuses to acknowledge paternity of the bastard child of "Dorcas Peascod," "Kitty's" rival. Meanwhile in a nearby field "Timothy," "Dorcas's" brother and "Filbert's" friend, will be shot for desertion: "When I was press'd, I told them the first Day, "I wanted Heart to fight, so ran away" (II.i.15–16), "Peascod" declares, recounting misdeeds remorsefully in the formulaic mode of popular ballads on about-to-be-executed criminals. Thinking this encounter with her doomed brother to be her last, "Dorcas" publicly confesses her baby to be, not "Filbert's", but the "Squire's": "The Squire betray'd me; nay,—and what is worse, / Brib'd me with two Gold Guineas in this Purse, / To swear the Child to *Filbert*" (II.iii.15–17). With "Filbert" therefore freed from compulsory recruitment, "Peascod" is likewise released when a constable—a witty deus ex machina for Gay's "modernized" pastoral—arrests the recruiting sergeant for stealing a horse. "Filbert" finds "Kitty," lovelorn and suicidal—another echo of popular ballad tradition—and brings her to the expected ending of comedy whether "low" or "high": a marriage. "A Wedding, a Bedding; a Wedding, a Bedding," the "Chorus of Haymakers" chants boisterously, voicing in the inner play of "Kitty" and "Filbert" the rhyme that has yet to be completed in the outer play of Katherine and Thomas.

The two plots converge in the dictates of Squire Roger—who "plays" himself. "Ay, now for the Wedding," he demands. When the curate refuses his gown as a costume—"for it is a Profanation" (II.x.7)—a reference to clerical disapproval of the theater in Gay's London—the squire exerts his authority:

> What, shall the Curate controul me? . . . Tell him that I will not have my
> Play spoil'd; nay, that he shall marry the couple himself—I say he shall.
> (II.x.19–21)

The parson agrees, but he will only perform the ceremony offstage. "Why, what's a Play without a Marriage?" the ruling squire insists (II.x.32), unaware that the wedding he has ordered will stick. "I wish you Joy of your Play, and of your Daughter," the steward triumphantly tells Sir Roger, presenting to him his new daughter-in-law, "I had no way but this to repair the Injury your Son had done my Child" (II,x,43-45). "Sure I must have been married some time or other," Thomas muses in a tone between rueful and agreeable. The play ends with a dance followed by a mock-moralizing epilogue in a single couplet that refuses didactic finality: "Our Stage Play has a Moral—and no doubt / You all have Sense enough to find it out" (II.x.71–72).

Christmas Mumming Plays

Critics have been alert to the echoes and allusions to high drama which pepper *The What-d'Ye-Call-It*. Only five weeks after the play opened, James Roberts published the anonymous *A Complete Key To the last New Farce The What D'Ye Call It*.[6] As Winton summarizes:

> [*The What-d'Ye-Call-It*] is a burlesque not only of blank verse tragedy but
> of all tragedy, indeed of the very spirit of tragedy. A published *Key*, pre-
> pared by someone who knew a fair amount about Gay and Pope, demon-
> strates that every scene, almost every line, burlesques some motif or some
> passage in stage tragedy.[7]

This ongoing allusion in Gay's parody to works of "polite" literature has preoccupied critics from the unnamed author of the *Key* until the present day.[8] The metaleptic panache of *The What-d'Ye-Call-It* is considerably more complex and pointed than *The Key* alone can disclose, for the play relies at least as consistently upon elements of popular culture for its forms as it does upon the tragedies of Addison, Dryden, or Lee. Looking culturally "down" and "sideways" with as much attention as he looks "up," Gay establishes points of view—placed in relationships with moral implications— at all levels. Using the materials, motifs, and structures of folk drama and

popular song, his giddy burlesque reveals the demarcations of rank and culture as configurations with ethical implication. The class world of the outer
play—that of the presiding squire with his cohort justices—stands accused
and upended by the outcomes of the steward's inner construction, whose
dramatic themes and argument speak from the popular realm of eighteenth-
century England, even as they echo Shakespeare, Dryden, and Otway.

The inner play, a "Christmas theatrical," cleverly reworks the traditional wooing play, a form of the ancient mumming dramas performed by
tenants, servants, and ploughboys during the holiday season, often for the
lord and lady of the great house. Rural people have performed such
pageantlike guising dramas in the British countryside and villages up until
recent times, and Gay's Drury Lane audience would have recognized the
reference immediately. In 1713 Gay, himself a domestic steward of sorts as
secretary to the formidable duchess of Monmouth, spent time at Moor Park,
her country house in Hertfordshire, just the kind of estate where tenants
performed holiday mummings.[9]

Folk mumming plays seem to have roots prior to the early modern era,
from whence they have survived in a puzzling profusion. In Britain they
fall into several types, of which Gay takes up two distinct patterns: (1)
hero-combat plays in which a hero "kills" an opponent who is then revived
by a comical doctor, a model for *Three Hours After Marriage*; and (2)
wooing plays, a model for *The What-d'Ye-Call-It*. In the wooing plays, a
woman rejects a hero in favor of a "clown" who is then accused by another
woman of fathering her bastard baby; when the clown denies this accusation, the action often moves into the hero-combat scenario in which a slain
disputant is revived by a doctor.[10]

The What-d'Ye-Call-It calls to mind such general features of all
mumming plays as the holiday context, the "sing-song" rhymes (which
Gay accentuates by the contrasting prose of the outer play), the formalized
and exaggerated entrances of characters, and a *quete*-like ending in which
the performers collect a reward from the audience as the drama ends in
music and dancing. *The What-d'Ye-Call-It* evokes the "wooing plays" or
"ploughplays" (so called because they traditionally happened on "Plough
Monday" after Twelfth Night when work was to resume after the midwinter holiday).[11] These customs, which survive mainly in the northeast midlands, loosely join the combat and cure episodes of the combat plays to a
sentimental drama which Chambers calls "The Fool's Wooing."[12]

The Christmas theatrical of Gay's clever steward contains the themes
of traditional wooing plays: a preoccupation with military recruiting, exaggerated courtings, lamenting ladies, bastard babies, sudden ghostly appearances, death sentences followed by inexplicable reprieves, and a jovial
if surprising wedding at the conclusion. Gay adopts a traditional form that

identifies common people at a subaltern social level. From their vantage, he critiques structures of custom, power, and thought occupying the "polite" level: the judicial system, the squirearchy, the military—and any form of theatrical and artistic self-importance.

Gay's play opens with the squire, Sir Roger, intoning a rhyming accusation against Filbert:

> Here, Thomas Filbert, answer to your Name,
> Dorcas hath sworn to you she owes her Shame:
> Or wed her strait, or else you're sent afar,
> To serve his Gracious Majesty in War.
>
> (I.i.1–5)

Setting the scene, the rollicking couplets and mocking formality call to mind the elaborate presentations which open traditional wooing plays. In them, the mummers announce themselves or, less frequently, are announced, in lilting rhyme and meter. One traditional play begins:

> In comes I noble Antony
> as mad and as milde and as blithe
> as your old Mantle Tree,
> make room for nob[le] Antony
> and all his jovel company.[13]

The first player in another manuscript announces himself:

> I am me Fathers eldest Son
> And Heir of all his land
> I hope in a short time
> It will all fall in my hand.[14]

The What-d'Ye-Call-It evokes both the manner and the matter of these holiday mummings.

However, *The What-d'Ye-Call-It* reverses the courtship dilemma that begins the conventional wooing plays. In these, "the Fool"—known in most traditional plays as "Thomas Fool" or "the Farmer's eldest Son"—enters the play, the unwelcome suitor of a disdaining lady. (In Gay's play, the disdain goes the other direction as "Thomas," the recruited "eldest Son," repudiates the courtship claims of the pregnant "Dorcas.") Conventional lines render from this lady's point of view the wooing play's standard presentation of the "hero":

> He swears if I don't wed with him
> As you will understand,

> He'll go and list for a soldier
> And go to some foreign land.[15]

Although it reverses the direction of the courtship and disdain in introducing the hero, Gay's play takes up the mocking connection the folk plays make between courtship and war (a theme he investigates thoroughly in *Polly*, the sequel to *The Beggar's Opera*). Moreover, the dynamic between "Thomas" and "Dorcas" in Gay's play mirrors the wooing plays, which inevitably bring on a second stock female character, who introduces the motif of bastardy that dominates *The What-d'Ye-Call-It*. This character, often called "Dame Jane," enters in the plight of Gay's wanton Dorcas:

> Here comes old Dame Jane
> Come dableing about the Meadow
> Comes Jumping about, to show you such sport
> Look about you old Maids and Widows
> Long time I have sought you
> But now I have found you
> Sarrah come take your Bastard.[16]

In the traditional plays, the fool rejects this woman and her baby in such farcical exchanges as the following:

> *Fool.* long time I've sought but now I'v found
>   my joy and only *arsturd*.
> *Jane.* but since you'v said so and calld me your Whore
>   Sarrah come take your Bastard
> *Fool.* Bastard t'is none of mine its not abit like me.
>   I'm a valient Knight just come from sea
>   you never heard talk of me before did ye.
>   I kill'd ten men with a mess of mustard,
>   ten thousand with my bright Sword.[17]

The farcical mock heroic of the Fool's boasting seems ready-made for Gay's sensibility. In particular, the mummings link the interdependence of heroic love and heroic war—an ongoing theme in Gay's satire—bringing the pretensions of this mutuality into laughable question with the resonance of "bastard" and deadly "mustard."

Using the materials, motifs, and structures of folk drama, *The What-d'Ye-Call-It* arrives at social comment through a burlesque mirroring of common and polite that looks forward to *The Beggar's Opera*. The play's reading of these stratified pairings, despite its hilarity, is satiric and ultimately moral. The plot unfolds metaleptically to reveal in its burlesque figures a dialectics of power. The figurative play within a play discloses the structural tensions, risks, and conflictual ironies—a "deep" play—in the pairings of mumming plays and tragedies, plaintiffs and judges, playwrights and critics, ruled and rulers, tenants and landlords, recruitees and recruiters, servants and masters, women and men. The traditional wooing play percolates up through both the matter and manner of *The What-d'Ye-Call-It* not just as an indirect influence, but as the point of departure. Recognizing a consolidating and sympathetic voice in the "low," Gay's play thus recognizes individual identity and subjectivity within a matrix of cultural expression at any level.

BALLAD TRADITION AND *THE WHAT-D'YE-CALL-IT*

The What-d'Ye-Call-It also resonates with the lines and themes of popular ballads, particularly in the speeches and actions of Kitty. Gay's fixation on music is, as we have noted, an ongoing preoccupation. Thematic conventions from balladry here include the visitant ghosts of murder victims; the breaking of the ninepence lovers' token; and the female true lover dying for the loss of her soldier or sailor love. Reaching deeper still than these surface invocations, ballad tradition shapes the representation of the heroine of the steward's inner play. As *The What-d'Ye-Call-It* laughingly makes plain, Kitty is a heroine straight from the ballads.

The Key attests that Gay's audience recognized in Kitty's drama the parody of such current tragedies as Ambrose Philips's *The Distress'd Mother* and Thomas Otway's *Venice Preserv'd*.[18] At the same time, playgoers would not have missed seeing Kitty as a common ballad type: the innocent, devoted heroine who will undergo any hardship or test for her love. She declares herself such in her attempts to best Dorcas's claims. Kitty will follow her hero to war to care for him as poetry's heroics prescribe, whether from the Muses of the court or the street:

> I can bear sultry Days and frosty Weather;
> Yes, yes, my *Thomas*, we will go together;
> Beyond the Seas together will we go,
> In Camps together, as at Harvest, glow.

(I.i.72–75)

Over Kitty's lines echo the voices of heroines of popular street ballads. "Whensoe're you march away, / In this Land I will not stay, / But thy true Comrade will be, / And freely live or dye with thee," declares the heroine of a ballad of about 1690.[19] Simultaneously invoking the mumming plays, *The What-d'Ye-Call-It* enlists a contradictory web of mimicry, for the resistant "Lady" of the wooing plays mocks such heroines as Kitty:

So now my love has listed
and enterd volunteer
I never will greive for him
nor for him shed one tear

I never will greive for him
I will let him to [k]now
I will have a nother sweetheart
and with him I will not go[20]

A play of reference and counterreference encircles the knowing audience of Gay's play, reinterpreting themes of love and heroism as allusions from one social level invoke yet contradict those from another: folk mummings evoke and contradict polite tragedies; polite tragedies evoke and contradict folk mummings.

Filbert's response to Kitty continues the citation of ballad tradition, where departing soldiers and sailors conventionally respond with rejoinders and tests that, with each devoted answer, heighten the suffering woman's heroism. Thus, "Thomas" of the ballad "The Souldiers Farewel to his Love" first objects to his (pregnant) lover, "It is too far for Peg to go with me;" later, "But Margarets fingers they are all too fine, / To wait on me when she doth see me dine;" then "But youl repine when you shal see me have / A dainty wench that is both fine and brave."[21] With each rebuff, Margaret declares her love and further willingness to suffer, finally declaring her desire for the conventional true-lover's death that Gay's Kitty seeks: "If nought wil serve why then sweet love adieu / I needs must die, and yet in dying true." Won over, the ballad's Thomas agrees to marry: "We will be wed, come Margaret let us go."

With a spate of wordplay and ironic resonance, Gay injects into the situation of *The What-d'Ye-Call-It* a further comic innuendo. *The Key* notes in Kitty's lines the echo of Belvidera's willingness to follow her Jaffeir in Otway's tragedy, *Venice Preserv'd*. "Though the bare earth be all our resting-place," Belvidera declares, "Its roots our food, some clift our habitation, / I'l make this Arm a Pillow for thy Head" (I.373–75).[22] The punning in Filbert's response brings on the laughter of a Restoration comedy even as it reminds its audience of the bawdy—yet dire—predicament of the outer play's Katherine. "Oh, *Kitty, Kitty*, canst thou quit the Rake," Filbert asks, "And leave these Meadows for thy Sweetheart's sake?" The pun on the word "Rake"—and the word, on stage, was undoubtedly followed by a pause—turns this line to the dilemma of the outer play's wanton, the pregnant (and thus demonstrably "rakish") Katherine, and the certainly more "rakish" Squire Thomas.

As Filbert continues this conventional testing, the parody jumps onto yet another track. Filbert's laughable reversal of such questions as the ballad Thomas raised abruptly turns from Kitty to an exposure of the less than heroic aspects of the warring army. Filbert's speech rests on the final thought that when he dies, however devoted she may be, Kitty will be cheated of his pension:

> Canst thou so many gallant Soldiers see,
> And Captains and Lieutenants slight for me?
> Say, canst thou hear the Guns, and never shake,
> Nor start at Oaths that make a Christian quake?
> Canst thou bear Hunger, canst thou march and toil
> A long long Way, a thousand thousand Mile?
> And when thy *Tom's* blown up, or shot away,
> Then—cast thou starve?—they'll cheat thee of my Pay.
>
> (I.i.84–91)

While Gay's play tips and turns with a laughable mimicry of the conventional postures of ballad, verse, and drama, its larger vision, like that of *The Shepherd's Week,* bestows a sympathetic rendering of those who suffer—amidst their own and our pastoral, tragic, and heroic fantasy—the real injustices of the world as it is. After all, in the remarks that prompt Kitty and Filbert's ballad-quoting outburst, Dorcas voices the all-too-unromanticized predicament of the "real" Katherine of the outer play: "How shall I weep to hear this Infant cry? / He'll have no Father—and no Husband I" (I.i.68–69). Of course, it is the trickster-steward's aim to bring Kitty's resolution in the inner play to Katherine, the Dorcas of the outer one. Its laughter notwithstanding, the play raises big questions: What is Art? What is Culture? How do they represent and express? How do they critique and protest? Identifying art as culture through his use of the "low", Gay actually brings to the fore the crux of satire: the relation of artistic expression (at any level) to the politics of its society.

The *What-d'Ye-Call-It* reaches its culminating turning point in " 'Twas When the Seas Were Roaring," a class-shuffling parody of popular balladry. The steward's play, in the course of its inner plot about preventing the abandonment of "Kitty" by the forced enlistment of her beloved "Filbert," will marry the "actual" Kitty and her seducer, the young Squire Thomas. " 'Twas When the Seas" was Gay's first collaboration with George Friedrich Handel, who composed the setting that probably served the original play.[23] " 'Twas When the Seas Were Roaring" is in the "flowery" style that Gay repeated in "Black-eyed Susan's Farewell to Sweet William." " 'Twas When the Seas" weaves language and music characteristic of elegant stage songs together with conventional ballad references—an interleaving of cultural strata that is, in fact, the theme of both inner and outer "plays" in *The What-d'Ye-Call-It.*

Scene 8 of act 2—part of the inner, mumming play—is devoted to "Kitty's" grief at "Filbert's" impressment. She is the conventional abandoned heroine of both high art and low, as Gay brings the two to a single level. With parodic reference to both realms (Dido meets the milkmaid), the allusive "Sighs and Groans" of the lamenting Kitty are funny. Yet the poignancy of mixed modes in this "tragi-comi-pastoral farce" is keen at this climax. The crux of the play's balance of laughter and sentiment lies in Kitty's ballad—which, as she says, she got from a broadside "bought at a Fair" (II.viii.19). From the play's parodic fabric, " 'Twas When the Seas Were Roaring" rises, a perfectly singable ballad on its own.[24] Indeed, the song was an immediate hit and remained popular in more than a dozen editions, including numerous broadside song sheets—possibly bought at fairs—throughout the century.[25]

"A Damsel" on the shore awaits the return of "her Dear," spies his "floating Corpse" in conventional fashion, and just as conventionally "bow'[s] her Head, and dy'[s]" (II.viii.22–61).

> 'Twas when the Seas were roaring
>   With hollow Blasts of Wind;
> A Damsel lay deploring,
>   All on a Rock reclin'd.
> Wide o'er the rolling Billows
>   She cast a wistful Look;
> Her Head was crown'd with Willows
>   That tremble o'er the Brook.
>
> Twelve Months are gone and over,
>   And nine long tedious Days.
> Why didst thou, vent'rous Lover,
>   Why didst thou trust the Seas?
> Cease, cease, thou cruel Ocean,
>   And let my Lover rest;
> Ah! what's thy troubled Motion
>   To that within my Breast?
>
> The Merchant, rob'd of Pleasure,
>   Sees Tempests in Despair;
> But what's the loss of Treasure
>   To losing of my Dear?
> Should you some Coast be laid on
>   Where Gold and Di'monds grow,
> You'd find a richer Maiden
>   but none that loves you so.

How can they say that Nature
    Has nothing made in vain;
Why then beneath the Water
    Should hideous Rocks remain?
No Eyes the Rocks discover,
    That lurk beneath the Deep,
To wreck the wand'ring Lover,
    And leave the Maid to weep.

All melancholy lying,
    Thus wail'd she for her Dear;
Repay'd each Blast with Sighing,
    Each Billow with a Tear;
When o'er the white Wave stooping
    His floating Corpse she spy'd;
Then like a Lilly drooping,
    she bow'd her Head, and dy'd.

(II.viii.22–61)

Ex. 2. Late-eighteenth-century songbook version of "'Twas When the Seas Were Roaring."[26]

The overwrought figure of "Kitty" and her dilemma mocks the over-sentimentalizing of ballad motifs, especially as these are adapted by "po-lite" imitators of them.[27] At the same time, "Kitty's" voice, especially in that poignant time-out-of-time experience that is the singing of the song, evokes genuine pathos and sympathy. Her predicament stands out amidst Gay's satire of the manor house: "Happy the Maid, whose Sweetheart never hears / The Soldier's Drum nor Writ of Justice fears" (II.viii.12). However parodically the ballad refers to the street song milieu, "'Twas When the Seas Were Roaring" sings quite beyond mockery, translating for a polite audience the sentiments and value of such people as the play's manor house "mummers." These are real people; their concerns are sympathetic, artful, kindred.

"'Twas When the Seas Were Roaring" marks the turning point of the play's inner plot. Kitty, directed by the sentiments of the song, considers how to carry out her destiny as a heroine. She takes up a suicidal "Penknife," as a ballad would have her. However, sister to Sparabella of *The Shepherd's Week*, she decides against such self-knifing and falling "as Pigs have dy'd" (II.ix.68); similarly, she chooses not to suffer the bestial death afforded by the noose, for "Curs are hang'd" (II.ix.71). Instead, she will simply close her "weary Eyes in Death," embracing the self-destruction that is the conventional fate of the Belvediras, Cleopatras, and Ophelias of high tragedy and the Nancys and Susans of popular ballads. "Kitty" faints. When she is revived, with the help of her water-splashing grandmother and aunt, she sees, amidst a swirling array of "Haycocks," "Bagpipes in Butter," "Flocks in fleecy Fountains," and so on, the image of "Filbert." "It is his Ghost," she cries, "or is it he indeed?" (II.ix.1). He assures her that he is no ghost and that "*Dorcas* confess'd; the Justice set me free" (XX.ix.5). Come, let's to church, to Church," he exhorts (8–9). "To wed," says "Kitty"; "To bed," replies "Filbert." The final episode, as we have seen, marries the steward's pregnant daughter to the squire's son, with obvious reference to the early eighteenth century's experience of and preoccupation with shufflings of rank.

The What-d'Ye-Call-It explores the delusions and dreams of aesthetic order with an ongoing and usually overlooked attention to their lack of fit with the world as it happens. Throughout, Gay constructs a satire that articulates this vision based on revealingly juxtaposed traditions from different sectors: Virgilian pastoral, tragedy and polite drama, antiquarian learning, street ballads, popular dances, holiday dramas of unlettered servants and ploughboys. Within the paradoxes and ironies posed by these mutually implicating traditions, we are brought to comic pleasure joined with a satirical perspective on social and political power in the unliterary day-to-day.

THREE HOURS AFTER MARRIAGE: MUMMERY AS A CLASS REFERENCE

Two years after the success of *The What-d'Ye-Call-It*, Gay brought to Drury Lane *Three Hours After Marriage*, another farcical satire that invokes customary mumming. In the advertisement to the published edition of 1717, Gay acknowledges "the Assistance" of "two of [his] Friends," Alexander Pope and John Arbuthnot, in the creation of this most Scriblerian of his plays. Although some critics—swayed, it would seem, by hostile contemporary reactions that were preoccupied with accusations of plagiarism— have doubted Gay's authorship, I agree with Winton and other recent commentators that *Three Hours After Marriage* is, as Gay said it was, his comedy. Like *The What-d'Ye-Call-It*, *Three Hours* pointedly draws attention to the social levels of customary expression in the domains of high art and low. Ben Jonson seems to have been on Gay's mind, especially his *Epicoene*—whose Morose seems a model of the grumbling, newly married senex, and *Volpone*—whose mountebank scene suggests the overdetermined science and doctoring in *Three Hours*.

The shaping of the play as "mummery," noticeable to a few recent critics, was certainly recognizable to Gay's London audience, especially given their familiarity with *The What-d'Ye-Call-It* of the previous season.[28] Indeed, Dr. Fossile, the central character, declares the connection. "Then why this Disguise?" his new bride asks, upon finding him disguised as his footman to spy on her. "Since it must come out," he blusters, "ha, ha, ha, only a frolick on my Wedding Day between *Hugh* and I. We had a mind to exhibit a little Mummery" (II.181–84). More glancing and intermittent in its references than *The What-d'Ye-Call-It*, *Three Hours After Marriage* nonetheless is shaped throughout by a burlesque conjunction of the underclass realm of mummery and the laughable literary, social, and political London that is being satirized. This, it should be noted, is a Georgian London of the middling sort, a feature of the satire that probably accounts for the hostility that it provoked. The play situates itself in a bourgeois household and takes up its mummery with reference to the doctors, lawyers, scholars, merchants, financiers, record-keepers, and so on, who were assuming increasing wealth, power, and importance in the shifting social order.[29] The target here, in contrast to the country squires in *The What-d'Ye-Call-It*, is the emerging realm of urban management. For its London audiences, *Three Hours* imagines as comical figures in a holiday mumming all-too-recognizable members of the new professional class: an antiquarian-physician who trades in knowledge and health, and a critic who trades in art and opinions.

The plot of *Three Hours* is an ingenious amalgam of conventional characters and topoi from a range of long-standing popular sources.[30] The old Dr. Fossile, an antiquarian-minded physician, has just married the young Susannah Townley—the conventional January-May marriage dilemma. The two have yet to consummate the union. In short order, Fossile discovers billets-doux for his bride from a flock of favorites. Meanwhile, the poetry-spouting Phoebe Clinket, Fossile's resident niece, employs a serving maid with a desk on her back as Clinket meanders through the abode writing verses. The bumbling *senex* schemes to catch Townley in her indiscretions, as his bride sets about to elude him. Two of her eager paramours, Plotwell and Underplot, arrive, vying for her favors on a wager they have laid with each other, even as they collaborate with her and each other to outwit Fossile. Posing first as a Polish doctor and a sick patient come to visit Dr. Fossile, they are eventually brought onto the stage disguised as a mummy and a crocodile—a sight gag that remained famous in theater lore for decades. As the plot resolves in a cavalcade of witty turns, "Jack Capstone of Deptford," a blunt, kindly Jack-Tar reminiscent of *The Shepherd's Week* and *The What-d'Ye-Call-It* arrives to present Fossile with a baby, eventually revealed to be Townley's. Meanwhile, the latter is found to be already wife to one Lieutenant Bengall, "just returned from the Indies." The buffoonish, tenderhearted Fossile, who at the outset had anguished whether he could produce an heir, finds one bestowed upon him. Philosophically he concludes the play: "What signifies whether a Man beget his Child or not? . . . It is better that the Father should adopt the Child, than that the Wife should adopt the Father" (III.556–60).

While *Three Hours* was a moderate success, running for a full seven nights, it provoked heated response to its pointed spoofs of antiquarian John Woodward and critic John Dennis. The play seems to have offended powerful Whigs in London and was something of an embarrassment to Pope. As Winton says, it was quietly dropped from the repertoire, probably by Richard Steele. Commentators today find the supposed caricatures of real people impossible to trace, and the satirical threat of the play difficult to understand.[31] However, the allusions to mummery that pepper the play have a social meaning that would have given the satire a bite that did not escape the original audience. An aura of plebeianism, similar to that in *The What-d'Ye-Call-It*, is in this case applied quite pointedly to persons and relationships among the middling sort in Hanoverian London. They were not amused.

Just as the outlines and themes of the wooing plays inform *The What-d'Ye-Call-It*, the ingredients and development of *Three Hours After Marriage* evoke an even more prevalent pattern of mummery: the hero-combat play. Mummers usually enacted this conventional scenario in house visits at sundry calendar feasts during the year throughout Britain. (Such mummings are still revived for certain village festivals today.)[32] The hero-combat scenario features contesting heroes—sometimes two, sometimes more—with an occasional dragon or monster, who announce themselves in verse and fight, usually with swords. When one such combatant is "slain," a doctor arrives on the scene and revives him. "Hocus, Pocus, Alecampain," says "doctor Quack" of a late-eighteenth-century play, "Take one of my Pills, Dead Man, rise and fight again."[33] The hero rises (sometimes to the joy of a female relation), usually to fight another combat in the same pattern. E. K. Chambers sees the structure of the combat plays as falling into three parts: first, the "presentation" of characters, who step forward with considerable formality; then, the "drama" which features the dispute, swordplay combat, a lament, and the cure; and finally, the *"quete,"* the collection of a reward from the audience as the drama ends in singing and dancing.[34]

These widely performed folk dramas are thought to be quite ancient forms modified from generation to generation. The earliest extant fragment of a hero-combat play dates from 1730s Devonshire. In it "St. George" announces his entrance:

> Oh! here comes I, St. George, a man of courage bold,
> And with my spear I winn'd three crowns of gold,
> I slew the dragon, and brought him to the slaughter,
> And by that very means I married Sabra,
>   the beauteous King of Egypt's daughter.[35]

The plot of *Three Hours* unfolds in the three acts as three climactic combats: (1) a battle of the "Ancients and Moderns" in act 1 between "Sir Tremendous" (an obvious caricature of the critic John Dennis) and Townley's paramour "Plotwell" (thought by some at the time to represent Colley Cibber) who, on behalf of Phoebe Clinket, pretends to be the author of Clinket's play; (2) a battle of learning and proposed cures in act 2 between the two physicians, "Fossile" and the supposed "Dr. Lubormirsky," who is really "Plotwell"; and (3) a competition in act 3 between the two paramours, "Plotwell" and "Underplot," as to which is the more desirable, an exchange which is then followed by a combative exchange of opinions between the antiquarians, "Nautilis" and "Possum," whose threatening swords finally prompt the "Mummy" and "Crocodile," to "leap from their Places" into life, bringing the play to its denouement.

Three Hours After Marriage called up for Gay's audience the comical battles of folk mumming plays, thus creating a socially resonant mock heroic. Just as such mumming plays self-consciously herald themselves with the entrance speeches of the various heroes, *Three Hours* introduces its first combative battle with the announcement by the ever-composing Phoebe Clinket: "I perceive here will be a Wit-Combat between these Beaux-Esprits. *Prue*, be sure you set down all the Similes" (I.400–401), whereupon the servant "Prue *retires to the back part of the Stage with Pen and Ink.*" The combat ensues:

Sir *Tremendous*. The Subjects of most modern Plays are as ill chosen as—
Plotwell. The Patrons of their dedications.
                              [Clinket *makes Signs to* Prue.]
Sir *Tremendous*. Their Plots as shallow—
Plotwell. As those of bad Poets against new Plays.
Sir *Tremendous*. Their Episodes as little of a Piece to the main Action, as—
Clinket. A black Gown with a Pink-colour'd Peticoat. Mark that *Prue*.
   [*Aside.*]
Sir *Tremendous*. Their Sentiments are so very delicate—
Plotwell. That like whipt Syllabub they are lost before they are tasted.
Sir *Tremendous*. Their Diction so low, that—that—
Plotwell. Why, that their Friends are forced to call it Simplicity. . . .
                                        (I.402–16)

A "Player" interrupts to suggest that they turn to the business at hand: the reading of the "Play" they are considering, "*The universal Deluge,* or the Tragedy of *Deucalion* and *Pyrrha*," supposedly by Plotwell, but really Clinket's. "O what Felony from the Ancients! What Petty-Larcenry from the Moderns!" bemoans Tremendous in an excoriation of supposed plagiarisms, one of the critic Dennis's well-known fixations. Eventually, Clinket's play is read aloud, then critiqued by Tremendous—"Such Stuff! [*strikes out.*] abominable! [*strikes out.*] most execrable!" (537-38)—until the overwrought Clinket faints: "Ah, hold, hold—I'm butcher'd, I'm massacred. For Mercy's Sake! murder, murder! ah!" (547-48). Fossile arrives and, "*peeping at the Door*," discovers them: "My House turn'd to a Stage! and my Bride playing her Part too!" (549). Furiously breaking up the rehearsal, Fossile flings Clinket's verses into the fire as the assembly disperses in haste; the first act ends with Fossile lamenting his cuckoldry even as fiddles, drums, and trumpets "Wish him much Joy of his Marriage" in an allusion to the traditional "rough music" for village weddings, a direct reference to a customary mumming context.[36] The metaleptic structuring of the play thus poses the arts as having mirroring expressions from "high" and "low" social contexts which will by the nineteenth century be understood—both from within and without—by the concept of class. Because culture, as E. P. Thompson and others have shown, forms such an important factor in this identification of distinct social levels, these early and influential demarcations by Gay become important to recognize as part of the history of the understanding of modern "class."[37]

Act 2 continues this attention to common people and their customs applied to the realm of the bourgeoisie, as Fossile enters disguised as his own footman. Eventually, upon discovery, he remarks that he had "a mind to exhibit a little Mummery"—just as the play has been doing. Once Fossile resumes his own attire, the farce turns to doctoring, evoking the conventional

"Quack Doctor" figure of hero-combat mumming plays and popular stage farces.[38] Plotwell enters, ostentatiously announcing himself in Latin, pretending to be "Doctor Cornelius Lubormirski" from "De famous University of *Cracow* in *Polonia minor*" who had "cur'd de King of *Sweden* of de Wound" (II.228–29). As he and Fossile encounter each other, "*they make many bows and cringes in advancing*," as another combative spoof is about to begin. Plotwell is, of course, intent on diverting Fossile from Townley in hopes of winning his wager with Underplot. Unable to persuade Fossile to "fetch some of de right *Thames* Sand date be below de Bridge" (II.256), Plotwell changes his tactics to a nonsensical combat of scholarly and antiquarian one-upmanship . . . with echoes of *The British Apollo*:

> *Plotwell.* This Bite wont take to send him out of the Way, I'll change my Subject. *[aside.]* Do you deal in Longitudes, Sir?
> *Fossile.* I deal not in impossibilities. I search only for the grand Elixier.
> *Plotwell.* Vat do you tink of de new Metode of Fluxion?
> *Fossile.* I know no other but by *Mercury*.
> *Plotwell.* Ha, ha. Me mean de Fluxion of de Quantity.
> *Fossile.* The greatest Quantity I ever knew, was three Quarts a Day.
> *Plotwell.* Be dere any secret in the Hydrology, Zoology, Minerology, Hydraulicks, Acausticks, Pneumaticks, Logarithmatechny, dat you do want de Explanation of?
> *Fossile.* This is all out of my Way. Do you know of any Hermaphrodites, monstrous Twins, Antidiluvian Shells, Bones, and Vegetables?
> *Plotwell.* Vat tink you of an Antidiluvian Knife, Spoon, and Fork, with the Mark of *Tubal Cain* in *Hebrew*, dug out of de Mine of *Babylon*?
> *Fossile.* Of what Dimensions, I pray, Sir?
> *Plotwell.* De Spoon be bigger dan de modern Ladle; de Fork, like de great Fire-fork; and de Knife, like de Cleaver.
> *Fossile.* Bless me! this shows the Stature and Magnitude of those Antidiluvians!
> *Plotwell.* To make you convinc'd that I tell not de lie, dey are in de *Turkey* Ship at *Vapping*, just going to be dispos'd of. Me would go there vid you, but de Business vil not let me.
> *Fossile.* An extraordinary Man this! I'll examine him further. *[Aside.]*
> (II.261–89)

A few lines later when the scheming Underplot arrives "*in a Chair like a sick Man*," Fossile and Plotwell parry and counterparry on the topic of how to cure him:

> *Fossile.* I am entirely for a Glister.
> *Plotwell.* My Opinion is for de strong Vomit.
> *Fossile.* Bleed him.

Plotwell. Make de Scarrification, give me de Lancet, me will do it myself, and after dat will put de Blister to de Sole of de Feet.

(II.353–58)

As they accrete, the remedies take on frenzied military metaphors until the pretend patient, Underplot, threatened by swordlike "Lancet" and "Poker," leaps up and exits:

Fossile. Your dolor proceeds from a frigid *intemperies* of the Brain, a strong Disease! the Enemy has invaded the very Citadel of your Microcosm, the Magazine of your vital Functions; he has sate down before it; yet there seems to be a good Garrison of vital Spirits, and we don't question to be able to defend it.

Plotwell. Ve will cannonade de Enemy wid Pills, bombard him wid de Bolus, blow him up with Volatiles, fill up de Trenches wid de large Inundation of Apozems, and dislodge him wid de Stink-pot; let de Apothecary bring up de Artillery of Medicine immediately. . . . Hoy, de Servant dere, make hast, bring de Pan of hot Coals; or de red hot Iron to make application to de Temples . . .

Underplot. Hold, hold, am I to be murder'd? [*starts up.*]

(II.359–84)

This giddy cataloging of cures against the backdrop of contestatory mock-heroic mumming casts over Fossile and Plotwell the aura of the farcical mock doctors of mumming plays. One such "doctor Quack" arrives on the scene of "The Islip Mummers' Play of 1780" on a hobby-horse, a "restive Nag," who "kicks the doctor off." ("Blame Salt Peter," the manuscript advises, "for giving the Nag to [*sic*] many Beans.") With much the same self-puffery that *Three Hours* so delights in, "doctor Quack" knocks at the door and announces himself:

> Come in doctor Quack
> I am not a Quack, as you may see
> I am Doctor Spinney with a Big M.D.

(ll. 26–28)

"Doctor Quack" then examines "the Dead Man," slain in the combat between "the Royal Duke of Blunderland" and "Earl or King Percy." (The manuscript gives "Instructions" earlier: "decide which is to be Dead Man, and make a good fight.) Taking up his "bag of Tools"—undoubtedly a collection of objects as hyperbolically grotesque as those of Fossile and Plotwell—"doctor Quack" declares:

> I am a Doctor, a Doctor Good
> Who's hand were never stained with Blood,

I can cure the itch, the Pox, the Palsy, and the Gout,
Pains within and pains without,
If the Devil in I can fetch him out.
I have Plaster and Potions poisons, and Pills,
Some to cure, and some to kill.
I have travelled thro' England, Ireland, France, and Spain,
been to Europe and back again
Hocus, Pocus, Alecampain
Take one of my Pills, Dead Man, rise and fight again.

(37–47)

Act 3 of *Three Hours* continues the theme of comical duelings. Locked
in the museum with the newly arrived mummy and crocodile—actually
Plotwell and Underplot in playhouse "Contrivance"—Townley witnesses
yet another of the play's mock-combats: "a Contest of Beauty" between
the two monsters. As they vie for her favor, she exclaims: "Well! Ye Pair of
Egyptian Lovers, agree this Matter between you, and I will acquit my self
like a Person of Honour to you both" (III.71–73). And combat begins.

Plotwell. Madam! If I don't love you above all your Sex, may I be banish'd
    the Studies of Virtuoso's; and smoak'd like *Dutch* Beef in a Chimney—
Underplot. If I don't love you more than that Stale Mummy, may I never
    more be proclaim'd at a Show of Monsters, by the Sound of a Glass-
    Trumpet.
Plotwell. May I be sent to '*Pothecary's Hall*, and beat up into *Venice-Treacle*
    for the Fleet and the Army, if this Heart—
Underplot. May I be stuff'd with Straw, and given to a Mountebank, if this
    Soul—
Plotwell. Madam, I am a Human creature. Taste my Balsamick Kiss.
Underplot. A Lover in Swadling-Clouts! What is his Kiss, to my Embrace!
Plotwell. Look upon me, Madam. See how I am embroider'd with
    Hieroglyphicks.
Underplot. Consider my beautiful row of Teeth.
Plotwell. My Balmy Breath.
Underplot. The strong Joints of my Back.
Plotwell. My erect Stature.
Underplot. My long Tail.

(III.74–94)

"Such a Contest of Beauty!" Townley declares, "How shall I decide it?"
(95). But the arrival of Fossile puts an end to the dispute. He enters with the
rival antiquarians, Dr. Nautilus and Dr. Possum, whose sparring about how
best to examine Fossile's new "antiquities" will unmask this last of the
play's "Mummeries." Nautilus and Possum tilt at every utterance. "To have
a *Mummy*, an *Alligator*, and a *Wife*, all in one Day," enthuses Nautilus as he

enters, "is too great Happiness for Mortal Man!" To which Possum sniffs: "This an *Alligator!* Alack a Day, Brother *Nautilus*, this is a meer Lizard, an Eft, a Shrimp to mine" (III.104–8). The two, brought by Fossile to attend to his new acquisitions, escalate their squabbles until one holds a sword to the alligator, the other a knife to the mummy. Remarking that his mummy is "hot in the first Degree, and exceeding powerful in some Diseases of Women" (147–48), Fossile launches the dispute.

> *Nautilus.* Right, Dr. *Fossile*; for your *Asphaltion*.
> *Possum. Pice-Asphaltus*, by your leave.
> *Nautilus.* By your leave, Doctor *Possum*, I say *Asphaltion*.
> *Possum.* And I positively say, *Pice-Asphaltus*.
> *Nautilus.* If you had read *Dioscorides* or *Pliny*—
> *Possum.* I have read *Dioscorides*. And I do affirm *Pice-Asphaltus*.
> *Fossile.* Be calm, Gentlemen. Both of you handle this Argument with great Learning, Judgment and Perspicuity. For the present, I beseech you to Concord, and turn your Speculations on my *Alligator*.
> *Possum.* The Skin is impenetrable even to a Sword.
> *Nautilus.* Dr. *Possum*, I will show you the contrary.
> > [*Draws his Sword.*]
> *Possum.* In the mean time I will try the Mummy with this Knife, on the Point of which you shall smell the Pitch, and be convinc'd that it is the *Pice-Asphaltus*. [*Takes up a Rusty Knife.*]
> *Fossile.* Hold, Sir: You will not only deface my Mummy, but spoil my *Roman* Sacrificing Knife.
> > (III.149–66)

Townley enters to divert such knifing, lest it discover Plotwell and Underplot within the Mummy and Crocodile. Temporarily distracted by her ploy to engage them with a telescope, the antiquarians return to their "experiments" until the paramours leap from their costumes, frightening the learned gentlemen, who think them ghosts or devils.

> *Nautilus.* I will insure your *Alligator* from any Damage. His Skin I affirm once more to be impenetrable. [*Draws his sword.*]
> *Possum.* I will not deface any Hieroglyphick.
> > [*Goes to the* Mummy *with the Knife.*
> *Fossile.* I never oppose a luciferous Experiment. It is the beaten Highway to Truth.
> > [Plotwell *and* Underplot *leap from their Places;*
> > *the Doctors are frighted.*] . . .
> *Fossile.* Gentlemen, wonder at Nothing within these Walls; for ever since I was Married, Nothing has happen'd to me in the common Course of Human Life.
> > (III.194–206)

At Townley's prompting, Phoebe Clinket here steps in to claim "the Invention": "I shall be proud to take the whole Contrivance of this Masquerade upon my self. [*To* Townley.] Sir, be acquainted with my Masqueraders. [*To* Fossile.]" "What mean you by these Gambols?" Fossile demands, "This *Mummy*, this *Crocodile?*" "Only a little Mummery, Uncle," she replies (210–17), underscoring the punning play of "mummy," "mumming," and "mummery." In "an extreme Palpitation," Fossile demands the departure of these "Diabolical Performers." "Nay, Sir," Clinket replies, "you shall see them Dance first" (244), invoking for her "Mummery" the conventional close ("All dance the Morris" concludes "The Islip Play"). Fossile insists. Underplot attempts to placate the furious "host," referring to the theme of hospitality with which visiting traditional mummers usually begin their gambols: "Let it never be said that the Famous Dr. *Fossile*, so renowned for his Charity to Monsters, should violate the Laws of Hospitality, and turn a poor *Alligator* naked into the Street" (255–58). But Fossile will have no more. As *Three Hours* comes to its close, the Crocodile and Mummy are turned out, just as the seaman "Jack Capstone" knocks at the door, baby in hand, for the play's last bit of foolery.

Like so many of Gay's works, *Three Hours After Marriage* inflects highly conventional materials with topical reference and relevance. Cues identifying such particular targets of Scriblerian satire as Woodward and Dennis are affixed to an amalgam of traditional topoi and structures—most notably traditional mumming—to take up general satiric preoccupations of Gay and his friends: pretension, ignorance, and chicanery in learning, clumsiness and self-important banality in art, and appetitive and dishonest self-interest in love.

Even though the play itself was not revived—perhaps, as Winton says, because it bit a little too hard—*Three Hours After Marriage* found its way in altered form into the popular theater as an afterpiece. *The Jealous Doctor; or, The Intriguing Dame* was first performed on 29 April 1717 at Lincoln's Inn Fields, "an Entertainment" later described as "Dancing in Grotesque Characters." Presumably *The Jealous Doctor* presents, as a unity, various elements from the Plotwell-Underplot scenes of Gay's play. The cast list names as characters Fossil, Plotwell, Underplot, Ptisan, and Mrs. Townley, giving in parentheses the formula names of pantomime—Punch, Scaramouch, Harlequin, Pierrot, and Colombine.[39] Though apparently never printed, *The Jealous Doctor* flourished as an afterpiece, becoming something of a commonplace. London theaters revived it more than three dozen times between 1717 and 1726.[40]

Both *The What-d'Ye-Call-It* and *Three Hours After Marriage* adapt the forms and themes of plebeian "Mummery," the earlier play with topics of hierarchy and political power obviously in mind. A discerning attention to the dynamics of cultural expression and social rank lies at the heart of Gay's mirroring of "high" art and "low" in both plays. Indeed, the class implications of burlesquing John Woodward by imagining him before a London audience as the "Dr. Quack" of a mumming play in a house full of "Mummery"—a realm of reference that has escaped scholarly commentators on *Three Hours After Marriage*—may help explain the seemingly overstated indignation heaped on the play by hostile contemporaries. It was one thing for Gay to stage mumming servants in a manor house; it was something else again for him to cast as mummers respected managers of the new science and criticism of a Georgian London in which such people of the middling sort were in the ascendant. As Winton notes (54), Woodward and Dennis had numerous friends in high places, most of them Whigs. Certainly, *Three Hours After Marriage* struck a nerve. The play's burlesquing application of plebeian identifiers to such stolid townsmen as Woodward and Dennis—two men who took themselves very seriously—may account for the sting.

Certainly the issue of class standing was on the minds of hostile commentators to the play. The spate of condemning critiques that immediately followed the staging of *Three Hours* all raise the question of his own status in their attacks on Gay. As noted above, his West Country background was ambiguous with regard to rank and compromised with regard to wealth. Coming to the defense of the duchess of Monmouth, who is said to be mocked in the play, the hastily published *A Complete Key To the New Farce call'd Three Hours after Marriage* by "E. Parker, Philomath" declares: "*Gay* justly deserves a Cudgel for abusing a Lady . . . who took him in when he was destitute of Meat, Drink and Cloaths."[41] The piqued writer castigates Gay and puts the poet in his place in a disparaging biographical sketch:

> *Gay* was a Serving-man, and never hop'd for any higher Preferment than holding a Plate at a *side Board*, till *Pope* took him into his Protection. *Gay* was born of honest, tho' mean Parentage, who by their Thrift and Industry made a shift to save wherewithal to Apprentice him out to a Stuff Man, but at the Expiration of his Time, being taken from that employ, he became *Amanuensis* to *Aaron Hill,* Esq; when that Gentleman set on Foot the Project of answering Questions in a Weekly Paper, call'd The *British Apollo*. Being dismist from Mr. *Hill's* Service, he was taken into the Family of the Lady *Monmouth*, whom he has thought fit to Banter. (7)

John Breval's equally hostile response to the play, *The Confederates: A Farce* focuses in similar fashion on this image of a servingman Gay of inferior rank. The end of scene 2 of Breval's mocking account of the staging of *Three Hours* refers to the earlier *Key* as a frantic Gay cries: "O that, contented with my Servile State, / At some Bufet I still had held a Plate!"[42] A few pages later, as the poets try to mount the play, and Pope asks, "What's to be done?" Gay replies, lamenting his poverty: "I, for my part, am poor, / Have clear'd my Lodgings, and my Ale-house Score" (31). In the same vein, another *Key to the New Comedy Call'd, Three Hours After Marriage* only published in 1758, identifies Phoebe Clinket—unconvincingly—as Anne Finch, perhaps to afford the opportunity to forward the following class-conscious castigation of Gay. The unnamed author, "a Person of Distinction in London," reports "To his Friend in the County of *Cornwal*" of Gay: "That unlucky lady [Anne Finch] was heard to say,—*Gays trivia show'd he was more proper to walk before a chair, than to ride in one.*"[43]

Throughout these condemnations a fixation on rank prevails. The heated attack on the poet with regard to his breeding and background fits the history of Gay's own reputation outlined in chapter 2. As the indignant objections to *Three Hours* in these pamphlets suggest, the nerve that was struck was a social one. Gay's metaleptic methods necessarily exposed the links between culture and social order. However rollicking the play appears now, the artificiality of social rank revealed in the ongoing play between "low" and "high" forms (which implied its revocability) was an idea that in 1717 seemed more than a little threatening.

6

Opera, Gender, and Social Strata: Gay and Handel's *Acis and Galatea*

The interplay of patrician and plebeian cultural forms in Gay is usually associated with his rollicking satiric muse. However, the metaleptic strategies we have found elsewhere can be seen to shape as well the structure, themes, and aesthetic of his operatic collaboration with George Friedrich Handel, *Acis and Galatea*, a poignant and serious work.[1] Conceived collaboratively, *Acis and Galatea* is a synergy of media, in which text and music together strengthen and comment upon each other. Throughout, media and message are linked as the work affirms the interdependence of mutually constructing realms.

Parody, as always, is fundamental to the structuring of *Acis and Galatea*. Its theme: the representation of a newly interiorized and self-expressive individual against a stratified backdrop of low and high cultures. When we identify the strategies in both text and music, we see the work's final focus on the heroine, Galatea, for the important shift it is. In the culminating artistry of the nymph's final arias, Gay and Handel articulate a profound transformation of language, musical form, and sensibility. Enacting a complex and socially charged interplay of popular and "high" art, *Acis and Galatea* presents in the figure of Galatea the poignant, ambivalent, and interiorizing onlooker of a very modern-seeming world.

In 1718, Gay and Handel created *Acis and Galatea*, a musical drama routinely categorized as a through-composed English pastoral masque, or more recently as an anglicized Italian serenata.[2] *Acis and Galatea* was originally composed for private performance in May 1718 at Cannons, the Edgeware estate of James Brydges, earl of Carnarvon and later duke of Chandos.[3] Literary scholars agree that Gay is principal author of the libretto, though one aria is known to be by John Hughes.[4] Gay's friends and colleagues, the Scriblerian circle of writers and wits, frequented the Cannons estate at this time, and the libretto of *Acis and Galatea* reflects their joint company just as do other of their works from these years, particularly those by Gay.[5]

The story, taken from Ovid, tells of the nymph Galatea's love for the shepherd Acis, whose suit to her is rivaled by the likewise smitten Cyclops, Polyphemus. After being spurned by Galatea, the amorous monster discovers the two courting lovers. Flying into a rage, he crushes Acis with a stone. (The story is an etiological tale linked to the eruption of Mount Etna.) By the semidivine power of the grieving Galatea, the dead Acis is transformed into a stream flowing from under the rock, a bittersweet presence "murm'ring still his gentle Love."

Acis and Galatea unfolds in a three-stage process that culminates in Galatea's empowered transformation of Acis. The work begins with a depiction of an Arcadia naive in its adherence to a mannered order. The shepherd Acis is elegantly identified with this realm. Next, words and music create a socially resonant portrait of a lower-order Polyphemus that parodies, then destroys this refined order. Thus the masque moves from a purposefully overwrought pastoral to a disruptive evocation of mock pastoral, bringing elements of high art and low into ironic and interdependent interplay. Acis and his burlesquing double, Polyphemus, mirror each other with a parodic nuance that looks ahead to Macheath and other of Gay's mock heroes, as it looks back to *The Shepherd's Week* and other mock pastorals. This parody sets up the undoing of forms and expectations which moves the work to its culminating third stage: Galatea's metamorphosing art. Changed by grief, Galatea voices in her final aria a sensibility new in its interiority and self-expression. To achieve his characteristically allusive parody, Gay engages the hierarchical implications of literary, musical, and artistic traditions at all levels.[6]

Brian Trowell has rightly situated *Acis and Galatea* in the context of eighteenth-century pastoral controversy.[7] The rendering of the pastoral topos in *Acis and Galatea*, particularly in its juxtaposition of a bumpkin Polyphemus amid the polish of Acis and Galatea's "happy plains," conforms exactly to Gay's themes and his methodic mixing and undermining of forms. Indeed, in its accomplishment and beauty, *Acis and Galatea* attests to the breadth and seriousness of Gay's aesthetic reconfiguration of the pastoral by means of the mock pastoral.[8]

AN ARCADIA POISED TO BE UNDONE

Throughout the first section of the work, preceding the disruptive entrance of Polyphemus, both words and music use the conventions of the Italianate pastoral to draw attention to the artificiality of its heightened order. Consciously contrived from the outset, Gay and Handel's Arcadia is poised to be undone. The opening overture moves directly into a chorus of shepherds and nymphs who praise "the Pleasures of the Plains." Repeatedly these rustics identify their innocence and joy: "Happy Nymphs and happy Swains . . . Harmless, Merry, Free, and Gay." The musical setting accentuates the little word "happy" with almost comic exigency, contrapuntally interjecting "happy, happy, happy nymphs" and "happy, happy, happy swains" among the five voices for some seven measures of the A section.

The B section of the chorus hints at the importunity and delusion of this bliss which will soon be questioned in burlesque, then finally undone by grief. The first tenor heralds the B section with a dotted melody which the five-part ensemble takes up. This dotted rhythm,

emblem of the Italian style, will appear with increasing resonance and ironic permutation as the masque proceeds, reaching its final permutation in Galatea's last aria. (See example 3, p. 148.)

This rhythmic pattern in the B section of the opening chorus sets a text which declares the sympathy and cooperation of Nature that typifies pastoral poetry. (In her final recitative, Galatea will relinquish this possessive pose.) Here, the bucolics catalog their entitlements:

> For us the Zephyr blows;
> For us distils the Dew;
> For us unfolds the Rose,
> And flow'rs display their Hue.
>
> (I.5–8)

A hint of presumption and overinsistence tinges the reiterative pattern as the chorus continues, the appropriating "For us" announcing each phrase. The B section closes with the foreboding image of blood:

> For us the Winters rain;
> For us the Summers shine;
> Spring swells for us the Grain,
> And Autumn bleeds the Vine.
>
> (I.9–12)

As we know, the Ovidian story itself troubles and undoes this presumptuous idyll, as the verb "bleeds" foreshadows. With its burlesque turn, Gay and Handel's *Acis and Galatea* will expose the conventions that make up this idyllic dream.

Ex. 3. Excerpt from "O the pleasure of the plains" from *Acis and Galatea*

To set up this oncoming subversion, both music and text accentuate the orderliness of the world of Acis and Galatea and their rural company. With relentless regularity, the musical settings for arias of the first section follow the ABA da capo form, as some critics lament.[9] In fact, the regularity works as an allusion to the Italian style, here codified to a predictable affectation as the work draws attention to its history and cultural antecedents. As Ellen Harris observes, "This is a throw-back to the Italian pastoral which emphasized regularity and consistency as musical and Arcadian virtues."[10]

Early in the masque Acis enters, identified with the conventions of the pastoral form and its manly protagonists. After the choral opening and the entrance of Galatea, he arrives, the leading tenor, singing of his romantic quest. Acis is on a heroic search. Energetically he seeks his "charming Fair" in the pulsing sixteenth notes and dotted eighths

recently intoned by the chorus. Reappearing in parody and transformation, this figure will accrue meaning in the course of the masque.

Ex. 4. Excerpt from "Love in her eyes sits playing" from *Acis and Galatea*

The text of the B section of this first aria of Acis foreshadows the bubbling fountain of the ending, particularly carried as it is on the recurring rhythmic pattern. "O tell me, if you saw my Dear?," Acis sings, "Seeks she the Groves, or bathes in Crystal Fountains?" (I.29–30) The rhythms of Acis' search amid "Groves" and "Crystal Fountain" will reemerge, as we shall see, first in parodic echo with Polyphemus and finally in the orchestral accompaniment of the story's ending.

Throughout the first section of the masque, Gay's text works with Handel's highly regularized music to create an overstylized Arcadia. The libretto pushes the language of Acis and Galatea and their shepherd cohorts to a poetry of overly contrived sounds and meanings. Alliteration prevails.

"O the Pleasure of the Plains" (I.1) begins the chorus, and the arias of the masque's first section continue with a heightened consonance and assonance exemplified in Galatea's simile of dove-like longing: "Billing, cooing, / Panting, wooing, / Melting Murmurs fill the Grove, / Melting Murmurs lasting love" (I.63–66). In the first section, a repetitious language of reiterated (and especially euphonious) sounds and words, and of recurrent grammatical constructions and phrases, works with the da capo musical form to create an art of contrivance and conventionality. In this overmannered scheme, Gay invokes images and themes typical of pastoral literature: purling streams, cool gales, warbling birds, groves, and fountains; the anguish and ecstasy of love; tragic jealousies and conflicts. Gay and Handel together fashion the waxed and perfect world of the stylized neoclassical pastoral, a Watteau-like landscape of "verdant Plains," "Crystal Fountains," "Melting Murmurs," and "painted Glories of the Field."

Galatea's aria *As When the Dove Laments her Love* (ll. 57–67), as apex of the deluding artfulness of this Arcadia, displays the musical and poetic conventionality of an empty naïveté. Lovely as it is, the aria typifies this overwrought realm. The predictable da capo setting carries words pointedly pastoral and, in this context, fallacious by design. The entire song is a deliberately unfinished simile cast in a poetry laden with figures of sound. An untethered vehicle, the text conveys just such cloying images of an emotive and sympathetic natural world that later critics would condemn in the pastoral as pathetic fallacy.

> As when the Dove,
> Laments her Love,
> All on the naked Spray;
> When he returns,
> No more she mourns,
> But loves the live-long Day.
> Billing, cooing,
> Panting, wooing,
> Melting Murmurs fill the Grove,
> Melting Murmurs lasting love.
>
> (ll. 57–66)

With no direct referent for their meaning, the "Murmurs" of this aria do indeed "Melt" into a semantic vapor carefully belied by Handel's sweetly uncomplicated accompaniment, whose very transparency masks how nonsensical the verses really are. Deliberately Gay sets up this illusory slippage of words and sense, as the premonitory water imagery and pun on the word "spray" ironically attest. Galatea's language reveals an ominous emptiness in her illusion.

Here, as elsewhere, awareness of artifice and of Galatea's lack of awareness prompts our recognition of the limitations and indeterminacy of signification in general. Preoccupied with perception, Gay (like others of his time) continually pondered modes of representation per se, especially as these can be seen to deceive or misapply. Such probings, as Barbara Stafford has shown, can be considered in hindsight to presage a worldview constructed by means of observation, measurement, and science. Certainly Gay is a most observant and self-aware "reader" of this querying of perceptual codes, as we see both from his insistent interrogations of figuration in language and from his ongoing collaborations with musicians and visual artists.[11]

PARODIC INSTABILITY AND THE BUMPKIN POLYPHEMUS

When Polyphemus enters soon after Galatea's aria, forms of high and low culture play off each other, urging that we acknowledge their interdependence.[12] The blithe world of the untethered simile breaks asunder. Allusion and diction immediately fasten the Cyclops to tangible and recognizable references from low culture that burlesque the artificial dream of Acis and Galatea. Handel's music conveys this disruption. In the second part of the masque, keys and scales move toward the minor, and the da capo aria form is interrupted. At the same time, Gay's language becomes earthy, comic, familiarly English, and redolent of popular songs and stories. Levels of culture collide. But this collision is complex, for text and music both oppose yet simultaneously connect Polyphemus to the elevated pastoral realm of literature and art which is the context for part 1. He functions as a parodic echo, replaying for our laughter and reconsideration the forms and values he burlesques.

Gay's Polyphemus owes much to Dryden's revered 1690s translation of Ovid's story. In fact, the Cyclops almost quotes verbatim from Dryden's well-known description of his enormousness, in which "A hundred Reeds, of a prodigious Growth, / Scarce made a Pipe, proportion'd to his Mouth."[13] In turn, "Bring me a hundred Reeds of decent growth," Gay's monster demands, "To make a Pipe for my capacious Mouth" (II.13–14). While the musical setting of this line about his gigantic shepherd's pipe and maw is utterly laughable, Gay wants us to recognize and appreciate the reference to Dryden as, with metaleptic verve, Polyphemus identifies himself with his most esteemed literary portrait. This burlesque moment in the text splices a cultural and social hierarchy of literary forms and traditions as we laugh at the disjunct mimicry before us: this Cyclops has read his Dryden. Even the most revered works of literature exist among us in an historical matrix (as we ourselves do), called up from their traditions by individuals as "little ghosts," to quote Adorno.[14]

Polyphemus is familiar in other ways. Even before he quotes Dryden, he enters evoking the realm of English popular theater and song. "I rage, I rage, I rage, I melt, I burn" he roars out, in his opening recitative.

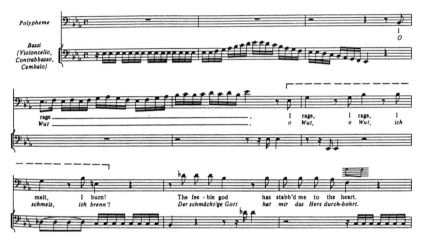

Ex. 5. Excerpt from "I rage, I rage, I melt, I burn" from *Acis and Galatea*

The inflamed text and its setting in brisk thirds ascending the triad would have reminded an early-eighteenth-century audience of "I Burn," the celebrated and much-published "mad-song" from "Part Two" of Thomas D'Urfey's *The Comical History of Don Quixote* (1694–96).[15] In act 5 of that play, the cruelly rejected Marcella enters onstage "mad as a March-hare" from unrequited love and sings "I burn, I burn, I burn, I burn."

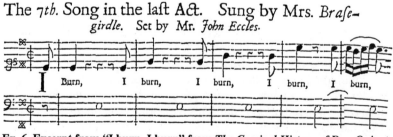

Ex. 6. Excerpt from "I burn, I burn" from *The Comical History of Don Quixote*

Polyphemus's triadic ascent on "I rage, I rage" (meas. 5–6) calls to mind D'Urfey's famously sizzling heroine. Indeed, the expectation that Polyphemus, like Marcella, will continue "burning" up, then down the triad heightens the effect of his early descent and "melting" into the dissonant tritone ending of his line on "I burn" (meas. 6–7). Thus the monster enters as a ludicrous mimic of the famously frail and lovesick heroine of D'Urfey's comedy. He has availed himself not only of Dryden's Ovid, but also of the flurry of broadsides that made Marcella's song recognizable to singers and theatergoers for decades.

Art thus is shown to be deeply social, embedded in the alliances and events of history and culture. Gay had already constructed Bowzybeus of *The Shepherd's Week* with metaleptically invoked antecedents that included D'Urfey, whose strong Whig identification hints at the possibility of party satire.[16] However, an inclination to anything but a playful jibe in that direction would have been tempered in this collaboration with Handel at the Cannons estate of James Brydges, whose Whig politics and ties to the Hanoverian court were explicit. As we shall see, Polyphemus is far from unsympathetic. With this invocation of prototypes and association, the bumpkinish Polyphemus of *Acis and Galatea* works metaleptically like his earlier "brother," Gay's Bowzybeus. Just as Bowzybeus parodies Virgil and Dryden's Silenus of the sixth eclogue, so Polyphemus brings into purposefully ill-fitting conjunction the legacy of Dryden's Ovid, reimagined through the lens of D'Urfey's distracted and ever-popular Marcella.

Polyphemus interjects a comic palpability into the stilted Arcadia of Acis and Galatea. For Gay's witty evocation of Dryden and D'Urfey, Handel composed some very funny music. The recitative underscores the text's parody of Dryden. The stepwise chant of the first line of the Dryden echo— "Bring me a hundred Reeds of decent growth"—becomes a musical phrase of lurching gaps and bumbling awkwardness.

Ex. 7. Excerpt from "I rage, I rage, I melt, I burn" from *Acis and Galatea*

Tumbling from the D above middle C, it falls all the way to low F by way of the dissonant tritone drop from B-flat to E-natural.[17] Joining amusing phonological and musical sounds, Gay wraps this wondrously grotesque melody around the words "my capacious mouth," whose exaggerated vowels push the phrase to a laughable enactment of its "capaciousness." A multimedia synecdoche, the figure encircles all who listen, treating us—by way of the enormous and self-doted-upon mouth—to the sight and sound of a very silly Cyclops.

This parodic Polyphemus continues a subversion already under way in Galatea's aria. Handel's setting for his first aria borrows from fellow-German Reinhard Keiser as the giant sings the continuo line, almost note-for-note, from "Wann ich dich noch einst erblicke" sung by Agrippina in Keiser's opera *Janus*. Handel's appropriation of this aria may have been suggested by Keiser's original scene (II.xii), which, like D'Urfey's, features an enraged outburst by a heroine, the imprisoned Agrippina. Polyphemus's entrance thus resonates with parodic allusions as he sings a recitative and first aria that identify him with not one, but two famously seething sopranos. Gay and Handel—the latter at least in his early years—each made frequent use of gender disguisings and reversals. Perhaps relevant to this preoccupation is recent scholarly conjecture on the sexual orientation of both.[18] Whatever their respective orientations, works of both Gay and Handel raise to our view key features of the gendered modes of understanding human sexual identity and expression that have marked the modern era off from, say, that of Shakespeare and Marlowe.

Gay's text for this aria further marks the Cyclops as a devotee of popular songs. Rendering love's similes in the Anglo-Saxon terms of English "country" song, Polyphemus lumbers over his angular bass line: "O ruddier than the Cherry, O sweeter than the Berry! . . . Like Kidlings blithe and merry" (II.17–22).[19] His language abounds with homely similes—cherry, berry, moonshine, kidlings. Indeed, Polyphemus burlesques just such overweening figures of nature as Galatea employed in *As When the Dove*. For his similes, the giant sings a laughably jagged melody that follows the bass, then falls into rhythms accentuating the humor of an ungainliness that is so frisky. "O ruddier than the cherry," capers along in hopping eighth notes whose eager phrases breathlessly follow each other with only eighth-note rests between them. Further undermining the monster's gravity, Handel seems to have intended the obbligato of "O ruddier than the cherry"—for which Polyphemus has just demanded his pipe of "a hundred Reeds of decent growth"—for the tiniest and highest of treble flutes, the "Flauto piccolo ottavo."[20] (See ex. 8.)

Polyphemus's lyrics evoke the world of popular pastoral songs, often comic and bawdy, that circulated on broadsides among lower-class people.

Ex. 8. Excerpt from "O ruddier than the cherry" from _Acis and Galatea_

Among the higher ranks, such songs were known in collections like Thomas D'Urfey's oft-printed _Pills to Purge Melancholy_.[21] A sampling of lines from such anonymous songs shows the familiarity of this Polyphemus with the world of street ballads and popular culture. "Her Colour's as fresh as a Rose in _June_, / Her Temper as kind as a Dove," sings "The Sound Country Lass" in D'Urfey's _Pills_.[22] A broadside street ballad, "The Discourse betweene a Souldier and His Love," similarly praises its heroine in a homely metaphor, "No Turtle to her mate,/could ever be more true."[23] Another song finds its celebrated heroine "Blyth as a Kid, / With Wit at Will;"[24] yet another sings of its Jockey: "His Cheeks were Cherry red."[25] An untitled "Scotch Song" describes its "bonny lass" in countryfied similes worthy of Polyphemus: "Her Skin like driven Snow, / Her Hair brown as a Berry, / Her Eyes as black as a Sloe, / Her Lips red as a Cherry."[26] Another, entitled "the Happy Shepherd," describes the eyes of its "Charming Jenny" as "Black as any Perry," a line that immediately tips rhymingly over into the ever-familiar refrain, "With a Hey down derry."[27] Gay's Cyclops exudes the lowbrow realm of English pub and countryside.

This plebeian Polyphemus is a far cry from Handel's earlier conception of the monster.[28] The shaping hand of Gay in the change is unmistakable. A decade before his collaboration in England, Handel had set an Italian version of Ovid's story. The heroic fanfare which announces Polifemo's entrance in this earlier setting stands in sharp contrast to that of Gay's bumpkin Polyphemus. The humor of Handel's 1718 music lies in the wit of exaggeration and surprise. Noting "the superbly dramatic conception of his character," Winton Dean calls Polyphemus "Handel's first immortal stage figure."[29] His Italian Polifemo of 1708 is, by contrast, an epic tyrant in a trumpet-sounding martial context who orders Galatea: *"Cadrai depressa e vinta al mio tenuto piede"* [You will fall vanquished at my dread feet].[30] Cruel, inhuman, and despotic, this earlier monster represents the heightened moral conflicts that typify Italian *opera seria*. He and the conflict he creates stand far distant from the witty, albeit disquieting parody and comedy of his English cousin.

Indeed, the English Polyphemus quickly reveals himself to be not just comic, but deflatingly mock-heroic. Following upon his first aria, Polyphemus invites the horrified Galatea to join him in the hero's conventional domains of conquest, "Empire" and "Love."

> Thee, Polyphemus, great as Jove,
> Calls to Empire and to Love,
> To his Palace in the Rock,
> To his Dairy, to his Flock,
> To the Grape of purple Hue,
> To the Plumb of Glossy Blue &c.
>
> (ll. 32–37)

This recitative entreaty sets up a disjunction between his Jove-like call to "Empire" (with all the elevated literary and political connotations that word conjures) and the homeliness of the domain he naively touts: his "Palace in the Rock," his "Dairy," his "Flock," and so on. Dotted rhythms take over Polyphemus's clownish invitation, and the lighthearted pulsing of the bass, both voice and continuo, makes this empire funny indeed. (See ex. 9.) Furthermore, these dotted rhythms are themselves a burlesque, for this call to "Empire and to Love" actually mimics—with a notable awkwardness—the dotted rhythms of Acis's highly mannered heroic entrance in his opening aria. (See ex. 4, p. 149.) Careening into this Italianate rhythm, Polyphemus draws attention to it as he stumbles comically through the conventional figure. It is precisely in the parodic character of its reappearance that this rhythm begins to accrue a deeper meaning which will carry through to the final transformative ending of the masque.

Acis thus has a burlesque counterpart in the mock-heroic Polyphemus, and the dotted rhythms at telling points in the masque underscore this correspondence. Polyphemus calls Galatea "to Empire and to Love" in a laugh-

Ex. 9. Excerpt from "Whither fairest, art thou running" from *Acis and Galatea*

able echo of the rhythm of Acis's search. Not only does this imitation disclose the interdependence of the two, hero and mock hero, but it also implicates our conventional expectations, as we laugh at the ludicrous yet familiar monster. Lurching precipitously into Acis's heroic meter, now reversed, the score calls attention to the clumsiness of Polyphemus, setting off his dotted rhythms as a comical attempt to sing like such elegantly Italianate shepherds as Acis. In a similar fashion, he breaks into sudden dotted eighths and sixteenths in the extended ornaments that end both sections of his later tantrum aria, "Cease to Beauty." These are parodic moments, as the farcical abruptness of the rhythmic shifts makes plain.

This burlesque Polyphemus was certainly Gay's project. Handel seems not to have been fully persuaded to the comic, antimasque character of the monster's disruptiveness, particularly as the composer's ties to the court and ministry strengthened over the years. Subsequent changes to the autograph manuscript suggest his desire to lessen the levity and burlesque, especially of Polyphemus. Handel seems to have intended a return to the more straightforwardly tyrannical Cyclops of his 1708 Italian serenata. An alteration in the manuscript illustrates this shift. In the original text, Acis declares in recitative midway through the masque:

> His saucy Love provokes my Rage,
> Weak as I am, I must engage.

> (II.56–57)

Replacing the word "saucy" with "hideous," the later manuscript emendation transforms this rakishly "saucy" Polyphemus into an unequivocally evil and terrifying tyrant, a "hideous" one.[31]

A parody of culturally cherished forms and values, especially those of the pastoral and the kindred epic, Gay's Polyphemus is more sympathetically comic than horrifyingly tragic. He is an ambivalent mix of the laughable, the pathetic, and the forbidden, and resembles other of Gay's burlesques on heroic ideals. Moments of vulnerability and suffering scatter throughout his blustering outbursts, starting with the first recitative where his *Furioso* "rage" and "burnings" (with all their resonant sexual and intertextual reference) are abruptly interrupted by a half measure of *Adagio*: "I melt," Polyphemus croons mournfully on an abruptly falling minor third.[32] (See ex. 5, p. 152.) A modern-seeming pathos thus replaces tragedy. As Gay's Polyphemus acquires the mixed-genre complexities of feeling and motive that seem somehow "psychological," he becomes a suffering victim of his own making, even as he victimizes others. This ambivalence of sentiment and effect continues through the masque in both text and music.

The painful power of Polyphemus's destructiveness emerges precisely because he engages our sympathy. Certainly, as Dean suggests, he is "still a monster"; we laugh in part because we sit at a distance.[33] Nonetheless, Polyphemus displays the dangers not of a tyrant but of a wild, clumsy, and childish lover. Nowhere in this treatment do we find the fiendish, premeditated cruelties of Handel's earlier Polifemo, an "inhuman tyrant" *(tiranno inumano)* whose "savagery" *(fiero)*, "vengeance" *(vendette)*, and "dreadful wickedness" *(empietà tremenda)* both words and music convey without ambiguity. By contrast, we may be moved to identify with and to pity this loutish English giant whose awakening to the sufferings of love erupts in a murderous outburst.

The operatic trio that brings the Arcadian lovers destructively together with their burlesque nemesis conveys the connections between the passionate, despairing, and uncontrollably hurt Polyphemus and his victims, Acis and Galatea. Gay's text in particular takes pains to give the Cyclops a sympathetic voice. Galatea and Acis begin a formal, ironically mournful love duet. Marching gravely and beautifully to Handel's *Andante* setting in c minor, the text tellingly hints of lines from Pope's pastorals as Gay continues his project of cultural reference and criticism. Having read their Pope, the lovers declare in harmonious counterpoint:

> The flocks shall leave the mountains,
> The woods the turtle dove,
> The nymphs forsake the fountains
> Ere I forsake my love.

(II.74–77)[34]

Overhearing, Polyphemus leaps into the duet with impassioned broken octaves each time Galatea and Acis repeat the word "love." The music imparts the force of his feelings and the power of his entry; the text speaks his feelings of anguish and suffering. "Torture, fury, rage, despair," he cries. "I cannot, cannot bear, I cannot, cannot bear, I cannot, cannot bear!" he repeats for some fourteen measures. His desperate sixteenth notes pulse frantically beneath the lovers' duet sounding above him.

Ex. 10. Excerpt from "The flocks shall leave the mountains" from *Acis and Galatea*

As the trio builds to its climax, the kindredness of Polyphemus—first as a laughable countryman, then as someone passionately vulnerable to love and suffering—prompts a pity that includes such monsters rather than a hatred that condemns them. "Fly swift, thou massy ruin, fly!" Polyphemus repeats furiously as he takes up the stone. The punning word "ruin" captures the self-implicating irony of his ruinous actions.[35]

GALATEA'S TRANSFORMATION: A NEW POETRY, A NEW MUSIC

From the death of Acis to the end, *Acis and Galatea* develops with powerfully moving features in both text and music the concept of metamorphosis that is at the heart of the story. Moreover, it is not just the physically transformed Acis, but Galatea who changes. Her interiority —a responsive self-expression in words and music—signals the change of sensibility that makes possible her art and power in the face of her loss. The disruption wrought by the burlesque Polyphemus is profound. Not only Acis is destroyed; the conventions of his heroic and pastoral world give way as well.

With Acis's death, Gay's poetry sheds figurative invocations of nature. Now a chorus of male voices takes up a language more associative than symbolic. Gone are the personifications and apostrophes, the similes and metaphors of birds, bees, trees, flowers, berries, cherries, fountains, mountains, and so on that pervaded the pastoral utterance of Acis and Galatea and its imitation by Polyphemus. Using allusion and metonymy, rather than the similes and metaphors of previous arias, the chorus sings:

> Mourn, all ye Muses, weep, all ye Swains;
> Tune, tune your Reeds to doleful Strains. . . .
>
> (II.88–89)

The tropes make clear Gay's attention to a new art in the language of the surviving Galatea. The poetry creates semantic relationships that are linear and culturally referential in contrast to the figurative, analogous, and parallel tropes of her earlier arias. Rhetorically more direct, the chorus eschews personifying apostrophes to nature and addresses fully human "Muses" and "Swains" in *this* world with lines that culminate in simple, literal words associated with the experience of grieving utterance:

> Groans, Cries, and Howlings fill the neighb'ring Shore;
> Ah! the gentle Acis is no more.
>
> (II.90–91)

Evocative of feeling rather than figure and tropological thought, this passage is also allusive. It suggests our grieving "neighborliness" here on the near shore of the river Styx, border of the classical netherworld that we know as part of our cultural geography. The poem situates itself in culture, rather than in a figurative nature.

Galatea's response continues this turn of language to express association, interiority, feeling, and experience for the individual in this demystified context. "Must I my Acis still bemoan," she asks, conveying in this rhetorical question no image beyond her felt experience. A single oboe at first anticipates, then echoes and answers her vocal line in a melody winding contrapuntally about hers.

Ex. 11. Excerpt from "Must I my Acis still bemoan" from *Acis and Galatea*

The polyphony of this interplay between voice and oboe contrasts with the strictly imitative echoings of voice and solo instruments in earlier settings (for example, in the mirroring oboe of "As When The Dove Laments Her Love").

Such intricacy in the musical design governs the aria as the stricken Galatea's heartfelt questions interlace with the elegiac consolations of the chorus. The questions pose Galatea's anguish with almost undisguised literalness:

> Must I my Acis still bemoan,
> Inglorious, crush'd beneath that Stone?
> ... Must the lovely charming Youth
> Die for his Constancy and truth?
> ... Say, what Comfort can you find,
> For dark Despair o'er-clouds my Mind?
>
> (ll. 92–103)

At the last word of each of her questions, the chorus sings: "Cease, cease, Galatea, cease to grieve." Tension heightens as the grieving soprano sings above the counseling lower harmonies. It peaks as she repeats the word "die" in a descent from f′ to e′ to d′ to c#′, each cry interjected between the insistent charges of the chorus: "Cease, Galatea, cease to grieve." (See ex. 12.) This deepening complexity in compositional strategies and in the new tension and interplay among the musical parts continues through the remaining movements of the masque.

In literal language, Galatea voices the loss and "dark Despair" for which she asks "Comfort." Responding in the block harmonies of church music tradition, the chorus urges the condolence of "Pow'r" and "Art." Galatea's "Comfort" will derive from her individual response in the context of familiar hymnal and poetic consolations here on "the neighb'ring Shore." The allusion to religious music makes an associative connection that is cultural and historical. The power of this choral response comforts as it resounds with the familiar reference of church music.

The chorus urges Galatea to use her art to release Acis and her grief:

> To Kindred Gods the Youth return,
> Through verdant Plains to roll his Urn.
>
> (ll. 104–5)

These lines closely echo Dryden's familiar Ovid. As the chorus here associates itself with familiar music, so does it call up familiar literary reference. And to the same purpose: comfort comes in recognition of oneself amidst the familiar. Both text and music carry simple allusions to "the real" world, to familiar "neighborly" traditions, musical and textual, that place Galatea—and her listeners—in a human community based on reference, knowledge, and felt experience rather than on figurative representations of Nature imagined as a literary echo.

The charge the chorus gives Galatea is successful. In recitative she declares: "'Tis done, thus I exert my Pow'r Divine, / Be thou immortal, tho' thou art not mine." (ll. 106–7) At this magical moment, the orchestra brings into life the dotted rhythms that will reverberate to the end of the masque in the bubbling fountain of Acis's presence. Key to her "Pow'r

Ex. 12. Excerpt from "Must I my Acis still bemoan" from *Acis and Galatea*

Divine" is the phrase "tho' thou art not mine" which reverses the presumptuous sentiments with which the masque opened: "For *us* the Zephyr blows"
(emphasis mine). Rather, as she learns, she has no absolute claim. With
this transforming line Galatea voices her own shift from the falsely enti-
tling and imitative mode of the opening. It is not just Acis, but she who
changes in the course of grief and the acceptance of loss. Her "Pow'r Divine" is in this change.

Noting the irregularity and artful surprise in Handel's music for
Galatea's final aria, Winton Dean describes it as "one of the most sublime
things Handel ever wrote."[36] The music from this moment in the masque
has received much admiring comment, particularly the orchestral accompaniment that "murmurs" through Galatea's aria and the choral finale, a
representation of the "crystal fountain" Acis has become. Of the sequencing
that governs the progression of this figure in Galatea's vocal line, Dean says,

> [T]he beautiful little sequence that first appears in bars 3 and 4 of the
> ritornello, instead of returning in its familiar two-bar form, soars to a *three-
> fold* repetition at the words "murm'ring still his gentle love." It is impos-
> sible to convey in words the compound of satisfaction and excitement pro-
> duced by this simple stroke.[37]

Ex. 13. Excerpt from "Heart, the seat of soft delight" from *Acis and Galatea*

Handel here creates the stream motive of the accompaniment using the
dotted rhythm in diminution

that occurred first in the B section of the opening chorus ("For us the zephyr
blows") and next in Acis's opening aria ("Where shall I seek the charming
fair?"), and that then appears in parody in Polyphemus's "calls to empire
and to love." The finale thus takes up and transforms in the stream motive

the memory of Acis, his parodic counterpart Polyphemus, and the naive stylized Arcadia of the first chorus. Mutually implicated, all three are undone and transcended in the eloquent art of Galatea, a powerful voice responding from within herself to the destruction and loss she experiences.

Undoing Arcadia in a collision of parody and prototype that resonated with social nuance in the evocation of both popular and polite forms, Gay and Handel push to transformation the poetry and music with which the work begins. An intricate collaboration of text, music, and cultural reference, *Acis and Galatea* engages pastoral and mock pastoral, as the Italianate masque of shepherd and nymph is countered and undone by the antimasque of the bumpkinish giant. Galatea is left to find a resolution to this two-sided failure of heroism and convention. The ambiguity typical of Gay's comic works resides here as well, but with a resolution that Handel and the nonsemantic power of music make possible. In the transformed and transforming Galatea we hear a voice of individual self-expression in an unheroic world of cultural and social collision and complexity.

The culminating artistry of Galatea's song reveals itself as the point to which the whole work leads. Both music and poetry are transformed as composer and poet alike discard imitative conventions in favor of inhering, self-generating forms and strategies of development and meaning. With a changed perception and sensibility, this eloquent female voice marks Galatea as a newly awakened witness to a world remarkably modern-seeming in its introversion and psychological disposition. Facing the loss of an old heroism, Galatea sings with a new sensibility: personal, interior, self-expressive.

7

Popular Songs and the
Politics of Heroism:
The "Beggar's" Operas

The ballad operas display most thoroughly the social character of Gay's vision as well as the unresolving mix of the celebratory comedic and the skewering satiric in its allusive enlistment of images and themes. *The Beggar's Opera* and *Polly* together offer one of the first and most insightful critiques of a world whose institutions and relationships are driven by a market-based individualism premised on capital and profit. What is it that remains so familiar about this drama of Macheath and Polly, with its ironic panoply of cultural "ghosts" and political applicability? More than any writer of his era, Gay reveals the underlying moral, political, and aesthetic design, the "deep play" of the new order taking shape around him. In contrast to his Scriblerian colleagues Swift and Pope, his satiric renderings, however skeptical their warnings, nevertheless remain ambivalent and bemused. *The Beggar's Opera* engages, with a good humor that manages to be at once genial and wry, in the very transmutations of value that it exposes. If the indeterminacy of the new order is risky, morally troubling, and sometimes dangerous, it is, nonetheless, exhilarating and affirming as well.

The Beggar's Opera and *Polly* carry to a new complexity the metaleptic mixing and mirroring of "high" and "low" culture that runs through Gay's writings. Together these two musical dramas can be read as a satiric meditation on Western heroic ideals as embodied in the "high" literary forms of tragedy and comedy, romance and epic. They continue the ongoing meditation in Gay's work as a whole on the history and function of art. Other works by contemporaries of Gay, as well as immediate predecessors and followers, showed a similar preoccupation with the heroic: Samuel Butler's *Hudibras*, John Dryden's *Macflecknoe*, and Aphra Behn's *Oroonoko* among the Augustans; Alexander Pope's *Rape of the Lock*, Jonathan Swift's *Gulliver's Travels*, Henry Fielding's *Tom Jones*, and Charlotte Lennox's *Female Quixote* in the Georgian era. None, however, introduce into the conventionally "polite" topic so wide-ranging, vibrant, and legitimizing a display of "low" cultural forms as Gay.

The ballad operas employ well-known heroic topoi from European literature, complete with characters and plots. These Gay recasts in metaleptic rereading with other citations that carry varied social valence—"high," "middle," or "low." The middle- and especially lower-valenced markers undermine the solemnity and revered status of the heroic models. Typically they reveal ironically the dynamics of power and exploitation in these familiar topoi, now "modernized" in a class-mixing social setting structured by desire, acquisitiveness, and expedience.

The Beggar's Opera thus burlesques the conventions of both tragedy and comedy (will the hero hang; or will he "marry" any or all of his faithful and emphatically plural wives, mistresses, and doxies?). This generic attentiveness culminates in the to-do over the ending. The execution of the condemned Macheath—which would make it "a downright tragedy," as the player in the drama's framing device protests—is upended at the last minute by an operatic "reprieve" that quickly propels a parody of the standard comic ending: the play concludes with singing and dancing on a stage full of the hero's supposed wives and children. With similar generic self-consciousness, *Polly* ruefully stages elements of pastoral romance in a pirate-ridden Jamaica, at the same time parodically exporting to this "New World" a famous and oft-rendered tragic topic: the Antony and Cleopatra story.

Love and glory, twin polestars of Western heroism, premise the heroic ideal that is undermined in both of "the beggar's" operas. Gay's satire exposes, in rather modern terms, the risks for women in the sphere of Love, the feminized side of the conventional heroic ideal. With regard to the masculinized realm of Glory, the arena of tragic and epic heroism, Gay, as usual, critiques a modern politics of corruption, social rank, and money. Trade defines the moral relations of one person to another at both personal and public levels, and in both plots: in the public, economic sphere, thieving and thief-taking in the first play and slavery in the second coexist with a personal (and sometimes familial) bartering for affectional and sexual favors. Traditional models of heroism and morality are revealed to be jarringly inapplicable amidst this unbrave new world.

Gay wrote *The Beggar's Opera* and *Polly* in tandem, both being prepared for production in a single year, 1728.[1] After being famously turned down by Drury Lane, "the beggar's" first "opera" opened at John Rich's Lincoln's Inn Fields the night of Monday, 29 January. It was still playing in May, an astonishing run for the time. As Winton notes (128), Gay may have had a sequel in mind from the beginning. In any case, *Polly* was ready for production by the autumn, fast on the heels of *The Beggar's Opera*.

Both plays take up the fortunes of Macheath and Polly Peachum, imagined in a single, two-part story that addresses itself to heroism and morality at home and abroad, in an institutionally restructuring Britain. This context forms an obvious backdrop, for *The Beggar's Opera* injects systematic reference to the events of recent history: the Stuart claimant to the throne and the Jacobite movement; the awkward and none-too-secure accommodation of the Hanoverian monarchy; the much-contended consolidation of the ministerial power of Robert Walpole around city-based business, banking, and trade; the South Sea Company stock scandal; and changes in institutions of law and penal justice. The sequel, *Polly*, took up more directly the corruptions of slave trading and empire. The banning of the latter in December attests that contemporaries considered the plays as two parts of a single message. Having suffered the jabs of the first play—as Lord Hervey remarked—Walpole intervened to keep from having to suffer its sequel.

Winton notes (103–8) that party satirists, including Swift, engaged in a journalistic flurry of political polemic from February 1728 onward, appropriating *The Beggar's Opera* in their salvos attacking Walpole. The prime minister's champions attacked the play in his defense. The presence of the "opera" in this skirmishing of party factions surely compounded the political innuendo Gay intended. At the same time, the play's role in the diatribe distorted the satire by localizing the focus to Walpole (something on the order of focusing on only a few bits of a mosaic). Despite the prominent role assigned to the opera from its first performances by eager polemicists and more neutral observers alike, the scholarly quest since then for direct allegorical application to particular policies—be they Walpole's in government or Handel's in *opera seria*—has yielded little.

Yet to see these plays as innocent comedy is to overlook both the discerning appraisal at the heart of all Gay's work as well as the telling reappearance of *The Beggar's Opera* in its biting modern and postmodern versions. Gay puts into vivid focus the general moral sensibility, the dynamics of social relationship, and the institutional organization and enforcement that found particular expression in a minister like Walpole, a king like George I, a colonizing presence of slave-owning in Jamaica, and the counterparts of all these in the twentieth-century Europe of Brecht, Havel, and Ayckbourn. *The Beggar's Opera* especially evokes particularities of history—that is, recognizable circumstances and people. At the same time, these function in the figurative way of Gay's allusions, as *exempla* to map the new moral dynamics of a world of individually earned, bought, or stolen—rather than inherited—power.

Songs in *The Beggar's Opera:* "Double-Capacities" in Private and Public

In the eighteenth century popular songs functioned more variously than they do today, when they serve us only for entertainment or ceremony. By means of songs eighteenth-century people processed the events, circumstances, sentiments, and ideas—both private and public—that made up their experience. Beyond their use as entertainment and ceremony, popular songs conveyed information, identified allegiances and constituencies, argued political positions, registered complaints of various sorts, fomented resistance, and mustered support. This cultural vitality of song traditions undergirds the force and meaning of single airs in *The Beggar's Opera.* Once again, Gay made key use of larger conventional patterns from the popular imagination as well. It is precisely through this appeal to communally recognizable and created forms that he read the deep changes in social organization, institutional structure, and individual behavior and sensibility that accompanied the shift to a ministerial government and a trade- and money-based economy.

Interjecting into the "present" circumstances of the drama a contemplative moment, songs supply "critical instants." Gay's are notably critical, for they beam multiple, often contradictory meanings drawn from the rich and often politically directed song culture of the time. Songs in a spoken drama stop the action and open the play out to a usually figurative consideration of themes and events. Such moments are perfectly suited for the complications of irony and satire. The phrase "critical instants" from Congreve's *Way of the World* captures the way the songs occasion "contemplation" of a particularly social sort.[2] Such "instants" establish the playwright, characters, players, and audience as a "company" engaged in shared discourse. The play itself—both text and performance—forms but one among many points of reference, expression, explication, and exchange. Gay's ballad operas stand in the line of development of such "critical instants" from the English operas of Purcell's era through the operas, pantomimes, and musical burlesques of the first decades of the eighteenth century.[3] Songs increasingly functioned as implicating intertexts which draw into the play other texts, authors, and contexts.

Gay's employment of familiar tunes in songs brought the "critical" nature of such "instants" to a new complexity. Like vibrant palimpsests where the old shows legibly through the recent, the original texts and associations for the tunes create the insistent polyvalent critique that accompanies our laughter. The songs in the plays supply referential excursions that contextualize the drama's "present" moment of plot and characters—say, Polly and Macheath—with resonating analogies—to a power-wielding Walpole or an exiled James Stuart. At the same time, the whistling familiarity of the songs and their conventional themes and images implicate the taste and preoccupations of the audience for whom they are everyday pastimes. Gay's meaning is always complex and, at some level, satirical of human failing and delusion. This satire usually extends in one direction to the particular—individual persons and famous or infamous events—and in another to the marketplace of a popularizing Everyman/Everywoman whose pastimes he invokes.

Through their singing of already familiar tunes, for example, the female figures Lucy and Polly illustrate Gay's lavishly rich and multilayered referencing of the interpersonal to historical and political dilemmas. After Lucy tells the jailed Macheath in act 2 of *The Beggar's Opera*, "'Tis the pleasure of all you fine men to insult the women you have ruined" (II.ix.20–21), she sings of the blackguard cruelty of theft in love:

> How cruel are the traitors
>   Who lie and swear in jest,
> To cheat unguarded creatures
>   Of virtue, fame, and rest!
> Whoever steals a shilling,
>   Through shame the guilt conceals;
> In love the perjured villain
>   With boasts the theft reveals. . . .

(II.ix.22–29)

The song uneasily yokes the usually contrasted realms of material gain on the one hand and of immaterial interior sentiment on the other: loyalty, affection, morality, and motivation. Lucy sings this lament to the tune of Gay and Handel's "'Twas When the Seas Were Roaring," the popular song from *The What-d'Ye-Call-It*, a theatrical favorite for decades after its earlier run in 1715. Lucy is thus immediately identified with the forlorn "Kitty Carrot" of the original farce discussed in chapter 5 above.

This identification is complex, for Kitty already had a double identity as the heroine of *The What-d'Ye-Call-It*'s play-within-a-play. Both Kitties—the "Kitty Carrot" of the inner mumming play and "Kitty," the Steward's pregnant daughter who plays her—have relevance to the pregnant Lucy's predicament. "Kitty" too sang of love's betrayals in the context of the earlier play's variant but not unrelated "perjured" and "boast[ing] villains." We view Lucy and Kitty as correspondent: they are, literally, singing the same tune. Yet the allusion accentuates both similarities and differences in their respective situations.

The identification of Lucy with "Kitty Carrot" takes on strategic relevance when, a few scenes later, Polly is similarly referenced to another of Gay's well-loved song heroines: she sings Macheath a fable (of a swallow pathetically faithful to her love) set to the poet's enormously popular ballad "Black-eyed Susan." These parodic echoes of "Kitty Carrot" and "Black-eyed Susan" in turn position Lucy and Polly as stock heroines who evoke the predicaments, stories, and contexts of their progenitors. A necessary reinterpretation accompanies these "ghosts" of types and prototypes, heightening audience awareness of the underlying pulls of resemblance and difference from one figure to the next. Underneath the play of individual allusions, we make out the systematic parallels that inform the politics of the situation.

Lucy's lament in *the Beggar's Opera* of "traitors" and "boasted thefts" takes a further twist of meaning amidst the echoing of other texts previously sung to "'Twas When the Seas Were Roaring." Soon after the first staging of *The What-d'Ye-Call-It* in 1715, the play's hit tune reappeared as anti-Jacobite satire, "The Pretender's Flight, and Sorrowful Lamentation for His Late Disappointment in Scotland."[4] For Gay's 1728 audience, Lucy's lament carried shadows of the earlier ballad's mocking depiction of the Jacobite claimant to the throne of England. The Whig satire sings of the disparaged James Stuart: "All melancholy lying, / Thus wail'd he for his Crown." With this tune-based reference, the tension between the two heroines hints at a political reading: as Lucy parallels Kitty, who in turn suggests a bereft James Stuart on one side, we might extend the parallel of Polly to Susan with an analogous reference to an accommodating George I on the other.

Lucy's situation and that of "Kitty" differ; nevertheless, they have overlapping features—pregnancy, lovelorn laments, aggrieved hopes of marriage. Even more provocative yet elusive are the echoing verses about a bereft (and feminized) "melancholy" and "wail[ing]" James Stuart. The reader/listener receives intersecting allusions that comment as satiric analogies one upon another.

Metaleptic design in Gay takes many forms, from the parody of Dryden's *Virgil* in the image of Bowzybeus in *The Shepherd's Week*, to the textual echoes of Otway's *Venice Preserv'd* in *The What-d'Ye-Call-It* or *The Beggar's Opera*, to the much-remarked linking of Lucy and Polly to the onstage spat in 1727 of the Italian divas Cuzzoni and Faustina.[5] Gay's songs illustrate most clearly how this mode makes possible a satire that is both individual and social, present and historical.

Gay's reliance on contemporary airs for the songs in *The Beggar's Opera* and other plays is well known.[6] Critics distinguish the ballad opera as a form from other dramas with music by this interjection of "low" materials performed by the "lowlife" characters in whose world the drama is set. The three ballad operas with which Gay invented the form establish a complex range of music tied to an identification with distinct social strata that is gradated from one play to the next. Gay's sixty-nine songs in *The Beggar's Opera* are set to familiar tunes, almost all of which would have been well known to people of the upper and middle levels from songbooks popularizing such airs, and to people of lower rank from cheap broadsides sold on the streets and from oral tradition. *Polly* and *Achilles*, in turn, display references to "higher" categories of popular music-making in dance tunes, glees, and concert pieces that represented a mid rather than low level of entertainment and marketing.

The "lowness" of the airs in *The Beggar's Opera* functions integrally to create the burlesque texture of Gay's oxymoronic "Newgate Pastoral" (to use Swift's phrase). The opera satirizes a false morality; the unequal terms of social rank establish unequal consequences with regard to "the similitude of manners in high and low life" because the "lower sort of people . . . are punished for them" (III.xvi.16–24). The underlayer of popular song traditions percolates up through Gay's own song texts, imbuing the entire drama with commenting subtexts, the sociocultural context.[7]

Air 9 of *The Beggar's Opera*, sung by Polly and her mother, works to interrogate the familial governance of love and sexuality. For the knowing audience, the song gains mightily in innuendo by the tune's original text, which renders the "toying" and "kissing," "teasing" and "pleasing" of *The Beggar's Opera* song with an explicitness that betrays the disingenuous coyness of the mother, the naïveté of the daughter. The euphemism that structures the song rules the Peachum household, a consuming "double capacity" in its feminized and domestic application (elaborated in both Brecht and Havel).

Act 1 of *The Beggar's Opera* centers on the Peachum family, focusing on Mr. Peachum's "trade" in stolen goods and law enforcement on the one hand, and on daughter Polly's secret marriage to the highwayman Macheath on the other. Distraught, the Peachum parents castigate, cajole, and inveigle Polly, trying to remedy this unprofitable match that threatens, most importantly, the family "business." "I did not marry him (as 'tis the fashion) coolly and deliberately for honor or money," Polly tells her parents, "But I love him" (I.viii.61–62). "Love him!," her mother cries, collapsing in a swoon, "Worse and worse! I thought the girl had been better bred. Oh husband, husband! Her folly makes me mad! My head swims! I'm distracted! I can't support myself.—Oh!" (63–66). At her father's direction, Polly brings "a glass of cordial," her mother's remedy of choice for what is obviously a standard family drama. Revived, Mrs. Peachum retrospectively advises in song, and Polly replies:

> *Mrs. Peachum*   O Polly, you might have toyed and kissed.
>   By keeping men off, you keep them on.
> *Polly.*   But he so teased me,
>   And he so pleased me,
>   What I did, you must have done.
>
>   (I.viii.76–80)

AIR IX

Ex. 14. "Air 9" from *The Beggar's Opera*

"Not with a highwayman. You sorry slut!" her mother retorts (81), with a force that shatters the lilting sweetness of the tune.

Deftly, Gay conjures a complex consideration of this exchange between Polly and her mother. The relation of the two women foreshadows the focus on women's relationships in mid- and late-century domestic novels. The song enacts, with delicious irony, a legacy of seduction in the interplay between the mother's (coy) admonition to coyness and the daughter's ingenuous insinuations. Neither stance, as Gay makes clear, is quite what it claims to be. The tune betrays the euphemism and unspoken, yet intended sexual enticement—calculated for power and profit—that mamma recommends. Thus, her first line leaps suddenly from "might" to "have" with dramatic shifts of harmony on "toyed" and "kissed": to the dominant harmony at "toyed" then with a surprising and suggestive fall to the subdominant harmony on "kissed." The tune mimics the charged "toying" and "kissing" of Mrs. Peachum that, "By keeping men off," will "keep them on"— what "might have" been.

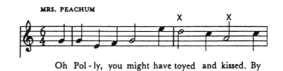

Ex. 15. Excerpt from "Air 9" from *The Beggar's Opera*

Polly's melody is similarly imitative and ironically self-commenting. Her response begins straightforwardly with a stepwise progression of even quarter notes: "But he so teased me, And he so pleased me." Suddenly, she too falls in gapping leaps to lingering half notes that distend with innuendo, as does her vocabulary's shift to an evasive abstraction: "What I did, you must have done." Her "must have" counters the advisory "might have."

Ex. 16. Excerpt from "Air 9" from *The Beggar's Opera*

The original words to the tune, titled "The Willoughby Whim," make fully explicit the unspoken innuendo to which Gay's song insistently directs us. Described as "A Scotch Song" in D'Urfey's *Pills to Purge Melancholy*, "The Willoughby Whim" is "a Dialogue between two Sisters" in which "Molly" questions "Jenny" concerning her whereabouts, fretfully accusing her of "ranting, playing the Wanton, / Keeping of *Jockey* Company."[8] As the song unfolds in conventional double entendres—"hear Mill clack," "grind Grist," "hang your Smickets abroad to bleach"—it becomes clear that Jenny has indeed been keeping considerably more "Company" than just the one lad. Throughout, the concrete language of *The Willoughby Whim* with its tangible, proverbial metaphors places sexual activity and its consequences in the context of a village community. The song concludes with one last double entendre from proverbial parlance—bell and clapper—that pointedly calls up the institutional structures of a waning order.

Molly. My Father you told you'd go to Kirk,
         When Prayers were done, where could you be?
Jenny. Taking a Kiss of the Parson and Clerk,
         And of other young Laddys some two or three.
Molly. Oh Jenny, Jenny, what wilt thou do,
         If Belly should swell, where wilt thou be?
Jenny. Look to your self for Jockey is true,
         And whilst Clapper goes will take care of me.

The earlier song supplies Gay a shadowing commentary on the sensibilities and circumstances of mother and daughter, full of linguistic contrast and hints of sociopolitical difference in the evocation of a village context that is nowhere in evidence in *The Beggar's Operas* pointedly urban underworld.

Polly's naïveté, juxtaposed to her mother's experience, insists that we consider the pressure of family life and of the private, domestic sphere on the public discourse and morality. The cloaking language of both daughter and mother, who understand even as they reject each other's viewpoints, makes possible the "double capacity" necessary to an individual woman's trade in love. The tangible representation of sex through proverbial metaphors like mill grinding and bell ringing in the earlier song contrast to the coyness in the later. With Jockey's "Clapper" and Jenny's bell/belly lurking in the tune, Mrs. Peachum's "teasing" and "pleasing" become prurient euphemisms answered by Polly's indirect "What I did, you must have done." The impertinent motherhood of *The Willoughby Whim* filters up through Gay's text, commenting upon the predicament of the naive Polly, juxtaposed to her more "knowing" mother. The text stands to its progenitor as does this Polly to her mother. Thus, in a single metaleptic figure Gay traces a history over three generations to the closetings of bourgeois decorum.

"Over the Hills and Far Away" (Air 16), the lovely duet that Macheath and Polly sing as they are about to part at the end of act 1, supplies an even richer example of the metaleptic complexity and power of Gay's songs. A complicated swirl of allusions attaches to this scene of amorous private parting. Such reverberations of satirical polemic and political innuendo both launched the play's reputation for dangerous critique and served as the model for satiric strategies in the "translations" of Brecht, Havel, and Ayckbourn.

As Donaldson notes, this song echoes the stock scenes of parting lovers that peppered sentimental tragedies and had already received parodic treatment in comedies by Gay and others.[9] Even audiences unaware of specific eighteenth-century prototypes cannot overlook the general ironic citing of the forms and influence of high literature and art. The naive Polly declares her trust in lines that portend Macheath's falsity, based as her faith is in her reading of sentimental stories: "Nay, my dear, I have no reason to doubt you, for I find in the romance you lent me, none of the great heroes were ever false in love" (I.xiii.15–17). Macheath, his affections markedly suspect after Polly's gullible reference to literary romances, sings of his fixation on Polly—as that of a "bee" to a "flower." These give us the very similes the "beggar" author identified in the introduction as key features "in all your celebrated operas" (17). (Indeed, the figures that Galatea surrendered in her final aria.) Hovering above the scene are the ghosts of literary and operatic prototypes of any age, attesting paradoxically both to the historical tangibility of such representations and their artifice.

The spoken remarks that follow shift the frame of reference completely. The next lines recontextualize this parting in the terms of transportation to the colonies, conjuring up both the expanding empire and the pressure of its criminal codes on the underclass at home. "Were you sentenced to transportation?" Polly inquires, "Sure, my dear, you could not leave me behind you, could you?" (24–25). Macheath answers with a series of similes that laughably link a lover's ardor and the images of banal self-interest in this new world of moneyed trade: "Is there any power, any force that could tear me from thee? You might sooner tear a pension out of the hands of a courtier, a fee from a lawyer, a pretty woman from a looking glass, or any woman from quadrille. But to tear me from thee is impossible" (26–30).

Macheath's response pushes to even more precision the reference to the politics of empire, for "pensions," lawyer's "fees," and the gambling card game "quadrille" would have put Gay's 1728 audience in mind of the stock market crash of 1720, the South Sea Bubble. This complicated web of investment scandals involved speculation on pensions, affected the politics of empire, trade, and colonization, and entailed elaborate government intrigues and cover-ups. Gay's lovers stand amidst an incongruity that has an ironic familiarity: on the one hand they appeal to templates of literature and art which, on the other hand, are quickly overturned by the mundane, not to say famously sullied images of pension investments, legal wrangles, and gambling. Macheath then begins the lovely, cuttingly ironic "Over the Hills and Far Away." To a tune that songsmith Allan Ramsay described in 1733 as an old Scottish song,[10] Macheath sings:

> Were I laid on Greenland's coast,
>   And in my arms embraced my lass,
> Warm amidst eternal frost,
>   Too soon the half year's night would pass.

The song opens with the ironic signifier "Greenland," which at one level connotes the innocent "green-world" of pastoral literature, especially framed

Ex. 17. Excerpt from "Air 16" from *The Beggar's Opera*

as it is in celebration of an all-saving love. At the same time, the realities of the actual "Greenland" intrude, both implied by the topic of "transportation" that prompted the song on the one hand, and brought into the text with the arresting image of a "half year's night" of "eternal frost" on the other. This irony, unmistakable for any audience, would have been especially keen for 1720s listeners cognizant of both pastoral literature and the famously icy wastes associated with the North Atlantic fishing grounds. The song encapsulates as the crux of its irony the lack of fit between a private pastoral "greenland" in which to love and the actual "Greenland" in the public sphere it signifies. At the same time, Macheath's dream—for all its ironies—enchants and persuades; it is one of the loveliest songs in the play.

To the same melody, Polly sings of a countering colonial context: a "burning day" on "Indian soil." The imagery arrests and troubles even as the tune beguiles. Intensifying Macheath's ironic depiction of the icy, new, mock-pastoral context of empire, she sings of love's ability to "mock the sultry toil" of slavery, pushing the idea of transportation to its further and more oppressive stage, a theme that returns in *Polly*.

> Were I sold on Indian soil,
>> Soon as the burning day was closed,
> I could mock the sultry toil,
>> When on my charmer's breast reposed.

Macheath and Polly then sing in tandem the invitation that ends the song, floating "Over the hills and far away" on the unresolving second note of the scale:

Macheath. I would love you all the day,
Polly. Ev'ry night would kiss and play,
Macheath. If with me you'd fondly stray
Polly. Over the hills and far away.

Ex. 18. Excerpt from "Air 16" from *The Beggar's Opera*

Enchanting and unsettling, a profoundly oxymoronic text set to a lulling, then unresolving tune, "Over the Hills and Far Away" exemplifies the poignant, almost painful melding of sentiment and satire, longing and critique in Gay's work, its "double-tongued utterance," to use Margaret Doody's phrase.[11] The song creates countercommenting reverberation between the spheres of private sentiment and behavior on the one hand—the love of Macheath and Polly—and of public history, circumstance, policy, and policy makers on the other—the transportation and slavery at the bottom rungs of the experience of empire. With this metaleptic move, Gay captures the unresolving crux of the dilemma of private and public morality in the demythologized new order.

"Over the Hills and Far Away" supplied Gay's 1728 audience an especially vibrant cluster of counter texts and contexts that accumulated a political application. Poised among echoing song texts of the previous two decades, Macheath and Polly sing this haunting invitation to transportation and slavery amid the charged overtones of Jacobite-Georgian history. Typically, it is not so much the specifics of Whig and Tory party politics that Gay addresses, but the larger dynamics of political power and socioeconomic change that his generation witnessed with the Hanoverian monarchy and the ascendancy of Walpole. A new order—commercial, urban, money and profit driven, ministerial—had begun.[12]

"Over the Hills and Far Away" situates the lovers within the history of this transformation. The tune Macheath sings to Polly envelopes him with a cumulative Jacobite resonance. It set a range of songs, most of them political and connected to the Stuart claimant: a Scottish lamentation of a lovelorn "Jockey"; class-scrambling "Verses upon raising Recruits" for the War of the Spanish Succession; pointedly Jacobite songs supporting James Stuart's claim to the monarchy; Whig countering songs, including a complaint at the 1711 dismissal of the duke of Marlborough from command of the army in the Spanish Succession war; and Thomas D'Urfey's popular "Hubble Bubbles" on the South Sea Bubble stock scandal of 1720. Macheath and Polly evoke their fantasized, mock-pastoral escape to an icy and burning overseas empire at the center of this constellation of allusion.

The tune takes its name from the refrain "'Tis o'er the hills, and far away, / The Wind has blown my Plad away" of "Jockey's Lamentation," a song that seems to appear first in D'Urfey's *Pills to Purge Melancholy* of 1706. Because "Jenny stole his Heart Away," "poor Jockey" is now "run mad" and, "griev[ing] both Night and Day," and can only sing the refrain, "'Tis o'er the Hills, &c." Together with "Jockey's Lamentation," D'Urfey published the recruiting song—"Being an Excellent New Copy of verses upon raising Recruits. To the foregoing Tune"—from George Farquhar's popular comedy of 1706, *The Recruiting Officer*.[13] Both would have been well-known to Gay's contemporaries, underscoring the "double-tongued" character of *The Beggar's Opera* song and extending its specificity as Macheath and Polly become identified with "Jockey" and "Jenny" of the Scots song, and with the class-scrambling enticements of "Flanders, Portugal and Spain" in Farquhar's recruiting song, which promises advancement to lowly "boys":

> Over Rivers, Bogs, and Springs
> We all shall live as great as Kings,
> And Plunder get both Night and Day,
> When over the Hills and far away,
>   Over the Hills and o'er the Main,
>   To *Flanders, Portugal* and *Spain,*
>   Queen *Ann* commands, and we'll obey,
>   *Over the Hills and far away.*
> . . . Come on then Boys and you shall see,
> We every one shall Captains be,
> To Whore and rant as well as they,
> When o'er the Hills and far away:
>   *Over the Hills, &c.*
> For if we go 'tis one to Ten,
> But we return all gentlemen,
> All Gentlemen as well as they,

> When o'er the Hills and far away:
> *Over the Hills, &c.*

Farquhar's song attached to the Scottish air an evocation of the War of the Spanish Succession that began under William III in 1701 and continued through Queen Anne's reign until 1713. This long and complicated dispute involved questions of European monarchical succession, including who would succeed the childless English queen: the exiled son of the Stuart James II, Catholic half-brother to the queen; or the heir of the Protestant house of Hanover. Already in D'Urfey's *Pills*, the old Scottish tune hinted of the Stuart cause. More pointedly political texts further emphasized this aura of Jacobitism in "Over the Hills and Far Away," an aura that clung to Macheath's "Over the Hills" in 1728.

A number of songs set to the tune circulated in the tradition of explicitly Jacobite prints and manuscripts. "A Song on the Birth-day of King James the VIII, 10 June, 1709" by "young Niddrie, to the Tune of, *Over the Hills and far away*" concludes with a ringing hope for the succession of the Stuart claimant:

> Hanover's tytle shall be gone,
> When the Right Heir's upon the Throne;
> We'll all be blyth, we s' a' be bra',
> When he comes home that's far awa'.
>   He's over the seas and far awa';
>   He's over the seas and far awa';
>   Of no man we will stand in awe,
>   *To drink his health that's far awa'*.[14]

"Granadiers, now change your Song," a Whig ditty from 1711 set to "Over the Hills," plays off the Jacobite resonance of the tune, expressing disapproval at the removal of John Churchill, duke of Marlborough, from command of the armies. As John McAleer observes, "Marlborough's Whig partisans thought his removal showed Anne's preference for the Pretender since Marlborough was a protégé of the Hanoverian Elector."[15] The Whig song suggests that the queen's removal of Marlborough was intended to halt English victories in the war in an effort to coax France and Spain to negotiate a peace. The "Second Part" of the Whig ballad begins:

> Granadiers, now change your Song,
>   Sing no more of Battels won:
> But break your Swords, and go to plough,
>   Since you have lost your *Marlborough*.
>   *Sing over the Hills and far away*.[16]

As Macheath and Polly sing of love in Greenland and the Indies, they invoke a complicated, encircling web of historical and political reference. The allusions make their way through a sequence of key events in the transformation: the long war begun under William III, the controversy over the monarchical succession, Whig and Tory party sparring, and the stock scandal. *The Beggar's Opera*'s "Over the Hills" proposes that such political issues are individually felt.

Already in 1714 Gay's *Shepherd's Week* had echoed the Marlborough ballad, with glancing reference as well to the "Shillings on the Drum" in Farquhar's recruiting song. At that time, the Treaty of Utrecht had just been signed, the succession to the throne was much in question, and both songs were in the air. In the prologue, Gay's "shepherd" persona celebrates the peace that the "Granadiers" singing of Marlborough in the Whig "Over the Hills" had decried:

> So forth I far'd to Court with speed,
> Of Soldier's Drum withouten Dreed;
> For Peace allays the Shepherd's Fear
> Of wearing Cap of Granadier.
>
> (ll. 45–48)[17]

Gay's celebration of the Tory peace of 1713 and dedication of *The Shepherd's Week* to Henry St. John, Viscount Bolingbroke, one of its principal architects, as we know, earned him the permanent disaffection of the House of Hanover, especially when Bolingbroke became associated with the Jacobite uprising of 1715. After living in exile, he returned to England in 1725. Though Bolingbroke himself had long abandoned his Stuart sympathies, he led the ongoing opposition to Walpole. Public rumors—probably encouraged by Walpole himself—spread upon the death of George I in 1727 that another Jacobite invasion and uprising threatened.[18] The opposition became identified with the Jacobite danger. The debonair Bolingbroke was certainly one of the references conjured in the figure of Macheath—particularly as the latter contrasts with the (Whiggish) shopkeepers, Peachum and Lockit. Moreover, Gay's own early experience of the personal effects of political events (in the repercussions of his dedication of *The Shepherd's Week* to Bolingbroke) find their way into the meaning of being transported "Over the Hills and Far Away."

The tune thus brings into the scene of Macheath and Polly's farewell a cavalcade of references—most of them political. Suggesting the presence of the Stuart "Pretender" as well as Bolingbroke's opposition to the ministry, this constellation of allusions reviews the history of the Hanoverian succession and the ministry that emerged in connection with it.[19] *The*

Beggar's Opera songs exemplify a process of ongoing reinscription described by William Donaldson, who notes, with regard to Jacobite political songs in general: "the ability of the parent text to colour the structure and tone of politically inspired derivatives."[20] Macheath and Polly's transportation—poignant enough as a personal story—enacts as well a community history that was sung about for more than a generation.

The final piece in this metaleptic design involves the South Sea Bubble stock market crash that dominated political discourse in the 1720s and whose resolution, more than any other single event, brought Robert Walpole to power. A spate of songs accompanied the stock scheme, extending from the founding of the company in 1711 through the investment bubble and crash of 1720. One of the most widely known was Thomas D'Urfey's "The Hubble Bubbles," again sung to "Over the Hills and Far Away" and providing the referent Gay's audience would have had most immediately to mind for this tune.[21]

The South Sea Company was founded in 1711 during the Tory ministry of Robert Harley to carry out English trade as stipulated by the Treaty of Utrecht which ended the War of the Spanish Succession. Identified with the Tory party, by 1719 the company had abandoned any pretense of trading and turned to speculative stockjobbing, the buying and selling of investment stocks, in order to convert some £50 million of government debt in the form of pensions into marketable stock shares.[22] At first, the company generated substantial profits by manipulating stock values and bribing key players at parliament and court. In the early months of 1720 the British public responded with a frenzy of stock purchasing. Values rose wildly, reaching a peak in the summer of 1720.

However, parliamentary moves to regulate the marketing of stocks and foreign withdrawals of investment triggered the collapse of the expanding "bubble." By autumn of 1720 the first modern stock market crash came, precipitating a ministry shakeup and an elaborate official cover-up that extended to the king himself. (Gay lost a considerable investment in the crash.)[23] Narrowly averting a national crisis that could easily have precipitated a change of monarch, Robert Walpole consolidated power largely through his skillful parliamentary salvaging—through payoffs and cover-ups—of both the new financial order and the Hanoverian monarchy. His screening protection of the court after the corruption of the Bubble was key to the control he maintained.[24] Indeed, his continued supremacy with the accession of George II in 1727, which could have been a moment of change, solidified his power and increased his stature in an unprecedented way. Rather baldly undermining his rivals and rewarding his friends, Walpole almost single-handedly seems to have maintained the stability of the emerging institutions and relationships of the new system. While he did not cause the deep changes in the financial and ruling order, he exploited them to advantage and came to be identified with them.

Picking up threads of Whig satire from the era of the Treaty of Utrecht, Thomas D'Urfey's "Hubble Bubbles" reminded people of the party politics embedded in South Sea Company history even as it critiqued the stock trading of 1720. "Ye Circum, and Uncircumcis'd, / Come hear my Song and be advis'd," "The Hubble Bubbles" begins.[25] A mélange of caricatured purchasers follows, commenting in its listed categories on the disturbing presence of suspect and previously excluded people in the trading: "Scotch men," "Irish who have Bulls to sell," "privy Councellors," "Nymphs of Gay desire," and "Italian Songsters."[26] The transforming values of paper stocks were effecting deep-seated shiftings of power and place, a new twist to the theme of Farquhar's recruiting song.[27]

"Hubble Bubbles" surveys typical investment proposals connected to the South Sea Company scheme: "insurance of ships," "project for emptying... houses," "insurance from fire," and so on. The "fishery hubble bubble" of the song alludes to a host of schemes centered on Greenland and the north Atlantic fisheries, certainly what Gay's "Over the Hills" evoked. As D'Urfey's ballad reaches its conclusion, the metaphoric bubble bursts with a pun on the word "Stocks":

> A bubble is blown up with air,
> In which fine Prospects do Appear,
> The Bubble breaks the Prospects lost,
> Yet must some bubble pay the cost,
>> Hubble bubble bubble hubble all is smoke
>> Bubble bubble hubble bubble all is broke
> Farewell your Woods your Houses Lands your
>> Pastures and your Flocks.
> For now you have nought but your Selves in ye Stocks.

D'Urfey crowds into the penultimate line of the resonant little tune a nostalgic list of landowners' losses—"Woods," "Houses," "Lands," "Pastures," and "Flocks"—from a world of land-based wealth that is slipping away. It is this world that the Stuart claimants came increasingly to represent, especially as the ministry persisted. The song's alliterative last sentence underscores the metamorphosing of value and relationship that, under that limited monarchy managed by Walpole, put into place a capitalist realm of striving individuals: "For *now* you have *nought* but your *Selves* in ye *Stocks*." The unresolving final note leaves us with the playful numerical pun on the word "nought": "now" = "nought."[28] (See ex. 19.) With this apprehensive lack of conclusiveness, D'Urfey figures forth in the singing, the floating insubstantiality of the new value of "nothing." In the same way, Polly's

Ex. 19. Excerpt from "Over the Hills and Far Away"

unresolving ending of "Over the hills and far away" floats uneasily over the horizon, trailing behind it, like kites on a string, a whole line of politically resonant texts.

This cavalcade of political songs functions in several ways in Gay's play. First, an unmistakably Jacobite tenor falls over Macheath and the image of exile he and Polly create, calling to mind the figures of James Stuart—himself "o'er the seas"—and such opposition figures as Bolingbroke. At the same time, the evasive suggestion—a tone, a coloring—evokes a correspondence with the displacements and ironies of history rather than the mythic continuities of allegory.

The political songs figuratively connect the private farewell of Polly and Macheath to the public events of some two decades of British political history. Polly's leave-taking resonates with England's farewell to the Stuart monarchy and the old order it represented. Gay increasingly marks the new order's careful division of spheres, public and private, at the same time that he exposes their overlapping dynamics and moral intersections. The politics and relations of individuals parallel the dynamics of polities propelled by appetite and trade, and the transvaluations such polities require. It was this coding of the public by the private, particularly when linked with the question of legitimate rule that Brecht and Havel found compelling and applicable in *The Beggar's Opera*: not so much what Gay signified, as how.

Gay's metaleptic method, exemplified richly in a song like "Over the Hills," creates in his works polyvalent figures of allusions. Like the vacillating figure-ground images that illustrate perceptual deception in psychology books, they accrue alternating meanings. Thus, Macheath can signify, by turns, a literary "Everyrake," any of us in love, James Stuart and the Jacobite cause, an England in the throes of transition, or Walpole poised between a Jacobite link to the past in Lucy and a Hanoverian Whig expediency in Polly.

It is no fluke that *The Beggar's Opera* has been read in its own time—and in ours—as a play about politics at every level. Throughout, the tunes carry the allusive bite we have seen in "Over the Hills." Gay creates for us "critical instants" that require the overlay of public on private, private on public. "If the heart of a man is depressed with cares, / The mist is dispelled when a woman appears," sings the faithless Macheath (II.iii.8–9), having just left Polly. To one side the tune conjures D'Urfey's bawdy "Would ye have a young Virgin of fifteen Years?"—a reinscription of Macheath at the private level.[29] On another, it suggests the political terrain in a Jacobite satire to the same tune: "Would you know what a Whig is, and always was?"[30] Combining the two in a single Macheath, Gay gives the noticeably modern presentation of a flawed, unremarkable, disempowered private individual read as a universal signifier against the backdrop of a larger public history.

HEROISM UNDONE:
POLLY AND THE BALLAD FEMALE WARRIOR

Gay's oxymoronic titling of his satirical genre "ballad opera" was more than an aesthetic joke coupling two disparate social spheres. *The Beggar's Opera* is shaped by its songs and, at its deeper and more satiric level, by the popular individual ballads and song traditions from which these emerge: stage pieces persisting as popular songs, political lampoons and rebuttals, foreign tunes that acquire English texts, dance tunes that are given words, traditional songs that become dances, and so on. The vibrancy and mettle of Gay's satire derives from its use of popular materials. These forms served the private lives and pastimes of ordinary citizens that increasingly constituted the power base of the new order. For the ballad operas especially, song traditions supplied the key to both Gay's method and his meaning. In *Polly*, this metaleptic mirroring of one citation by another is carried out in particular moments in the text—that is, individual songs and speeches—but also in the larger architecture of the play, which hinges on a dismantling conjunction of conventional paradigms from "high" art and "low": the Antony and Cleopatra topos of tragedy and the female warrior motif from the sphere of popular balladry that is so prevalent in *The Beggar's Opera*.

Polly takes to a structural level Gay's method of allusion, with his concomitant examination of private morality in the context of community expectations and values on the one hand and divisions of rank on the other. The play borrows from popular song traditions at a deeper and more general level than *The Beggar's Opera*, for *Polly* is structured along the lines of the conventional female warrior motif whose heroine—in this case, Polly Peachum—dresses as a man and ventures to war for the sake of her beloved. This prototypical narrative and thematic pattern governs a whole group of similar lower-class popular ballads.

Polly concurrently employs a prototypical pattern from "high" art: the Herculean dilemma that is played out in the Antony and Cleopatra story of John Dryden's *All For Love*, whose tragic pair Gay parodically relocates in

Jamaica as the pirate Macheath and the strumpet Jenny Diver. The satire of
Gay's *Polly* extends beyond *All For Love*, its immediate reference, and
works to question the basis for Dryden's tragedy, which summoned—besides Antony and Cleopatra and any number of seventeenth-century protagonists—such renowned biblical and classical pairings as Samson and
Delilah, Paris and Helen, Odysseus and Circe, and Aeneas and Dido.[31]
Polly's romance quest, juxtaposed to Macheath's Herculean dilemma, exposes the seams, so to speak, of those categories which costume the two
interlocking sides of European heroism: male and female, Mars and Venus.
In *Polly* Gay both unmasks the political "heroes" around him—the most
conspicuous being Walpole—and indicts the Western heroic blazon of love
and glory in the mock pastoral context of the colonial West Indies. Indeed,
he poses the problem with the heroic that has dogged European-derived
literature since Milton's *Paradise Lost:* the inability of the post-Renais-
sance sensibility to imagine itself as epic.

From the outset, the "Second Part of *The Beggar's Opera*" achieved
notoriety, though not box-office success. Walpole suppressed the play, and
it remained unstaged for half a century. Since then, it has been more per-
plexing than controversial. With a few exceptions, literary critics pass over
it.[32] Gender politics lie at its core. *Polly* is a strenuous satire that exposes
the European heroic ideal as an ethos of slavery: an enslaving masculinist
ideology in the private sphere and an enslaving will to empire in the public
arena, which encode and construct each other. This ideal—whether for men
or women, for Antonys or Cleopatras—conquers and owns. Conquest of
the "other" is in the private sphere a matter of gender, and, in the public
realm of empire, of race. Disguisings of the two are pivotal in the play:
Polly disguises her gender; Macheath disguises his race. *Polly* takes up the
fortunes of the pair after the last curtain of *The Beggar's Opera*. The celebrated duo are separated by Macheath's transportation to the West Indies—
"Over the Hills and Far Away" indeed. Polly arrives in the New World in
search of her man. Hers is the quest of ballad and romance, a venturing
heroism made available to women by the trope of gender disguise. She is a
female warrior.

When Macheath appears in act 2, Gay continues the preoccupation
with heroism begun in *The Beggar's Opera*. With his Cleopatra, Jenny
Diver, Macheath has run off from a plantation where he was indentured,
and remains hiding in blackface disguise as "Morano," the "Neger" leader
of a group of pirates. Act 2 centers on Macheath and Jenny as Antony and
Cleopatra, but with a difference. Gay retells their story from the point of
view of Polly in the position of Octavia, Antony's abandoned wife. While
Polly enters act 1 as the heroine of romance, act 2 applies this conventional
paradigm to the Octavia of Dryden's well-known tragedy. How different

this story looks when seen, not with Antony at center, but rather from the perspective of an heroic and sympathetic Octavia, a venturing female warrior. (This strategy resembles Gay's decentering of Virgil's "Pollio" in "The Birth of the Squire.")

Act 3 undoes these two heroic prototypes—Polly's romance and Macheath's tragedy—as a battlefield collision exposes the delusions of the heroic expectations of both genres. Macheath and his pirate band of plundering New World "Alexanders" engage in battle with the victims of their unruly conquest: noble Indians, on whose side we find Polly disguised as a white man. Ironicaily, she is the only admirably "manly" European in the play. Macheath's disguise makes him unrecognizable to Polly, who is equally unrecognizable in her men's clothes. Unwittingly she conquers him in battle: he looks nothing like the hero for whom she has ventured. After the destruction of her hero, Polly awakens, it would seem, to the failure of the European enterprise, and leaves at play's end with her Indian allies.

THE FEMALE WARRIOR MOTIF

The female warrior sold as a "pop song" fashion from the Elizabethan era to the mid-nineteenth century and persists (albeit marginally) in Anglo-American folk song tradition to our own day. The figure suited Gay's predilection for ironic mirrorings: highwaymen/ministers, beggars/poets, low/high, private/public, females/warriors. The cross-dressing lover/fighter explicitly enacts the gendered terms of heroism, love and glory, as the play explores with a fresh urgency the idea of gender as a category and its implications for heroism in the "new world."

Gay's identification of Polly in *The Beggar's Opera* with "Black-eyed Susan" (mentioned above) hints at her disguised venturing in *Polly*. Many popular cross-dressing ballads open with just such farewells as William and Susan's, although often to have the woman follow the man in active adventuring. Female warrior ballads are typically success stories. Their cross-dressing heroine, a model of beauty and pluck, proves herself deserving in romance, able in war, and rewarded in both. A centuries-long cliché in British commercial songs, the motif governs more than 120 separate ballads which circulated on cheap song sheets among the lower classes in the early modern era. The first such ballad in Anglo-American tradition is *Mary Ambree*, which flourished as a "hit" from about 1600 and remained popular into the nineteenth century. Folk song versions of ballads from the eighteenth and nineteenth centuries—*Jack Monroe*, *Polly Oliver*, or *The Handsome Cabinboy*, to name a few titles—are being sung somewhere in the English-speaking world to this day.

The female warrior motif subverts the European heroic ideal of male glory rewarded by female love. Although based upon this icon, the motif confounds the opposition between male glory and female love, for the heroine plays out both terms herself. "When Mars and Venus *conjunct* were, / 'tis thought that she was born"—so one ballad describes its heroine.[33] She represents an encompassing, hermaphroditic Venus and Mars, simultaneously loving and warring. Female warrior stories present the familiar terms of epic and romance transposed and conflated: the loving heroine; the venturing hero in arms; the battlefield setting; the glory-and-love-rewarded ending.

Not only do the idealized categories of "woman" and "man" represented by Venus and Mars articulate conventions of gender attribution (what "men" and "women" are supposed to be like) but cross-gender reciprocity as well—that is, the relationship women and men supposedly have to each other. Men conquer empires to woo, win, and maintain women, who have conquered male hearts. However, the female warrior subverts this construct. One ballad heroine explicitly identifies the two aspects of the Venus/Mars conjunction:

> Come all you young virgins attend to my song,
> See how boldly I ventur'd my life for a man,
> I took up arms and a soldier did become.[34]

The song's second line, "I ventur'd my life *for* a man" (italics added) is a pun: the female warrior ventures *on behalf* of a man, and *as* a man. Such wordplay captures the oxymoronic motif's inherent irony. Dissembler that the "female warrior" is, she unfixes the coded conventions of gender. After all, she cannot be a man—or can she? Dressed as a man, she plays the hero; playing the hero, she is taken for a man. Masculine and feminine identity and heroism, private and public, mutually construct each other; this trickster commandeers both. Thus, she also undermines the idealized reciprocity of women and men: who wins wars and who wins hearts. Not coincidentally, she flourished during the early modern era, when gender roles were in the process of redefinition.

However provocative the ballad female warrior's exploitation of the heroic ideal, it is in the main naively so. Whatever satire one finds in ballads is equivocal, ambiguous, localized, intermittent. Fanciers of female warrior ballads were lower-class song makers and their audiences, who either did not hold up for scrutiny the motif's deconstruction of gender and heroism, or, if they did, left us no record of their thoughts on the matter.[35] Yet the female warrior's implied critique of the heroic did not go unnoticed, as John Gay's *Polly* attests. Unlike the heroines of the ballads, the *Polly* that makes use of them is deeply self-aware and satirical.

Key to Gay's deconstructive reading of *All For Love* is his use of the female warrior motif to decenter Dryden's tragedy. The "Second Part of the Beggar's Opera" is entirely Polly Peachum's play, a feature that seems to have stymied the play's (mostly male) critics who have struggled to locate the drama's central subject where it "ought to be," with Macheath.[36] Like all female warriors, Polly is the story's center and subject, and the play renders its events from her perspective. Moreover, Gay's Octavia enters the familiar arena of European tragedy, epic, and romance not only from a margin now become center, but as a paradoxically dressed-up transformation of the heroic ideal.

Separated from Macheath, Polly goes to the Indies in search of her hero, eerily characterizing her love quest in terms that call up *Hamlet:* "I love him, and like a troubled ghost shall never be at rest till I appear to him" (I.v.45–47).[37] The play opens with the female warrior motif's customary separation of lovers, develops the characteristic tests of the heroine's love and prowess, and brings her to a final encounter and test of her hero. But *Polly* leads not to the comedic reunion of lovers that the pattern prompts us to expect, but instead—rather in the vein of *Hamlet*—to a severing revenge.

The problem of slavery permeates the play, supplying the key to the interlocking conquests of gender and race. Early on, slavery defines Polly's womanhood; by play's end it emerges as the European raison d'être whether in love or in empire. (Indeed, Gay may have already had *Polly* in mind when he penned her verse to "Over the Hills.") Polly is threatened with slavery *as a woman,* that is, with sexual assault and exploitation.[38] Here, the "toying and kissing" of *The Beggar's Opera* are revisited in a darker key. The faithful Polly, arriving penniless in the New World in search of Macheath, gets employment on a plantation. Soon she discovers that, ostensibly hired as a servant to the mistress, she is in reality a slave to the master. Barring the door, the slave-owning (and monetarily named) Ducat claims her services: "A kiss on those lips" (I.xi.33). Polly refuses. In the struggle which ensues, she and the audience awaken to her predicament: she is a slave.

> *Ducat.* I shall humble these saucy airs of yours, Mrs. *Minx.* Is this language for a servant! from a slave!
> *Polly.* Am I then betray'd and sold!
> *Ducat.* Yes, hussy, that your [*sic*] are; and as legally my property, as any woman is her husband's, who sells her self in marriage. . . . Your fortune, your happiness depends upon your compliance.
>
> (I.xi.55–64)

Protesting her "vertue and integrity," Polly stands firm despite Ducat's threat of a more obvious slavery, "work in the fields among the planters."

A crisis without interrupts them. "The whole country is in an uproar!" a servant cries, "the pyrates are all coming down upon us" (I.xii.105–6). Amidst the crisis, Polly escapes a female slavery by running into the battle-ready countryside in men's attire. A virtuous Polly will have none of her mother's "teasing and pleasing," refusing to act the slavish part of Ducat's concubine. Her resistance will in the acts to come contrast with the acquiescence of the willing slaves, Jenny and Macheath.

Act 2 opens with an ironic look at the necessary contingency on a man of a woman's heroic behavior. Her final motivation must be love. Polly observes with irony how Macheath's fate—life or death—rules her own. His death would require hers according to the conventional heroic paradigm. This prescription for female heroism, we might note, permeates literature at all levels, fitting a plethora of street ballad heroines, the suicidal "Kitty Carrot" of Gay's *What-d'Ye-Call-It*, as well as the suicidal Cleopatra. A flippant Polly summarizes the requirements:

> When Papa 'peach'd him,
> If death had reach'd him,
> I then had only sigh'd, wept, and dy'd!
>
> (II.i.4–6)

Yet the fact that he is not dead requires something more complicated than "only" to sigh, weep, and die. When her man is "far from his home, and constant bride," a virtuous woman may undertake the conventional heroism of the female warrior. With simple dying not in order, Polly will venture after Macheath, donning the necessary guise: "With the habit, I must put on the courage and resolution of a man; for I am every where surrounded with dangers" (II.i.8–9).

Slavery is key to the love between Gay's parodic Antony and Cleopatra, centerpieces of act 2. Polly's disguise as a hero—spurred by selfless love and a desire to escape virtual slavery—has its counterpart in Macheath's disguise as a slave, spurred by his and Jenny's mutual conquest of each other. "I disguis'd my self as a black," he says, "to skreen my self from women who laid claim to me whereever I went" (II.iii.34–35). Gay's critique of love as enslaving ownership derives explicitly from Dryden's tragedy, as a few excerpts show. In *All For Love* Cleopatra declares: "I'm to be a Captive: *Antony* / Has taught my mind the fortune of a Slave" (II.i.14–15).[39] Polly's journey to recover her "enslaved" Macheath/Antony becomes ironically explicit when we recall (as Gay's generation certainly did) the declaration of Octavia in *All For Love*:

> He was a *Roman*, till he lost that name
> To be a Slave in *Ægypt;* but I come
> To free him thence.

(III.i.421–23)

For Dryden this bondage of love creates a tragic tension within the (gendered) ideal of love and glory. For Gay, nobility strips away to delusion and self-interest. Dryden saw a sympathetic and tragic Antony: Mars entrapped by Venus, vanquished by his own and her all-too-human, all-too-female weakness. "We have loved each other / Into our mutual ruin," Antony tells Cleopatra elegiacally. For Gay, Macheath's "skreening" exposes an expedient and willful slavery: he is Jenny's property, thus usefully "skreened" from ownership by other women.

In his costumed burlesque of Dryden's elevated enslavement of love, Gay sees not the heroic failure of individuals that Dryden imagined. Rather, the ideology of interlocking love and glory itself fails in a literalizing age of South Sea Company slave trading and ministerial buy-offs and cover-ups. Macheath's enslavement to Jenny literalizes and extends the crucial (and beautiful) speech in *All For Love* in which Antony, believing the misreport that Cleopatra is dead, surrenders his will to fight and even to live. For Dryden, this abdication is tragedy—an emblem of the Herculean conflict. Antony cries:

> What shou'd I fight for now? My Queen is dead.
> I was but great for her; my Pow'r, my Empire,
> Were but my merchandise to buy her love;
> And conquer'd Kings, my Factors. Now she's dead,
> Let Caesar take the World. . . .
> for all the bribes of life are gone away.

(V.i.269–76)

Even in the original, the mercantile imagery tumbles problematically from "Power," and "Empire" to "Merchandise," "Factors," and finally "bribes" for love. It is a short step for Gay to take his parodic Antony from Dryden's imagined commodities to a willing slavery that exchanges literalizing claims of ownership between female love and male glory.[40]

Polly makes resonant use of Georgian song culture to identify and satirize its mock heroes. Gay pushes Dryden's imagery to a laughable debasement as his Macheath/Morano—a New World "hero" in the style of Peachum and Ducat—echoes Dryden's in lines set to a stage tune by Thomas D'Urfey:

> To deck their wives fond tradesmen cheat;
> I conquer but to make thee great.

(II.iii.23–24)[41]

Jenny replies that ". . . if my hero falls,—ah then / Thy Jenny shall ne'er know pleasure again!" (26).

Macheath accounts for his disguise as "a black" in a moment in which, again, we see a burlesque literalizing of Dryden's imagery—here, of love as slavery. "Was it not entirely for you that I disguis'd my self as a black, to skreen my self from women who laid claim to me where-ever I went?" asks Macheath, with a nod to the "claims" of Dryden's Octavia. His blackface "skreening" makes him a ridiculous image that conflates slavery in love and the burgeoning slavery in trade, governed by the banalities of profit-totting account books in the hands of the world's Peachums and Ducats.

In similar fashion, Macheath's Cleopatra, Jenny, speaks in the voice of the new Venus, a tradesman's consort, using the language of bourgeois economics and respectability:

> You have a competence in your power. Rob the crew, and steal off to *England*. Believe me, Captain, you will be rich enough to be respected by your neighbours.
>
> (II.iii.49–52)

Macheath at first resists when Lieutenant Vanderbluff, the counterpart to Dryden's Ventidius, presents the "glory" side of the Herculean dilemma. "See her not; hear her not," pleads Dryden's Roman general, "the breath of a woman has ever prov'd a contrary wind to great actions" (II.iv.45–47). Vanderbluff, Gay's burlesque of this "old true-stamped Roman" of the tragedy, spins out this message in a rollicking string of lowbrow clichés:

> For shame, Captain, what, hamper'd in the arms of a woman, when your honour and glory are all at stake! while a man is grappling with these gil-flirts, pardon the expression, Captain, he runs his reason a-ground; and there must be a woundy deal of labour to set it a-float again.
>
> (II.iv.1–5)

Caught between Mars and Venus, Morano/Macheath sings of his conflict to another popular tune by D'Urfey:

> Tho' different passions rage by turns,
>   Within my breast fermenting;
> Now blazes love, now honour burns,
>   I'm here, I'm there consenting.
> I'll each obey, so keep my oath,
>   That oath by which I won her:
> With truth and steddiness in both,
>   I'll act like a man of honour.
>
> (II.iv.55–62)

With a subverting gender play, D'Urfey's original text filters through Macheath's declaration of honor, an apt prompt for the focus in the next scene on Polly's travesty romance. D'Urfey's song, "Since all the world's turn'd upside down," sings, in the voice of an old serving maid, of the glories of "ancient Modes and former ways. . . . In good Queen *besses* Golden Days."[42] Each of its seven stanzas ends with "When I was a Dame of Honour," an ironic mirror of Macheath's "I'll act like a man of honour." This reference, in addition to contextualizing the play historically and conjuring D'Urfey (yet again), also continues the association of Macheath with Bolingbroke, whose political ideas included an elaborately argued nostalgia for Elizabethan era values and structures.[43]

Private and public, love and glory, conflate in this burlesque extension of Dryden's Herculean dilemma. Jenny persuades both Vanderbluff and Macheath that flight is the expedient course: "You may talk of honour, as other great men do: But when interest comes in your way, you should do as other great men do" (50–52). As for Jenny, so committed to slavery is Gay's Cleopatra, that at play's end she begs for bondage: "Send me back again with him into slavery, from whence we escap'd" (III.xiii.32). And later: "Slavery, Sir, slavery is all I ask" (III.xiii.64). This relentless craving contrasts with Polly's stalwart resistance.

However, Polly's love is itself far from clean. The play's final unmasking discloses that Polly's story (and our faith in it) remain defined and corrupted by the New World's updated paradigm of Mars and Venus, whose men must be pirates and slavers and whose women must be trulls. Gay's satire neatly fosters the ultimately false hope that the familiar ideal of love and glory will work itself out in expected and satisfying ways. We have learned to expect the deserved union of "the Brave" and "the Fair," to quote Dryden's *Alexander's Feast*, whether in tragic destruction or comedic renewal, in lofty plays about ancient Romans or humble ballads about female warriors. In overturning the happy ending of Polly's female warrior romance, Gay exposes the ultimate failure of these long-standing expectations and the heroic ideal which governs them.

Polly's problem is Macheath: he is not the hero he is supposed to be. This difficulty can be solved in two conventional ways, both of them working out of the ideal's system of gender reciprocity, the relationship of women and men vis-à-vis love and glory. First, the resolution implied in the Herculean dilemma itself: male glory should withstand the soft debilitation of female love—the conflict of Antony and Cleopatra. Tragic "ruin" occurs when glory fails to stand up and be "manly." The countervailing view presents female love as preserving, redemptive, reforming. Fallen or stumbling male glory can be restored by the power of female love. Gay's play deliberately entertains, then discards both solutions.

The Herculean conflict poses the first possibility: Macheath really *is* a hero; the problem, simply and traditionally, is his "arrant Cleopatra," and manly glory is rendered servile in the thrall of womanly love. Gay entices us with elements of the familiar portrait. Jenny is, after all, a most unattractive contrast to the sympathetic Polly, whose pluck and fidelity bolster confidence that there is something heroic in Macheath. Indeed, the Herculean dilemma works precisely because the paradigm is weighted against siren love in favor of heroic glory. It is weakness in Dryden's Antony to deny his soldier-aide Ventidius and favor the sexy Cleopatra. But Gay overturns the Herculean solution because Vanderbluff and Jenny agree: self-interest outweighs valor. In this shabby world of Walpolean Alexanders, conquests of lovers and of nations are altogether alike: an ignoble slave trade.

More complex, however, is the critique of Polly's female warrior romance and the hope for salvation of a fallen hero. Gay postulates the redemptiveness of Polly's female love, fast on the heels of her battlefield success as a male "hero." Her final plea for Macheath, stemming from womanly devotion, brings about the disclosure of her man's disguise. Captured by the boy-clad Polly, "Morano" has been led off to be punished for his crimes. But Jenny reveals Macheath's true identity, posing the one convention left that might save him, the intercession of a loving woman:

> He is no black, Sir, but under that disguise for my sake, skreen'd himself from the claims and importunities of other women. May love intercede for him?
>
> (III.xiii.43–45)

Momentarily, it does. The astonished Polly, soldier hero of the day, claims his life as reward for her warring: "*Macheath*! Is it possible? Spare him, save him, I ask no other reward" (III,xiii,46-47). But she is not in time. He has been executed. Her intercession comes too late to save the ideal which requires, if not his actual heroism, at least the hope of it.

For all her good intentions, Polly's allegiance to love as conquest and claim catches her in a falsifying web of vice. Asked to reconcile her request for Macheath's release with her admission that he was "the most profligate of mankind," Polly proposes to reform him:

> He ran into the madness of every vice. I detest his principles, tho' I am fond of his person to distraction. . . . Sure my love still might reclaim him.
>
> (III,xii,85–89)

But Polly's declaration turns deludedly upon itself. If Macheath is run into a vicious "madness," Polly's language betrays that she runs right along with him: driven to "distraction" by his "possession" of her; imagining in her "distraction" that she will "reclaim him."

This "sureness," that love "might reclaim" the antihero for whom Polly has taken the hero's role, is the last unsteady feature of the heroic paradigm to be undone. In short order, we are awakened to the conventionality, contradiction, and real viciousness of this attempt to preserve the ideal. Immediately after Polly's plea, the ignoble Jenny voices the identical claim of womanly love's hero-making power: "I have so much power over him, that I can even make him good" (III.xiii.7–8). The onlooking Indian, Pohetohee asks the obvious: then why didn't she? Jenny replies lamely that she was "too indulgent," "loth to balk his ambition," and herself possessed the "frailty of pride." The Indian ponders this acceptance of vice in Jenny's hopes and, as we realize, in Polly's as well: "With how much ease and unconcern these *Europeans* talk of vices, as if they were necessary qualifications" (III. xiii.15–16).

In Gay's analysis, they are. Polly's goals coincide with Jenny's. Her female heroism ultimately depends upon Macheath and the paradigm of love and glory from which she has yet to extricate herself. Even Polly's female warrioring must fail. For, Gay insists, these 1720s plantation pirates *are* European heroes. Before his final exit, Macheath declares, "*Alexander* the great was more successful. That's all" (III.xi.59).

Even recognizing the ambitious and sometimes ingenious sweep of the satire, one hardly finds *Polly* a conventionally satisfying play. How can it be when it deliberately thwarts, frustrates, and overturns so many cherished conventions? Moreover, Gay does not shed entirely those heroic notions that the play undermines, though he insists upon the failure of eighteenth-century Europe's conquering enterprise. Seeing Polly go off with the Indians, we project at the end an eventual relationship with the "Prince" Cawwawkee which seems not so much an alternative, as a modification of the heroic ideal that has unraveled before us. If Gay recognized the need for a point of reference altogether outside the European ethos, he could not quite imagine a voice for that perspective. It is telling that *Polly* does not depict even one non-European woman.[44]

Gay dismantles the European heroic ideal of love and glory by means of the female warrior motif of balladry. As the female warrior reveals, heroism itself is a matter of gender. Gay's story of female glory prompted by love ultimately implies not only the maleness of heroism, but an economy of conquest. Love and glory construct each other; the ideologies of both are far from clean. Even Polly's female warrior heroism must fail. Exiting into a "Third World" of hopeful, if vaguely conceived alterity, Gay's female warrior and her play attempt to flee altogether the bounds of a failed European civilization.

With the invention of ballad opera, Gay shaped his satire by means of the socially valenced expressive arts of his day, notably song cultures. *The Beggar's Opera* and *Polly* construct complex, allusive "critical instants," especially with the songs. Moments of ironic and paradoxical counterreading, these musical references place the dramatic scene within a wider, politically charged field of reference as well. In *Polly*, an interplay of sociocultural levels of reference is set into motion through the structuring of the drama as an intersection of two readily recognizable conventional paradigms: the Herculean dilemma of Dryden's tragic *All for Love* from high art, and the female warrior motif of popular balladry from low. Thus contemplating a world of two-tiered cultural expression, *Polly* critiques the ethical failure of both in a debased mock-pastoral New World of self-aggrandizing planters and pirates.

8

Country Dancing and the
Satire of Empire in *Polly*

Polly was banned before its opening night and remained unstaged for half a century.[1] Although perplexed commentators have treated Gay's satires on Walpole as a mysterious personal animus, not all historians are sanguine about the changes the ministry brought about. E. P. Thompson suggests that a purely ethical opposition to Walpole was hardly unwarranted. In his study of the privatizing of the forests in the 1720s, Thompson remarks in general:

> Someone must have benefited from Walpole's administration; although having read most of the state papers and most of the surviving newspapers for the years 1722–4, I am at a loss to know who this was, beyond the circle of Walpole's own creatures.[2]

Gay's analysis was systemic rather than personal. Indeed, as we have seen repeatedly, Walpole usually emerges in any given textual moment as one of a host of referenced figures. Nevertheless, he is frequently there, supplying in 1728 one of the most readily recognized (and undoubtedly least tolerant) of Gay's contemporary allusions. The sequel to *The Beggar's Opera* denounces the greed, dishonesty, and exploitation that drive profiteering in a pastoral New World being plundered by English planters and pirates identified with Walpole and his "creatures." It was not inexplicable that the government suppressed the play before it opened. With its damnation of Macheath and like antiheroes, *Polly* was obviously *not* simply the joke about aesthetic forms and operatic performers that literary critics have tended to imagine it. Its "deep play" entailed a strong dose of condemnation for a world whose conventions and values were being transformed by profiteering.[3] At the same time, the play summons elements of popular culture to widen the satire to what we would call a sociocultural politics of class: the

197

power dynamics evident in the pastimes of every day, especially in this case for people of the middling sort.

In addition to employing the female warrior motif from the ballad tradition of the lowest classes, the play cites forms of middlebrow entertainments throughout. The refractive mixing of well-known traditions from various social levels marks the "social" character of the satire as it brings into pointed relation both the semiotics and the power dynamics that relate people at the different levels to each other: those at the "top" who know their Dryden and Plutarch; those at the "bottom" who march off to Flanders singing their street ballads; and those in the "middle" who sing their catches and dance their country dances. At the same time, this coding of social relations in terms of such expressive, intersemiotic forms as tragedies, ballads, and dances, creates the socially resonant category of "culture" (which in fact must at center be understood as "cultures," because of the diversities of class, region, gender, and so on). The incorporation of dance tunes adds to the mock-pastoral tone of *Polly* since, for the middle and upper classes, "country dances" constituted, from the seventeenth century on, an urban and courtly *idea about* a bygone countryside. It was precisely this countryside—as Bolingbroke's opposition party continually objected—that ministry policies were transforming. But as Thompson (and Gay) demonstrate, it was not only the gentry who suffered.

Gay's ballad operas point to a political dimension infusing private life and interpersonal relations. In a newly complex and intimate social satire, a markedly modern ethical sensibility emerges: socially defined, individual, interior, and self-examining. Gay brings this about by rendering satirically directed figurative and allusive tropes—Adorno's "little ghosts"—largely drawn from customary behavior. Such tropes in *Polly* to popular dancing represent a "step up" in the social frame of reference from the ballad subtexts of *The Beggar's Opera*. Well over half of the seventy-one tunes in *Polly* refer to dances, most of them traceable to 1720s editions of John and Henry Playford's *Dancing Master*, which by 1728 had gone into its eighteenth edition.[4] These "country dance" references suggest a courtly and bourgeois pastime carried on by such dancers as could (1) afford manuals like *The English Dancing Master*, (2) read the dance instructions, and (3) attend the assembly halls where such dancing was the fashion. This context was a cut above the underclass milieu of the first play's "beggar," whose songs circulated on cheap broadsides in the streets and public markets. The figurative use of dancing makes the application of vehicle to tenor an intensely intimate and individually applied experience: the figure, as a dance, *embodies* in the act of dancing the meaning of the text, thus "bringing home" the satire in a notably personal way for members of an audience who had performed the patterned movements to the tunes with their own bodies. The play thus applies its story to its audience, invoking their pleasures with a new proximity, individuality, and intimacy. The onlookers themselves—as dancers of the patterns—become the metaleptic referents.

Dance references identify the targets of the satire, clarify its meanings, build its ironies, and establish its sociopolitical character. Popular dances function as subtexts both metonymically and metaphorically in relation to events in the play. Gay focuses his attention—and ours—on ironic correspondences among (1) a mock-heroic narrative of empire, (2) uncomplimentary allusions to Walpole and rule by profiteering, and (3) the pastimes and products of bourgeois domestic life.

The country dances in *Polly* knit together a lively and provocative image of a world of notably interpersonal political tension. The forces shaping interrelationships among people operate within a tiered social context whose dynamics encompass more than merely textual traditions. To burlesque the relationships of that world, Gay enlists its everyday patterns, especially those that are undertaken without serious examination and imagined as frivolous and innocent. *Polly* shows its audience their own pastoral-citing pastimes as a mocking mirror of heroic themes gone parodic. It implicates their everyday selves in the larger political structures of family, trade, and empire.

Gay ingeniously interrelates mimicking macro- and microworlds—political and economic empires on the one hand, and dances and other "personal" diversions on the other. These two construct—and in his parodic rendering, deconstruct—each other. The individual, as the embodied spectator, becomes the satire's target, prompted to reflect upon his or her enactment and participation in the newly forming "body politic" that is metaphorically rendered by the dance figures. The participatory sensibility evoked in *Polly* supplies an anticipatory model for this modern engagement of the individual citizen in a definition of politics that, though not yet in place with regard to political representation, foreshadows its extension well below the level of monarchs, courtiers, and ministers.

COUNTRY DANCES AS FIGURATIVE REFERENCES

Like *The Beggar's Opera*, *Polly* intersperses spoken drama with songs set to well-known popular tunes. For an eighteenth-century listener the majority of song tunes in *Polly* would have recalled familiar square, circle, and especially line dances. Kate Van Winkle Keller and Genevieve Shimer characterize these lively entertainments:

> [C]ountry dances are created from a vocabulary of often symmetrical floor
> tracks along which the dancers move with or around one another. . . . The
> weavings and turnings create a kaleidoscopic effect on the floor and the
> steps used are secondary to the figures, and vary with changing fashion. . . .
> Two distinguishing characteristics are that the country dance is a group
> dance in which there is interaction between two or more couples and it is a
> democratic dance in that the couples often change positions in the set and
> take turns leading the figures. . . . From 1650 to 1850 [country dancing]
> was a significant medium of social expression for rising bourgeois society.[5]

The songs in *Polly* resonate as polyvalent markers of the everyday cultural traditions and experience of 1720s Londoners. Air 11 provides a rich example. The tune invokes a dance, as well as a three-part catch (i.e., a round or canon at the unison for three voices).[6] Both forms—country dance and catch—represent the burgeoning of "social music" in bourgeois circles of Georgian England. The two Henry Playfords—father and son—published collections of dance music and catches, and the younger initiated tavern catch clubs early in the century.

Air 11 comes just after Polly Peachum's entrance. She arrives in the West Indies in search of Macheath, who has been condemned for some undisclosed crime and transported as forced labor. Encountering the entrepreneurial Diana Trapes, Polly is told that her wayward husband has married Jenny Diver, run off, and "turn'd pyrate." Trapes arranges for the destitute Polly to be taken into service at a nearby plantation of the Ducats. Trapes sets up the deal for the master's pleasure, and Mrs. Ducat is not deceived by his claims that the pretty servant was hired for her benefit. "I will have none of your hussies about me," she declares (l. 39); "But I bought her on purpose for you, Madam," Ducat replies (l. 42). "For your own filthy inclinations, you mean," she retorts (l. 43). He then proclaims his household rule: "I will have the directions of my family. 'Tis my pleasure it shall be so. So, Madam, be satisfy'd" (ll. 46–47). He then breaks into song to the canon and dance tune of "Christ-Church Bells": "When a woman jealous grows, / Farewell all peace of life" (ll. 48–49). His wife replies, taking up the catch tune, "But e'er man roves, he should pay what he owes. / And with her due content his wife" (ll. 50–51). The spouses bicker through the course of the tune, whose tingling bells become wittily explicit at Ducat's injunction, "Let your clack be still" (l. 57).

The canonic figure enacts the quarrel, suggesting the sexual triangle at the center of the argument. "Upon Christ Church Bells in Oxford" first appears in collections of the late seventeenth century and has been attributed to Henry Purcell.[7] It continued in print in Gay's time and after, published by the indefatigable John Walsh in his *The Second Book of the Catch Club, or Merry Companions* (1731). Most people in 1729 London, familiar with "Christ-Church Bells," could imagine the voices resonating in simultaneous opposition, as they would interrelate polyphonically in the catch. (It is likely that Gay had some canonic singing of the argument in mind—perhaps with Polly joining in for the third voice.)

Ex. 20. Three-part catch "Upon Christ Church Bells in Oxford" with Gay's text from *Polly* added[8]

The original text of the catch percolates up through Gay's scene in ironic and telling ways. Like the Ducats' quarrel, the song is about having the last word. Ducat makes plaintive claims to rule, which are noticeably overruled by Gay's text when Mrs. Ducat ignores her husband's order, "Let your clack be still." "Not till I have my will," she retorts, and carries on, "clacking" her way to the tune's ringing conclusion on its lowest note, "the mighty Tom." This musical "last word" of Mrs. Ducat pointedly reverses the usual gendering of musical range: low notes for men; high notes for women.

In "Christ-Church Bells," archaic symbols identify material facets of a social order undergoing rapid transformation in the new ministerial England. The original canon rings out with images of an old authority seen in medieval customs, labors, and hierarchies: the tolling of the changes to mark prayers at the canonical hours of the day; the customs, objects, and postures that signal ecclesiastical ranks; the work and respite of laboring people (who do not carry pocket watches). A contemporary audience or people (who do not carry pocket watches). A contemporary audience or reader would hear the irony in Mrs. Ducat's flippant retort to her husband's declaration of rule—"but sweet kind husband, not today"; she sings these lines at exactly that point in the tune where the original text describes a properly subordinate "Verger troop[ing] before ye Dean."

Lyrics and tune are not the only intertexts; "Christ- Church Bells" was also a popular dance. Thus, Gay creates a poignantly self-implicating site for the public's imaginative participation in his satire. The dance for "Christ-Church Bells" enacts the key feature of the Ducats' quarrel: at no time in the three sections does a person dance with his or her own partner. All dancers (not just lofty prime ministers) are thus prompted to recognize their behaviors as metaphorically resonant and potential targets for satire.

Playford's *Dancing Master* gives the tune and the following directions for "Christ-Church Bells in Oxon":

> The first Man Sett to the 2 Woman and turn single, then turn her with both Hands. Then the 1. Woman do the same to the 2. Man. Then the 1. Man change place with the 2. Woman, and the 1. Woman with the 2. Man, and go quite round and clap as they go, then all four Sett down and clap five or six times quickly, and all four jump up, and Right and Left half round into the 2. cu's place.[9]

A set of dancers is a line of women facing a line of men (their partners). In a duple minor, every two couples perform the figures of the dance as a foursome. A triple minor takes three couples for the figures. Here is a conjectural translation of "Christ-Church Bells" into modern directions for English country dancing.

> Duple minor longways for as many as will:
> A 1st Man and 2nd Woman set (i.e., step quickly right-left-right, then left-right-left), moving toward each other, turn single back to places, and turn each other with both hands once round (diag. 1.1).
> A´ 1st Woman and 2nd Man the same (diag. 1.2).
> B 1st M and 2nd W change places; 1st W and 2nd M change (diag. 1.3). All four clap, join hands, and circle to the left once round (diag. 1.4).
> B All face the center of their foursome and advance setting while clapping (perhaps on their own knees—i.e., "down") in rhythm with the tune. Then all four retire (four small steps back), straightening up as they go. Neighbors change places giving right hands (diag. 1.5), partners change giving left hands (diag. 1.6), neighbors change once more by the right hand to progress (diag. 1.7), ready to dance the entire pattern again with a new pair of neighbors.[10]

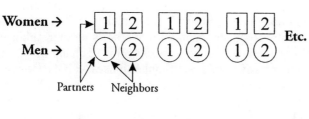

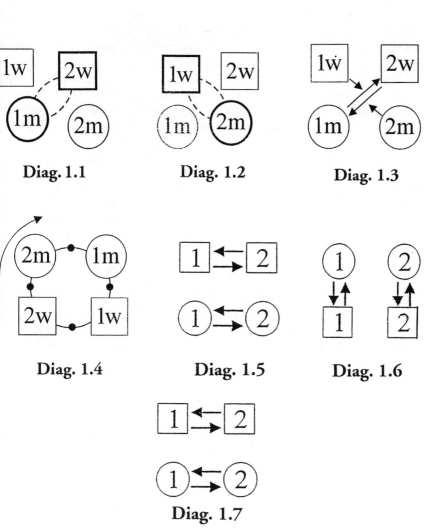

Diag. 1.1

Diag. 1.2

Diag. 1.3

Diag. 1.4

Diag. 1.5

Diag. 1.6

Diag. 1.7

Diag. 1.1–1.7. "Christ-Church Bells" country dance

The first part of the dance thus figures forth in its movements the "roving" and the implicated "jealousy" of the bickering Ducats, as the couples in the set venture to dance, each with another's partner rather than his or her own. The second part continues this notion of changing partners within each set, as the man of couple one changes places with the woman of couple two, even as the woman of couple one and the man of couple two exchange. Thus, all four carry out a rambunctious scurrying of "roving," "having [their] will," and "asserting [their] right." Still joined to their original partners, but reconfigured in the set, both couples proceed to "go quite round and clap as they go": all four vividly, tactilely embodying the "clacking" of Gay's text and the bell ringing of the original.

This hand-clapping figuring-forth of the "clacking" quarrel becomes even more "woundy" (i.e., excessive) in the third part of the dance, where "all four Sett down and clap five or six times quickly, and all four jump up" as the dance figure concludes with couple one moving into "the 2. [couple's] place" so that the dancers progress up or down the line. People dance this entire figure with everyone nearby *with the notable exception* of their partners.

Other tunes call up dances that function similarly as allusive figures. One reference explores the figurative collapse of gender and sex on the one hand and race and work on the other in the dealings of this world of "trade." In scene 11, Ducat reveals his true intentions to the resisting Polly with a declaration that identifies her as a slave: "I shall humble these saucy airs of your[s], Mrs. *Minx*. Is this language for a servant! from a slave!" (I.xi.55–56) "Am I then betray'd and sold!" exclaims Polly. "Yes, hussy, that your [*sic*] are," Ducat replies, "and as legally my property, as any woman is her husband's, who sells her self in marriage" (ll. 57–60). "Your fortune, your happiness depends upon your compliance," he declares a few lines later (ll. 63–64). Then he sings of the mercantile workings of this slavery joining to it the monied flatteries of court:

> Maids like cou[r]tiers must be woo'd,
> Most by flattery are subdu'd;
> Some capricious, coy or nice
> Out of pride protract the vice;
>   But they fall,
>   One and all,
> When we bid up to their price.
>
>   (I.xi.67–73)

The song proceeds out of the slave trade context into a familiar similitude drawn between courting and courtiers. With Gay's characteristic dispatch and surprise, the song's last line casts over all three of these relations of

compliance and subduing—"one and all"—the new language of investment and trade: "When we bid up to their price."

By means of its dance referent, "Bobbing Joan," the tune to Ducat's
mercantile rule conjures both the movement and the power dynamics in
these analogously imagined trade-identified relationships of Ducat and Polly,
purchaser and slave, husband and wife, king and courtier.[11] As with "Christ-
Church Bells," the country dance figure implicates both court and city,
catching political dynamics in ordinary pastimes. "Bobbing Joan" involves
much changing of places to the repeating of the A part of the tune, with
siding and arming movements accompanied by finger snapping, all of which
suggest the "wooing," "flattery," and "subduing" of Gay's text.[12] The B
part of the dance, which corresponds to Ducat's lines "But they fall, / One
and all, / When we bid up to their price," brings about the "tumbling" of the
top couple in the set to the very bottom of the line. Casting over Ducat's
abusive threat to the innocent Polly the systematic shiftings of the dance,
Gay overlays the "slavery" of plantation trade onto the "gender" politics of
private relations, politicizing each category by the other in the context of
the domestic pastimes of 1720s London.

Coming immediately after this allusive dance-song, Ducat's next remarks suggest the tensions and pulls of gender-based courting that underlie the patterns of country dancing. "Besides, hussy, your consent may make
me your slave; there's power to tempt you into the bargain" (I.xi.74–75).
Gay moves the concept of "power" to the fore as Ducat calls attention to its
complex dynamics. While the potential for power may at times appear paradoxically reciprocal in an otherwise unequal sexual relationship, Gay quickly
reveals the self-serving deceptiveness of this offer; instead, Ducat intends
an unequivocal slavery for Polly based on his own unbridled sway. "Sure
you only mean to try me!" Polly says, "but 'tis barbarous to trifle with my
distress" (I.xi.77–78). To this Ducat declares the stark literalness of her
slavery and the market-driven absoluteness of his ownership:

> I'll have none of these airs. 'Tis impertinent in a servant, to have scruples
> of any kind. I hire honour, conscience and all, for I will not be serv'd by
> halves. And so, to be plain with you, you obstinate slut, you shall either
> contribute to my pleasure or my profit; and if you refuse play in the bed-
> chamber, you shall go work in the fields among the planters. I hope now I
> have explain'd my self.
>
> (I.xi.79–85)

The title of Ducat's previous tune, "Bobbing Joan," hints at the force
Ducat implies, for the term "bobbing" is commonplace in children's games
of slapping, hitting, and stamping which the targeted child "bobs" or dodges
to avoid.[13] (Early in the twentieth century Cecil Sharp collected "Bobby

and Joan," a tune for a traditional "stick dance.")[14] Polly responds to Ducat's threat with a firm declaration:

> My freedom may be lost, but you cannot rob me of my vertue and integrity: and whatever is my lot, having that, I shall have the comfort of hope, and find pleasure in reflection.
>
> (I.xi.86–89)

Lest we slip too easily into an unreflective belief in Polly's heroism and virtue, Gay uses another tune reference to contextualize the song that follows these remarks, in which she reminds us of the romance that has prompted her quest. Gay's purpose is to undo romantic as well as epic heroism. Polly sings:

> Can I or toil or hunger fear?
> For love's a pain that's more severe.
> The slave, with vertue in his breast,
> Can wake in peace, and sweetly rest.
>
> (I.xi.90–93)

Polly's tune, "A Swain long tortur'd with Disdain," carries words that undercut her romantic pretensions, foreshadowing the play's exposure of her delusion in act 3. The corresponding lines of the tune's original text are:

> A swain, long tortur'd with disdain,
> That daily sigh'd, but sigh'd in vain,
> At length the god of wine addrest,
> The refuge of a wounded breast.[15]

This subtext moves through Polly's text with satiric effect as her consoling "vertue" calls to mind the "god of wine" of her tune's original words. The parodic echoing calls to mind the imprisoned and mock-reflective Macheath who drinks up his bottled "courage" in Newgate at the end of *The Beggar's Opera*. Threatened in a situation signified by the familiar "Bobbing Joan," Polly responds with reference to a romantic "refuge" that the play will eventually undo. The song reminds us that both her predicament and her response are socioculturally determined.

Dance references in *Polly* code characters along lines of social rank, using the dances as markers to explore the dancers' mutual—but unequal—exploitations. For example, in scene 2 of act 2, a ragtag band of pirates arrives on stage in search of "either booty or intelligence." Polly lies sleeping nearby, disguised in boy's clothes, the better to seek her husband Macheath. The pirates, finding her, take her for "booty" to their leader—

who happens to be Macheath, disguised in blackface as "Morano." As we know, this "Antony" has run away with Jenny Diver, his "Cleopatra": Gay cites heroic "high" literature in this evocation of the Antony and Cleopatra story. He links the pirate gang to traditions of the rural underclass, yet simultaneously loops them up to bourgeois midlevel, with dual dance references.

The pirates enter the play (II.ii) as subversive servants. "Morano," soon to be revealed as Macheath, demands booty. However, when they get it, his pirate underlings agree to "lye" to their own advantage as "every common servant." "[N]o man ever speaks what he thinks, but what is convenient," declares Laguerre (ll. 12–13), after which Cutlace sings, to the tune "Three Sheep-skins":

> Of all the sins that are money-supplying;
> Consider the world, 'tis past all denying,
> >   With all sorts,
> >   In towns or courts,
> The richest sin is lying.
>
> > (II.ii.14–18)[16]

Ex. 21. "Air 24" from *Polly*

The song employs a familiar burlesque reversal for its mock "moral": extolling the "virtue" of greedy expediency. The melody, "Three Sheep-skins," is a rustic tune such as accompanied the ceremonial stick, handkerchief, and sword dances performed as part of seasonal customs in rural areas. This tune at once connotes two dances: the more plebeian and probably earlier folk dance and an English country dance from the middle ranks.

Most immediately, Gay's audience would have recognized an allusion to the country dance, made popular in *Playford's Dancing Master*. There, "The Three Sheep-skins" consists of an opening figure that brings two people in a couple to set—that is to confront in a face-to-face step—a single person, first the man of another couple, then the woman. The directions for the dance are as follows:

> The first Couple take Hands and sett twice to the second Man, and then go the Hey till they come into their own Places again. *The Tune throw twice.* The first Couple do the same to the second Woman, then all four Hands a-breast, go the Figure thorow in the second Couple's Place, the same as before.[17]

In contemporary dance terms: Couple One join hands and set to the Second Man (diag. 2.1), then those three dance a winding hey, coming back to their own places (diag. 2.2). Couple One then do the same with the Second Woman. All four join hands abreast with Couple One in the middle, and dance forward and back (diag. 2.3). Couple One dance a figure eight around the standing Couple Two, who step up at the last moment so that all end in progressed places (diag. 2.4).[18]

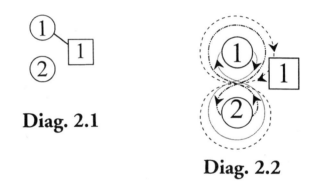

Diag. 2.1

Diag. 2.2

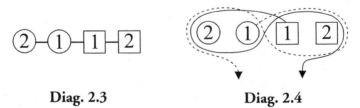

Diag. 2.3   **Diag. 2.4**

Diag. 2.1–2.4. "The Three Sheep-skins" country dance

The movement in the dance of one person being accosted by others—"The first Couple take Hands and sett twice to the second Man"—is about to be enacted in the play, as the pirates come upon the sleeping Polly and take her as "booty." The connotations of the dance thus mimic the play, and vice versa. The play reads into the dance the dynamics of conquest and the habits of empire, which are directed back to the drawing rooms where the audience have enacted these motions themselves.

The tune also would have brought to mind a "Three Sheepskins" morris that renders an even more pointed side to the satire that the scene suggests. Morris dances are traditional English versions of older ritualized dances, widespread throughout Europe, performed as customs in connection with specific seasons and feasts—Twelfth Night, Plough Monday, Whitsunday, May Day, and so on. These dances entail various longways and circling formations; employ combinations of steps, leaps, and kicks; and often include sticks, swords, and handkerchiefs.[19] Thus, the morris association of the telltale "Sheepskins" tune identifies these pirate "servants" with the rural underclass, linking them to the plowboys of such earlier works by Gay as *The Shepherd's Week* and *The What-d'Ye-Call-It*. In 1838, publishing a version of "Thrie Sheips Skinns" from "a manuscript of the reign of King James VI," William Dauney links the tune to the skinning trade—certainly an apt allusion for Gay's purposes. Dauney says: "The worshipful body who lay claim to it are, as may be supposed from the name, the incorporation of 'Skinners'; and we are told that it used to be played on the bells of St Giles's Church on the day on which they had their annual procession."[20] The morris dance to the "Three Sheepskins" tune persists in Britain as a pub tradition: the dancer who loses his way and stumbles out of the confusingly intertwining hey buys drinks for the rest.

A rowdy "Three Sheepskins" morris (with associations to the skinning trade) certainly makes an apt figure for the pirates' ludicrous dreams of conquest. The European presence in the Americas becomes a Rabelaisian tavern antic by rabble morris dancers of the skinning trade. In Gay's text, social rank quickly comes to the fore along with the tune. After Cutlace sings it, the pirates discuss their "profession": "What can be more heroic," declares Hacker, "than to have declar'd war with the whole world?" (II.ii.26–27). The theme of social mobility—in both directions—is taken up as they share "career" stories that feature a shared trajectory: from servant positions; to less savory services (gaming and pimping) drawn by ambitions "of a gentleman's profession"; to outright thieving; to transportation to the Americas.

This thieving becomes a trope for European New World policy as the pirates fall into a squabble over "Mexico," "Cuba," and "Cartagena" that resembles nothing so much as the scrambling disarray of a drunken "Sheepskin Hey." After declaring that Morano's "Cleopatra" must be "hawl'd from him by force,"

Hacker proclaims: "Then—the kingdom of *Mexico* shall be mine. My lot shall be the kingdom of *Mexico*" (II.ii.93–94), whereupon the squabble begins.

> *Capstern*. Who talks of *Mexico*? [*all rise*] I'll never give it up. If you out-
> live me, brother, and I dye without heirs, I'll leave it to you for a legacy.
> I hope now your [*sic*] are satisfy'd. I have set my heart upon it, and no
> body shall dispute it with me.
> *Laguerre*. The island of *Cuba*, methinks, brother, might satisfy any reason-
> able man.
> *Culverin*. That I had allotted for you. *Mexico* shall not be parted with with-
> out my consent, captain *Morano* to be sure will choose *Peru;* that's the
> country of gold, and all your great men love gold. *Mexico* hath only
> silver, nothing but silver. Governor of *Cartagena*, brother, is a pretty
> snug employment. That I shall not dispute with you.
> *Captstern*. Death, Sir,—I shall not part with *Mexico* so easily.
> *Hacker*. Nor I.
> *Culverin*. Nor I.
> *Laguerre*. Nor I.
> *Culverin*. Nor I.
> *Hacker*. Draw then, and let the survivor take it.
>   [*they fight.*]
>
>   (II.ii.95–112)

In *The Morris Ring: A Handbook of Morris Dances*, Lionel Bacon gives directions for "Three Jolly Black Sheepskins," a morris collected in Herefordshire early in the twentieth century. He characterizes the "various tunes" for this and other dances as performed on fiddle or melodeon—not sung—with the possible addition of triangle and tambourine.

> Three dancers. Place hats in row 4–5 ft apart. Start standing in file (see fig),
> and all, led at first by No.1, dance a straight hey between the hats. At X, the
> last dancer (No.3), instead of following No.2, turns l[ef]t round the middle
> hat and so becomes the leader. At Y, on the return journey, the new tail man
> (No.2) turns l[ef]t round the middle hat, and so becomes the leader. At X
> No.1 takes the lead, and so on. "Dance continues until someone makes an
> error in casting off."[21]

Bacon diagrams this simple, rambunctious hey as follows:

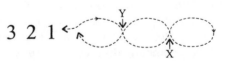

Diag. 3. "Three Jolly Black Sheepskins" morris dance

This traditional tavern morris dance enacts, in miniature, the conquering claims to Mexico, Cuba, Peru, and so on in the Americas by Europeans. Three dancers drunkenly circle a line of hats to a rowdy morris tune, competing for leadership of the line until one of them, losing track of the dizzying shifts of direction, collides into the others. For this interruption of the game, he is allotted the charge of buying the round of drinks before the next dance. Conquest of the Americas is, by analogy, a drunkenly competitive and reeling morris dance—neither a heroic nor an ethical endeavor.

The burlesque center of *Polly* comes in act 2 as the disguised Polly and Macheath enact the intersection of the play's two readily recognizable narrative templates: the ballad and romance pattern of the female warrior (the cross-dressing Polly), and the Herculean dilemma from Dryden's *All for Love* of the hero caught between the demands of love and glory (the blackfaced Macheath/Morano). The recognizability of the interlocking features—Dryden's play, the classical story, the ballad motif, the dance figures, and the song subtexts—constitutes the grounding principle for the satire, which resides in this familiarity. We are all too thoroughly implicated to leave the satire pure and simple—it must be applied to ourselves.

The next scene (II.iv) brings the disguised Polly onto the stage, with the burlesque collision of the two heroic topoi, Polly's female warrior romance and Macheath's Herculean dilemma. The disguise indulges Gay's frequent preoccupation with gender reversals and homoerotic innuendo. Underscoring the pastoral context for Polly's quest, *The Dancing Master* supplies a tune and dance that render her predicament, in a burlesque light, as a squirrel hunt. The dynamic of "squirrel hunting" enacted in the dance aptly represents the situation of Polly herself, first as slave and sexual prey to Ducat, then as "booty" to the underling pirates, and—as becomes apparent—as an enticing sexual captive to Jenny who finds her "a mighty pretty man."

Bringing the masquerading and unknown Polly before the disguised and unrecognized Macheath, Hacker says: "We found him upon the road. He is a stranger it seems in these parts. And as our heroes generally set out, extravagance, gaming and debauchery have qualify'd him for a brave man." "What are you, friend?" Macheath/Morano asks. With an ironic characterization that fits Gay's depiction of the debased conquest of this New World "pastoral," Polly replies: "A young fellow, who hath been robb'd by the world; and I came on purpose to join you, to rob the world by way of retaliation. An open war with the whole world is brave and honourable. I hate the clandestine pilfering war that is practis'd among friends and neighbours in civil societies. I would serve, Sir" (II.v.18–23). Polly voices the equivalency between the "pilfering" dynamics of bourgeois "friends and neighbours" and the profit-driven expansions of such "civil societies."

Gay's enlistment of the dance tune "Hunt the Squirrel" brings the point home.

"The world is always jarring," Polly sings. Her words continue the theme of conflict in everyday life.

> The world is always jarring;
>   This is pursuing
>   T'other man's ruin,
> Friends with friends are warring,
>   In a false cowardly way.
> Spurr'd on by emulations,
>   Tongues are engaging,
>   Calumny, raging,
> Murthers reputations,
>   Envy keeps up the fray.
> Thus, with burning hate,
> Each, returning hate,
> Wounds and robs his friends.
>   In civil life,
>   Even man and wife
> Squabble for selfish ends.
>
> (II.v.24–39)

At the cadence, Jenny voices as an aside her sudden libidinous (and unfaithful) interest in this "mighty pretty man." The dance figure conjured by the tune "Hunt the Squirrel" is all about venturing, especially across gender borders. The dance in Playford goes as follows:

> The first Man Heys on the We. side, and the 1. Wo. on the Men's side at the same time. Then 1. Man Heys on the Men's side, and the Wo. on the We. side, till they come into their own Places. Then 1. cu. cross over and turn. Then the 2. cu. do the same.
> The 1. Man goes the Figure of 8 on the Men's side, his Partner follows him at the same time; then she slips into her own Place. Then 1. Wo. cast off on the outside of the 3. Wo. and half Figures with the 3. and 2. We. her Partner follows her at the same time; then the Man slips into his own Place. The 1. cu. being at the top, the 1. Man then goes over with the 2. Wo. and the 2. Wo. with the 2. Man, then all four Hands half round, then the 1. cu. being at the top, cast off. Then Right and Left quite round, and turn your Partner.[22]

The dance reconstructed is as follows:

Triple Minor longways, for as many as will:
A Crossover heys: Couple One cross to dance a hey with the 2 persons on the opposite side (diag. 4.1).

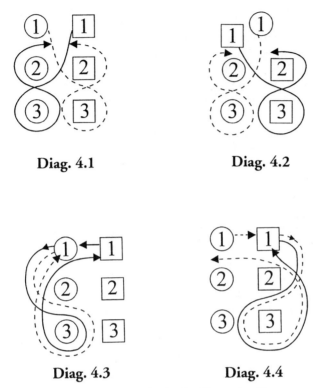

Diag. 4.1   **Diag. 4.2**

Diag. 4.3   **Diag. 4.4**

Diags. 4.1–4.4. "Hunt the Squirrel" country dance

A Hey on one's own side: As Couple One finish the heys on the opposite sides, they coss to their own sides to begin the second hey. Couples Two and Three continue dancing the hey without crossing (diag. 4.2).

B Couple One cross and cast (i.e., dance down the outside of the line) one place as the dancers of Couple Two dance up into first place. Couple One turn each other with both hands once-and-a-half to their own sides.

B Couple Two (now in the place of Couple One) do the same.

A The First Man casts down into a figure eight around the standing Second and Third Men, the First Woman following (diag. 4.3). As he finishes his figure eight, his partner scoots across to her own place and

A The First Woman leads a figure eight around the standing Second and Third Women, the First Man following until both arrive at their own places (diag. 4.4).

B First diagonals change places; second diagonals change; taking hands, the four dancers circle halfway round.

B Couple One casts off one place; Couples Two and One dance four changes of Right and Left.[23]

An unusually active and transgressive dance, "Hunt the Squirrel" requires the dancers to crisscross from side to side in the set. The figure opens with the lead couple crossing to opposite sides of the set to begin weaving hey figures down each line. The woman of couple one moves to the men's side of the set and weaves down the line—an echo of Polly's disguise. At the same time, her partner crosses to the opposite line of the set and weaves in a hey down the women's line. With the repeat of the tune's A strain, the two interlopers cross back to their original sides and start the hey again, the woman down the women's line, the man down the men's. With the B strain of the tune, first and second couples switch places amidst some dizzying turns—their own and those of the other dancers.

As the directions to the tune note, each of the two strains "must be play'd twice over to each Part of the Dance." With the return of the A strain of the tune comes a chasing figure that is as pointedly significant to the play's meaning as the opening cross-gendered heying. The second half of dance begins with an agitated movement wherein the man of the lead couple begins a "Figure of 8" down "the Men's side," while his partner crosses from the women's line to follow him in hot pursuit. With the repeat of the tune's A strain, this "Figure of 8" pattern is reversed, the man of couple one crossing over to chase his partner down the women's line. With the return of the B strain of the tune, the couples switch partners in the final disarranging figures. This dance graphically embodies the "jarring" that is explicit in Polly's text, implicit to her situation in the play, and everywhere enacted in the political and—more to the point—the bourgeois social "world" which the players disclose for critique.

Dance references supply provocative tropes for the play's social and political tension. Gay enlists everyday patterns to implicate familiar contexts. Thus he interrogates the informal and the unstudied, and through pointed references to social rank, he politicizes for the audience their usually unpoliticized distractions. The intimate and private become public and political even as they are defined in a dialectic relation. Moreover, an awareness of the allusiveness and interpretive significance of song and dance references reveals the extent to which the text of the play forms only one of a number of dimensions of performance. Gay has created a pan-sensory interplay of media; reverberating points and levels of reference simultaneously implicate each other. Catching the audience "in the act" of engaging in usually unnoticed and unpoliticized leisure, the satire takes on a probing intimacy that implicates the intimate and private in the public and political.

Gay's is an incipiently modern "take" on values, manners, and relationships as his works provoke not only laughter and irony, but introspection and self-scrutiny as well. In *Polly*, as elsewhere, the expressive forms of different social levels echo and burlesque each other—morris tunes and epic dramas, Handelian opera and bawdy ballads, archaic popular canons and country dancing. Social stratification is a self-referencing identification based on cultural forms of a shared nature. This is a world of individual agents who are inextricably linked. In the "introduction" to *Polly*, the "Player" warns the "Poet" of the intimacy of this satiric implication: "Though your Satyr, Sir, is on vices in general, it must and will give offence; every vicious man thinks you particular, for conscience will make self-application." (ll. 58–60) "Self-application" applies to all of us, not just princes and prime ministers. Thus we dance our empire's values, and vice versa.

9

Sexuality, the Middling Sort, and the Invention of "Camp": Achilles in Petticoats

Achilles plays upon the cultural valence of rank—decorum, manners, sensibility, and preoccupations—among the middling and upper classes. The songs especially, both texts and tunes, evoke this social context. Here Gay did not create the low burlesque of *The Beggar's Opera*, but moved up to target the playgoing community to which the work was directed. With pointed reference to the new genre he had himself invented, Gay took up and reused tunes from the spate of imitative ballad operas that filled the London stages in the four years between *The Beggar's Opera* of 1728 and the creation of *Achilles* in 1732. Thus, he drew the noose of the satire, as it were, tighter and tighter around his audience. At the same time, this self-awareness underscores even as it revels in the market dynamics that catch up and turn to a profit even a critique of political (or market) corruption, in the consumer society emerging around him.

Achilles takes up lofty subject matter: Greek heroes and the Trojan War. However, the play burlesques its epic subject in a notably domesticating fashion: it dramatizes a story in which the goddess Thetis hides her hero son from involvement in the Greeks' war on Troy by dressing him as a girl and sequestering him in Scyros at the court of Lycomedes. The "prologue" confesses, "His Scene now shews the Heroes of old Greece; / But how? 'tis monstrous! In a Comic Piece" (ll. 15–16). A 1733 review of the play, published as *Achilles Dissected: Being a Compleat Key of the Political Characters In that New Ballad Opera*, summarizes the plot from Statius:

> "ACHILLES was the Son of PELEUS, by THETIS, Goddess of the Sea; who, being told by an ORACLE, that if the Youth went to the *Trojan* War, he would acquire great Glory, but lose his Life. His Mother, for his Preservation,

carries him, drest as a Virgin, and in that Garb secretes him, at twelve Years old, in the Court of Lʏᴄᴏᴍᴇᴅᴇs, King of *Scyros*. He took upon him the Name of Pʏʀʀʜᴀ; became enamoured with the beautiful Dᴇɪᴅᴀᴍɪᴀ by whom he had a Son, named Pʏʀʀʜᴜs. The Hero being missed, and Uʟʏssᴇs sent in quest of him; upon his Arrival at *Scyros*, he charges Lʏᴄᴏᴍᴇᴅᴇs with se-creting Aᴄʜɪʟʟᴇs. The King utterly denies the charge, (and herein ignorant of this *Strategem* of *Thetis*;) but Uʟʏssᴇs, by another *Artifice*, of making some Presents to the Daughter of Lʏᴄᴏᴍᴇᴅᴇs, among which was a fine Set of Armour, Sword, and Buckler. Upon the Sight of these, our Hero forgets the Character he was persuaded to assume, throws off the woman, most dexterously brandishes the Sword, and poizes the Buckler." Thus, *by the Aʀᴍᴏᴜʀ, is* Aᴄʜɪʟʟᴇs *found out.*[1]

But Gay's preoccupation here—apparently his own addition to the story—is the attractiveness of the burlesque Pyrrha to the men in the play, notably the "formidable Hero General *Ajax*" (III.i.24) and the king, Lycomedes, who, with the help of his minister, attempts to seduce and then to rape "the Lady Pyrrha." Gay thus foregrounds a homoeroticism suggested by the ancient story. This topos becomes a courtship made farcical by a burlesque Achilles, whom Gay depicts with a simultaneous play of extravagance and vulnerability that calls to mind a present-day drag queen. The attractive-ness of Achilles to the "heroes" is reimagined in terms in which we see the emergence of what will be to us recognizable forms of male or female identity, gender-identified desire, and bourgeois marriage and domestic life. *Achilles* is a surprisingly up-to-date farce. The intimate, vampish banality of its gendered, sexual, and familial burlesques smacks of a situation com-edy. In its "petticoats," Gay's *Achilles* introduces into drama the interplay of gender identity, sexual orientation, and commonplace "pop" culture that are the beginnings of "camp."[2]

Aʟʟᴜsɪᴠᴇ Tᴜɴᴇs ᴀɴᴅ Sᴏᴄɪᴀʟ Mɪʟɪᴇᴜ

The tunes in *Achilles*, in contrast to those in *The Beggar's Opera* and *Polly*, show the shift in Gay's musical references to a higher social rank. Most of the tunes in *The Beggar's Opera* come from popular sung street ballads, many of them anthologized in Thomas D'Urfey's *Pills to Purge Melancholy*. The majority in *Polly* are dance tunes from John Playford's *The English Dancing Master*, redolent of everyday pastimes of the mid-dling ranks. The tunes in *Achilles* evoke the realm of concert composers, of pointedly theatrical sources, and of the newly fashionable ballad operas. Virtually all of the tunes in *Achilles* circulated at this "higher" level of song materials. Only twelve of the fifty-three tunes in *Achilles* were known in the street-level ballad milieu cited in *The Beggar's Opera*; and of these twelve, ten appear in ballad operas between 1728 and 1732, while the other two ballad tunes circulated as well in instrumental and keyboard versions. Therefore, all refer to a "polite" context of theater and instrumental performance, two arenas that increasingly marked haute-bourgeois culture in London.[3]

Throughout, *Achilles* evokes its own ballad opera identity, audience, and market. "Come Open the Door Sweet Betty" (air 22 in *Achilles*) had been heard in Ryan's *The Cobler's Opera* (1729) and Hippisley's *Flora* (1729). "Harvest Home" (air 16 in *Achilles*), a Henry Purcell tune composed originally for Dryden's *King Arthur* (1691), set songs in Gay's own *Polly* (1729), as well as in Chetwood's *Lover's Opera* (1729), Odingsells's *Raree Show* (1730), the anonymous *Jovial Crew* (1731), and Fielding's *The Mock Doctor* (1732). The ballad and dance tune "Mall Peatly" (air 18 in *Achilles*) appears in Ralph's *The Fashionable Lady* (1730), Gataker's *The Jealous Clown* (1730), Lillo's *Silvia* (1731), and the anonymous *Calista* (1731). We might enumerate many more examples.

Six of the tunes in *Achilles* come from the concert-hall gavottes, minuets, and sarabands of such well-known Italian composers in London as Corelli and Geminiani. (This compares with two unattributed minuets in *Polly* and no identified instrumental pieces in *The Beggar's Opera*.) These Italian masters and their instrumental music supplied the performance alternative for that part of fashionable London that found Handelian opera unpalatable. Gay's use of a familiar catch tune, "My Dame hath a lame tame Crane," for air 47, sung by his Grecian heroes toward the end of the play, further targets the newly emerging musical taste of middling London. To underscore this allusion to the burgeoning of men's glee and catch clubs in the city—mentioned above as a context for the "Christ-Church Bells" canon in *Polly*—the play directs that the heroes repeat the air "as before, Sung in Four Parts as a Catch" (III.x.114).

The popular dance tunes in *Achilles* have dancing-master and concert-hall connections. "Richmond Ball" (air 42) refers to a country tune and dance devised by one "Mr. Lane" in 1695.[4] Similarly, Gay used for companion airs the two parts of "The Dutch Skipper," a popular country dance tune that was choreographed for performance and by the 1740s had become a stage standard for the celebrated Madame Auretti, a dancer from a famous touring family.[5] The two parts of the tune set the argument between the king Lycomedes, enraptured by the disguised Achilles, and the jealous queen, Theaspe, who declares of the "Lady Pyrrha": "The Men, it seems, think the aukward Creature handsome" (I.vi.17–18). Deflecting her focus from his attraction to the "aukward Creature," Lycomedes responds with a song set to the "First Part" of "The Dutch Skipper" that attacks woman's censorious "Pride": "By her Envy she does herself alone expose" (I.vi.27). To the tune's "Second Part," Theaspe responds with an attack of her own: "'Tis strange that all Husbands should prove so blind, / That a Wife's real Merits they ne'er can find" (I.vi.41–42).

A few lines later—lest the play's allusions to marks of polite taste escape notice—Theaspe owns her fixation on social level: "[G]ive me leave to tell you, Sir, that was I of a lower Rank it wou'd keep you in some Awe, because you wou'd then know I cou'd take my Revenge" (I.vi.51–54). She refers here to the increasingly codified restrictions of decorum to which higher rank subjected people, especially women. "You forget your duty, Child," Lycomedes patronizingly retorts. Thus the use of songs to cite familiar elements of a "polite" haute bourgeoisie of 1730s London is made explicit. As we shall see, the play parodies the new cult of domesticity in this familial sphere.

A new social and economic mobility forced upon individual behavior a new function: that of delineating, relationally, access to or exclusion from social and political power. Gay uses taste as an indicator of social division and identity precisely because expressive forms—songs, texts, images, sartorial fashions—were accruing new representational importance. Gay's burlesque resituated the gender- and sex-charged Achilles story in the domestic sphere, presenting the newly emerging bourgeois identity as "a discursive event," to use Joan Scott's term, created out of the materials and meanings of language and cultural forms.[6] No longer born to power, people striving for power acquired commodities or imitated behaviors—as best they could—that signified their own advantageous identity in rank and power relationships.

Gay's portrait of Ulysses draws attention to this new mentality toward the material world: rather than sacramental links to an immaterial divine, objects were trade commodities in a secular world of market consumption.[7] As the play's "prologue" declares, "mighty Chiefs must speak but common Sense" (l. 18). For a world of stock bubbles and colonial trade, "common Sense" is the sense of profit and purchase. The crafty Ulysses arrives *selling* ladies' clothes, and Achilles is seduced by consumer products he cannot ignore: a sword and shield. Gay continues the critique—already begun by Dryden—of the new order as a necessarily corrupting ethos whose naive and whining "heroes" buy their kingdoms rather than conquer them. In the England of pedestrian Georges, kings have diminished to business-minded squires from Hanover who turn over their affairs to such stock-jobbing ministers as Walpole.

Contemporary audiences assumed the presence of political satire in the play. "Mr. Burnet's" *Achilles Dissected* draws a parallel between kings and prime ministers in Scyros and in London: "LYCOMEDES has a staunch

Prime Minister [Diphillis], who makes every Thing *possible* for his *Monarch* to attain, either Love by Force or Taxes by Excise" (3).[8] "Burnet" continues this parallel (between Lycomedes and George II, Diphilis and Walpole), quoting the views of "a North-British-Seer" with regard to air 21, in which "Pyrrha" calls Lycomedes' conniving minister "the greater knave":

> Can any Thing be plainer, than the *song* of the Lion and the Ass? is it not directly applied to a Monarch engrossed by his Prime Minister? Does he not even tell his Master, that sometimes *Plots* are necessary? (13)

The play, like *The Beggar's Opera* and *Polly*, refers to the considerable intrigues and machinations of Walpole's domination of the country. At the same time, it is the bigger picture, the "deep play," that Gay really has on his mind. *Achilles* turns our attention—as would donning petticoats—from the public world of empire to the private, feminized, domestic household.

Domesticity, Intimacy, Family, and "Camp"

Into the "Matter of Troy" Gay brings comically jarring expressions of the intimacies and concerns of private life. The play opens with the much-discussed topic of Achilles' "Honor." However, the speeches of the hero and his mother lurch risibly between the high, public language of heroic discourse, and the diminutive addresses, conventional sentiments, redundancies, and clichéd expressions of familiar domestic conversation. Thetis begins the play in the voice of a fretful mother dressing her child for an outing in St. James's Park:

> Before I leave you, Child, I must insist upon your Promise, that you will never discover yourself without my Leave. Don't look upon it as capricious Fondness, or think (because 'tis a Mother's advice) that in Duty to yourself you are oblig'd not to follow it.
>
> (I.i.1–5)

Hers are the vocabulary and tone of polite conversation: the punning redundancy on the word "leave," the apostrophic "Child," the distended indirection in her commands: "must insist . . . never discover . . . don't look . . . or think . . . oblig'd not to follow."

Achilles responds with concerns of "Character" and "Honour" in exactly that heroic vein of "Duty" ("Duty to yourself") that Thetis prohibits. "But my Character! my Honour!" Achilles cries, "Wou'd you have your Son live with Infamy?" (6-7) Quickly, however, this new Modern hero,

quite like his mother, slips into the conversational clichés of just such bourgeois "young Fellows" as sat in the audience at just such a Covent Garden
ballad opera. "On the first Step of a young Fellow depends his Character
for Life.—I beg you, Goddess, to dispense with your Commands" (8–9).
The combination of intimacy and banality in this burlesquing conversation
requires as its point of departure the customary codes and habits of bourgeois decorum.

Thetis remains firm in her resolve to save her son. "Have you then no
Regard for my Presentiment?" she demands. "I can't bear the Thoughts of
your going, for I know that odious Siege of *Troy* wou'd be the Death of
thee" (10–12). With an hilarious yoking of the banal and the heroic, the
prose of Gay's goddesses and "Heroes of old Greece" intersperses reso-
nantly public expressions with hackneyed private conversation. "Character" becomes "a young Fellow['s] . . . Character for Life"; "the Siege of
Troy" is, with hyperbolic deflation, "odious"; and the perils of battle prompt
a warning such as one might receive for an outing without an overcoat: it
"wou'd be the Death of thee."

The play's "Prologue," with a knowing nod to controversies over language between the rival Ancients and Moderns, notes (in a humorous couplet) Achilles' modernity: "And whatsoever Criticks may suppose, / Our
Author holds, that what He spoke was Prose" (23–24). Gay's Achilles speaks
a pointedly domestic prose that places him, with notably reduced stature,
in a family of the upper-middling sort: a petulant child in relation to his
scolding mother. (One almost catches sight of Sigmund Freud's bowler on
the horizon.)[9]

The mode in Gay's *Achilles* even more accurately fits the current delineation of "camp" than a traditional definition of literary burlesque. Susan
Sontag says of "camp":

> To camp is a mode of seduction—one which employs flamboyant manner-
> isms susceptible of a double interpretation; gestures full of duplicity, with
> a witty meaning for cognoscenti and another, more impersonal for outsid-
> ers. Equally and by extension, when the word becomes a noun, when a
> person or a thing is "a camp," a duplicity is involved. Behind the "straight"
> public sense in which something can be taken, one has found a private
> zany experience of the thing.[10]

The "camp" sensibility hinges upon the boundaries between public and
private and the connected "mappings of secrecy and disclosure," to quote
Eve Sedgwick.[11] Pertinent to the redefinition of individual sensibility and
behavior we have been tracing, this distinction was part of the eighteenth-
century's reconstitution of institutions as well.[12] In recent time, the themes
of "secrecy and disclosure" are at the heart of the recent *Beggar's Operas*

by Havel and Ayckbourn. *Zebráká Opera* begins and ends with the framing of the play by mirroring scenes of domesticity: the identical kitchens of Will Peachum and Bill Lockit.

Sexually referential inversions and reversals are also integral to definitions of camp and its emergence in and ties to a parallel "queer" world of hidden and half-hidden meanings. As Jack Babuscio notes of the modern cinema, passing for straight "heighten[s] awareness and appreciation for disguise, impersonation, the projection of personality, and the distinctions to be made between instinctive and theatrical behavior."[13] Individual personalities thus submerge and emerge. As Jonathan Dollimore says, camp "renders gender a question of aesthetics."[14] "Camping" parodically juxtaposes the grandly public and powerful, with the private and banal. Today, it is the drag queen's self-consciously theatrical fixing of bra straps that proclaims what is pointedly *not* Marilyn Monroe about the performance. Further, "camp" playfully traverses the border between the naive and the deliberate, coming "to life," to quote Dollimore, "when and where the real collapses into artifice, nature into culture" (312). As we have seen, these are exactly the developing preoccupations of Gay's refinement of the burlesque way of seeing into a mode of self-awareness that casts itself back and forth in often ironic ways across a screen of mimicking cultural analogues.

Throughout *Achilles*, Gay interrogates a naively serious taste by interrupting the evocations of a revered antiquity with clichés and cultural referents that introduce the banalities of modern, middle-class life.[15] Thus, the bourgeois playgoer is encouraged to "identify with" and to laugh at a vexed Thetis, a yearning and frustrated Lycomedes, an ungainly and hormonal Pyrrha/Achilles; at the same time, both identification and laughter are critiqued in the parodic, self-reflexive prototype of camp, the elusively challenging offspring of burlesque in the modern and postmodern world.

The eighteenth century's ongoing philosophic and literary discussion of the comparative value of "the Ancients" and "the Moderns" raised the far-off "Matter of Troy" to a public concern. The reading, playgoing partisans of Gay's ballad operas drove and defined the new market for a revered antiquity.[16] In *Achilles*, the ancients and moderns coexist in a laughable and mutually undermining interrelation, as Gay renders a revered heroic tradition of antiquity in the new terms of a private, daily life of the middling sort. This vamping of the classical story makes the rhetorical move that Sue-Ellen Case recognizes as "the camp assimilation of dominant culture," which in our own time involves "identification with movie idols."[17] A revered classical heritage supplied Gay with a parallel demarcation and assimilation of a "dominant culture."

GENDER AND HOMOEROTICISM

Achilles takes up the old story, reimagining it in terms of a male/male sexual desire that becomes gendered here—as, indeed, it does in the early modern period. The homoeroticism of the classical story is rendered as humorously counterpoised "feminine" and "masculine" affectional and interpersonal modes. The lustful and preying Scyrian king, Lycomedes, is feminized along with his minister, Diphilis. By contrast, the product-peddling Greeks arrive, swaggering with an overdetermined masculinity—especially the doltish Ajax, who, like Lycomedes, is smitten by the petticoated Pyrrha. With its genderizing of sexual desire, made plain in the burlesque representations of male-male attraction, *Achilles* opens to view the sexualized person-categories of the modern world: man, woman, and homosexual.[18] This gendering, along with its setting in the private, domestic sphere of the "nuclear" family (to use our term), brings Gay's *Achilles* to propose a "modern" gendered homoeroticism in a burlesque relationship to the "ancient" heroes of epic tradition.

As Yvonne Noble shows, *Achilles* not only displays a preoccupation with the personal politics of gender relations and sexual desire; it does so against the backdrop of the sexual relations of persons in the news and at the court of George II.[19] Owing to the sensational trial of one Colonel Francis Charteris for the rape of a recently hired serving maid, London in 1729–30 was in a ferment on the subject of rape, particularly the rape of servants and underlings by masters and guardians. For Gay's audience, the Pyrrha/Lycomedes portion of the plot would have prompted thoughts of the events that culminated in a royal pardon for Charteris from the sentence of hanging.

Achilles continues the interest in the politics of gender that we have traced in other of Gay's works. Here he casts the hero in the position of the preyed-upon Everywoman, yet gives Achilles the power to respond to such preying with an effective anger. As Noble argues, Gay's addition of this extensive episode of the victimization of Pyrrha/Achilles by the concupiscent Lycomedes "invokes by inversion . . . the rape of Deidamia *by* Pyrrha in Ovid's version, where the idea of rape was added to the old tale" (205). This Ovidian addition remained popular in Gay's time both as it appeared in Ovid's *Metamorphoses*, and with more development in *Ars amatoria*, where it supplied an example of the "date-rape" recommended to the poem's addressee, an amorous but inexperienced pupil who is being advised on the strategies for sexual conquest. (The latter text was "modernized" by Henry Fielding in the 1740s.) Just before citing the Achilles-on-Scyros story, *Ars amatoria* advises:

quaecumque est Veneris subita uiolata rapina,
gaudet, et inprobitas muneris instar habet.
at quae, cum posset cogi, non tacta recessit,
ut simulet uultu gaudia, tristis erit.[20]

... Rough seduction
Delights them, the audacity of near-rape
Is a compliment—so the girl who *could* have been forced
yet somehow
Got away unscathed, may feign delight, but in fact
Feels sadly let down.[21]

Applying his instruction a few lines later to his famous example, Ovid says of Deidamia:

uiribus illa quidem uicta est (ita credere oportet),
set uoluit uinci uiribus illa tamen.

(699–700)

Her seduction must have been forceful,
but to *be* forced was what she desired.

Throughout his satire Gay displays and critiques vice as rendered in the private, relational tyrannies of individuals, one over another. The hierarchy of gender with the victimization of women by men is a familiar topos for this preoccupation. Gay's addition of the Lycomedes-Pyrrha episode to the Achilles-in-Scyros story repositions Achilles from the role of the perpetrator of such a rape to the role of the victim. Indeed, Gay removes the rape of Deidamia from the story except in oblique references that pointedly avoid any mention of roughness or force. As Noble remarks:

Gay calls up this passage [from Ovid's *Ars amatoria*] ... and by moving Achilles from agent to recipient enforces a reassessment of the advice from within the consciousness of the woman whom Ovid keeps silent until she has been subdued. The burning male consciousness of Achilles invites his fellow Fieldings, or Ovids, to recognize what it might be to suffer and be silent, while, for those of Gay's audience gendered female, the concealed power replots Ovid's tale so that the would-be rapist becomes the booby object of ridicule. (207)

This reading is altogether persuasive with regard to the play and typical of Gay's exploration of gender roles elsewhere in his work. We may additionally note that the sexual politics in *Achilles* are consistently wrapped up in a display of homoerotic desire.

"Mr. Burnet," for one, directs his readers to the play's homoeroticism, especially with reference to persons and events at court, and perhaps with reference to Gay himself. Ostensibly quoting his *"North-British-Seer,"* Burnet poses the question: "Is not the *Duel* fought between that Hero AJAX and a *Great* LORD, a plain Representation of what lately happened between a *Little* LORD and a *Great* COMMONER?"[22] The reference is to a duel fought in 1731 between William Pulteney and John, Lord Hervey, Walpole's vice chamberlain, over the former's suggesting in print the sexual character of the homosexual Hervey's passion for one Stephen Fox.[23] It seems likely that more than a few audience members would have laughed with this referent in mind at such lines of the play as the following by Periphas: "Our Duel, *Ajax*, had made a much better Figure if there had been a Woman in the Case" (III.xii.33–34). Whether the "dissection" of Burnet and his "Seer" accurately reads authorial intention, there is no doubt that *Achilles* heightens a preoccupation with homoeroticism that characterized Gay's era and appears repeatedly throughout his work.[24]

As David Nokes suggests, this theme seems linked to Gay's own life and his ongoing association with men we today would identify as homosexual or bisexual.[25] Burnet's "Key" repeatedly brings up the topic through innuendo, insinuating, for example, that the rapacious Lycomedes knew full well the *"Sex of* ACHILLES" (12). Coy remarks at the outset of the "Key" might be taken to refer to either common or personal knowledge of Gay's own ambisexual and ambigendered turn of mind, identifying the bisexual eroticism in the works cited with the person of their author. Describing the play of sexual desire in *Achilles,* Burnet refers to "Damon and Cupid," a song by Gay (from 1720) in which Cupid speaks. The emphases of Burnet's sentence, however, conflate "Cupid" with "Mr. GAY" as it simultaneously conflates the bisexuality in the song with that in *Achilles:*

CUPID begins his Rendezvous; and, as Mr. GAY, upon *another* Occasion, makes him justly boast,
> At *Court* I never fail,
> To scatter round my *Arrows*;
> *Men* fall as thick as *Hail*,
> And *Maidens* love like *Sparrows*.

So *here* no less than *Three* are wounded: our young Hero burns for his DEIDAMIA, and she sighs for her ACHILLES: Struck likewise is LYCOMEDES for his PHYRRHA.

(2–3)

In well-known earlier poems, Gay had explicitly identified himself with such descriptions as the song gives to this "Cupid" who has left the countryside for the court. The most notable of these self-characterizations occurs in the "prologue" of *The Shepherd's Week*, Gay's popular and influential mock pastoral of 1714.[26] By 1730 with the success of the ballad operas of his "beggar" poet, such personae were something of a trademark. Certainly readers in 1733 would have brought such self-descriptions of Gay readily to mind.

In any case, Burnet calls attention to the play's depiction of rampant sexual desire that is busily *both* homoerotic and heteroerotic (in our terms). The prominence of Gay's addition to the story—the various assaults on and competitions for Pyrrha—suggests that a new feminizing of "homoerotic" passion commanded his interest.[27] In both arenas of sexual desire Gay reframes the story in terms of a gendering that feminizes contexts and key characters and, with regard to actions, accentuates the woman's point of view.

The division of desire into what we would term homoerotic and heteroerotic in *Achilles* follows the classical narratives, particularly the principal source for the story, the Roman Statius (c. 40–c. 96 C.E.). Yvonne Noble thoroughly sets out the sources for the story and Gay's use of them (pp.185-91), including the best translation to date of the (pseudo-)Bion fragment. Gay's drama elaborates and updates the tension built into the story between the sphere of war, fate, and classical heroism—a homoerotically charged manliness—on the one hand, and the heteroerotic home front of peace, prosperity, and women on the other. Thus, *Achilles* revisits the Herculean dilemma that faced the rakishly heterosexual Macheath. This play undertakes a consideration of homoeroticism in the terms of both bourgeois gender identity and heterosexual family structure, particularly as these are juxtaposed to the "Greek love" that threads through the classical sources for the story.

Gay, as usual, builds upon earlier texts as parodied sources and references, recasting and reformulating their content in consciously discrepant new forms that mark their transformation in the present from earlier appearances in the past. The result is a burlesquing, intertextual repartee between the cultural world that produces and receives his drama, and the values and worldview of its echoing precursors. The story of Achilles hiding in the dress of a girl appears in an array of ancient sources: Apollodorus, Pseudo-Bion, Euripides, Paulus Sileniarius, Pausanias, Philostratus the Younger, Horace, Hyginus, Ovid, Pliny, Seneca, Sidonius, and Statius. As Noble shows, Gay demonstrates familiarity with many of these.[28] The story often appears with suggestions of the homoerotic warrior traditions of Greek antiquity. Thetis drags Achilles out of his apprenticeship with the centaur Chiron where he trained alongside Patroclus. The most extended classical account by the Roman Statius emphasizes certain Bacchic rites in which Achilles is described as being beautifully, androgynously attractive— "*niveo natat ignis in ore / purpureus fulvoque nitet coma gratior auro.* (A radiant glow shimmers on his snow-white countenance, and his locks shine more comely than tawny gold)."[29] This attention in Statius to Achilles' charms seems to forecast Gay's exploration of the comely boy's cross-dressing appeal.

Gay's Achilles takes the stage like a male transvestite performer whose camp posturings of the feminine simultaneously elevate and deflate its classical referent. This Achilles signals a knowing plunge into the homoeroticism that is both disguised and revealed in drag. It at once subscribes to and pokes fun at the condemning phobias of bourgeois sex and gender taboos. The juncture of the homoerotic charge with an emerging ethos of bourgeois domestic life—a notably gendered, indeed, feminized ethos—identifies Gay's purpose. This play probes the new configuration of sexual desire as played out by a gendered, individual within the domestic context of the modern family. Gay's burlesque rewrites the homoeroticism of classical sources to accentuate the new private and gendered terms of desire as expressed in a feminized seduction. The emphasis in *Achilles* on feminization and the power of seduction marks the development in Gay from literary burlesque to the modern-seeming sensibility of camp. Sontag's definition of camp opens with the idea of seduction. Sue-Ellen Case even more pointedly identifies seduction as the point of modern camp:

> The point is not to conflict reality with another reality, but to abandon the notion of reality through roles and their seductive atmosphere and lightly [to] manipulate appearances. In other words, a strategy of appearances replaces a claim to truth.[30]

Same-sex Desire in the Achilles-in-Scyros Tradition

In the play's opening scene, Achilles arrives onstage with Thetis, who has removed him from his warrior training in the wilds of Thessaly under the tutelage of the centaur, Chiron. The opposition between Thetis and Chiron resonates with sexual topics in the classical story, for it signals gendered puberty customs and rites of passage in an ancient world possessing highly developed traditions of homoeroticism. Gay and his audience were aware of the reference. The play poses the idea as Achilles ponders himself caught in a moral predicament that was outlined for him from medieval schoolbook traditions onwards: obedience to his mother or to his heroic fate.[31] At the outset, Gay's *Achilles* renders the "Love" of Chiron, the abandoned "Preceptor," comically imagined "galloping" in a lovelorn "distress" so headlong as to lead to his "founder[ing]." Achilles demands of his mother:

Why was I stolen away from my Preceptor? Was I not as safe under the
Care of *Chiron?*—I know the Love he had for me; I feel his Concern; and
I dare swear that good Creature is now so distress'd for the Loss of me, that
he will quite founder himself with galloping from Place to Place to look
after me.

(I.i.51–56)

This laughably equine rendering of the centaur creates a fablelike contrast
of the competing spheres of Thetis and Chiron. At the same time, the burlesque directs our attention to the "distress" of love's "Loss," suggesting
the familiar context of "Greek love" between men and boys. Statius identifies his Achilles-in-training in these terms.

Gay knew and relied upon his audience's awareness of the classical
and medieval traditions of the Achilles-at-Scyros story. Those traditions
include a long-standing presentation, especially in Statius, of the two competing eroticisms. Gay satirically "updates" these in the new gendered terms
of Georgian England. Pierre Vidal-Naquet places the story in its ancient
context:

It is well known that in archaic Greek societies, as well as in other societies, dressing up as a woman . . . was a means of dramatizing the fact that a
young man had reached the age of virility and marriage. The classic example in Greek mythology is the story of Achilles on Skyros.[32]

Statius identifies Achilles as an ephebe, an adolescent boy engaged in military training under the centaur Chiron, famed tutor of heroes, in the border-
lands beyond settlement. At work in the ancient story, as Nicole Loraux
observes, is a "principle of inversion [i.e., gender reversal] that is called to
play in rites of passage in the Greek world—particularly those of passage
from childhood to adulthood."[33] This involved erotic expression and representation of what we would term sexual behavior. As scholars note, the
terms differ between the ancient world and ours. John Winkler observes,
"the homosexual as a person-category is a recent invention."[34] It is precisely the historical process of this "invention," particularly as it intersects
with the invention of the "person-category" woman, that Gay's *Achilles*
opens to view through its reimagining of the ancient story.

Statius presents Achilles' transvestism as the customary ritualized inversion that marks the hero's passage from boyhood to manhood. This is
dually marked by his desire for Deidamia and by his longing for the armor,
which allows the Greeks to recognize him and incorporate him into the
warrior ranks.[35] Both parts of this transformation of Achilles' identity are
key. In Statius, both entail a "sexual dynamic," to quote Noble. The im-
pregnation of Deidamia is, of course, literal and obvious. More remark-

ably, when Ulysses recognizes the hero and commands that the trumpet sound, as Noble says, "Achilles simply grows huge and dominant: as his womanly garments fall away, *he* (his whole body) erects":

> *illius intactae cecidere a pectore vestes,*
> *iam clipeus breviorque manu consumitur hasta,*
> *—mira fides!—Ithacumque umeris excedere visus*
> *Aetolumque ducem . . .*

In Noble's translation: "From his breast the garments fall away untouched, now the shield and puny spear are swallowed up by his hands—marvellous to believe!—his head and shoulders loom up above those of Ulysses and Diomede."[36] Noting the hero's "combat stance" a few lines later, Statius remarks: *Peleaque virgo quaeritur* (I.884)—"The daughter of Peleus is sought." Meaning, of course, that the *son* of Peleus has overtaken and eclipsed "her."

Central to the *Achilleid* of Statius is the ancient Mediterranean world's ideology of masculinity. To quote Maud Gleason, "Manliness was not a birthright. It was something that had to be won."[37] As Winkler observes, "masculinity is a duty and a hard-won achievement," premised on "the reversibility of the male person, always in peril of slipping into the servile or the feminine."[38] This ideology underpins the transformation from ephebe to hoplite in ancient culture and such myths as that of Achilles at Scyros. Statius's image of Achilles' person becoming an heroic "erection" conveys a key aspect of this change: for an individual, the passage from boyhood to manhood in the ancient world entailed sociopolitical changes as well as the shift to the active, penetrating role in sexual relations with women and boys.[39] Passages throughout the *Achilleid* pointedly orchestrate this transformation with a doubly directed eroticism—same-sex and other-sex—that probably accounts for the poem's long-lived popularity in schoolbook traditions from the Middle Ages to Gay's generation and may have suggested the story for his own exploration.

At key moments the *Achilleid* is charged with erotic descriptions—such as the one regarding Achilles' body noted by Noble—that serve to oppose the womanly sphere dominated first by Thetis and then by Deidamia on the one hand, and on the other the manly sphere of warring to which Achilles is destined as he moves from Chiron's tutelage on the frontier to full heroic status on the ships bound for Troy. Throughout, the language is elevated and serious.

Early in the story, Thetis journeys to Thessaly where with Chiron she awaits her son's return from the wilds. Arriving with two lion cubs he has snatched from their mother, the figure of Achilles rises from the highly eroticized passage about his "radiant glow" and "snow-white countenance"

already mentioned above. The radiantly desirable Achilles stands poised
between the goddess and the centaur, an opposition that carries with it connotations of gendered realms. Into the scene comes his comrade-at-arms
Patroclus, who figures importantly in Statius as well as in other accounts:
"insequitur magno iam tunc conexus amore Patroclus." Both "insequitur"
and "conexus" are potentially erotic words in this passage which, in an
understated rendering, the Loeb edition translates: "Patroclus follows him,
bound to him even then by a strong affection."[40] Statius, thus, poses in
Achilles an eroticized figure poised between two realms. As night falls and
Thetis prepares to steal her son away, Achilles beds down with Chiron in
lines which suggest an emotional intensity equal to that in Gay's burlesque
image of the "foundering" Centaur, but without the parodic deflation:

> *nox trahit in somnos, saxo conlabitur ingens*
> *Centaurus blandusque umeris se innectit Achilles,*
> *quamquam ibi fida parens, adsuetaque pectora mavult.*

Night draws them on to slumber: the huge Centaur lays him down on a
stony couch, and Achilles lovingly twines his arms about his shoulders—
though his faithful parent is there—and prefers the wonted breast.

                                                                (I.195-97)

The rape of Deidamia as portrayed by Statius brings together this schema
of oppositions. In the context of the famously nonheterosexual Bacchic
rites, Achilles appears again—this time in disguise—as an eroticized, cross-
gendered beauty whose dancing captivates the gazing crowd (Statius, I.606–
18). Then, moving apart from the group in the moonlight, the troubled hero
addresses the absent Patroclus—pictured as now in possession of Achilles'
horses and bow—even as the would-be warrior chafes in his women's spinning and Bacchic dancing, as well as in his concealed desire for Deidamia
(I.632–39). Immediately after this impassioned apostrophe to Patroclus,
Achilles rapes the unsuspecting Deidamia: *"vi potitur votis et toto pectore
veros / admovet amplexus* (he gains by force his desire, and with all his
vigour strains her in a real embrace)" (I.642–43). As her screams fill the
night, the Bacchic revelers mistake them for a signal to resume the dancing, so that this first of Achilles' proofs of "manhood" in the account is
carefully situated not only with impassioned reference to his comrade
Patroclus and the context of his earlier ephebic tutelage under Chiron but
also pointedly within the celebration of the Bacchic rites.

This opposition of erotic contexts governs Statius; certainly Gay did
not overlook it. At the same time, he altered the emphasis, not only in the
interests of a mock heroic, but, as Noble observes, in shifting attention
away from the tradition of the rape toward an exploration of Deidamia's

point of view. Gay supplies no suggestion that the sexual activity between the cross-dressed Achilles and Deidamia was other than mutually consensual.

The *Achilleid* of Statius was known in England in both Latin and English. For men, Statius's account of a young hero's coming-of-age supplied a favorite grammar school teaching text that had, over the centuries, accrued a tradition of elaborate textual glosses focused both on the language itself and, somewhat nervously, on the charged themes of the story.[41] Indeed, the *Achilleid*—undoubtedly long subject to schoolboy jests and distortions—was just the sort of classical-text-in-common-parlance that Gay favored for his satiro-comic refigurings of revered models. For women of Gay's time, not schooled in Latin—and non-Latin-reading men, too—an Englished *Achilleid* was also available in the verse translation of Robert Howard, published first in 1660 and reissued in 1696.[42] Howard's translation actually carries on in elaborate and studious annotations the long practice of professorial glossing, which Gay loved to parody. Further, the Howard version makes clear that Augustan and Georgian readers brought to the *Achilleid* expectations of such ambidextrously erotic currents as Burnet identifies and Gay exploits.

Howard's 1660 volume of poems was introduced to the public by a single commendatory poem, "To My Honored friend, Sir Robert Howard" by the young John Dryden, who would in a few years become the former's brother-in-law.[43] This ambiguously worded recommendation of Howard's poesy is the earliest of Dryden's many poems of dubious compliment. He remarks (ll. 68–70), surely with such overly "bold" passages in mind as those I have noted above:

> Your kindnesse great *Achilles* doth confesse,
> Who dress'd by *Statius* in too bold a look,
> Did ill become those Virgin's Robes he took.[44]

In addition to its ironic denigration of the poetry of both Statius and Howard, Dryden's poem suggests the paradoxical fixation the *Achilleid* held for readers of his time: it was repellent or at least worrisome, and simultaneously riveting and worthy of extensive comment. As Dryden notes, Howard's translation distances his English readers from the heatedness of the Latin.

At the same time, Howard's annotations gloss his source with commentary that delves into classical lore—place names, persons, stories, and cultural practices of the ancients—particularly as these can be juxtaposed to biblical and Christian traditions. Pointing to this weaving of "fable" and "sacred," Dryden observes

> Your curious Notes so search into that Age,
> When all was fable but the sacred Page,

> That since in that dark night we needs must stray,
> We are at least misled in pleasant way.
>
>   (83–86)

As Dryden's language directs us to suppose, Howard's comments let readers "stray" in a "pleasant way" through the "dark night" of curious and exotic pre-Christian stories, beliefs, and customs. Indeed, Howard's couplet restrains Achilles' rape of Deidamia: "She now no more his feign'd embraces found, / Whilst he by force his burning wishes crown'd" (III.269–70). At the same time, the annotations for this section examine "*Bacchus and his rites*" and "consecrated Groves" (wherein "abominable ceremonies were practised") for some ten pages of close-packed commentary on geographical locations, the origins and descriptions of curious and repellent customs, mythic and biblical parallels, and so on.[45] As Dryden's oblique "praises" attest, Howard takes up the *Achilleid* with considerable attention to the inversions at the center of the story. Moreover, the ethnographic-mindedness of his annotations, with their focus on customs and beliefs as well as texts, exemplifies the early modern antiquarianism that would, in time, become the discourse of such modern disciplines of cultural study as folklore, anthropology, and ethnomusicology. In Howard we see not only the richness of Gay's textual borrowings and allusions, but a context for his attention to cultural forms. These bespeak the importance of his burlesques in the intellectual construction of the concepts of "popular" and "polite" literature and of "culture" in general.

Same-sex Desire in Gay's Play

As Burnet notes, the play focuses our attention on same-sex attraction as "*Men* fall as thick as *Hail,/* And *Maidens* love like *Sparrows.*" The idea of a single, male-to-female inclination as the cast of desire is compromised by telling glances at homoeroticism in the ancient world, and by the attractiveness to other men as well as women of the disguised Achilles. Expressions of love, especially songs, between Deidamia and Pyrrha pose the image of female-female desire in Gay's play.[46] At the same time, the fiery attraction of both Lycomedes and Ajax for the sturdy Pyrrha—known by us to be Achilles—posits male/male desire. Both images counter and complicate an easy or seamless view of "nature" and personal desire in Gay's updating of the famously homoerotic classical story.

Even pregnant, Deidamia continues to call Achilles Pyrrha, obliged by her lover, as she says, "still to call [him] by that Name" (II.x.42–43). One result is to hone to a frivolous—indeed "campy"—extravagance the fine points that Gay's Achilles had put to his "Honour" and "Resolution" at the outset of the play. "Only imagine what must be the Consequence of a Month or two . . . ," Deidamia says. "To save my Shame (if you are a Man of Honour)," she insists of her Pyrrha, "you must then come to some Resolution" (ll. 43–46), that is, to marry her and save her from unwed disgrace. Achilles responds with a petulant redirection of the word "Resolution" to withhold his identity, his remarks seemingly made for Eve Sedgwick's "mappings of secrecy and disclosure":

'Till I deserve these Suspicions, *Deidamia*, methinks it wou'd be more becoming your Professions of Love to spare 'em.—I have taken my Resolutions; and when the time comes, you shall know 'em: till then be easy, and press me no farther.

(ll. 47–51)

Deidamia responds with a love song to her Pyrrha. As a critical instant, the song presents a woman's voice singing her love for another woman—an aspect underscored as the clichéd text of the original filters through it.[47] The original text begins: "My Time, Oh ye Muses! was happily spent, / When *Phebe* went with me wherever I went."[48] Gay's Deidamia echoes this devotion to her Pyrrha:

How happy my Days and how sweet was my Rest,
Ere Love with his Passions my Bosom distrest!
Now I languish with Sorrow, I doubt and I fear:
But Love hath me all when my Pyrrha is near.

(ll. 52–55)

This song of the lovelorn Deidamia opens to view a lesbian love scene: not the conventional boy-clad female page and a duped woman, but two lovers who appear to be women. The song thus sets before us the love of woman-identified Deidamia for woman-identified Pyrrha.

At the same time, the disguise of Achilles is hardly forgotten. Through it, however, the play emphasizes the contrasting social circumstances of the female Deidamia and the male Pyrrha/Achilles. As Noble demonstrates, the play unfolds from the sympathetic vantage of a woman: the trials of "the feminine-gendered Pyrrha, whose treatment and circumstances the audience must evaluate in terms of the smouldering male consciousness that must endure them."[49] For example, referring to queen Theaspe's determination to marry Pyrrha to Periphas, her nephew, after Lycomedes has assaulted his ward, the exasperated Achilles exclaims: "I have no sooner escap'd being ravish'd but I am immediately to be made a Wife" (ll. 67–68). The frustrated hero finds himself between the two pivotal—and very seriously imagined—possibilities for a woman's life. His burlesque quip, a combination of offhandedness and extravagance of feeling, voices their limitations. What is not a laughing matter becomes so, but with an exposure of its absurdity. Richard Dyer describes the sensibility of camp as "hold[ing] together qualities that are elsewhere felt as antithetical: theatricality and authenticity ... intensity and irony, a fierce assertion of extreme feeling with a deprecating sense of its absurdity."[50] Certainly "a deprecating sense of absurdity" is evoked by Achilles' impassioned observation.

The play considers, with similarly revealing parodic disjunctions of form and content, the obstacles to and dangers of a public disclosure of erotic feeling, the pressure to relegate it to the private sphere, the idea of Sedgwick's "mappings." Shortly after Achilles' outburst, Deidamia observes with "violent Apprehensions" that she fears discovery because her lover's "Swearing...upon certain Occasions, sounds so very masculine" (84–85) and because he "very often look[s] so agreeably impudent" upon her (89–90). Deidamia would "closet" such dynamics.

As to the swearing, Pyrrha (Achilles) reminds her that "there are Ladies who, in their Passions, can take all the Liberties of Speech" (87–88). The idea of manly "Liberties of Speech" in women is given added weight at this point in the play, occurring as it does after Achilles' spirited defense of himself against Lycomedes. To the question of gaze, he responds with a resonating question: "May not one Woman look kindly upon another without Scandal?" (ll. 93–94). The lovers' circumstances, of course, suggest not. However, like the term "Liberties of Speech" with its resonance of individual "civil" rights, Achilles' question directs itself beyond the play to the public and political arena. The first decade of the century saw a flurry of erotic rumor involving Queen Anne and her female favorites. Achilles' remark conjures this famously polemical history of erotic dynamics between women and women. An audience in the 1730s, attuned as it was to consider a background of court and party politics, would have placed Deidamia and Pyrrha in the context of such steamy roman à clef renderings of the "scandals" as *The New Atalantis* of Delarivière Manley or the bawdy attacks on Abigail Masham, the queen's favorite, in Whig opposition propaganda.[51] The allusion thus draws attention to the image of female/female desire posed by Deidamia and Pyrrha.

In like fashion, the play focuses attention on male/male desire in the new episode Gay adds to the story, the assault on the disguised Achilles by the king, Lycomedes. Gay feminizes the character of this guardian-king, especially with regard to his passion for the young Pyrrha/Achilles. Lycomedes is desperately, hysterically aflutter in his love for this "Girl" whom his sycophant minister Diphilus can only regard as a "Termagant," "Tigress," and "Spit-fire" (II.ii.2–6). Diphilus counsels—with notable resemblance to *Ars amatoria*—"To save the Appearances of Virtue, the most

easy Woman expects a little gentle Compulsion, and to be allow'd the De-
cency of a little feeble Resistance. . . . You will have no more trouble but
what will heighten the Pleasure" (II.iii.36–42). Lycomedes responds to this
Ovidian advice with heart palpitations, a feminizing reference to his
"Breast," and a request that Diphilus touch him in a notably intimate, potentially erotic gesture. "*Pyrrha!*—This is beyond my Hopes.—*Diphilus*,
lay your Hand upon my Breast. Feel how my Heart flutters" (ll. 43–44).
Here, in burlesque (both because of their dramatic exaggeration and their
male identity) the characters enact recognizable gestures, mannerisms, remarks, and attitudes of female delicacy.

The family context now becomes an accentuated feature. Amidst this
expression of the effeminate king's passion for someone the audience knows
to be the most virile of male heroes, Gay draws attention to Lycomedes'
role as father in the family. The play thus anticipates the older male-younger
female incest dynamic that Ruth Perry discovers in Gothic novels of the
late-eighteenth century.[52] Querying after his daughterly heartthrob,
Lycomedes establishes where to find Pyrrha in relation to his (nuclear)
family: the Queen, Deidamia and his "other Daughters."

> *Lycomedes. Deidamia* too not with her!
> *Diphilus.* She is with the Queen, Sir.
> *Lycomedes.* My other Daughters, who seem less fond of her, are in the
>   Garden; so all's safe.—Leave me, *Diphilus*, and let none, upon Pain of
>   my Displeasure, presume to intrude.
>
> (II.iii.47–50)

When Achilles enters immediately after this remark, the king assumes a
fatherly tone: "Lady *Pyrrha*, my dear Child, why so thoughtful?" (II.iv.1).
The homoerotic and incestuous overtones of Lycomedes' passion for Pyrrha/
Achilles are presented in gendered terms, both by feminizing the king and
by placing this love within the (domestically feminine) context of the bourgeois family. In precisely those enclosed familial circumstances that Perry
analyzes, the assault scene begins with a fatherly Lycomedes summoning
his "dear Child," the "Lady *Pyrrha*." But Lycomedes is no match for the
manly outrage of Achilles whose resistance, as Noble suggests, both encourages sympathy for the woman's plight and models her resistance. Certainly the play presents as a triumph of justice the trouncing of the preying
Lycomedes by the preyed-upon Pyrrha/Achilles.

The play also foregrounds male homoerotic desire in the figure of Ajax,
representing the businessman-soldiers on their way to Troy. His blustering
erotic fixation on Achilles/Pyrrha supplies a masculinized counterpart to
the effeminate desire of Lycomedes. Ajax is subject to physical responses
quite as intense as those of the *"fluttering"* Lycomedes; his *"blustering*

Soldier's Valour" marks this difference (emphases mine). Artemona, the queen's serving maid, remarks to Periphas, the nephew selected to marry Pyrrha:

> How I have seen that formidable Hero general *Ajax* suffer upon your Account!—Of all his Rivals [for Pyrrha's favors] you are his eternal Torment.—He reddens, sighs, and (as much as is consistent with such a blustering Soldier's Valour) languishes whenever you are near [Pyrrha].
>
> (III.i.24–28)

This predicament of jealous rivalry is another of Gay's additions to the story. The tormented Ajax declares, "'Tis not her Consent, but my Sword, that must decide the Question" (III.iii.54–55). The reluctant Periphas, set up by Theaspe, responds: "Sure never a Rival (as you will call me) had a better Reason for fighting than I have at present; for if I am kill'd, I shall be out of danger of having the Woman" (III.iii.56–58). They fall into the fight that Burnet linked to the duel of Hervey and Pulteney. Periphas declares: "Since my own Honour calls upon me.—Take notice, *Ajax*, that I *don't* fight for the Woman" (III.iii.95–96). The duel is interrupted by palace guards just as the arrival of the Greeks introduces the well-known final episode.

The ending brings to this house, steaming with intrigues of same-sex desire, the theme of an intersecting relation of trade and domestic consumption of goods on the one hand and expansionist soldiering on the other. A servant announces to the young "ladies," Achilles, Deidamia, and her sisters: "The Anti-chamber, Madam, is crowded with Trades-People" (III.ix.8–9), including "those foreign Merchants who lately came into Port" (13–14). The ladies summon them, with a nod to Londoners' voracious taste for imports: "There must be something pretty," Artemona declares, "in every thing that is foreign" (III.ix.64–65). The merchant Greeks enter. Ulysses calls for the ladies, as principal household consumers: "Wou'd you command the things, Ladies, to be brought here, or wou'd you see 'em in your own Apartment?" (III.x.36–37). "Here—immediately," Philoe commands (l. 40). The "Goods" are displayed, and the ladies ferret through them. Finally, the packet of armor is opened, to which Lesbia quips, with a sidelong glance to the female warrior: "You see, *Philoe*, they can at least equip us for the [military] Camp" (III.x.74–75). With the ladies enrapt in their shopping, the stage directions complete the scene: "Achilles is handling and poising the Armour, Ulysses observing him" (l. 80).

The disclosure of Achilles' true identity unfolds in a melodramatic crescendo of events that reaches a rollicking musical climax. As Achilles, the avid consumer, studies the famous sword and shield just emerged from the salesmen's packet, Ulysses proclaims: "That intrepid Air! That Godlike Look! It must be He! His Nature, his Disposition shews him through the

Disguise. Son of *Thetis*, I know thee, *Greece* demands thee, and now, *Achilles*, the House of *Priam* shakes" (III.x.87–91). Agyrtes reaches for "a Trumpet which lay amongst the Armour, and sounds." However, these new Greek heroes have familiar British tastes and pastimes: they are fanciers of catch clubs. With the trumpet's sound Ulysses rouses the four warriors in a call to arms sung to the tune of "My Dame hath a lame tame Crane," a four-part catch popular from the 1660s to our own time.

With this burlesquing, catch-club reference framing the scene, the warriors take up the tune by turns: "Thy Fate then, O Troy, is decreed," intones Ulysses. Diomedes chimes in, "How I pant!" Achilles follows, "How I burn for the Fight." "Hark, Glory calls," Diomedes proclaims; "Now great Hector shall bleed," Achilles adds; and Agyrtes concludes, "Fame shall our Deeds requite" (III.x.102–7). Filtering through Gay's text, the irresistibly rhyming words joined to the known tune subvert these blazing exhortations to glory—along with the halting entrances of the singers that must have been intended for the performance. The original catch is a rollicking—and notably unheroic—request by a servant on behalf of his/her dame's domestic possession: an ungainly bird, and a crippled one at that: "Good gentle *Jane*, let my Dames lame tame Crane feed and come home again."

> My Dame hath a lame tame Crane,
> My Dame hath a Crane that is lame:
> Good gentle Jane, let my Dames lame tame Crane feed
> and come home again.[53]

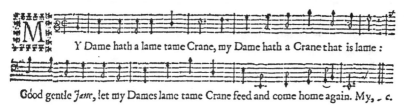

Ex. 22. "My Dame hath a lame tame Crane" from *Catch that Catch Can* (1667)

The legendary heroics of Troy here conflate, in a fabling mode, with the "feeding" of a "lame tame Crane" who can then "come home again."

The parodic enactment of the scene in musical terms continues. With Agyrtes' cadence on "Fame shall our Deeds requite," Achilles "turns and looks on Deidamia." Once more the Herculean dilemma rears up. Here the hero's struggle is taken up with tunes that invoke the dually gendered spheres of 1730s bourgeois musical culture: the catch clubs of London's male citizens on the one hand, and the drawing-room singing and keyboard playing of their wives, daughters, and sisters on the other. As the "lame tame Crane" reaches its final cadence, Achilles responds in solo to the pull of Deidamia singing to the tune of "Geminiani's Minuet." Glory and love are opposed in a burlesque juxtaposition of catch and minuet.

Italian violinist, composer, and theorist Francesco Geminiani (1687–1762) was prominent in the London musical scene from 1714 to 1732, and was mentioned in the same breath as Handel and Corelli. Involved in the burgeoning business of bourgeois music making, he organized societies and subscription concerts.[54] His enormously popular compositions were typically directed toward an audience of amateur players and singers.

Geminiani's minuet is found in various instrumental and vocal forms, testament to its popularity and familiarity. Pertinent to Gay's use of it, the minuet appears with "Gently touch the warbling Lyre," *A New Song The Favorite Air Compos'd by Sig.^r Geminiani The Words by M.^r A Bradley*. This sentimental song from about 1725 elicited a mocking response, "Gently stir and blow the Fire," *The Warb'ling Lyre Burlesqu'd by Sir W.Y.*[55] As the conflicted Achilles intones his solo in contrast to the catch tune, he situates the female side of the Herculean dilemma on the hearth of the private drawing rooms of bourgeois London, a space increasingly coded as "feminine."[56]

Gay's *Polly* critiqued the Herculean dilemma in terms of gender and the individual allegiance and behavior of Polly and Macheath. In *Achilles* that gendering takes a more social turn, as Gay marks the pastimes of a recognizable group of women and men—indeed, an emerging social class of the middling sort—whose increasing political and economic power as well as aesthetic and moral sway were reconfiguring legacies of heroism both at home and abroad. Gay's immensely popular works identified this shift in power by participating in it even as he called attention to new delineations and premises of value, sway, social identity and organization, sensibility, and so on.

The Herculean dilemma, however it is reconfigured or burlesqued, is a conventional motif with a predictable outcome. It typically supplies an ABA form that a witty formalist such as Gay could not fail to exploit: the hero is called to glory (A); love pulls him back (B); manliness and duty call again, and, even more heroic because of his suffering as an individual, he ventures to glory (A). Gay's musical burlesque of this is gloriously comic.

Picture the scene. Achilles, the most heroic of heroes, is in a dress, recently discovered by his Greek comrades who have been posing as peddlers to the ladies. When the trumpet sounds, the heroes one after another intone a call to perform their famous warrior "Deeds" at Troy. The tune is a popular and very silly catch. Spurred by "Honor," Achilles is "going off," as the stage direction says, then "turns and looks on Deidamia." The music turns with him to "Geminiani's Minuet" and the familiar sway of woman and love. Achilles croons, "How can I leave her? my Heart feels her Anguish. / Hence, Fame and Glory. Love wins the Day" (XXX.x.110–11) and "drops the Sword and Shield."

AIR XLVIII. *Geminiani's* Minuet.

Ach. *Beauty weeps. — Ah, why that Languish?*
See she calls and bids me stay.
How can I leave her? my Heart feels her Anguish.
Hence, Fame and Glory. Love wins the Day.
[He drops the Sword and Shield.

Ex. 23. "Air 48" from Gay's *Achilles*[57]

But the "Trumpet sounds. He takes 'em up again" as the heroes, in Pavlovian response, take up their "feeding" on Troy "as before, Sung in Four Parts as a Catch." In a zany burlesque of the ABA form intrinsic to both aria and minuet, Gay recasts the Herculean dilemma, one of the central tenets of the European classical legacy, in terms that invoke the gendered markets for 1730s popular music of the middling sort. This is a very campy moment.

Through its ongoing use of such cultural references, *Achilles* reveals an emerging social system that posits sexual desire and gender identity within a domestic order, with the nuclear family at its center. Delineations of public and private simultaneously closet and enforce the sexualizing of relations—in both hetero- and homosexual terms—in this household sphere. As *Achilles* draws to its close, Lycomedes and Theaspe introduce the enforcing rubric of "Disgrace." "You must own, Madam," Lycomedes tells his spouse, "that 'twas your own Jealousies that were the Occasion of *Deidamia's* Disgrace." "How can you have the Assurance to Name it?" she responds, "Does it not put you in mind of your own?—Let her Marriage to *Achilles* make us forget every thing past" (III.xi.15–19). Thus, "father" and "mother," rulers of this new order, euphemistically refer to the eroticizing of this domestic sphere—both as hetero- and homosexual expression. Applied equally to daughter and father, the enforcing rubric of "Disgrace" closets both the dynamic of sexual desire of Pyrrha/Achilles and Deidamia and that of Lycomedes for Pyrrha/Achilles. Individuals together choose to abide by an agreed-upon ethos of propriety and privacy: the divergent, unruly sexiness of it all is put in a closet.

A reinterpretation of the meaning of the natural world accompanied the shifting of values and structures of power that Gay's satires continually raise to view. The dynamics of the order of human systems were increasingly linked to the order of a "nature" that would, in time, be imagined to operate with quite as businesslike a system of supply and demand, survival of the fittest, and natural selection as the early investment schemes of Georgian bankers. Images of animals and fabling permeate all of Gay's ballad operas. This use of satirical animal parallels reaches a kind of climax in *Achilles*. Ulysses brings the play to its close as a dance—notably a minuet—begins: "We may for a while put on a feign'd Character," that famously wily businessman of antiquity declares, "but Nature is so often unguarded that it will shew itself.—'Tis to the Armour we owe *Achilles*" (III.xii.77–79). But as Noble observes, this last phrase ironically suggests that the heroism, far from being a nature, "lodges not in the man but in the armour" (195). The concluding song—in ABA form to minuet and saraband tunes of Corelli—rather ominously reimagines our hero through a fable, that most conventional of similes: he is a cat, and the sway of his glory, the irresistible chase of a mouse. "Let's with Achilles our Genius obey," the chorus sings at the cadence of the minuet, part A of the finale. To which Ulysses responds with the fable:

> Thus when the Cat had once all Woman's Graces;
> Courtship, Marriage won her Embraces:

> Forth lept a Mouse; she, forgetting Enjoyment,
>   Quits her fond Spouse for her former Employment.
>   (III.xii.84–87)

This fable and its saraband setting echoes in our ears *sans* subtexts, for these are instrumental tunes. When the minuet returns, this reduction of heroic tradition to the antics of feline appetite hovers, with a grim irony, over the artful little tune:

> Nature breaks forth at the moment unguarded;
>   Through all Disguise she herself must betray.
> Heav'n with Success hath our Labours rewarded;
>   Let's with Achilles our Genius obey.

10

Lessons of the "Natural" World from Gay to William Blake: The Animal Fables

A fabling narrative presents an illuminative parallel to its reader, so that the parable yields a moral lesson. As we have seen, implicative creatures and objects permeate Gay's work, especially the satires, from the preyed-upon fish and fowl of *Rural Sports* to the admonitory cats and mice, bees and butterflies of the ballad operas. In Gay's verse fables proper, composed in the last five years of his life, the worrisome social "leveling" noted by eighteenth-century commentators reaches an intricate culmination in the figurative play of the fable form.

Jayne Lewis shows that the creation of ironic parallels to human behavior from the animal and plant world engrossed Gay's Britain, where hundreds of fables and fable collections appeared between 1651 and 1740.[1] For the eighteenth century, Aesopian fables still served as commonplace figures for real history; the presence of anthropomorphic animals immediately placed a work in a political register.[2] In Gay's writing, the chattering sparrows, roses, elephants, dogs, and barley mows supply a multilevel world of speaking subjects connected to each other in relations of power and interdependence which, for their readers' sake, they live out, ponder and dispute. Here, expressive individuals self-consciously interrelate from within diverse, stratifying levels of prestige or subjection, importance or ignominiousness. The fables explore the dynamics of survival and morality in this world, insistently calling its hierarchies into question.

Reprinted in more than 350 editions from 1727 to the 1880s, Gay's *Fables* had currency among English speakers at every rank for generations.[3] Illustrated by artists of the caliber of Thomas Bewick and William Blake, they were remembered and quoted by apprentices and magistrates, children and grown-ups at all social levels in the eighteenth and nineteenth centuries.[4] The fables' exploitation of parody, allusive method, and popular tropes and materials earned them their long-standing and widespread appeal, and eventually their censure as moral and proverbial templates.

Not uncommon in his earlier writing, fabling parables fill Gay's late satires, signaling both their political bent and their affinities to popular lore. To give just a sample from the ballad operas: In *The Beggar's Opera* Peachum draws lessons from foxes and hens (air 11), Macheath sings of bees (air 15), and Polly of turtles (air 13), sparrows (air 18), and swallows (air 34). In *Polly*, the eponymous heroine croons of the sportsmen's hawks and hounds that prey upon the woodcocks and stags of the woodland (air 48), while Morano/Macheath cautions of tigers threatening timorous flocks (air 53). *Achilles* concludes with Ulysses' arresting ditty of the unconcealable natures of cats and mice (air 54). These parables heighten the referential range of the songs as "critical instants" by invoking the well-known Aesop and the long, politicized tradition of fables. In addition, they call to our awareness the simple day-to-day interacting of creatures in the nonhuman world.

While creating the ballad operas, Gay was composing verse fables. His first volume of fifty was published with lavish illustrations in 1727, the year in which George II succeeded to the throne. Written in 1725–26, these fables were exactly contemporary with Swift's *Gulliver's Travels*. Both works combine far-fetched renderings of "nature" with fancifully mock exaggerations of moral exposition. With the fables, dedicated to the five-year-old Prince William, Gay obviously hoped for patronage and influence at court. In this he was disappointed.[5] However, his fabling appears to have been on the order of a general, ontological preoccupation, for it continued into the later plays and generated a second series of sixteen longer fables constructed as verse epistles, that he was writing at the time of his death. Published in 1738 with even more lavish engravings than the earlier set, this posthumous collection opens with the following elegiac "Advertisement":

These FABLES were finished by Mr. GAY, and intended for the Press a short time before his Death; when they were left, with his other Papers, to the Care of his noble Friend and Patron, the DUKE of QUEENSBERRY: His grace has accordingly permitted them to the Press, and they are here printed from the Originals in the Author's own Hand-writing. We hope they will please equally with his former Fables, though mostly on Subjects of a graver and more political Turn: They will certainly shew Him to have been (what he esteemed the best Character) a Man of a truly honest Heart, and a sincere Lover of his Country.[6]

Shifting Vantage and Gay's Fabling

Gay's work consistently shifts point of view from the expected to the unexpected. Inversions of "high" and "low" oblige us to reimagine stock narratives and topoi and to undertake the moral critique such reversals inevitably entail. Among other themes, the fables develop the awareness of rank and entitlement that the Beggar pinpoints in his closing remarks about the "revised" ending of his *Opera*: the unequally rewarded "similitude of manners in high and low life." As noted above, Eliza Haywood had observed already in the 1740s that there is in Gay "a constant Strain . . . of putting the whole Species pretty much upon a Level."[7]

Jayne Lewis remarks on the positive response this leveling received from readers—"often women, children, and colonials"—who found in such fables as "The Elephant and the Bookseller" a claim to "the printed page as ground common to two very different links in the chain of being." As Lewis observes,

> While cultural subalterns might naturally have warmed to such exhibits of parity, it is a very small wonder that, even though the speaking animal pretense remained an acceptable literary convention, the loftier custodians of eighteenth-century literary culture came to regret Gay's *Fables* in general, and "The Elephant and the Bookseller" in particular, as "a fiction wherein no regard is had to the nature of things."[8]

At the heart of Gay's method, this irreverent leveling—a playful identification of and with various points of reference—gives his worldview a striking indeterminacy that questions the positive "certainties" about to be laid down when Gay wrote. In this destabilizing view, thinking, reading, culture-bearing individuals make their way through a social order that, whatever its cruelties, is nonetheless at crucial points unfixed and permeable. Its ironic deep logic and rewards, however elusive, are universal to all.

Burlesque and the satirical mock heroic supply the aesthetic and formal ingredients for this notably sociopolitical move of "putting the whole Species pretty much upon a Level." An early Scriblerian frolic demonstrates the link between the mock heroic and Gay's fabling animals. "The Country-Post, From Tuesday August the 12th. to Thursday August the 14th" appears unattributed in the *Miscellanies in Prose and Verse* published by Swift and Pope from 1727 to 1732.[9] Like many pieces in the collection, the authorship of "The Country Post" is not certain. In his edition of 1824, however, Walter Scott states unequivocally: "This burlesque gazette was written by Gay."[10] The "Post," possibly written with collaboration by Pope, may date to August 1718, when the two poets spent time at the country estate of Lord Harcourt in Oxfordshire.[11]

"The Country-Post" parodies reports of foreign news for the urbane English reader. *The Weekly Journal: or, Saturday's Post* supplies examples of the model to be skewered. In July and August news spread of renewed hostilities with Spain.[12] The report for 26 July begins: "All the Eyes of Europe seem now to be turn'd towards Italy; the Spaniards, who, as we formerly gave an Account had Landed at Palermo, have not only possess'd themselves of the Royal Palace of the King of Sicily, and of the Fort of Donjon here, but have spread themselves throughout the whole Island" (504). On 9 August, news on "the Affairs of Italy" continues with report of a Spanish Viceroy's flight "so fast towards Syracusa that the Dragoons could not come up with him, tho' they had the good Fortune to overtake his Baggage, which they plunder'd to the great Satisfaction of the Soldiers" (516). Alarming news from other regions typically follows such "headlining" reports. *The Weekly Journal* for 16 August, with a delicate restraint, informs readers: "They write from Normandy, that the People continue to die in such Multitudes, that the Relation of it is frightful, and we care not to repeat it, for we do not covet to be the Messengers of evil Tidings" (522). The issue for 23 August says: "Our People are alarm'd here at a Piece of News from the Baltick, viz. that the Czar of Muscovy and the king of Sweden have agreed to have an Interview in the Island of Aland, and to sign, ratify, and exchange the Peace made between them all at the same Time" (528).

"The Country-Post" burlesques such reports with a sensibility empathically comic as well as satiric. Notwithstanding a laughable anthropomorphizing of the barnyard, this parodic "Post" creates the sympathetic, if ironically constructed speakers typical in Gay's later animal fables.[13] This spoof "fables" as it exposes in its animal actors familiar human webs of accident, suffering, and betrayal. Its recognizable, Scriblerian preoccupation with the mock heroic applies an inflated military discourse to the mundane activities of the barnyard. In so doing, "The Country-Post" reveals the pretensions, even dangers, of this discourse. The result: the mix of comic sympathy and satiric awareness typical of Gay's writing.

"The Country Post" reports "From the Hen-roost" on recent events from the perspective of the distraught eyewitness hens:

Two Days ago we were put in a dreadful Consternation by the advance of a Kite, which threaten'd every Minute to *fall upon* us; he made several *motions* as if he design'd to attack our *left Wing*, which cover'd our *Infantry*. We were alarm'd at this approach, and upon a general Muster of all our Forces, the Kitchen-Maid came to our relief; but we were soon convinc'd that she had betray'd us, and was in the Interest of the Kite aforesaid; for

she twisted off two of our Companions necks, and stripp'd them naked:
Five of us were also clapp'd in a *close Prison*, in order to be sold for Slaves
the next Market-day. (2:285)

With a simultaneously funny and pathetic irony, the preyed-upon "Hens"
render quotidian and notably unmomentous—from our point of view—
barnyard events in the hyperbolic language of military conquest. With Gay's
usual "tweak" on the urban fashion for pastoral scenes, "The Country-Post"
distances these barnyard doings, which would have had a slight exoticism—
familiar in literary or dramatic reference, but less so in fact—for, say, an
urban audience in Georgian London. With ironic misapprehension, the reporting hens suspect in the appetitive predations—altogether similar from
their point of view—a conspiracy between the circling Kite and the businesslike Kitchen-Maid. Like *The Shepherd's Week*, "The Country-Post"
punctures lofty pastoral expectations with the often grim and gritty facts of
country life. Even more pointedly, this "burlesque gazette" upends the habits
of the epic imagination with deadpan application of military terminology
to the fortunes of hapless, stew-destined hens. Most unsettlingly, the rendering fits.

Rhetorical figures, personifications, and wordplay tickle our reception
of a naively steadfast herald who contributes further installments to the
gazette. With prankish irony, this dispassionate reporter intones "From the
Garden": "The *Boars* have done much Mischief of late in these Parts, to
such a degree, that not a Turnip or Carrot can lie safe in their *Beds*" (286).
A bulletin "From the great Pond" takes up the language of military exploit
and penal discipline—"large Sail," "Resistance," "Enterprize," "retired,"
"Crime," and so on—rendering the interactions of animals and humans as
a complicated state of war.

> Yesterday a large *Sail* of Ducks pass'd by here; after a small Resistance
> from two little Boys who flung Stones at them: They landed near the Barn-
> door, where they *forrag'd* with very good Success: While they were upon
> this Enterprize, an old Turky-Cock attack'd a Maid in a red Petticoat, and
> she retired with *great precipitation*. This Afternoon being somewhat rainy,
> they set Sail again, and took several *Frogs*. Just now arrived the *Parson's* .
> *Wife*; and twenty Ducks were brought forth before her in order to be Tried,
> but for what Crime we know not. (286–87)

The shifted point of view has particular comic effect when applied to
the homely animate and inanimate creatures of Aesopian fables. Because
this "burlesque gazette" consists only of prose narratives uncomplicated
by either verse formations or moral comment, the effect of this shift becomes obvious. With its hens and ducks speaking from alternative subject

positions, "The Country-Post" reframes familiar actions and power relations for us in terms of their felt effects on the barnyard recipients of those actions. This move is necessarily satirical as it reimagines heroic topoi and diction and the ruling position these represent in terms of the sentiments of the normally ruled and notably humble and unheroic subjects. As comic as it is, "The Country-Post" locates our readerly affinities with the understandably anxious "Hens" reporting "From the Henhouse." It draws attention both to the artifice and predilections of its model as well as the cultural, social and generic functions of such news. While inducing laughter, it provokes cultural- and self-awareness for a reading and thinking individual in a social context. This basic move governs Gay's verse fables.

The Fables: Contingencies of Media and Message

The fables use conventional images and proverbial language accessible to a wide range of readers. As commentators observe, they are shot through with folkloristic allusions, popular beliefs and customs, and common proverbs and proverbial expressions.[14] At the same time, Gay fits them to a tight and complex organization. Ironic waggishness and paradoxical ambiguities prevail, especially as these verse narratives probe the limitations and contradictions of language itself on the one hand, and the moral and perceptual limitations and self-deceptions of speakers on the other. Both sets of fables take up issues of moral decision and behavior in a Hobbesian world of appetitive acquisition. Individual speakers and actors struggle to survive, in stories of power relationships seemingly unmoored from institutional authority—a thematic preoccupation that must have seemed especially pertinent and useful to readers in eighteenth-century Britain.

Speaking animals and objects—with pointedly different interests, sensibilities, and ranks—grapple with questions of power, knowledge, and personal moral response. For example, "Fable 7" of the first set of 1727 records a peripheral voice of dissent at the acclaim for a newly named Viceroy Fox—a transparent reference to Walpole and Walpole-like appointees—proverbially put in charge of the henhouse. A goose standing at a distance from the acclaim for the new Viceroy, notes that "'twas a fox who spoke th' oration." From the perspective of this onlooking spokes-goose, foxes on top bode small good for some in the realm: "When ev'ry petty clerk in place, / To prove his taste, and seem polite, / Will feed on geese both noon and night." Such carefully wrought and often ingeniously humorous vignettes held people's attention for generations. With amusing facetiousness—and each with an engaging illustration—the fables posed dilemmas that readers of all ranks could recognize in the new market-driven society of striving, scrabbling individuals taking shape around them.

In general, the fables are characterized by their simple, aphoristic language and a reliance on traditional images, topoi, themes, and proverbial expressions. Like Gay's songs, the fables are poised between the forms of oral and written expression at a key moment in European cultural history, which saw the widespread adoption of reading and writing at all levels. Against the backdrop of this cultural transformation, Gay's popular fables seem to have functioned importantly to mediate this change for individual readers. The fables do not set reading apart from speaking precisely because they insistently implicate the reading reader in the ongoing—and often witty and undermining—production of meanings, both conceptual and especially moral. As Lewis observes, Gay's fables explore the proliferation of a written and read culture among individuals.[15]

Throughout, the familiar pretensions of the mock heroic, so prevalent elsewhere in Gay's satire, reappear in barnyard contexts reminiscent of "The Country-Post." But the fables move beyond the mock heroic to explore the ironic deceptions of moralizing itself. Routinely contradicting their own fixities, they insist upon the instability of anyone's perspective, reliant as it is upon language, individual standpoint, and power in relation to others. More than most fables, Gay's interrogate fabling itself. Their morality is mock-moral.

Consequently, throughout both parts of the fable collection, the advice that prevails concerns honesty and self-awareness. The celebrated Elephant of the 1727 collection's "Fable X. The Elephant and the Bookseller" asks: "Can he discern the diff'rent natures, / And weigh the pow'r of other creatures, / Who by the partial work hath shown / He knows so little of his own?" (ll. 39–42).[16] The strategically placed penultimate fable of the 1727 collection, "Fable XLIX. The Man and the Flea" recommends a humble self-knowledge that brings humans to an immanent participation in rather than a transcendent dominance of the world around them. A man stands on a cliff after sunset and expounds with soon-to-be-punctured grandiosity. His flourish suggests such oft quoted declarations of human grandeur as Shakespeare's "What a piece of work is man! . . . the beauty of the world! the paragon of animals!" (*Hamlet*, II.ii.305–10):

> When I behold this glorious show,
> And the wide watry world below,
> The scaly people of the main,
> The beasts that range the wood or plain,
> The wing'd inhabitants of air,
> The day, the night, the various year,
> And know all these by heav'n design'd

> As gifts to pleasure human kind,
> I cannot raise my worth too high;
> Of what vast consequence am I!
>
> (29–38)

Immediately he receives the following flea's-eye-view "comeuppance":

> Not of th'importance you suppose,
> Replies a Flea upon his nose:
> Be humble, learn thyself to scan;
> Know, pride was never made for man.
> 'Tis vanity that swells thy mind.
> What, heav'n and earth for thee design'd!
> For thee! made only for our need;
> That more important Fleas might feed.
>
> (39–46)

The fable thus ends with the flea's caustic deflation of human vanity.

Such critiques of individual vainglory and benightedness often combine with satire on heroic pretension. In "Fable XX. The Old Hen and the Cock," an old mother hen warns her grown son to avoid a well, lest he drown like his younger sister, a "giddy chick" who fell when trying her wings. The fable takes up gender in its mock-heroic treatment of the hot-tempered "macho"-cock. "Why was this idle charge? he crys: / Let courage female fears despise" (29–30). "His bosom burn'd to disobey" (24), and eventually he heads for the rim of the well. As he looks down, a "foe with ruffled plumes appears" (42), his own unrecognized reflection in the well-water. "With wrath his ruffled plumes he rears . . . Threat answer'd threat, his fury grew, / Headlong to meet the war he flew" (41–44). Of course, he charges into the water to a "watry death," a mock-heroic example for the fiery Hotspurs of the world. To this image of deluding contentiousness comes a further twist on the theme of self-deceit. This empty-headed hero adds to his ridiculousness by blaming his mother: "I ne'er had been in this condition / But for my mother's prohibition" (ll. 47–48). This final couplet bounces with ironic absurdity back to the moralizing admonition that began the fable: "Restrain your child" (1). This opening "moral" becomes fully mock-moral when joined to the portrait of an offspring so unrestrainable and doltish.

Allusions in some fables touch on the burlesque overturning of conventional heroic topoi that Gay used in other works, especially the ballad operas. For example, fable 6 of the second set, "The Squire and his Cur" describes in mock-heroic terms a notably unsavory dog seduced to follow when "a fav'rite bitch was in the wind": "Thus by untimely love pursuing,

/ Like Antony, he sought his ruin" (153-54). Fable 33 of the first collection, "The Courtier and Proteus" mockingly likens a courtier's provincial building ventures to the oft-quoted desire of Alexander the Great for more worlds to conquer.[17] The fable further undermines the respectability of such conquest with the terms "plunder" and "ruin," along the lines of the satire on "heroic" New World piracy in *Polly:*

> [The courtier] builds new schemes, in hope to gain
> The plunder of another reign;
> Like Philip's son would fain be doing,
> And sighs for other realms to ruin.
>
>   (5-8)

Gay—a familiar visitant to such estates as Burlington House and James Brydges's Cannons—had ample opportunity to note the connection between such building projects at home and the new forms of money-making conquest abroad. With a startling transformation of both the lands and the institutions of Britain, fortunes made in the Indies funded estates, manor houses, titles, and influence at home.

Indeed, Gay's eye is ever on the trading and consumer culture emerging around him whose morality and dynamics the fables probe in terms of greed and especially appetite (as above busy "doing" and "pursuing" are deflatingly rhymed with "ruin"). Depicting affairs of state and human society through the predations of forest and barnyard, the fables represent this founding of the polity upon an expanding national rapacity with an eye to discovering in this world the moral course for individuals. Especially targeted are the ironic self-satisfactions of moralizing speakers who ennoble this systemic rapaciousness. Thus, the Ratcatcher of fable 21, "an Engineer, of noted skill," mulls over the problem of competition in trade. Were the "interloping" cats "extinguish'd, or expell'd the land," he declares: "We rat-catchers might raise our fees, / Sole guardians of a nation's cheese!" (39-40). The comically zeugmatic image of a zealously guarded national stock for a nation of cheese eaters would have brought to the minds of Gay's readers conventional satires of Dutch and German burghers, with obvious application to the house of Hanover.

Similarly, fable 38 refers to the slave trade and the hierarchically appetitive interrelations that make such predation possible. With his usual call to self-awareness, Gay also depicts the obliviousness of consumers to their own indulgence. "Tir'd of common food," a mother Turkey takes her brood to an anthill. "Behold, the busy *Negro* race," she enthuses with unmistakable reference to the traffic in enslaved Africans. She goes on to lament "that curst man on turkey preys," especially at Christmas when

"turkey smoaks on ev'ry board." An Ant offers the subaltern voice so typical in Gay, reproaching the Turkey's lack of self-reflection in lines that
apply, with obvious intention, to the colonial enterprise:

> Ere you remark another's sin,
> Bid thy own conscience look within.
> Controul thy more voracious bill,
> Nor for a breakfast nations kill.
>
> (27–30)

The grimly comic notion of committing genocide "for breakfast" condemns
the consuming appetite of the new commerce-based economy, replacing
responsibility at the individual level. Moreover, mindlessness of the "kill-
ing" is heightened by its "breakfast" context, a meal that connotes intimacy, privacy, a kind of safety. The burlesque image "gets at" something too
recognizable: the numbing, euphemistic banality that cloaks and institution-
alizes cruelty in its modern forms. This feature of Gay's satire is furthered
in Brecht with the image of Peachum's grotesquely regimented industry of
begging; it is what Ayckbourn captures when the hapless Guy can explain
nothing about what it is that happens at (the boring? or sinister?) BLM.

Several fables allude to the South Sea Company fiasco which, more
than any other single event in England, brought the terms and dynamics of
investment capitalism into widespread parlance. "Fable XXXV. The Bar-
ley-Mow and the Dunghill" complains of "Proud rogues, who shar'd the
South-sea prey, / And sprung like mushrooms in a day!" In fable 42 Vice
wins her contest with a Juggler thanks to transformations that move through
the new semantic sphere of liquid assets and their crime-and-punishment
corollaries: a "senator's" disappearing banknote, a purse that changes into
a hangman's halter as a thief closes his fingers about it, a money counter
that "Grew twenty guineas at command," and so on. Fable 3 from the 1738
set laments the mysteries of the new, participatory politics: "Thus oft the
cheated croud adore / The thriving knaves that keep 'em poor" (ll. 19–20)
until "The bubble breaks, the gewgaw ends" (l. 53).

With aptness to present-day concerns about vanishing species and eco-
logical depletion, the fables apply the theme of exploitation to dynamics
among creatures and to the relation of human beings to the natural world.
They expose not only individual benightedness in humans, but the effects
of the attitude of entitlement to which the Flea responded in fable 49. Typically, the fables consider relations of creatures to their use as commodities—of sheep to their shorn wool, oxen to cooking spits, horses to the bit,
and so on. They imagine the relation from the sensibilities of the creatures
who, as commodities, are sacrificed to human uses and appetites.

Human folly in the fables has its sad effects on that "lower world" of creatures that Anne Finch described poetically in her well-known "Nocturnal Reverie."[18] Fable 12 of Gay's later set warns a "Young Heir" of the gaming that will transform his estate into cash through the "gen'ral massacre" of logging and other money-making designs on his estate:

> The forest (a whole cent'ry's shade)
> Must be one wasteful ruin made...
> Fall'n are the elm and rev'rend oak;
> Through the long wood loud axes sound,
> And eccho groans with ev'ry wound."

(ll. 63–74)

This exploitive relationship of humans to the natural world is perhaps most ironically expressed in "Fable XLV. The Poet and the Rose." As Lewis observes, Gay made particular use of the fable as "an animate, mediatory, and self-reflexive figural device" (185).

"The Poet and the Rose" looks at love poetry's long tradition of plucking roses—from the point of view of the plucked. In the process, the poem of course implicates the fabling poet himself, particularly as the text imagines him a songsmith. Seeking "the sweets of *May*," as centuries of poetic convention have dictated, the love-prompted poet goes to the garden, plucks a rose, and begins a song replete with the most traditional of Petrarchan comparisons: "Go, Rose, my *Chloe's* bosom grace. . . . You die with envy, I with love" (19–30). Just as we settle into the familiar tropes, a cranky voice jolts us out of complacence: "Spare your comparisons," a peeved Rose interrupts:

> Does it to *Chloe's* charms conduce,
> To found her praise on our abuse?
> Must we, to flatter her, be made
> To wither, envy, pine and fade?

(31–40)

This fable, like others, does not release us from the ironic bind in which it wraps us. Gay requires that we consider the limits of language itself, for this critique of abuse takes aim not primarily at the material realm in which roses get plucked, but at the conventions and indeed semiotics of simile making that underpin this action, bringing into relation—to the sentient rose's chagrin—guilty poets and victimized roses. The poetical becomes political.

As critics have observed from Samuel Johnson on, a compromised self-contradiction permeates Gay's fables which insist upon critiquing, not from an imagined space *above* the contingencies of language and custom, but from *within* them. Lewis points out,

> Gay wove compliance with contemporary print culture together with criticism of it . . . [and] established literary authority by displaying its vulnerability. . . . Like *The Beggar's Opera* (1728), the *Fables* forge powerful bonds with the "lower" phylogenetic, social, and literary orders. But the *Fables* also explore the ties that bind these orders to the ones above them. (158–59)

With often delicious comic effect, these fables laugh at those who naively or manipulatively position themselves—usually through moralizing—above the necessary compliances of language, custom, and living in a body. Two owls in fable 32 ponder the superiorities of ancient wisdom. However, the couplet rhyme of "fowls" and "owls" in which the fable sets their sententious ponderings hilariously undermines the self-satisfaction of their project: "They weigh'd the dignity of fowls, / And pry'd into the depth of owls" (7–8).

Similarly, in "Fable XXIX. The Fox at the point of death," a dying vulpine patriarch, tormented by the phantoms of his guilty conscience— "murder'd geese," "bleeding turkeys," and slain chickens—admonishes his sons to rein in their "passions" and redeem their good name. His progeny reply that such a change "shall never be believ'd" (46). At this objection, the feeble old moralizer reconsiders his dictum, especially when he hears a chicken nearby. ("But, hark! I hear a hen that clocks," the old fox remarks in a parenthetical aside before moving on to adjust his moral.) His final advice alternates comically between otherworldly remonstrances of conscience, and the appetitive, this-world immediacy of being a fox with a stomach. "Go, but be mod'rate in your food," he commands (48–49). Then, with a laughable shift of diction, morality disappears altogether as the fable facetiously concludes with his musing: "A chicken too might do me good" (49–50) .

Popular Elements and the Leveling of the Fables

"The Ravens, The Sexton, and the Earth Worm" (1738), the last of the posthumously published fables, flippantly takes up the familiar theme of the vanity of human power and self-importance in the face of death. With the equivocation at which Gay excels, the fable treats this topos at once parodically and elegiacally, as the poem enacts the very leveling it bespeaks. Throughout, strategic textual oppositions subvert the expected forms of social power and value. Authority and power shift to the customarily disempowered sides of opponent pairings: a woman and her (presumably male) flatterer, women and men, beggars and kings, crows and gentlemen, a horse and a squire, an earthworm and a sexton—these final pairs emphasizing the overriding opposition always at work in beast fables, animals and humans. But these oppositions are themselves unstable. Each pairing dissolves into the next as Gay exposes the irony, illusion, and vanity—as well as the injustice—of these very structures of power and class. The poem spirals down the Chain of Being and ends with a parodic graveside image: a solemn earthworm delivers a mock pronouncement on the death of a fat squire.

The fable opens with the speaker's flattering address to "Laura," a beautiful woman "singular" in her disdain for the kind of praise for which the verses keep reaching. This first section commends Laura for being so beautiful as to attract its "tribute" of praise, yet so "virtuous" as to reject it. The relationship of Laura and her genteel flatterer is the first of the poem's many oppositions. The speaker says:

> If you the tribute due disdain,
> The muse's mortifying strain
> Shall, like a woman, in mere spite
> Set beauty in a moral light.
>
> (ll. 19–22)

Laura's indifference exposes the vain poetic gaze of her insistent (male) flatterer (another rose-plucker?). From this initial opposition, the poem circles and recircles the theme of human vanity, finally concluding in an earthworm's ironically "sage opinion."

Toward the end of the preliminary address to Laura, the fable takes up its dialectic in terms of women and men. Into a hitherto feminized scene of beauty, the poem interjects images of masculinity and a language of stratification and tyranny. Feminized nature and masculinized society are at odds. "What's beauty?" the poem asks (l.55), still invoking the realm of the woman, Laura. The querying answer—"A flow'r that fades as soon as blown?"—(l. 56) gives way to the genderizing and power-coded shift: "What's man in all his boast of sway? / Perhaps the tyrant of a day" (ll. 57-58). Here follows a flurry of socially resonant words: "laws," "monarch," "regal line," "raised," "force," "pow'r," "destin'd." These signifiers of a stratified society tumble to a final, fervent warning that prompts the fable set within Gay's framing verse epistle: "Consider, man, weigh well thy frame; / The king, the beggar is the same" (ll. 69–70). The inner fable fixes steadily on relations of power. An ongoing insinuation of popular materials into the poem accentuates this maneuver: the subaltern—"the beggar"— becomes not only an empowered subject in this leveling "moral," but its source and voice as well.

The fable proper at the poem's center begins by paraphrasing a long popular ballad. This reference brings with it a constellation of texts and parodic maneuvers that, drifting up from the realm of traditional culture, encircle and enrich Gay's permutation of the story. His tale begins:

> Beneath a venerable yew,
> That in the lonely church-yard grew,
> Two Ravens sate. In solemn croak
> Thus one his hungry friend bespoke.
> Methinks I scent some rich repast,
> The savour strengthens with the blast;
> Snuff then; the promis'd feast inhale,
> I taste the carcase in the gale.
> Near yonder trees the farmer's steed,
> From toil and ev'ry drudg'ry freed,
> Hath groan'd his last. A dainty treat!
> To birds of taste delicious meat!
>
> (ll. 73–84)

This little conversation of hungry crows pondering a dead carcass paraphrases "The Three Ravens," a traditional English ballad which first appeared in print in 1611, apparently already an old song.[19] Since that time, the song has persisted in Anglo-American song tradition in a complex array of forms, most of them parodies, right up to our own day. The following eighteenth-century version was known to sheep shearers and harvest workers in Lincolnshire:

> There was three ravens in a tree,
> As black as any jet could be.
>   A down a derry down
> Says the middlemost raven to his mate,
> Where shall we go to get ought to eat?
> It's down in yonder grass-green field
> There lies a squire dead and killed.
> His horse all standing by his side,
> Thinking he'll get up and ride.
> His hounds all standing at his feet,
> Licking his wounds that run so deep.
> Then comes a lady, full of woe,
> As big wi bairn as she can go.
> She lifted up his bloody head,
> And kissed his lips that were so red.
> She laid her down all by his side,
> And for the love of him she died.[20]

This representative version of the ballad depicts a stable and accepted social order: the ruling squire mourned by horse, hawks, and hounds (his public possessions as hunter-warrior), and by his pregnant woman (his domestic possession as husband). Even in such straightforward, unparodic form, the ravens threaten this order by their scavenging presence and by the parody interjected into the scene by their speaking beaks. Nonetheless, the song renders in approving terms the key elements of this hierarchy. Its vanity is precisely targeted by Gay.

His fable of hungry crows undermines the original along several lines of social comment. First, its language is redolent of high society: "rich repast," "savour," "snuff," "taste," "steed," "dainty treat," "delicious meat." His carrion-feeding ravens wear the waistcoat and breeches of eighteenth-century England's manor houses. Moreover, the fable immediately opposes to its gentlemen-crows a realm "beneath," as these well-mannered ravens matter-of-factly project the probable identity of their upcoming feast: "the farmer's steed, / From toil and ev'ry drudg'ry freed" (ll. 81–82). Gay injects social critique into the ballad-borrowing as this world splays into opposing realms: preying gentleman-crows, oppressive farmers, and overworked horses whose "drudgery" only death can relieve. With his familiar maneuver of opposition, Gay divides his ballad reference in terms of rank, calling to our attention an oppression defined explicitly in terms of social position and work.

By citing the "Three Ravens," Gay situates his fable within a history of burlesque association. Satirical forms of the old ballad, more widespread and popular than the original, and almost as old, irreverently overturn the order and solemnity of their prototype. The first of these burlesques to reach print seems to be the Scottish *Twa Corbies* which appears in Walter Scott's *Minstrelsy of the Scottish Border* (1803). Here, crows observe that the slain knight's subjects abandon him at the first opportunity:

> His hound is to the hunting gane,
> His hawk to fetch the wild-fowl hame,
> His lady's ta'en another mate,
> So we may make our dinner sweet.[21]

But Gay's transformation of the "Three Ravens" has more telling affinity to another comic permutation: a burlesque which reduces the squire to a horse (as Gay's ravens mistakenly do at first). This parody seems not to have been printed before the middle of the nineteenth century. However, the song's form reveals an affiliation—presumably long-standing—with mock sermons, a popular tradition extending back to the late Middle Ages and a folk form in which the ballad still flourishes today.[22] Here is the song as it appears in a nineteenth-century minstrel show songster, the performance a parody of hymn singing:

Spoken (slowly and precisely).
There were three crows sat on a tree,
And they were black as black could be.
                              Brothers, sing!

Quartette.
There were three crows sat on a tree,
And they were black as black could be.
     Spoken.
One of them said unto his mate,
"What shall we do for grub to eat!"—
                              Brothers, sing!

Quartette.
One of them said unto his mate,
"What shall we do for grub to eat?"
     Spoken.
There lies a horse on yonder plain,
Whose bod-y has been late-ly slain.
                              Brothers, sing!

Quartette.
There lies a horse on yonder plain,
Whose bod-y has been late-ly slain.
     Spoken.
Let's perch ourselves on his back-bone,
And pick his eyes out, one by one!
                              Brothers, sing!

Quartette.
Let's perch ourselves on his back-bone,
And pick his eyes out, one by one!
     Spoken.
The devil thought to in-jure me,
By cutting down my apple-tree,
                              Brothers, sing!

Quartette.
The devil thought to in-jure me,
By cutting down my apple-tree.
     Spoken.
He did not in-jure me at all,
For I had apples all the fall.
                              Brothers, sing!

Quartette.
He did not in-jure me at all,
For I had apples all the fall.[23]

This burlesque mocks the church custom of "lining out" a hymn (also known as "deaconing"). Current since the seventeenth century, "lining out" involves the speaking (or chanting) of each line of a hymn by the song leader before it is sung by the congregation.[24] Such "deaconing" versions of the "Three Ravens" continue to be featured today in the parodic sermon, a long-standing folk jest tradition.[25]

Gay's parody of the "Three Ravens" leads explicitly to the ecclesiastical realm. Quickly the image of the overworked horse shifts to that of a parish sexton who, busy at his gravedigging "trade," overhears the ravens' "chat" (ll. 85–86). Again, Gay fixes his eye on hierarchy and work. Death gives this sexton in the employ of the church "no farther thought, / Than merely as the fees he brought" (ll. 87–88)—indeed, an image reminiscent of Ayckbourn's Guy at BLM. Temporarily distracted by the ravens, he demands that these "Blockhead" crows "learn more respect" (l. 91). (Such a man as the sexton would sing the original ballad with its dutiful hawks and hounds.) What these birds smell is no horse's carcass, but rather the "somewhat fat . . . squire, that yon fair hall possest" (l. 95). "Sure some diff'rence must be found" between horsemeat and squires, the sexton insists, "Or where's the dignity of man?" (ll. 101–4). The chatty ravens busily take up the sexton's question and decide that, as to the dignity of man, in the matter of tasty carcasses, dead horses are in fact preferred to fat squires. An argument ensues between these "disputing friends." An ironic and most undignified quarrel regarding "taste" and "the dignity of man" ensues.

The ravens refer the "case" to an authoritative arbiter, an earthworm who, "huge of size, unroll'd / His monstrous length." "To th' experience of his jaws / Each states the merits of the case." This selection of so vulnerable an arbiter—since birds routinely eat earthworms—is not without its irony. With great solemnity, the parodic judge undertakes a mock legal argument (cousin to the mock sermon, among traditional parodies). Peter Burke describes these widely popular mimickings of the forms of institutional power:

> Parodies of legal forms were almost as common as ecclesiastical parodies [such as mock sermons]. There were mock proclamations, mock trials, such as the trial of Carnival (or, in England), *The whole trial and indictment of Sir John Barleycorn*: most common of all, there were mock testaments—the cock's, the Pope's, the Devil's, Philip II's, Frederick the Great's, and many more. . . . [T]he creators of popular culture took over ready-made forms from the official culture of the church and the law. . . .[26]

With matchless self-importance, Gay's mock judge delivers an utterly leveling verdict: the worm distinguishes not at all between human and equine carcasses. Death confounds all hierarchy: "The prince," "the judge" (worms included), "The rich, the poor, the great, the small, / Are levell'd. Death confounds 'em all" (ll. 143-46).[27] Nor are the worm and his fellow "reptiles" so deluded as to imagine that the "real good of man" were a matter of "taste." Rather, value is "virtue" that "Mounts with the soul we know not where" (l. 154). Thus, the parodic worm returns the poem to its opening, to "virtue"—and to ironic negation. As Gay hinted at the outset, "virtue," rather than being a positive entity such as "goodness" or—even more to the point—"righteousness," is instead a *non*entity, a renunciation: Laura *refuses* to be fooled; she will not feed on flattery, the carrion of language.

Brought to worm level, Gay's fable voices a profound and self-implicating skepticism. Leaving the scavengers' dispute unresolved, the worm's parting remarks are the most castigating of all, indicting as they do the sexton and the predatory social structure which commands his allegiance.

> So good-man Sexton, since the case
> Appears with such a dubious face,
> To neither I the cause determine,
> For diffrent tastes please diff'rent vermine.
>
> (ll. 156–57)

The loyal sexton is identified: he is but a "diff'rent vermine." Moreover, in a manner typical of Gay, the fable encircles itself in this deepening spiral. Its proposition from the outset—the "dignity" and superiority of "man" framed within a "moral light"—erodes utterly through the course of the poem, particularly as it savors of the vulturism of the deluded sexton. All power arrangements stand mocked and indicted as the verse makes its way from the courtly realm of female beauty and male tyrants, on through the ballad-based fable which eventually undoes itself when "dignity" is found nowhere in sight, least of all in the sexton's churchyard. Thus, the facetious little poem spirals down the social system, undoing all forms of carrion-feasting and power-parsing artifice, even its own.

In "The Ravens, the Sexton, and the Earthworm," as in so many of Gay's works, popular traditions pervade the satire. They are crucial to Gay's metaleptic method and his sociohistorical sensibility. A *bricoleur* with these materials, Gay borrows from them and builds with them from the very center of a work. Indeed, the structure and scope of his satire can hardly be appreciated without identifying these stones, tiles, boards, and beams that make it up. "The Ravens, the Sexton, and the Earthworm" absorbs popular parodic traditions—mocking ballads, sermons, and legal arguments—and hones to a fine point their gestures of leveling reversal. It turns the irreverent stance of the ballad parody into a deeply and consciously held moral position, and one with harrowing poignance when we remember that "The Ravens, the Sexton, and the Earthworm," with its message of surrender

amidst a cherishing swirl of jokes and popular references, is the last of
Gay's fables.

Illustrations of a Changing Sensibility

As previously described, the *Fables* were enormously popular for generations. According to William Irving, the collection "almost acquired sanc-
tity by its juxtaposition with the Bible on all Victorian parlor tables."[28]
Their ready interest to the increasing market of readers at the lower ranks
was enhanced by the fact that they were short and easily reproduced in
cheap, abbreviated editions that common people could afford. Their ab-
sorbing illustrations further ensured widespread popularity, especially in
the burgeoning trade of children's literature.[29]

Gay seems to have taken an active part in arranging the illustrations.
The drawings for the 1727 collection were designed by two prominent artist friends, John Wootton and William Kent, the protégé of Gay's intimate,
Lord Burlington. Paul Fourdrinier, Michael Van der Gucht, and others were
the original engravers, whose delays of the project provoked from Gay
several complaints.[30] His scowling about them notwithstanding, the engravings are generally skilled and add a tangible dimensionality to the poems. For the monumentalizing posthumous edition of 1738, the duke and
duchess of Queensberry engaged two of the most esteemed engravers in
London, Hubert Gravelot and his collaborator Gérard Scotin. Through the
eighteenth and nineteenth centuries, a cavalcade of illustrators, both ac-
complished and indifferent, refitted the illustrations of the fables for numerous editions that tumbled yearly from the print shops. The most notable artists are Thomas Bewick and William Blake, whose images disclose key turns in the cultural meanings of the fables.

Thomas Bewick (1753–1828) of Northumberland supplied woodcuts
for *Fables of the Late Mr Gay*, an edition published in Newcastle by Thomas Saint in 1779. These early cuts, some of which Bewick began as an
apprentice, gained the young artist a premium from the national Society
for the Encouragement of the Arts, marking the beginning of his career.[31]
Bewick's illustrations exemplify the earthy vividness and appreciation for
the natural world that characterize his work in general. They show as well
the ever widening appeal of Gay's fables. Saint, a prominent north country
publisher, carried on a considerable trade in the cheap, woodcut broadside
and chapbook ballads and histories that catered to the lower ranks. His
edition of the fables with the young Bewick's simple yet masterful illustrations addresses an audience of common readers.

Bewick's depiction of the first fable, "The Lion, the Tyger, and the

Traveller," demonstrates his plebeianizing departure from the original engravings. Kent's image of 1727 combines the classical ambiance of the ancient Aesop with the swirling tension of the Baroque pastoral: beneath a leafy bower, a toga-clad traveler converses with a ferocious lion astride his vanquished foe. In contrast, Bewick's woodcut of 1779 brings us face-to-face with a hat-and-plaid-bedecked British walker with a well-maned lion pacing companionably at his side, the prone tiger in the background. We see the realistic depiction of plants and animals for which Bewick was to become famous. The woodcut encircles the scene with the everyday tools of country life for laboring people—rakes, shovels, hoes, and picks. (See fig. 10.)

Others of Bewick's scenes similarly draw attention to details of working life. The 1779 illustration for "Fable XLI. The Owl and the Farmer" fills the empty barn of the 1727 scene with an assortment of sheaves, rakes, pitchforks, and other farming implements. Bewick's rendering of "Fable XXXVI. Pythagoras and the Countryman" adjusts the scene rather to favor the countryman, whose neatly fenced farmhouse is not found in Kent's image and whose barn seems more sturdy than "weak" (as the fable would have it). Humans and animals are caught in action, sharply contrasting with the dead kite on the wall: as the visitor approaches, a small dog barks realistically while the countryman stands poised near the top of the ladder, the striking hammer in his upraised hand. (See figs. 11 and 12.)

In similar fashion, "Fable XXIV. The Butterfly and the Snail" transforms the manorial garden of Kent's image to a simple farmyard where two workmen are busy digging. In the last fable of the second set, "The Ravens, the Sexton, and the Earth-Worm," the busy urban scene of Gravelot's original becomes for Bewick a quiet rural churchyard; the sexton's country hat and coat are placed carefully to the side of a scene that renders everyone—human, crows, and worm—realistically to scale. In all of these, Bewick has created scenes familiar to and evocative of the readers who were in the process of identifying themselves as the English working "class" in the modern sense of, say, E. P. Thompson's analysis. The burlesquing politics of Gay's fables and other satires figure into that social, cultural, and literary history. (See figs. 13 and 14.)

William Blake (1757–1827) supplied twelve engravings for John Stockdale's 1793 *Fables by John Gay*.[32] Blake's luminescent images stand in striking contrast to the tangible, "this-worldly" particularity of Bewick's woodcuts. Indeed, Blake's otherworldly vision departs significantly from the ironic morality of immanence in the fables themselves. Yet, some of Blake's poems, especially in *Songs of Innocence and Experience*, betray in their ironies, underclass sympathies, and unresolving, almost fabling figures, the legacy of Gay.

W.ᵗ Kent inv.   P.ᵗ Fourdrinier sculp.

Fig. 10. Fourdrinier's engraving of Kent's illustration for fable 1 of John Gay's *Fables* (1727) and Bewick's woodcut illustration for *Fables of the Late Mr Gay* (Newcastle: Thomas Saint, 1779). Courtesy of the William Andrews Clark Memorial Library, University of California, Los Angeles, and the Department of Special Collections, Stanford University Libraries.

Fig. 11. Van der Gucht's engraving of Wootton's illustration for fable 41 of Gay's *Fables* (1727) and Bewick's woodcut illustration for *Fables of the Late Mr Gay* (1779). Courtesy of the William Andrews Clark Memorial Library, University of California, Los Angeles, and the Department of Special Collections, Stanford University Libraries.

W. Kent inv.   P. Fourdrinier sculp.

Fig. 12. Fourdrinier's engraving of Kent's illustration for fable 36 of Gay's *Fables* (1727) and Bewick's woodcut illustration for *Fables of the Late Mr Gay* (1779). Courtesy of the William Andrews Clark Memorial Library, University of California, Los Angeles, and the Department of Special Collections, Stanford University Libraries.

W. Kent inv.   P. Fourdrinier sculp.

Fig. 13. Fourdrinier's engraving of Kent's illustration for fable 24 of Gay's *Fables* (1727) and Bewick's woodcut illustration for *Fables of the Late Mr Gay* (1779). Courtesy of the William Andrews Clark Memorial Library, University of California, Los Angeles, and the Department of Special Collections, Stanford University Libraries.

Table XVI

H. Gravelot inv. et delin.   G. Scotin Sculp.
Published Sep. 29. 1738. by J. & P. Knapton & T. Cox.

Fig. 14. Scotin's engraving of Gravelot's illustration for fable 16 of Gay's *Fables* (1738) and Bewick's woodcut illustration for *Fables of the Late Mr Gay* (1779). Courtesy of the William Andrews Clark Memorial Library, University of California, Los Angeles, and the Department of Special Collections, Stanford University Libraries.

Blake's illustrations of the fables themselves bring to them a vision of transcendence. The image for "The Ravens, the Sexton, and the Earthworm," for example, positions Gay's surly sexton as the dazed and radiant center of a town or city setting. The scene contrasts in its urbanity and abstractness to Bewick's rural simplicity on the one hand, and in its order and piety to Gravelot's baroque skepticism on the other. For Blake—seemingly oblivious here to Gay's ironic moral position—the grandeur of man is not to be undermined. (See fig. 15.)

Fig. 15. Blake's engraving for fable 16 of *Fables by John Gay* (London: John Stockdale, 1793). Courtesy of the Huntington Library, San Marino, California.

With brilliant and beautiful abstraction, Blake's images tend to sidestep the satiric social levelings of the fable texts themselves. Thus, the exchange in fable 24 between an "upstart" butterfly and "his now forgotten friend, a Snail" (who awkwardly recalls the former's caterpillar background) becomes in Blake a beautifully poised tension between contrasting shapes of light. (See fig. 16.) Gay's satire on attitude and self-awareness disappears

Fig. 16. Blake's engraving for fable 24 of *Fables by John Gay* (London: John Stockdale, 1793). Courtesy of the Huntington Library, San Marino, California.

as the glowing wings of Blake's butterfly hover above the curving snail and the memory of its earthbound origins. The castigated owl of "Fable XLI. The Owl and the Farmer" becomes for Blake similarly apparitional: a mysteriously glowing spot that bypasses Gay's meaning altogether. Blake's is quite a different creature from Wootton's original owl, who looks every bit the stolid "blockhead" of the text. (See fig. 17.)

Gay's fables became set pieces of cultural discourse, almost as readily called to mind as biblical passages in their shaping familiarity and widespread relevance. Like biblical episodes, Gay's well-known scenes supplied artists such as Blake and Bewick a point of departure for their own independent visions. This is nowhere more apparent than in the illustration by Blake that opens the fables, "The Shepherd and the Philosopher." William Kent's original image straightforwardly depicts Gay's mutually respectful conversation between a "deep Philosopher (whose rules / Of moral life were drawn from schools)" (ll. 11–12) and a modest Shepherd whose "little knowledge . . . Was all from simple nature" (ll. 33–34). Obviously proceeding from the familiar design, Blake's image transforms the original

Fig. 17. Blake's engraving for fable 41 of *Fables by John Gay* (London: John Stockdale, 1793). Courtesy of the Huntington Library, San Marino, California.

with his characteristic use of white to accentuate the standing philosopher. Robed and bearded and linked visually to the sheep, now become much more prominent, the philosopher takes on a transcending Biblical resonance as he points, prophet-like, to the cottage added in the distance. Blake's engravings are brilliant, if willfully distorting, visual transformations of Gay's message. Shaped by a determinate and unifying aesthetic, Blake's changes suggest the inaccessibility, even unpalatability, of the earlier poet's moral vision of an ironic and paradoxical immanence. (See fig. 18, p. 270.)

RESISTANCE TO GAY'S FABLES

By the end of the eighteenth century, Gay's *Fables* began to provoke uneasiness among certain of the morally minded. While *The Beggar's Opera* had triggered complaints of impropriety from the beginning, *The Fables* were at first recognized as moral satire. Thus, the writer of *The Egg; or, The Memoirs of Gregory Giddy . . . Conceived by a Celebrated Hen* (c.

IV. Kent inv.   C. Fourdrinier sculp.

Blake sc

Fig. 18. Fourdrinier's engraving of Kent's illustration for "The Shepherd and the Philosopher" of Gay's *Fables* (1727) and Blake's engraving for it in *Fables by John Gay* (1793). Courtesy of the William Andrews Clark Memorial Library, University of California, Los Angeles, and the Huntington Library, San Marino, California.

1728) voices the standard view of Gay's contemporaries: "I don't imagine that the morality contained in Mr. Gay's 'fables' will ever eradicate the seeds of vice, sown by his 'Beggar's Opera.'"[33] By the century's end, however, *The Fables* joined *The Beggar's Opera* in the eyes of disapproving commentators, many of whom echoed and expanded Johnson's criticisms. The preface to a 1797 edition of Gay's poetry catalogs those features of the poems deemed morally and stylistically unacceptable. The list is instructive.

> The pieces omitted in this publication are the greatest part of his fables, the morality of which cannot tolerate the human speeches of quadrupeds and birds, or of a barley-mow and dunghill; those founded on nature are only retained. The other parts deemed exceptionable, are descriptions of savage sports, heathen mythology, and pieces, temporary, local, and indelicate.[34]

While this preface does not really explain the "morality" that has dictated the omissions, the words "savage" and "heathen" resonate with Johnson's remarks in his "life" of Gay cited in chapter 2 above. The objection to "pieces . . . indelicate" calls to mind as well the ongoing controversy about *The Beggar's Opera* and the moral uneasiness about appropriate behavior and rank to which Warton gave voice.

Their widespread popularity at all social levels as children's fare ensured that Gay's *Fables* increasingly drew the scrutiny of moralists, educators, and authors of conduct books. Eventually, editorial censorship followed. In 1815 and 1816 the *European Magazine* published a series of letters on "the defective morality" found there. Written by the educator and clergyman, John Lettice, the letters are inscribed "to the Misses Mathews, Governesses of an Establishment for the Education of Young Ladies, at Union-place, Regent's Park."[35] Lettice's criticism actually throws into relief Gay's own moral purpose. Indeed, Gay's satire articulates a morality that runs counter to the depoliticized individual striving of Johnson and the constrained subservience of Lettice. Like Johnson, Lettice maintains that it is the moralist's business to advocate a dutiful, rationally idealized heroism. As he says, "It is much less the business of the moralist, to tell us what the world is, than what it ought to be."[36] For Gay, of course, quite contrary lessons emerge: see the world as it is, especially one's own limitations; recognize injustice, appreciate the jokes, and behave honorably and without cruelty. Lettice's "Letters on Gay's Fables" preach a morality of hierarchy and social control completely at odds with the ironies and exposed deceptions in Gay's world of indeterminacy.

This line of criticism and editorial pruning of Gay in the nineteenth century is even more apparent in James Plumptre's edition of the *Fables* of 1823, as mentioned in chapter 2, above. In his introduction, Plumptre declares:

The Fables of Gay have ever been esteemed for their easy flow of versifi-
cation, for their wit and humour, and for containing a considerable portion
of moral and worldly instruction. They are not however, without a very
considerable portion of alloy.[37]

Quoting Johnson and Lettice in support of his moral reconstitution of the
poems, Plumptre submits his "selection" for the approval of "the Special
and Subcommittees of the Society for promoting Christian Knowledge"

with such omissions and alterations as he judged necessary to make an
exceptionable book for the youth of both sexes. . . . The omissions and
alterations have been made upon the same principles which have guided
the editor in his former works; that is, that nothing should remain which
can occasion a blush on the cheek of modesty, or grieve the heart of piety;
in short, that nothing should appear inconsistent with the faith, the conversation, and the practice of a Christian. (ix–x)

The bowdlerizing of the disparaging Plumptre takes place in a world much
changed from 1738, when the two-set collection of *Fables* appeared as
testimony that Gay was "(what he esteemed the best Character) a Man of a
truly honest Heart, and a sincere Lover of his Country." As popular as the
verse tales continued to be through the nineteenth century, the shifting ironies, political satire, and universal morality across ranks and categories
became increasingly "unnatural" and inaccessible to readers in an earnest,
industrializing Victorian world. Illustrations by Henry Heath (*fl.* 1824–50)
from about 1830 show the nineteenth-century resistance to the talking owls
and butterflies of Gay's earlier era.[38] In cartoons that render the fables in
the slapstick of music-hall comedy, Heath fully humanizes the characters.
The conversing avians of fable 32, who take up with solemnity "the dignity of owls" in contrast to a frivolous sparrow, become in Heath's imagining owlishly human professors on a Cambridge street, eyeing a dandy on
the sidewalk. The snail and butterfly of fable 24 become for Heath a plod-
ding, big-footed old gent partnered with a toe-dancing, feather-flouncing
ballerina. Heath circumvents altogether the turning of the fable form in
Gay's texts to an interrogation of Poovey's "classificatory thinking" cited
earlier. Bypassed as well is their preoccupation with morality as self-awareness in a complex and interactive natural world.

   The reflexivity of the fable as a genre, together with its proverbial and
popular bent, must have been irresistible to the notably ironic Gay. Not
surprisingly, the self-implicating slippery slope of their pervasive and often funny indictments of benighted moralizing became unpalatable to earnest preceptors of a later era. But Gay's fables speak freshly as we self-
referential postmoderns move into the twenty-first century. Like all of his

Fig. 19. Fourdrinier's engraving of Kent's illustration for fable 32 of Gay's *Fables* (1727) and Heath's engraving for *Illustrations of Gay's Fables* (London: S. Maunder, c. 1830). Courtesy of the William Andrews Clark Memorial Library, University of California, Los Angeles, and the Harvard Theatre Collection, Houghton Library.

satire, the fables take up the issue of abusive power relations, especially targeting the unthinking human exploitation of the earth and its plants and animals. Gay paints a South Sea Bubble world of capitalist venture that has at base ethical problems stemming from unchecked individual appetite and irresponsible self-aggrandizement. Like *The Beggar's Opera*, the fables undercut their misapprehending speakers, especially the moralizing ones, including the fabulist himself. Self-delusion and the honesty and humility that are its antidotes are the favorite topic. Now seems a good time to take Gay's fables up again.

Epilogue

This book has examined John Gay's sensibility as it reflects, recasts, and comments upon a contextualizing matrix of polite and popular forms and materials of the eighteenth century. In their play upon and between these levels, Gay's satires show how what we now identify as "cultural forms"—people's customary modes of expression and behavior—came to express stratifying categories in an emerging socioeconomic system of striving individuals: social ranks, ethnic identities, genders, sexual orientations, and so on. Popular songs, images, stories, dramas, dances, and sayings are used to mark social place and to express the point of view from that position. Throughout Gay's works, speaking subjects from one level mirror those from another through parodic irony, allusion, and the historical reflections of metalepsis. This socially resonant poetics still reverberates through our own demarcations of "polite" from "popular" art.

More specifically, a range of plebeian forms—ballads and songs, country dances, catches, mumming plays, beliefs and sayings, fables, stories, and legends—are brought by Gay to comment on "polite" opera, drama, and literature. Such satires as *The Beggar's Opera*, *The Shepherd's Week*, and *Achilles*, are best understood in and illuminate this context of "under-" "middle-," and "upper-" class expression. In Gay's hands, such mock pastorals, genre-confounding dramas, fables, and songs disclose an ethical and political questioning that continues to apply to the modern and post-modern world, as the "Beggar's Operas" by Brecht, Havel, and Ayckbourn attest. The juxtaposed materials Gay employed effectively made his a significant voice at a pivotal historical moment.

Gay's multimedia satires place us within a kaleidoscopic mirroring and reverberation of early modern forms. These spectra of citation bring into focus human beings—women *and* men—who encounter each other as historical and cultural selves. Like his fabling roses, birds, and barley mows, we speak from the contexts of our kind. In the marketplace of a rather unbrave new world, our predicaments emerge from transactions involving

275

private desires and personal relations. But these dynamics are political, bearing on larger relations of power and questions of justice. The good, when encountered apart from the self-justifying, is ingloriously humble, fair, and honest: the beauty of the song in the midst of its frail and failure-ridden setting.

John Gay fashioned his art at the cusp of the modern era. With enduring insight, it opens to our view the whole matrix of literature, drama, culture, music, popular lore, and history of his early-eighteenth century. Its satiric and aesthetic preoccupations reveal how that Georgian moment put into place key intellectual and sociopolitical underpinnings for the modern era, now questioned in our postmodernity. Gay's satire is a call to contextualized self-reflection. "Gentle Reader," he exhorts in "The Proeme" of *The Shepherd's Week*, "turn over the Leaf, and entertain thyself with the Prospect of thine own Country" (ll. 87–88). The punning phrase "entertain thyself" is the mirror at the center of a richly cultural and historical "Prospect." Bid to diversion, we are called as well to self-awareness.

Notes

PROLOGUE

1. Geertz, "Deep Play: Notes on the Balinese Cockfight," in *Interpretation of Cultures,* 412–53.

2. Jeremy Bentham, *The Theory of Legislation,* ed. C. K. Ogden, trans. R. Hildreth (London: Kegan Paul, Trench, Trubner and Co.; New York: Harcourt, Brace and Co., 1931), 106. See also Lon L. Fuller, *The Morality of Law,* rev. ed. (New Haven: Yale University Press, 1964), 9.

3. E. B. Tylor defines the term in *Primitive Culture: Researches into the Development of Mythology, Philosophy, Religion, Art, and Customs,* 2 vols. (London: John Murray, 1871), 1: "Culture or Civilization, taken in its wide ethnographic sense, is that complex whole which includes knowledge, belief, art, morals, law, custom, and any other capabilities and habits acquired by man as a member of society." This meaning reached common parlance in the Victorian era after gradually developing out of the eighteenth-century intellectual and artistic context, especially with the writings of Herder. See Williams, *Keywords,* 76–82. Gay should be recognized as an important voice in this developing context.

4. See E. P. Thompson, "Patrician Society, Plebeian Culture," *Journal of Social History* 7 (1974): 382–405 and "Eighteenth-Century English Society: Class Struggle without Class," *Social History* 3 (1978): 152–64. For background on this topic, see Preston, *Folklore, Literature, and Cultural Theory.*

5. Thompson's recent work focused on this realm of popular culture. See *Customs in Common.*

6. Winton, *John Gay and the London Stage;* Lewis and Wood, *John Gay and the Scriblerians;* and Nokes, *John Gay.*

7. Thompson, "The Poverty of Theory or an Orrery of Errors," in *Poverty of Theory,* 171. On the importance of analyzing texts in a cultural context, see also Jauss, *Aesthetic Experience,* and *Toward an Aesthetic of Reception.*

8. Joan W. Scott, "The Evidence of Experience," *Critical Inquiry* 17 (1991): 784.

9. Gayatri Spivak, *In Other Worlds* (New York: Methuen, 1987), 241.

10. Hutcheon, *Theory of Parody.* See also *Irony's Edge.*

11. Metalepsis or Transumption" in *The New Princeton Encyclopedia of Poetry and Poetics,* ed. Alex Preminger and T. V. F. Brogan (Princeton: Princeton University Press, 1993), 759–60.

12. On the increasing separation of belles lettres from the sphere of popular and customary forms, see Burke, *Popular Culture;* and Peter Stallybrass and Allon White, *The Politics and Poetics of Transgression* (Ithaca: Cornell University Press, 1986).

13. David Nokes stresses this idea in his recent biography, *John Gay,* 470–532.

CHAPTER 1. *THE BEGGAR'S OPERA* IN THE TWENTIETH CENTURY

1. With this book already in press, I note my gratitude to Calhoun Winton for bringing to my attention the existence in the Ellington Collection of the Smithsonian Archives another twentieth-century "translation" of Gay's *Beggar's Opera*. *The Beggar's Holiday*, with music by Billy Strayhorn and Duke Ellington and libretto by John Latouche, was produced by Perry Watkins, opened in New York on 26 December 1946, and ran through March 1947. For an overview of the production and Billy Strayhorn's contribution, see David Hajdu, *Lush Life: A Biography of Billy Strayhorn* (New York: Farrar Straus Giroux, 1996), 100–105. This biracially collaborative American play— "too daring for its time," according to George Abbott, one of the directors (ibid., 104)—further demonstrates the importance of *The Beggar's Opera* and Gay's sensibility for modern and postmodern sociocultural critique.

2. Donaldson, " 'A Double Capacity': *The Beggar's Opera*," in *World Upside Down*, 159–82.

3. John Gay, *The Beggar's Opera*, ed. Edgar V. Roberts (Lincoln: University of Nebraska Press, 1969), introduction, line 15. All subsequent quotations are from this source, the only readily available edition of the play that includes the music.

4. Langford, *Walpole and the Robinocracy*, 22. Of course, much has been written on Walpole and his ministry. For general introductions, see Jeremy Black, *Robert Walpole and the Nature of Politics in Early Eighteenth-Century Britain* (London: Macmillan, 1990) and Langford's opening chapter in *Excise Crisis*, 4–25. Bertrand Goldgar's *Walpole and the Wits* argues that Walpole's administration severed a longstanding political function for art and literature, a shift that accounts for the keenness and pervasiveness of literary attack. Certainly the outlines of this argument hold, especially if it is enlarged to encompass not just issues of patronage and function for literature, but a larger shift in the relationship of representation and expression to the structures of power. See B. W. Last, *Politics and Letters in the Age of Walpole* (Newcastle upon Tyne: Avero, 1987).

5. For a general summary of the social and political context for Gay's plays, see Bryan Loughrey and T. O. Treadwell's introduction to *The Beggar's Opera* (London and New York: Penguin, 1986), 7–34. For more detailed treatment, see Schultz, *Gay's Beggar's Opera*. On the South Sea Bubble, see Carswell, *South Sea Bubble*.

6. On Wild, Walpole, and the criminal milieu of the 1720s, see Gerald Howson, *Thief-Taker General: The Rise and Fall of Jonathan Wild* (London: Hutchinson, 1970).

7. As Langford and others note, Gay's use of Walpole as a glancing cultural referent in *The Beggar's Opera* was turned to more direct attack on him in opposition political writing that followed and exploited the play (Langford, *Walpole and the Robinocracy*, 23).

8. Nathan Bailey, *An Universal Etymological English Dictionary* (London: E. Bell, 1721).

9. On the complicated origins and textual history of the play, see Stephen Hinton, "'Matters of intellectual property': The Sources and Genesis of *Die Dreigroschenoper*," in Hinton, *Kurt Weill*, 9–49. Elisabeth Hauptmann's collaborations with Brecht are well known, if difficult to document. See Paula Hanssen, *Elisabeth Hauptmann, Brecht's Silent Collaborator* (Bern: Peter Lang, 1995). Hauptmann began translating Gay in 1927, after spending time in London. See Sabine Kebir, *Ich fragte nicht nach meinem Anteil* (Berlin: Aufbau, 1997), 102. The manuscript of Hauptmann's rendering of Gay seems not to have survived, and scholars remain unsure about exactly what she translated and how, and what relation her work has to Brecht's play. See Hanssen, *Elisabeth Hauptmann*, 30–32. *The Beggar's Opera* came to Hauptmann's attention through Nigel Playfair's London productions of the early twenties. Playfair revived *The Beggar's Opera* in 1920 with great success and staged

Polly as well in 1922–23, the latter being played for the first time since its original (much delayed) performance in 1777. See Winton, *John Gay and the London Stage,* 128–48. For Playfair's account, see Nigel Playfair, *The Story of the Lyric Theatre Hammersmith* (London: Chatto and Windus, 1925), 135–44.

10. Patrick O'Connor, "Turning Points: Fifty Works that Shaped the Century," *London Times,* 15 May 1999, sec. A, 6.

11. The transformation of the play into the film entailed changes to the work as well as controversy and a much-publicized legal dispute between Brecht and Weill on the one hand, and Pabst and the filmmakers on the other. Despite Brecht's vociferous complaints, critics tend to see Pabst's transposition as articulating the original play's sociopolitical critique, but with more attention to the characters and sentiments in a media that is visual rather than verbal. See Lee Atwell, *G. W. Pabst* (Boston: Twayne Publishers, 1977), 83–103; and Thomas Elsaesser, "Transparent Duplicities: *The Threepenny Opera* (1931)," in *The Films of G. W. Pabst,* ed. Eric Rentschler (New Brunswick, N.J.: Rutgers University Press, 1990), 103–15.

12. The high-budget film was originally planned to be released in three versions—German, French, and English—a common practice before the invention of dubbing. The German film premiered in Berlin in 1931, and it and a French version met with initial success. The German film (Warner Brothers/Nero-Films/Tobis) was banned in 1933, and negatives were confiscated and destroyed. However, the film was discovered and is currently available on videocasette. See Atwell, *G. W. Pabst,* 94–95; Elsaesser, "Transparent Duplicities," 104; and Hans-Michael Bock, "Georg Wilhelm Pabst: Documenting a Life and a Career," in Rentschler, *Films of G.W. Pabst,* 225–26.

13. The remarks were made near the time of the suppression of the play in December of 1728 by the courtier Lord Hervey. See John, Lord Hervey, *Lord Hervey's Memoirs,* ed. Romney Sedgwick (London: Batsford, 1963; reprint, New York: Penguin, 1984), 20. For discussion of the production history, see Dianne Dugaw, *Warrior Women,* 194–96. See also Schultz, *Gay's Beggar's Opera,* 208–20.

14. Theodor Weisengrund-Adorno, "Zur Dreigroschenoper," translated by Stephen Hinton, in Hinton, *Kurt Weill,* 131. Adorno's essay appeared in *Die Musik* 22 (1929): 424–28.

15. Bertolt Brecht, "On *The Threepenny Opera,*" in Manheim and Willett, *Collected Plays,* 2:323–24. This essay appeared as "Über die Dreigroschenoper—I" in Brecht's *Schriften zum Theater.* Dated 9 January 1929, it was an article in *Augsburger Neueste Nachrichten* to introduce a production of the play. The translation is from this edition.

16. Michel Foucault's *History of Sexuality* first mapped the general outlines of this emergent modern ideology of Western sexuality in the eighteenth century and its social and institutional contexts.

17. In "'Matters of intellectual property'," Hinton traces Brecht's development of a "less debonair" Macheath through several early versions of the play (30–31).

18. For a recent edition, see Sarah Fielding, *The Governess: or, Little Female Academy* (London: Pandora, 1987).

19. Brecht, *The Threepenny Opera,* translated by Ralph Manheim and John Willett, in Brecht, *Collected Plays,* ed. Manheim and Willett, 2:147. All references to the play will be to this edition.

20. From the "Closing verses of the ballad" that Brecht composed for *Die Buele* (The bruise), his proposed treatment for Pabst's *Threepenny Opera.* The transformation of the gang into bankers under Polly's direction is part of this treatment. Brecht's idea for the script departs completely from the original play and was unwelcome to the producers, who dismissed him from the project. See Manheim and Willett, introduction to Brecht, *Threepenny Opera,* xxv–xxvi.

21. On Hogarth's series, see Ronald Paulson, *Hogarth: His Life, Art, and Times*, 2 vols. (New Haven: Yale University Press, 1971), 1:180–95.

22. Calhoun Winton, "John Gay's *Beggar's Opera* and Václav Havel's," in *Augustan Subjects: Essays in Honor of Martin C. Battestin*, ed. Albert J. Rivero (Newark: University of Delaware Press; London: Associated University Presses, 1997), 145. Winton discusses Havel's play—which was suppressed after the first performance on 1 November 1975—in terms of the playwright's political criticism of the regime and imprisonment, particularly for his being a founding member of the "Charter 77" human rights movement of the mid 1970s. Thus, Macheath's signing of Lockit's agreement at the play's end resonates with the Husák regime's "Anti-Charter" pledge of loyalty "For New Creative Deeds in the Name of Socialism and Peace" and repudiation of the original document's declarations of freedom (140–42).

23. Václav Havel, "The Beggar's Opera" (in manuscript), 5. This is a translation by Michal Schonberg and Josef P. Skala of the Czech original published by Sixty-Eight Publishers Corp., Toronto, Ontario in 1977. I am grateful to the translators for permission to cite their work. I must also thank Marketa Goetz-Stankiewicz and Norma Comrada for helping me to locate it. The English version of the play was premiered in Vancouver, B.C., Canada on 22 April 1992 by Kitsilano Theatre under the direction of Kico Gonzalez-Risso. All citations are from this version.

24. For relevant passages in Ovid, see *Artis amatoriae* (Oxford: Oxford University Press, 1989), 1:675–78.

25. As Winton observes, the latter probably alludes to the pressured signing of a document of repudiation of an earlier human rights statement.

26. Alan Ayckbourn, *A Chorus of Disapproval* (London: Faber and Faber, 1986). All quotes are from this text. Ayckbourn collaborated on the screenplay with Michael Winner (Scimitar Films, 1989). The movie version of *A Chorus of Disapproval* (Cinema Seven Productions, Ltd.), produced by Eliot Kastner and directed by Michael Winner, features Anthony Hopkins and Jeremy Irons in the roles of Dafydd and Guy.

27. For the famous account of the meteoric public infatuation with Gay's "Polly" and her original actress, Lavinia Fenton, see Schultz, *Gay's Beggar's Opera*, 23–25.

28. This detail is changed in the film version, which thus takes on a notably lighter ending. Although he collaborated on the film screenplay, Ayckbourn has voiced disappointment about the film, the transformed ending in particular. See his discussion of the adaptation in Bernard F. Dukore, "An Interview with Alan Ayckbourn," in *Alan Ayckbourn: A Casebook* (New York and London: Garland Publishing, 1991), 15–17.

Chapter 2. Dangerous Sissy

1. With regard to women's authorship and publishing, see Catherine Gallagher, *Nobody's Story* (Berkeley: University of California Press, 1994). In recent years, scholars are reconsidering Gay and the importance of his art. See Winton, *John Gay and the London Stage;* and Lewis and Wood, *John Gay and the Scriblerians*.

2. See Guillory, *Cultural Capital;* and Jonathan Kramnick, "The Making of the English Canon," *PMLA* 112 (1997): 1087–1101. See also Weber, *The Rise of the Musical Classics*.

3. For full-length biographical treatments of Gay, see Irving, *John Gay, Favorite of the Wits;* and Nokes, *John Gay*. Nokes's biography uncovers new information on Gay's background, particularly with regard to business affairs in his extended family and his affectional relations.

4. Nokes, *John Gay*, 16–35.

5. Gay's relations with the Scriblerian circle of Swift and Pope have received some scholarly attention. However, two of his closest, most enduring, and especially shaping friendships were with Henrietta Howard, countess of Suffolk, and Catherine Hyde, duchess of Queensberry. For his collected letters, see Gay, *Letters*, ed. Burgess.

6. See Yvonne Noble, "John Gay's Monument," in Lewis and Wood, *John Gay and the Scriblerians*, 216–18.

7. This appendage of over two hundred pages is attached to Thomas Whincop's *Scanderberg: or, Love and Liberty. A Tragedy* (London: W. Reeve, 1747), 87–320.

8. Gay is favorably contrasted with Pope: "It is plain that Mr. Pope esteem'd himself a Writer only of that Sort of Pastoral which painted the Golden Age. Mr. Gay, on the contrary leaves that behind, and gives his Shepherds and Shepherdesses a Turn altogether modern and natural." See William Ayre, *Memoirs of the Life and Writings of Alexander Pope*, 2 vols. (London: Printed for the Author, and Sold by the booksellers of London and Westminster by his Majesty's authority, 1745), 2:129. Ralph Straus suggests in *The Unspeakable Curll* (London: Chapman and Hall, 1927), 194–97, that Edmund Curll may have authored these *Memoirs*.

9. Theophilus Cibber et al., *The Lives of the Poets of Great Britain and Ireland*, 5 vols. (London: Printed for R. Griffiths, 1753), 4:259. This work was compiled by Robert Shiels with additions by Cibber.

10. Oliver Goldsmith, *Works*, ed. J. W. Gibbs, 5 vols. (London, 1884–86), 5:156. His review of *The Beggar's Opera* in *The London Chronicle; or, Universal Evening Post* 4, no. 278 (7–10 October 1758) observes that "so sweet and happy a genius as Mr. Gay possessed of could achieve anything."

11. John Gay, *The Beggar's Opera . . . To which is prefixed the Life of the Author* (Glasgow, 1772), 7. This editor finds Gay "universally read" and "represented."

12. David Erskine Baker (continued from 1764 to 1782 by Isaac Reed), *Biographia Dramatica, A New Edition Carefully Corrected, Greatly Enlarged, and Continued from 1764 to 1782*, 2 vols. (London: Printed for Mess. Rivingtons, &c., 1782), 2:401. Reed notes that this "good-natured burlesque" was still "frequently performed" in 1782.

13. Tobias Smollett, *The History of England from the Revolution to the Death of George II*, 5 vols. (London: T. Cadell and R. Baldwin, 1790), 2:460.

14. Most twentieth-century concern with morality treats *The Beggar's Opera*. See Winton, *John Gay and the London Stage*, 109–27; and Schultz, *Gay's Beggar's Opera*.

15. John Gay, *The Works . . . To Which Is Added an Account of the Life and Writings of the Author*, 4 vols. (Dublin: James Potts, 1770), 1:vii.

16. [Eliza Haywood], *The Parrot* (London: T. Gardner, 1746), no. 9, 2v.

17. See Hunt, *Middling Sort*.

18. Joseph Warton, *An Essay on the Genius and Writings of Pope*, 5th ed., 2 vols. (London: W. J. and J. Richardson, &c., 1806), 1:245–46; first published in 1756.

19. Irving contextualizes this story with discussion of trade in Barnstaple and in Gay's family in *John Gay, Favorite of the Wits*, 17–27.

20. David Nokes, "The Smartness of a Shoe-boy: Deference and Mockery in Gay's Life and Work," *Times Literary Supplement*, 20 January 1995, 13–14. See Nokes, *John Gay*, 42–50, citing John Dunton's "The He-Strumpets," a poem describing Willets' clientele as "Men worse than goats / Who dress themselves in petticoats . . . / These doat on men, and some on boys, / And quite abandon female joys."

21. Nokes, "Smartness of a Shoe-boy," 13. Nokes proposes that "the urgent attempts of Pope and Swift to suppress and sanitize the details of Gay's early private life would seem to confirm a suspicion that there was something they wished to conceal more shameful than a mere background in trade" (*John Gay*, 44). This "something" Nokes believes to be that Gay was "at least a latent homosexual" (50). Whatever the poet's affectional life and sexual

expression, Nokes stands squarely within the tradition of discussing Gay in terms of "manliness" and a gendered identity.

22. Ayre, *Memoirs,* 2:97.

23. John Gay, *Plays ... To Which Is Added an Account of the Life and Writings of the Author* (London: J. and R. Tonson, 1760), iii–iv.

24. Gay, *Works* (Dublin), 4:ii.

25. Samuel Johnson, *Lives of the English Poets,* ed. George Birkbeck Hill, 3 vols. (Oxford: Clarendon Press, 1905). Quotes are from this edition. Commissioned by Johnson's publishers, *Lives* reflects the period preoccupation with retrospective collecting and cataloguing in sundry dictionaries, memoirs, and checklists. Johnson infused this codification with a compelling morality. On Johnson and biography, see William H. Epstein, *Recognizing Biography* (Philadelphia: University of Pennsylvania Press, 1987), esp. 52–70. See also Honan, *Authors' Lives,* 17–25.

26. See Michael McKeon, "Writer as Hero: Novelistic Prefigurations and the Emergence of Literary Biography," in Epstein, *Contesting the Subject,* 17–41. See also Robert Folkenflik, "The Artist As Hero in the Eighteenth Century," *Yearbook of English Studies* 12 (1982): 91–108.

27. By the early nineteenth century, Johnson's "Life" appeared—without attribution—in disparate publications of Gay's works. See, for example, editions of *The Fables ... with the Life of the Author* published in Vienna by R. Sammer in 1799 and in Dublin by William Porter in 1804.

28. Johnson, *Lives,* 2:282.

29. Jeffrey Plank, "Reading Johnson's *Lives*: The Forms of Late Eighteenth-Century Literary History," in *The Age of Johnson: A Scholarly Annual,* ed. Paul Korshin (New York: AMS Press, 1989), 1:351.

30. As Plank observes, Johnson's "lives" may counter, sometimes even parody authors' works. He notes that "the life of Milton is thus a parody of *Paradise Lost, Paradise Regained,* and *Samson Agonistes.. . . .* If the life of Milton is a moral tale that parodies the epic and the epic hero . . . then the life of Pope is a moral tale that demonstrates the superiority of the moral tale to the mock epic for dealing with the figure of the poet" (ibid., 343–44).

31. Johnson, *Lives,* 2:267–68.

32. See Lewis, "Risking Contradiction: John Gay's *Fables* and the Matter of Reading" in *Fables,* 156–84.

33. As Annabel Patterson shows, the pastoral up to the Romantic era conventionally carried moral and political implication. See *Pastoral and Ideology.* See also Armens, *John Gay, Social Critic;* and Empson, *Some Versions of Pastoral.*

34. See Samuel Johnson, *The Works of the English Poets,* 58 vols. (London: C. Bathurst, J. Buckland, &c., 1779–80), 41: frontispiece. See also *Catalogue of Engraved British Portraits Preserved in the Department of Prints and Drawings in the British Museum,* 6 vols. (London: Longmans & Co., &c. by order of The Trustees, 1908–25), 2:291.

35. I am indebted for my work on portraits of Gay to the Archives of the National Portrait Gallery, London and to the Department of Prints and Drawings of the British Museum, London. For a summary of printed images, see John Chaloner Smith, *British Mezzotinto Portraits, being A Descriptive Catalogue,* 4 vols. (London: Henry Sotheran, 1883), 2:789–90.

36. Gay, *Letters,* 6 July 1728.

37. *The Bystander; or, Universal Weekly Expositor by a Literary Association* (London: H. Thomas, 1790), 195.

38. William Coxe, "Life of Gay," in Gay, *Fables Illustrated with Notes and the Life of the Author by William Coxe* (London: T. Cadell, jr. and W. Davies, 1796), 65–66.

39. *The Poetical Works of John Gay . . . to Which Is Prefixed the Life of the Author* (Edinburgh: Mundell and Son, 1794), 262.

40. Gay's works were popular across class lines from the beginning. Their appropriation by publishers marketing children's literature—for example, the Bow Churchyard printshop of William and Cluer Dicey—contributed to and reflected this popularity. Eventually moral reformers promulgated literature for lower-class people and children. The cautionary presentation of Gay's works fits into the context of this development in the field of popular literature as a whole. See Dugaw, *Warrior Women*, 140–42.

41. In *Resemblance and Disgrace* Helen Deutsch has examined Pope's physical appearance and disabilities in connection with his work. As she observes, Johnson depicts Pope as a "feminized cripple" (33). However, Pope himself—and eventually his supporters—tended to see his work as a surmounting heroism whereby he became a "warrior in the fight for good" (32).

42. Mack, *Alexander Pope,* 652–71.

43. On this problem for scholarship on Gay, see Nokes, *John Gay*, 535–38.

44. As Nokes observes, it was not only Gay's apprenticeship with Willett that discomfited Pope. He was equally anxious to cover over the young Gay's service in 1713 to the duchess of Monmouth (ibid., 44). This preoccupation of Pope with the possibility that "commoness" might be suggested hints at uneasiness among his friends about Gay's background and rank.

45. Gay, *Fables . . . with a Life of the Author,* 2 vols. (London: J. Stockdale, 1793), 2:163–64.

46. Gay, *Poems . . . with the Author's Life* (Poughmill, U.K.: George Nicholson, 1801), i.

47. See the editor's remarks about the fables in *Poems by John Gay . . . to Which Is Prefixed, A Sketch of the Author's Life* (Manchester: G. Nicholson, 1797), 2.

48. *The Beggar's Opera . . . the Objectionable Poetry Altered . . . with New Symphonies and Accompaniments for the Piano-forte by John Barnett* (London: Library of Standard Music, [183?]). See also letters by the Reverend John Lettice on "the defective morality" of Gay's *Fables*, in *European Magazine* 68 (1815): 17–18, 114–15, 213–14, 325–26, 407–8, 505–6, and 69 (1816): 29–30, 119–21, 218, 314–15, 415–16.

49. Gay, *Selection from Fables,* iii, ix–x. Plumptre cites both Johnson and Lettice as authorities.

50. Plumptre's unpublished biography of Gay (Cambridge University Library, Manuscript Add. 5829) is quoted by Winton, *John Gay and the London Stage,* 107.

51. John Aikin, *Select Works of the British Poets* (London: Longman, Rees, &c., 1849), A1r.

52. Charles Cowden Clarke, ed., *The Poetical Works of Joseph Addison; Gay's Fables; and Somerville's Chase* (London: Cassell Petter and Galpin, [1875]).

53. William Makepeace Thackeray, "The English Humourists of the Eighteenth Century: A Series of Lectures Delivered in England, Scotland, and the United States of America" (1853), in *The Oxford Thackerary*, ed. George Saintsbury, vol. 14 (Oxford: Oxford University Press, 1908).

54. Austin Dobson, *Miscellanies* (New York: Dodd, Mead, and Co., 1899), 241.

55. Duncan Tovey, "John Gay," in *Reviews and Essays in English Literature* (London: George Bell and Sons, 1897), 136.

56. Arthur Salmon has an admiring chapter on Gay in his *Literary Rambles in the West of England* (London: Chatto and Windus, 1906), 72–86. In a letter of 1906, he says, "You may be surprised to hear that the *Times* reviewer censured me for including this writer at all in my book; but to my mind he is a most interesting literary character, and my fear is that I hardly did him justice." (From MS card to E. L. Gay, 6 September 1906 in Harvard University, Widener Library copy of Salmon's *Literary Rambles.*)

CHAPTER 3. APOLLO, BOWZYBEUS, AND MOLLY MOG

1. This shift can be seen as part of what Pocock describes as the emerging ideology of civic humanism. See *Virtue, Commerce, and History.* See also Brewer, *Sinews of Power.*

2. Of course, others of Gay's generation were part of this early moment in cultural studies, notably Joseph Addison, whose *Spectator Papers* on popular ballads have received considerable comment. See, for example, Friedman, *Ballad Revival.* Such discussions, however, rarely recognize the importance of Gay to this history, both in the formulation of its concepts and in his contributions to popular traditions themselves.

3. See Brewer, *Pleasures of the Imagination,* which devotes considerable attention to Gay. See also Bermingham and Brewer, *Consumption of Culture,* especially John Brewer, "'The most polite age and the most vicious': Attitudes towards Culture as a Commodity, 1660–1800," 341–61.

4. Defining "traditional lore" or "folklore" is a complex task. In Leach, *Dictionary of Folklore,* 1:399, Theodore Gastor writes: "Folklore is that part of a people's culture which is preserved, consciously or unconsciously, in beliefs and practices, customs and observances of general currency; in myths, legends, and tales of common acceptance; and in arts and crafts which express the temper and genius of a group rather than of an individual. Because it is a repository of popular traditions and an integral element of the popular 'climate,' folklore serves as a constant source and frame of reference for more formal literature and art; but it is distinct therefrom in that it is essentially of the people, by the people, and for the people." See 398–408 for extensive discussion of the topic. For a preliminary consideration of Gay and tradition, see Gene Wiggins, "The Uneasy Swain: Folklore in John Gay," *Tennessee Folklore Society Bulletin* 46 (1980): 45–62.

5. For a reconsideration of the interplay of print and oral forms in Anglo-American folksong, see Dianne Dugaw, "Anglo-American Folksong Reconsidered: The Interface of Oral and Written Forms," *Western Folklore* 43 (1984): 83–103.

6. Bertrand Bronson supplies examples of this ironic interplay between texts in *The Beggar's Opera* and the popular words originally linked to the tunes that Gay used. See his essay "*The Beggar's Opera,*" in *Facets of the Enlightenment,* 62–68. Because his purpose is to link Gay's play and Italian operas of the 1720s, Bronson does not pursue the question of the provenance of these popular songs beyond their appearance in D'Urfey's collection. For an overview of broadside balladry, see Simpson's introduction in *British Broadside Ballad,* ix–xvii. For discussion of D'Urfey's *Wit and Mirth,* see Cyrus Day's introduction to the 1959 edition (New York: Folklore Library Publishers, Inc., 1959), i–xii.

7. *The Letters of Philip Dormer Stanhope, Fourth Earl of Chesterfield,* ed. Bonamy Dobree, 6 vols. (London and New York: Eyre and Spottiswoode, 1932; reprint, London and New York: AMS Press, 1968), 2:461.

8. Still current, this proverb is L506 in Morris Palmer Tilley, *A Dictionary of the Proverbs in England in the Sixteenth and Seventeenth Centuries* (Ann Arbor: University of Michigan Press, 1950), 396. See also F. P. Wilson, *The Oxford Dictionary of English Proverbs* (Oxford: Clarendon Press, 1970), 490; Wolfgang Mieder, *The Prentice-Hall Encyclopedia of World Proverbs* (Englewood Cliffs, N.J.: Prentice-Hall, 1986), 286; and B. J. Whiting, *Early American Proverbs and Proverbial Phrases* (Cambridge:: Belknap Press of Harvard University Press, 1977), 269.

9. This is L515 (p. 397) in Tilley, *Dictionary.* See Also Wilson, *English Proverbs,* 491.

10. These are W231 (p. 715), H196 (p. 293), C663 (p. 120), and B396 (p. 50) in Tilley, *Dictionary.* See also Wilson, *English Proverbs,* 490, 875, 515; Mieder, *World Proverbs,* 521, 314, 32; and Whiting, *American Proverbs,* 477, 84, 33. The dialogue or flyting is a

typical folk framework not only for proverbs, but also for such other traditional forms as riddles and songs.

11. See Wayland D. Hand, ed., *Popular Beliefs and Superstitions from North Carolina*, vols. 6 and 7 of *The Frank C. Brown Collection of North Carolina Folklore*, 7 vols. (Durham, N.C.: Duke University Press, 1952–64), 6:4234, 4134–35, 4146, 4148.

12. See E. Radford and M. A. Radford, *Encyclopedia of Superstitions*, ed. Christina Hole (Chester Springs, Pa.: Dufour Editions, 1961), 189. The Radfords record the following rhyme—which puts one in mind of Gay's—to accompany the ritual: "Hempseed I sow, / Hempseed, I grow. / He that is to marry me, / Come after me and mow." See also Robert Hunt, *Popular Romances of the West of England* (London: Chatto and Windus, 1916; reprint, New York: B. Blom, 1968), 384–85.

13. See *Frank C. Brown Collection*, 6:4536-39; see also Radford and Radford, *Encyclopedia of Superstitions*, 313; and Wayland D. Hand, Anna Casetta, and Sondra B. Thiederman, eds., *Popular Beliefs and Superstitions: A Compendium of American Folklore from the Ohio Collection of Newbell Niles Puckett*, 3 vols. (Boston: G. K. Hall, 1981), 1:12981–82. (This collection will be designated as *Puckett Collection*.)

14. See *Frank C. Brown Collection*, 6:4594–99; *Puckett Collection*, 1:12987-91; and Radford and Radford, *Encyclopedia of Superstitions*, 17.

15. See *Puckett Collection*, 1:13023, 13567–60, 14284, 13555, 13557–59; *Frank C. Brown Collection*, 6:4404, 4533, 4545, 4589–90, 4639; and Radford and Radford, *Encyclopedia of Superstitions*, 17, 212, 252, 260–61. Nor are love portents the only components of custom and belief in Gay's works. In *Fable 37* (1727), a fretful widow ponders widely reported bad omens: "The salt is spilt . . . / My Knife and fork were laid across, / On Friday too!" (ll. 6–9) Later, a traditionally feared raven makes an "ill-betiding" appearance (ll. 26–27). (See *Frank C. Brown Collection*, 6:2879-80, 3551, and 7:5994, 5996–98, 6002, 7289; and *Puckett Collection*, 1:3426, 15923–43, 16432, 16434, 16448, 16491, and 2:30680; and Radford and Radford, *Encyclopedia of Superstition*, 281.) Another "boding Raven" betokens death in *The Shepherd's Week* ("Friday," l. 103) along with other traditional portents: "tolling bells" (ll. 99–100), "shrilling Crickets" and other "clicking" insects (ll. 101–2), and swarming bees (l. 107). (See *Frank C. Brown Collection*, 7:5320, 5337–38, 5049; *Puckett Collection*, 2:28211–12, 28730, 28252–53, 28259, 28261–62, 28279; and Radford and Radford, *Encyclopedia of Superstitions*, 39–40, 120, 132.) Supernatural folklore likewise occurs in Gay. Ghosts are signaled by "jingling chains," "blood-stained planks," spectral identifications of murderers, bluish-burning candle-flames, the smell of sulphur, and so on. *An Answer to the Sompner's Prologue of Chaucer* (1717), ll. 20-26, 53-56; *A True Story of an Apparition* (1720), ll. 17-26, 74-76, 84, 94-124; and *The Wife of Bath* (1713), III.i.79–100. For traditional correspondents, see *Frank C. Brown Collection*, 7:5710, 6:3699–700, 6:3694-96, 7:5166, 7:5764, 7:5082; *Puckett Collection*, 2:29665, 20593, 29607, 26297.) *Fable 3* (1727) centers on beliefs about infant-stealing fairies (*Puckett Collection*, 1:3356–59). *Fable 23* (1727) catalogs safeguards against witches: objects set across a path, horseshoes nailed in the doorway, and the drawing of a witch's blood (ll. 29–34) (*Frank C. Brown Collection*, 7:5562, 5634, 5627–28, 5727; and *Puckett Collection*, 2:25957, 25977, 25986–87, 26010). Gay shows an easy familiarity with weather signs. "Pricking Corns" foretell rain in *The Shepherd's Week* ("Monday," l. 28) and *Three Hours after Marriage* (1717) (II.65) (*Frank C. Brown Collection*, 7:6414, 6641, 6916; and *Puckett Collection*, 2:34140). High-flying swallows signal clear weather in *The Shepherd's Week* ("Monday," ll. 29–30) (*Frank C. Brown Collection*, 7:6245; *Puckett Collection*, 2:33841). In *Trivia* (1716) Gay repeats the traditional tenets that weather on St. Paul's and St. Swithin's days predicts future storms and warfare (ll. 175–86). *Frank C. Brown Collection*, 7:6435; *Puckett Collection*, 2:34755; Radford and Radford, *Encyclopedia of Superstitions*, 277. For the legend of St. Swithin, see Marjorie Rowling, *The Folklore of the Lake District* (Totowa,

N.J.: Rowman and Littlefield, 1976), 103. In *The Shepherd's Week* Gay notes, with face-tious double entendre, the saying that when "the Heifer's Tail" is "stuck aloft . . . showers ensue." ("Monday," ll. 25–26), parodying the saying that one knows of a storm "if a cow raises her tail over her back and runs" (Harry M. Hyatt, *Folklore from Adams County Illinois* (N.p.: n.p., 1965), no. 727.

16. On these forms and terms, see Leach, *Dictionary of Folklore*, 1:106–11, 431-39, 1032-50, and 2:753, 761, 902–6, 938–44.

17. Mary Poovey, "The Social Constitution of 'Class'" in Dimock and Gilmore, *Rethinking Class*, 15–56.

18. Hoyt Trowbridge, "Pope, Gay, and *The Shepherd's Week*," *Modern Language Quarterly* 5 (1944): 84.

19. See Congleton, *Theories of Pastoral Poetry*. See also Dearing and Beckwith's headnote to *The Shepherd's Week* in Gay, *Poetry and Prose*, 510–15.

20. Spacks notes this complexity in *John Gay*, 39–40. Other studies of Gay's social criticism touch on it as well, though none explore the strategic ways that Gay uses folk forms. See Adina Forsgren, *John Gay, Poet "of a Lower Order"* (Stockholm: Natur och Kultur, 1964); and Armens, *John Gay, Social Critic* .

21. Ian Donaldson discusses this ambiguity of genre in "'A Double Capacity': *The Beggar's Opera*," in *World Upside Down*, 160–61.

22. For discussion of this ballad motif, see Dugaw, *Warrior Women*. For analysis of Gay's use of the motif in *Polly*, see ibid., 191–211. The play was stopped in rehearsal in December of 1728. Published by Gay in a subscription edition in 1729, it was not brought to the stage until George Colman's production of 1777.

23. On *The British Apollo*, see Irving, *John Gay, Favorite of the Wits*, 40–56. See also Nokes, *John Gay*, for a detailed discussion of the contributors (60).

24. "The Present State of Wit, in a Letter to a Friend in the Country" (ll. 251–55), in Gay, *Poetry and Prose*, 2:455–56.

25. *British Apollo*.

26. "Saturday" of *The Shepherd's Week*, ll. 45–120 in Gay, *Poetry and Prose*, 1:120–23. Gay identifies himself with Bowzybeus in ll. 87–90 of the "Prologue" (1:95). All quotations from poems by Gay are from this edition.

27. It was the dedication of these pastorals to Bolingbroke (1678–1751) that was believed to be the "original sin," to quote Swift, that permanently clouded Gay's prospects with the Hanoverian monarchs. After Queen Anne died, just as Gay's *Shepherd's Week* was finished, Bolingbroke did not support the new Hanoverian king George I and was eventually implicated in efforts to reinstate the Stuart claimant to the throne in the uprising of 1715. Bolingbroke fled to France and remained there until he was pardoned in 1723. When he returned to England, he was part of the opposition circle which took up Gay's satire in the sharp polemic of the 1720s against Walpole.

28. Gay's involvment with *The British Apollo* presumably ended when Hill sold it toward the end of 1709. See Irving, *John Gay, Favorite of the Wits*, 28, 49–50.

29. *Spectator*, no. 85 (1711). See Friedman, *Ballad Revival*, 84–113.

30. See William D. Ellis Jr., "Pope, Gay, and *the Shepherd's Week*," *Modern Language Quarterly* 5 (1944): 79–88; and idem, "Thomas D'Urfey, the Pope-Philips Quarrel, and 'The Shepherd's Week'," *PMLA* 74 (1959): 203–12.

31. Gay supplies two footnotes: an attribution to John Denham (which is probably correct), and a reference to Silenus's consolation of Pasiphae in Virgil's Eclogue 6. On the song "All in the Land of Essex," see Simpson, *British Broadside Ballad*, 712. Simpson says of the song: "This sordid tale of buggery, aimed at Quaker hypocrisy, was based on a notorious event of c. 1653."

32. Winton, *John Gay and the London Stage*, notes throughout his study Gay's impor-

tance as a songwriter. See, in particular, 11-47 regarding songs in *The Mohocks*, *The Wife of Bath*, and *The What-d'Ye-Call-It*.

33. See Friedman, *Ballad Revival;* and Dugaw, *Anglo-American Ballad*.

34. See the entry for "ballad" by James Moreira in Green, *Folklore*, 81–84; and in Leach, *Dictionary of Folklore,.*106–11. Scholarship on popular balladry is staggering. For bibliography, see W. Edson Richmond, *Ballad Scholarship: An Annotated Bibliography* (New York: Garland, 1989).

35. See Gay, *Poetry and Prose*, 596. The song also circulated on various undated broadsides from the same 1720s period.

36. Ibid., 613–14.

37. See Laws, *American Balladry*, "Ballads of Faithful Lovers (O–1 to O–41)" and "Ballads of Crime and Criminals (L–1 to L–22)."

38. See entries on "broadside ballad" by Roger deV. Renwick and on "chapbook" by Michael Preston in Green, *Folklore*, 103–9, 117–20. See also Dugaw, *Warrior Women*, chaps. 1–3; and Shepard, *Broadside Ballad*.

39. See Dianne Dugaw, "The Popular Marketing of 'Old Ballads': Eighteenth-Century Antiquarianism Reconsidered," *Eighteenth-Century Studies* 21 (1987): 71–90.

40. Dearing (Gay, *Poetry and Prose*, 596) mentions Leveridge, Hayden, and Sandoni. However, see Edythe Backus, *Catalogue of Music in the Huntington Library Printed before 1801* (San Marino, Calif.: Huntington Library, 1949), 389. Hayden's tune seems, in fact, a diverging paraphrase of Carey's. See the Huntington Library broadsides 90318 ("Sweet William's Farewell to Black-Ey'd Susan, The Tune by Mr Carey") and 81013, vol. 1 ("A New Song by Mr Huddy to Mr Haydon's Tune to blackEyd Susan").

41. Friedman, *Ballad Revival*, 158.

42. G.Malcolm Laws, *American Balladry*, 239.

43. Helen Creighton and Doreen H. Senior, eds., *Traditional Songs from Nova Scotia* (Toronto: Ryerson Press, 1950), 132.

44. See Laws, *American Balladry*, 239–41. For further discussion of this dialogue pattern, see Dugaw, *Warrior Women*, 104–5; and idem, "The Female Warrior Heroine in Anglo-American Popular Balladry" (Ph.D. diss., University of California, Los Angeles, 1982), 135–67, 345–459.

45. Gay, *Poetry and Prose*, 249.

46. Neil Rosenberg, letter to author, 10 February 1989. "Dark-eyed Susan" appears in *Come and I Will Sing You: A Newfoundland Songbook*, ed. Genevieve Lehr, songs collected by Genevieve Lehr and Anita Best (Toronto: University of Toronto Press, 1985), 47–49. Anita Best says of the ballad: "My mother brought this song with her from Tack's Beach when she moved to Merasheen, Placentia Bay. Lillian Pittman learned it from her and wrote it down in her song scribbler. The scribbler was lost in the move to Placentia during the Resettlement era, but the song survived" (49).

47. For excellent discussion of the ballad in these terms, see Winton, *John Gay and the London Stage*, 75–82.

48. Gay, *Poetry and Prose*, 289, stanzas 5, 6, and 7.

49. On the song's history and texts, see Dearing's discussion in ibid., 616–18. This song has also been collected from oral tradition.

50. See Irving, *John Gay,* 215–16.

51. Alfred Williams included a version of the song in a 1914 column in *The Wiltshire and Gloucestershire Standard*: "obtained of Thomas Baughan, South Cerney [Gloucestershire]. The song was a favourite of his father's, and of his grandfather's, who bought it on a broadside at Cirencester Mop, where it was sung at least as early as the year 1793." I am grateful for this information to Roy Palmer, who cites the article from "a scrapbook in the Local Collection, Gloucester City Library, p. 13" (letter, 6 August 1996).

52. See Gay, *Poetry and Prose*, 376.
53. Wheelock, *Haydn's Ingenious Jesting with Art,* .202–3.

CHAPTER 4. VIRGIL UPENDED

1. On the enclosure process and related issues, see Snell, *Annals of the Labouring Poor.* See also Barrell, *Dark Side of the Landscape;* and B. J. Davey, *Rural Crime in the Eighteenth Century* (Hull: University of Hull Press, 1994), esp. 110–19, 128–38; and Thompson, *Whigs and Hunters* on the policing of forest lands with discussion of an incident of 1722 linked to Alexander Pope (278–94). This process of regulation and privatization accelerated with the Whig ascendancy after the Hanoverian succession of 1714.
2. Letter from Pope and Thomas Parnell to Gay dated 4 May 1714, in *The Correspondence of Alexander Pope*, ed. George Sherburn, 5 vols. (Oxford: Clarendon Press, 1956), 1:223.
3. "Metalepsis or Transumption," in *The New Princeton Encyclopedia of Poetry and Poetics*, ed. Alex Preminger and T. V. F. Brogan (Princeton: Princeton University Press, 1993), 759-60.
4. Hollander, *Figure of Echo*, 114. Hollander's appendix supplies a short history of this overlooked trope, 134–39. In discussing "allusion" in Preminger and Brogan, *New Princeton Encyclopedia*, Earl Miner remarks that "no comprehensive study [of allusion] exists. A fully comparative study would be very valuable" (40).
5. Hutcheon, *Theory of Parody,* 6–8. See also Rose, *Parody.*
6. Patterson, *Pastoral and Ideology,* 194.
7. See Congleton, *Theories of Pastoral Poetry,* .53–65.
8. John Gay, *Rural Sports: A Poem, Inscribed to Mr. Pope* (London: J. Tonson, 1713). All quotes from the 1713 poem are from this edition. The only modern republished version of the poem is in *The Poetical Works of John Gay*, ed. G. C. Faber (London: Oxford University Press, 1926), 655–65.
9. See J. Nichols, ed., *Bibliotheca Topographica Britannica*, 8 vols. (London: 1780–90), 3:xxi n.
10. John Gay, "Rural Sports. A Georgic: Inscribed to Mr. Pope," in *Poems on Several Occasions* (London: Jacob Tonson and Bernard Lintot, 1720), 1–25.
11. Hutcheon, *Theory of Parody*, 11.
12. In 1713 Pope was known for his pastorals, which appeared in *Dryden's Miscellany* of 1709 and came to represent the ancient "Golden Age" advocated by the French theorist Renée Rapin. See Congleton, *Theories of Pastoral Poetry,* 79–84.
13. The two original lines are as follows: *"silvestrem tenui musam meditaris avena"* ("wooing the woodland Muse on slender reed") from Eclogue 1.2; and *"agrestem tenui meditabor harundine Musam"* ("now I will woo the rustic Muse on slender reed") from Eclogue 6.8. The translation is from Virgil (Publius Vergilius Maro), *Eclogues, Georgics, Aeneid 1–6,* trans. H. R. Fairclough, Loeb Classical Library (Cambridge: Harvard University Press, 1953).
14. Gay, *Poetry and Prose*, 492.
15. John Dryden, *Poems: The Works of Virgil in English 1697*, ed. William Frost, in *The Works of John Dryden*, ed. H. T. Swedenberg Jr., Alan Roper, and Vinton Dearing, 20 vols. (Berkeley and Los Angeles: University of California Press, 1956–2000), 5:107.
16. Virgil, *Eclogues,* trans. Fairclough, 42.
17. This poetic construct refers to the situation of Virgil himself, whose farm in Mantua was exempted by special order from being dispersed with those around it to the returning troops as pay. This sociopolitical background threads through the pastorals. See Patterson, *Pastoral and Ideology,* 33–38, 95–102.

18. Pope's pastorals are titled "Spring. The First Pastoral, or Damon," "Summer. The Second Pastoral, or Alexis," "Autumn. The Third Pastoral, or Hylas and Ægon," and "Winter. The Fourth Pastoral, or Daphne." For these poems and discussion of them, see Alexander Pope, *Pastoral Poetry and an Essay on Criticism*, vol. 1 of *Works*, ed. E. Audra and Aubrey Williams (London: Methuen; New Haven: Yale University Press, 1961), 58–95. For discussion of them, see 37–55. See also Pope's "A Discourse on Pastoral Poetry," in *Pastoral Poetry,* 22-33. This discussion was published in 1717, but Pope claimed to have written it at the time he wrote the pastorals, which were published in 1709.

19. Barrell *Dark Side of the Landscape,* 37–40, 46–47, notes the opposition between Gay's leisured poet "swain" and the sweating laboring "swains" he sees, but overlooks the poem's conscious ironies and disjunctions.

20. Thomas Bullfinch, *The Age of Fable or Beauties of Mythology*, ed. J. Loughran Scott (Philadelphia: David McKay, 1898), 43–44. Calisto's story hinges upon this theme of the perceptions of the hunted: "One day a youth espied her as he was hunting. She saw him and recognized him as her own son, now grown a young man. She stopped and felt inclined to embrace him. As she was about to approach, he, alarmed, raised his hunting-spear, and was on the point of transfixing her, when Jupiter, beholding, arrested the crime, and snatching away both of them placed them in the heavens as the Great and Little Bear" (44).

21. See Adina Forsgren, *John Gay, Poet "of a Lower Order": Comments on his Rural Poems and Other Early Writings* (Stockholm: Natur och Kultur, 1964), 69–81. Rather than shaping his poem by this connection to the peace, Gay alludes to it among the constellation of referents with which the poem is in metaleptic relation.

22. Gay's "rural sports" are the most plebeian—fishing, fowling, and hunting the hare. The poem omits chasing deer and fox as well as hawking. The hunting of the hare was termed by Richard Blome in *The Gentlemans Recreation*, 2 vols. (London: S. Roycroft, 1686) "every man's Sport" (2:67, 87, 91). Fishing, likewise, is popular rather than gentlemanly, and certainly would have been recognized as such in Gay's poem. See Forsgren's discussion in *John Gay,* 81–87, 90–92.

23. Jacob Tonson and Bernard Lintot published this folio edition of Gay's collected poems by subscription, with a long list of prominent subscribers. For discussion of this publication and period in Gay's life, see Irving, *John Gay,* 173–82.

24. Recent commentary on Gay has sought ways to read the ironies of *The Shepherd's Week* more effectively. See, for example, Nigel Wood, "Gay and the Ironies of Rustic Simplicity" in Lewis and Wood, *John Gay and the Scriblerians*, 94–121.

25. Owen Ruffhead, *The Life of Alexander Pope, Esq.*, 2 vols. (Dublin: S. Powell, P. Wilson, J. Exshaw, H. Saunders, W. Sleater, B. Grierson, D. Chamberlaine, J. Potts, J. Hoey, J. Williams, and C. Ingham, 1769), 1:39. This level of satire in *The Shepherd's Week* has drawn the attention of critics such as Hoyt Trowbridge, "Pope, Gay, and *the Shepherd's Week*," *Modern Language Quarterly* 5 (1944): 79–88; and William D. Ellis Jr., "Thomas D'Urfey, the Pope-Philips Quarrel, and 'The Shepherd's Week'," *PMLA* 74 (1959): 203–12.

26. See, for example, Donna Landry's mention of Gay in *The Muses of Resistance: Laboring-Class Women's Poetry in Britain, 1739–1796* (Cambridge: Cambridge University Press, 1990), 1–3.

27. On the collaboration of Pope and Gay, see Maynard Mack, "Two Variant Copies of Pope's *Works . . . Volume II:* Further Light On Some Problems of Authorship, Bibliography, and Text," *The Library*, 5th ser., 12 (1957): 48–53.

28. See Dearing's remarks in *Poetry and Prose*, 531ff.

29. Gay's comic *Wife of Bath* was produced in 1713. See Winton, *John Gay and the London Stage,* 26–40.

30. Quoted from Dryden's prefatory "Argument" to the eclogue (*Poems,* 107). The

original epigraph to *Rural Sports,* as noted, quotes a line from this eclogue of Virgil, underscoring the links between the two poems. As Dearing and Beckwith note (Gay, *Poetry and Prose,* 535), the name "Bowzybeus" is "a compound of bowzy, drunken, and Meliboeus."

31. Dryden, *Poems,* 106.

32. Virgil gives the promise: "You shall have your songs, she another kind of reward" (*Eclogues,* trans. Fairclough, 6.25–26).

33. The ducking stool was a chair in which scolds were tied and put under water in a customary punishment extending back into the medieval era. See Thomas Faulkner, *An Historical and Topographical Description of Chealsea and its Environs interspersed with Biographical Anecdotes,* 2 vols. (Chelsea: Faulkner, 1829), 2:160.

34. Spacks, *John Gay,* 41.

35. Critics incline to resolve this ambiguity in telling ways with regard to gender, reading the male walker as unambivalently reliable, the female rustics as unambivalently ridiculed.

36. Dearing and Beckwith supply many of the classical parallels (Gay, *Poetry and Prose,* 549) See also Dianne S. Ames, "Gay's *Trivia* and the Art of Allusion," *Studies in Philology* 75 (1978): 199–222.

37. Gay removed this facetious scholarly framework in the second edition of 1720.

38. Mack, *Alexander Pope,* 134.

39. Virgil, *Eclogues,* trans. Fairclough, 3.26–27.

40. Virgil, *Eclogues,* trans. Fairclough, 1.1. Moeris is a farmer, coming to town, on foot.

41. John Dryden's translation of 1696 heightened this theme of political disenfranchisement with reference to the ousted Stuart monarch, James II. See Annabel Patterson, *Pastoral and Ideology,* 188–89.

42. Gay, *Poetry and Prose,* 557.

43. It adds, for example, a serious dimension to the paradox and playfulness emphasized by Tom Woodman, "'Vulgar Circumstance' and 'Due Civilities': Gay's Art of Polite Living in Town," in Lewis and Wood, *John Gay and the Scriblerians,* 83–93.

44. Gay's references to bookstalls, books, and the book trade echo similar images in Dryden's satire. More than a few readers have found the Cloacina story unacceptable. Already in the eighteenth century, Joseph Warton sniffed: "The fable of Cloacina is indelicate. I should think this was one of the hints given him by Swift." See Joseph Warton, *An Essay on the Genius and Writings of Pope,* 2 vols. (London: W .J. and J. Richardson, &c., 1806), 2:244. As recently as 1974 David Lindsay published the poem's earlier version, *sans* Cloacina and bootblack, in *English Poetry, 1700–1780: Contemporaries of Swift and Johnson,* ed. David Lindsay (London: Dent, 1974), 14–41.

45. See Winton, *John Gay and the London Stage,* 66–72, particularly for his discussion of lesbian sexuality in *Dione* (62–63).

46. James Sutherland, "John Gay," in Clifford and Landa, *Pope and His Contemporaries,* 211.

47. Marcus Walsh, introduction to *John Gay, Selected Poems* (Manchester, U.K.: Fyfield Books, 1979), 14.

CHAPTER 5. VILLAGE MUMMING ON AN URBAN STAGE

1. See "Mumming," in Green, *Folklore,* 2:566–67. See also, "mummers" in Leach, *Dictionary of Folklore,* 761.

2. John Gay, *Dramatic Works,* ed. John Fuller, 2 vols. (Oxford: Clarendon Press, 1983), 1:416–17. All quotes are from this edition of the play. Opening on 23 February 1715,

the play had seventeen performances in the season and continued to be one of the most frequently performed afterpieces of the century. It was published in March, when Gay added a long Scriblerian preface, in the vein of "The Proeme" to *The Shepherd's Week*, which takes up—with "owlish seriousness," to quote Winton—the facetiously mocking generic identities of the piece: tragedy, comedy, pastoral, farce.

3. Peter Lewis, "The Beggar's Rags to Rich's and Other Dramatic Transformations," in Lewis and Wood, *John Gay and the Scriblerians*, 140.

4. For a nostalgic upper-class description of such Yuletide gatherings of owners and tenants, masters and servants, see the anonymous *Round about our Coal Fire* (London: James Roberts, c. 1730).

5. Peter Lewis, "The Beggar's Rags," in Lewis and Wood, *John Gay and the Scriblerians*, 137.

6. *A Complete Key to the last New Farce The What D'Ye Call It* (London: for James Roberts, 1715). On the much-discussed and as yet uncertain authorship of this pamphlet, see Gay, *Dramatic Works*, 1:418–19.

7. Winton, *John Gay and the London Stage*, 43–44.

8. Fuller, for example, annotates his edition (Gay, *Dramatic Works*, 1:418–35) with line-by-line references to *Complete Key*.

9. Irving, *John Gay, Favorite of the Wits*, 68–70. Gay was in Moor Park in October, as a letter from him to William Fortescue attests. See Gay, *Letters*, ed. Burgess,.3–5. As noted above, this was one of the episodes of "service" in Gay's background from which Pope deflected attention. In "Plough Plays in the East Midlands," *Journal of the English Folk Dance and Song Society* 7 (1953), M. W. Barley says that household account books suggest widespread eighteenth-century performance of such plays: "The practice of visiting the great house to perform the play must certainly have been common" (73).

10. An early survey of these dramas is Chambers, *English Folk-Play*, though much has been written since this work. Cawte, Helm, and Peacock, *English Ritual Drama*, 94–132, contains an extensive bibliography. See also Helm, *English Mummers' Play;* Barley, "Plough Plays in the East Midlands," 68–95; Michael J. Preston, "The Revesby Sword Play," *Journal of American Folklore* 85 (1972): 51–57; and Martin Lovelace, "Christmas Mumming in England: The House-Visit," in *Folklore Studies in Honour of Herbert Halpert*, ed. Kenneth Goldstein and Neil Rosenberg (St. John's: Memorial University of Newfoundland, 1980). Although we know that such plays were performed in villages and manor houses well into the nineteenth century, texts do not survive from before the eighteenth century. (See Chambers, *English Folk-Play;* and Barley, "Plough Plays.") We can only imagine from later collected versions the outlines and preoccupations of these plays as they must have been passed down. These however are apparent, as is their resonance, in Gay's construction of *The What-d'Ye-Call-It*. For a recent survey that is useful in placing mumming within the context of other seasonal customs, see Hutton, *Stations of the Sun*, 70–80, 124–33. Hutton is too eager to dismiss out of hand the dating of these (and other) traditions to earlier than the surviving manuscripts for particular performances. While projected claims for the survival of mumming from ancient pagan rites are unwarranted, early references to them, particularly in connection with village relations to the manor house, certainly date them to well before the eighteenth century. Indeed, they are identified with exactly that older world order whose cultural forms Gay's satires freely use for metaleptically employed designs and allusions.

11. Chambers, *English Folk-Play*, 89–91. Sketchy on the wooing plays, Chambers is misleading in his assumption of the "normality" of the combat schema. On the wooing play traditions, see Charles Baskervill, "Mummers' Wooing Plays in England," *Modern Philology* 21 (1924): 225–72; Barley, "Plough Plays," 68–95; and Jerry V. Pickering, "The English Plough Plays," *Western Folklore* 32 (1973): 237–48. Pickering notes the "strong comic element"

running through all the plough plays, which he sees as "marvelous examples of rustic parody" of the other plays and the customary ritual of mumming in general (242). Gay's play opened at Drury Lane in late February during the season of such traditional mummings.

12. During this early period of his life, Gay had links to the northeast midlands, and traditions there, through his friendship with Maurice Johnson (1688–1755) of Spalding, Lincolnshire. The young Johnson was admitted to the Inner Temple in 1705 and called to the bar in 1710. Part of the London literary circle in which the young Gay traveled, Johnson may have been a contributor with Gay to Aaron Hill's *British Apollo*. Johnson eventually became well known as an antiquarian, founding a number of literary and antiquarian societies both in London and the Midlands. Johnson's father was steward for the Lincolnshire manor of the duchess of Monmouth, his family customarily entertained the duchess and her family in their own mansion in Spalding, and it was probably through Johnson that Gay received his appointment as her secretary in 1712. See *Dictionary of National Biography*, 2d ed., s.v. "Maurice Johnson." See also Irving, *John Gay*, 68–71.

13. From an undated manuscript play reproduced in Baskervill, "Mummers' Wooing Plays," 259–62.

14. From a manuscript play dated 1823, reproduced in ibid., 241-45.

15. Barley, "Plough Plays," 82.

16. Baskervill, "Mummers' Wooing Plays," 242.

17. From an early-nineteenth-century text (in three variants) in ibid., 256.

18. *Complete Key*, 6. See Fuller's notes in Gay, *Dramatic Works*, 1:423–24.

19. "A Protestant Souldier and His Love: The Damsels Resolution at Length to Take Up Arms against the Irish Rebels for the True Enjoyment of Her Dear," in *The Pepys Ballads*, ed. Hyder E. Rollins, 8 vols. (Cambridge: Harvard University Press, 1929–32), 4:350. Apparently written in 1689, this ballad circulated in print into the first decade of the eighteenth century.

20. From a nineteenth-century text in Baskervill, "Mummers' Wooing Plays," 265.

21. "The Souldiers Farewel to His Love. Being a Dialogue betweixt Thomas and Margaret," in *A Pepysian Garland,* ed. Hyder E. Rollins (Cambridge: Cambridge University Press, 1922), 173. This mid-seventeenth-century ballad continued in print late in the century.

22. *Complete Key*, 6. See Gay, *Dramatic Works*, 1:424.

23. Versions of the song printed during the eighteenth century attribute the setting to Handel, who seems to have supplied it for the play. How the collaboration happened is not known, and the frequent attribution is not utterly certain. See Gay, *Dramatic Works*, 1:432–33.

24. For discussion of the text as it demonstrates Gay as "a superior lyricist," see Winton, *John Gay and the London Stage*, 45–47.

25. See Gay, *Dramatic Works,* 1:432–34.

26. *Amaryllis*, 2 vols. (London: J. Tyther, c. 1778), 2:79.

27. Gay had in mind such contemporaries as Ambrose Philips. See Hoyt Trowbridge, "Pope, Gay, and *The Shepherd's Week*," *Modern Language Quarterly* 5 (1944): 79–88; and Ellis, "Thomas D'Urfey, the Pope-Philips Quarrel, " 203–23.

28. In their introduction, Richard Morton and William M. Peterson tentatively suggest as a model "the Mummers' Play, with its king of Egypt, his daughter and the dragon, as well as its comic Doctor waving his bolus and reviving the dead." See John Gay, *Three Hours after Marriage . . . with The Confederates and The Two Keys*, ed. Richard Morton and William M. Peterson (Painesville, Ohio: Lake Erie College Studies, 1961), xii

29. See Hunt, *Middling Sort;* and Earle, *Making of the English Middle Class.*

30. See Morton and Peterson, introduction to Gay, *Three Hours*, vi–xx.

31. See Winton, *John Gay and the London Stage,* 53–56; Morton and Peterson, introduction, ii–vi; and Gay, *Dramatic Works,* 1:438–43.

32. See Alan Gailey, *Irish Folk Drama* (Cork: Mercier Press, 1969) and Rippon, *Discovering English Folk Dancing*.

33. From "The Islip Mummers' Play of 1780" from Oxfordshire in the Bodleian Library, Ms. Top. Oxon. d. 199.301v-306v. The play is reproduced in Michael Preston, "The Oldest British Folk Play," *Folklore Forum* 6 (1973): 169–71.

34. See Chambers, *English Folk-Play*, 13–71.

35. Quoted from G. T., "Christmas Pastimes in Exeter Sixty Years Ago," *Western Antiquary* 3 (1883): 166. Cawte, Helm, and Peacock, *English Ritual Drama,* cite the source (101) as Andrew Brice, *The Mobiad or Battle of the Voice* (Exeter: Brice and Thorn, 1770), 90, a mock-heroic poem from 1738.

36. See Thompson, "Rough Music," in *Customs in Common,* 467–531. See also "Charivari" in Leach, *Dictionary of Folklore*, 1:120–21.

37. Thompson, *Customs in Common;* and idem, *Making of the English Working Class.* See also John Smail, *The Origins of Middle Class Culture: Halifax, Yorkshire, 1660–1780* (Ithaca and London: Cornell University Press, 1994); and McKendrick, Brewer, and Plumb, *Birth of a Consumer Society;* and Melling and Barry, *Culture in History*.

38. Among plays that Morton and Williams identify as possible models for the ongoing spoof on scientific pedantry are Marmion's *The Antiquary* (1641), Shadwell's *The Virtuoso* (1676), D'Urfey's *Madam Fickle* (1676), Behn's *The Emperor of the Moon* (1687), and Ravenscroft's *The Anatomist* (1696) (Gay, *Three Hours,* vii–viii). Several shorter works in a more popular vein were certainly equally influential. For example, "The Infallible Doctor" (also known as "The Infallible Dr Anthony"), a song published first in *The Pleasant Musical Companion* reappears on broadsides and in D'Urfey, *Pills to Purge Melancholy,* editions of 1707 (1:35–36) and 1719 (3:30–32). Peter Motteux's *The Mountebank: or, The Humours of the Fair,* a musical interlude of 1707, was published with his comedy *Farewell Folly: or, The Younger the Wiser* (London: James Round, 1707), 61–69. Motteux's "Quack" possesses a "Pill" to cure "the Love-sick Maid" that calls to mind the "Touchstone of Virginity Liquor" that Lubomirski supplies Fossile to test Townley and the other women. Of his "Pill" the "Quack" cautions: "But be sure You're a Maid; / Or as soon as 'tis swallow'd, 'twill choak you—you're dead" (68).

39. See Avery, *London Stage,* 448–49, 604.

40. Ibid., 460–73, 475–76, 479, 484, 489, 494, 534, 570, 572, 577–78, 580–81, 604–6, 612, 614, 620, 628–29, 648, 654, 658, 671, 696, 701, 703, 719, 769, 771, 776, 778, 781, 876, 877.

41. E. Parker, *A Complete Key To the New Farce, call'd Three Hours after Marriage* (London: E. Berrington, 1717), 7.

42. [John Breval], *The Confederates: A Farce* (London: R. Burleigh, 1717), 22.

43. *A Supplement to the Works of Alexander Pope, Esq. . . . To Which Is Added . . . A Key to the Three Hours after Marriage, and a Letter Giving an Account of the Origin of the Quarrel between Cibber, Pope, and Gay* (Dublin: W. Whitestone, 1758), 213.

CHAPTER 6. OPERA, GENDER, AND SOCIAL STRATA

1. For the standard version of Gay's libretto, see Gay, *Dramatic Works*, ed. Fuller, 1:265–76. For Handel's score, see George Frederic Handel, *Acis and Galatea,* ed. Wolfram Windszus (Basel, London, New York: Bärenreiter Kassel, 1991). All passages of text and music in this essay are from these sources.

2. Often placed in the genre of the English masque, the work is operatic in that the music is through-composed, made up of recitatives, arias, and choruses. See Windszus's preface (xiv–xv) to Handel, *Acis and Galatea,* ed. Windszus, which relies heavily on Brian Trowell's discussion of the work as a concert serenata: "Acis, Galatea and Polyphemus,"

31–93. See also Dean, *New Grove Handel,* 24. For additional discussion of the various terms designating the work, see Gay, *Dramatic Works,* 1:451–52.

3. Although the exact date is unknown, most scholars agree that it must have been in 1718. See Handel, *Acis and Galatea,* ed. Windszus, xvii. A letter of 27 May 1718 by Sir David Dalrymple refers to a "little opera . . . as good as finished" thought to be *Acis and Galatea,* whose "words are to be furnished by Mrs Pope and Gay, and the musick to be composed by Hendell." See Patrick Rogers, "Dating *Acis and Galatea.* A newly discovered letter," *Musical Times* 114 (1973): 792. Winton Dean suggests the summer in *Handel's Dramatic Oratorios and Masques,* 159. George I named Brydges first duke of Chandos in 1719. On Chandos and the estate at Cannons, see C. H. Collins Baker and Muriel I. Baker, *The Life and Circumstances of James Brydges, First Duke of Chandos, Patron of the Liberal Arts* (Oxford: Clarendon Press, 1949). On music, musicians, and performances, see 129–40. Handel's connections to Brydges as a patron are well known, as are those of Gay and the other Scriblerians. On Gay's collaboration with Handel, see Winton, *John Gay and the London Stage,* 41–59.

The early history of *Acis and Galatea*—performances, manuscripts, and first publications—is exceptionally complex and uncertain, principally because of its sequestered private origins. Recently Brian Trowell has suggested it was not originally staged at all but presented in concert performance. See Trowell, "Acis, Galatea, and Polyphemus," 39–54, for a detailed exposition of this complex history and array of evidence. See also Dean, *Handel's Dramatic Oratorios,* 629–31; and W. C. Smith, "*Acis and Galatea* in the Eighteenth Century," in *Concerning Handel, His Life and Works* (London: Cassell, 1948), 197–265. The first public performance in London, a benefit for which only advertisements survive, did not occur until 1731. In 1732 the work was staged in London in competing forms and amidst controversy. Thomas Arne produced a highly publicized version of the Gay/Handel collaboration at the Haymarket without authorization. Immediately Handel mounted a competing composite production consisting of portions of the 1718 work (some translated into Italian), together with sections from his own 1708 Neapolitan *Aci, Galatea e Polifemo,* and sundry other pieces new and preexisting. While Arne's 1732 production brought public recognition of the work, this version—now the standard reference—diverges somewhat from libretti in surviving earlier manuscripts and publications, and almost certainly does not represent in detail Gay and Handel's original conception. I will, however, use this libretto for my discussion since an acceptable alternative is not yet available. My analysis of the work is not affected by discrepancies among different versions of text and music.

4. See Pat Rogers, "Gay and the World of Opera," in Lewis and Wood, *John Gay and the Scriblerians,* 152–53; and Winton, *John Gay and the London Stage,* 56–59.

5. Gay's authorship of works has been frequently reassigned to his colleagues, especially Alexander Pope. David Nokes takes up this issue in *John Gay* and, with regard to *Acis and Galatea,* 275–76. Conjecturing on the basis of textual style, Trowell ("Acis, Galatea, and Polyphemus," 83) suggests that Pope, Hughes, and John Arbuthnot supplied many of the arias. This argument on the basis of reverberations and borrowings from other poems is unconvincing, since Gay's texts invariably contain just such echoes of his contemporaries as we find in *Acis and Galatea.* In both style and thematic conception the libretto displays throughout an imagination altogether characteristic of Gay.

6. For discussion of Gay's parody with regard to gender, see Dianne Dugaw, "The Anatomy of Heroism: Gender Politics and Empire in Gay's *Polly,*" in *History, Gender and Eighteenth-Century Literature,* ed. Beth Fowkes Tobin (Athens and London: University of Georgia Press, 1994), 39–63. Commentary on *Acis and Galatea* is similar to critics' dismissive misreadings of *Polly.* Just as commentators did not recognize that Polly is the protagonist at the center of Gay's sequel to *The Beggar's Opera,* they do not recognize Galatea at the center of *Acis and Galatea.*

7. Trowell, "Acis, Galatea, and Polyphemus," 83. Because his discussion is focused solely on Pope's poetry and theory, Trowell leaves unexplored the important ways that Gay, certainly the principal librettist of this work, contributed to the refashioning of pastoral ideology in Georgian England.

8. In *Acis and Galatea*, Gay and Handel bring together aspects of Italian opera on the one hand and English music drama on the other. The interjection of pastoral or mock-pastoral elements that featured rustics making music with popular connotations was common in seventeenth-century English theater. The entrance of "Comus *with three Peasants*" singing "Your Hay it is Mow'd" in Dryden and Purcell's *King Arthur* (1691) is an example. See John Dryden, *The Dramatic Works*, ed. Montague Summers, 6 vols. (London: Nonesuch, 1932), 6:284, and Henry Purcell, *King Arthur* (Melville, N.Y.: Belwin Mills [Kalmus Vocal Scores], n.d.), 107–8. The "Songish parts" in late-Restoration plays were typically performed by characters from realms separate from that of the characters in the plot: deities, magicians, native priests, servants, lower-class rustics. See Dugaw, "'Critical Instants,'" 157–75. A short *Masque of Acis and Galatea* featuring "Clowns and Country Lasses" and a rustic "Bride" and "Bridegroom" was written by Peter Anthony Motteaux (text) and John Eccles (music) to be interpolated into a 1701 revival of *The Mad Lover* by John Fletcher. See Motteux and Eccles, *The Rape of Europa by Jupiter (1694) and Acis and Gallatea (1701)*, introduction by Lucyle Hook, Augustan Reprint Society publication no. 208 (Los Angeles: William Andrews Clark Memorial Library, 1981). Roger Fiske in *English Theatre Music in the Eighteenth Century*, 14, describes this masque as having "a clodhopping underplot in which Joan is briefly diverted from her betrothed Roger, by the charms of Acis." Gay and Handel's *Acis and Galatea* develops from this English tradition of underplots with their reference to "low" culture. Handel's 1708 Italian version of the Acis and Galatea myth contains no hint of this intersecting of "high" and "low" worlds.

9. See, for example, Dean, *Handel's Dramatic Oratorios.*, 166.

10. Harris, *Handel and the Pastoral Tradition*, 204.

11. See Stafford's *Body Criticism*. For analysis of Gay's *Fables* in these terms, see Jayne Lewis, "Risking Contradiction: John Gay's *Fables* and the Matter of Reading," in *Fables*.

12. This artfully constructed interdependence sets Gay and Handel's invocation of the popular mock pastoral apart from such farcical "underplots" as that of Motteux and Eccles'.

13. John Dryden, "The Story of Acis, Polyphemus, and Galatea, from the Thirteenth Book of Ovid's *Metamorphoses*," in *Works of John Dryden*, ed. Swedenberg, Roper, and Dearing, 4:414–21.

14. Theodor Weisengrund-Adorno, "Zur Dreigroschenoper," translated by Stephen Hinton, in Hinton, *Kurt Weill*, 131. Adorno's essay appeared in *Die Musik* 22 (1929): 424–28.

15. Thomas D'Urfey, *The Comical History of Don Quixote, Parts I, II and III* (London: For Samuel Briscoe, 1694-96). Parts 1 and 2 were staged in May of 1694, part 3 in November of 1695. Henry Purcell and John Eccles composed the music. Curtis Alexander Price discusses the plays with emphasis on the music in *Henry Purcell and the London Stage* (Cambridge: Cambridge University Press, 1984), pp.205-22. For discussion of "I burn," see 210 and 215–16. The plays were revived in many forms between 1700 and 1717. In addition, the song "I burn" appeared independently in entr'acte performances with productions of other plays. From 21 December 1715 it played with Gay's *What d'Ye Call It* as an afterpiece. See Avery, *London Stage*, 72, 93, 128, 211–13, 254, 278, 304, 354, 359, 370, 382, 386, 395, 399, 409, 439, cxxxix.

16. See Ellis, "Thomas D'Urfey," 210–12, and chapter 4 above.

17. In medieval music theory this dissonant interval of an augmented fourth/diminished fifth, conventionally called "the devil in music," was to be avoided both melodically and harmonically.

18. On Handel's use of Keiser, see John Roberts, "Handel's Borrowings from Keiser,"

in *Göttinger Handel-Beitrage*, Band II (Basel and London: Barenreiter-Verlag Kassel, 1986), 51–76. For the aria from which Handel borrowed, see "Wann ich dich noch einst erblicke" in Reinhard Keiser, *Adonis and Janus*, Handel Sources Series, vol. 1 (New York: Garland, 1986), 278–79. The basso continuo part beneath Agrippina's aria becomes, almost without alteration, Polyphemus's angular vocal line. For scholarship on sexual orientation, see Nokes on Gay in *John Gay*, esp. 36–50. On Handel, see Rousseau, "Threshold and Explanation," 127–52; and Gary C. Thomas, "Was George Frideric Handel Gay?: On Closet Questions and Cultural Politics," in Brett, Wood, and Thomas, *Queering the Pitch*, 155–203.

19. Polyphemus's taste for rustic similes extends through traditions of the story of the Cyclops to Theocritus's Idyll 11. See the translation in Thomas Creech, *The Idylliums of Theocritus with Rapin's Discourse of Pastorals* (Oxford: L. Lichfield, 1684), 62–66.

20. Handel, *Acis and Galatea*, ed. Windszus, xxi. Dean (*Handel's Dramatic Oratorios*, 77, 163) proposes the flageolet. For discussion of this scoring as imitation of a whistle, see John Solomon, "Polyphemus's Whistle in Handel's 'Acis and Galatea,'" *Music and Letters* 64 (1983): 37–43. Solomon proposes that it is not his pipes to which the recorder line refers, but a whistle (which Dryden's poem supplies). The difference in reference does not obviate the ironic reading which I favor (along with Dean), particularly given the frolicsome humor of the music and its comic interplay with the aria's vocal line. Solomon's proposal, however, seems unlikely. For an exchange with regard to Solomon's essay, see Anthony Hicks, "Semele's Mirror and Polyphemus's Whistle," *Music and Letters* 65 (1984): 213–16, and Solomon's response, "Handel's Mythological Sources," *Music and Letters* 65 (1984): 321–22.

21. On the complex publication history of this collection, see C. L. Day, "*Pills to Purge Melancholy*," *Review of English Studies* 8 (1932): 177–84. On the contents, see Friedman, *Ballad Revival*, 131–35.

22. D'Urfey, *Wit and Mirth*, 4:207. As Fuller notes (Gay, *Dramatic Works*, 1:453), Dryden's Ovid suggests some of these details. Gay, however, pushes these suggestions into explicit borrowings from popular balladry which contribute to the parodic character of his Polyphemus.

23. This ballad is on a late-seventeenth-century broadside from the collection of Samuel Pepys. It is reprinted in Hyder Rollins, ed., *The Pepys Ballads*, 8 vols. (Cambridge: Harvard University Press, 1929–32), 2:253.

24. From "Bessy Bell and Mary Gray," in *A Collection of Old Ballads*, 3 vols. (London: J. Roberts, 1723–25), 3:243–44.

25. From "The bonny Grey-Ey'd Morn," in *Collection of Old Ballads*, 2:261–62.

26. *Collection of Old Ballads*, 2:244–45.

27. Ibid., 2:265–66.

28. George Friedrich Handel, *Aci, Galatea e Polifemo*, in *The Works of George Frederic Handel*, ed. Friedrich Chrysander, 97 vols. in 84 (Leipzig: for the German Handel Society, n.d.; Ridgewood, N.J.: Gregg Press, 1965), 1:11. Handel wrote this Italian "serenata" in Naples in the summer of 1708. Harris (*Handel and the Pastoral Tradition*, 207–8) briefly discusses some of the many ways this earlier musical version of the myth contrasts with the later English masque.

29. Dean, *Handel's Dramatic Oratorios*, 163.

30. Handel, *Aci, Galatea e Polifemo*, 19. For a recent compact disc of this serenata, see Harmonia Mundi, HMC 901253.54. The translation here is from the libretto to this recording.

31. The composer's changes to the libretto, most of them in his famously awkward English, mitigate the ribaldry and parodic excess of Gay's bumpkin. (See Fuller's notes to II.44 and II.56 in Gay, *Dramatic Works*, 1:453–54.) The manuscript contains an impudently rakish response by the Cyclops to Galatea's disdain, presumably as Gay originally intended:

> Who would bear a woman's toying,
> Who would be a whining lover?
> Force her if she's worth enjoying,
> She'll forgive you when 'tis over.

These rapacious lines are replaced with an awkward and barely meaningful stanza which Fuller suggests "might well be Handel's own effort to make the meaning less direct, resulting in an unacceptably unnatural syntax" (1:453).

> Cease to sue the scornfull Beauty,
> Whining lover still desdaining,
> Women mocking humble duty
> Laugh to see the strong complaining.

This stanza, in a slightly less clumsy and more coherent form, appears in the 1732 publication of the libretto and is the text we inherit for this aria:

> Cease to Beauty to be suing,
> Ever-whining Love disdaining,
> Let the Brave, their Aims pursuing,
> Still be conqu'ring, not complaining.

For discussion of these various texts and Handel's evident dissatisfaction with the aria, see 1:450 and 1:453–54, and Dean, *Handel's Dramatic Oratorios,* 189–90. Gay died in December 1732 and seems to have had no connection with the publication of the masque in this last year of his life.

32. Dean notes the comic exaggeration and contrast of this abrupt shift (*Handel's Dramatic Oratorios,* 163).

33. Ibid.

34. While Dean—like other critics—certainly overreads Gay's dependence on Pope's *Autumn* for these lines (ibid., 161), there may indeed be a poignant evocation of the polished realm of these early pastorals.

35. The word also recalls Damon's query just following Acis's opening aria: "Shepherd, what art thou pursuing? / Heedless, running to thy Ruin" (ll. 36–37). Trowell ("Acis, Galatea, and Polyphemus," 54–93) proposes that the arias for Damon were added to a work originally conceived for three voices and suspects another author wrote the texts. (One of these arias is attributed to John Hughes.) Trowell's analysis of the performance and manuscript evidence more convincingly argues the case than his conjectures with regard to the mannerisms of the poetry. Nonetheless, even if another librettist—Hughes or John Arbuthnot—contributed this aria, the occurrence of "ruin" in both arias carries a meaningful resonance with its repetition.

36. Dean, *Handel's Dramatic Oratorios,* 166.

37. Ibid., 166–67.

CHAPTER 7. POPULAR SONGS AND THE POLITICS OF HEROISM

1. For the composition and early history of the plays, see Winton, *John Gay and the London Stage,* 87–144. For the most detailed summary of the history of the *Beggar's Opera,* with some discussion of *Polly,* see Schultz, *Gay's Beggar's Opera.*

2. The term is used by Mrs. Fainall in the opening of the famous fourth act of

Congreve's play (IV.i.77–79). For application of the term to and analysis of the increase of music and spectacle as socially relevant in late seventeenth-century plays, see Dugaw, "'Critical Instants,'" 157–81.

3. See Winton, *John Gay and the London Stage*, 73–86, on the pantomime dance tradition and Gay's ballad "Newgate's Garland" sung in the pantomime *Harlequin Sheppard* (1724) written, and presumably danced by John Thurmond. As Winton shows, "the conjunction here of pantomime and Gay's ballad is . . . a significant step on the way to *The Beggar's Opera*" (75).

4. *A Pill To Purge State-Melancholy*, Part the Second (London: J.Graves, 1718), 25–27.

5. On the Otway connection, see Ian Donaldson, *World Upside-Down*, 159–82. On the singers, see Bertrand Bronson, "The Beggar's Opera," in *Facets of the Enlightenment*, 69.

6. For a survey of scholarship on this subject, see Edgar Roberts's remarks in John Gay, *The Beggar's Opera*, ed. Roberts and Smith, xxviii–xxix.

7. Winton discusses some of these relationships in *John Gay and the London Stage*, 113. See also Bronson, *"Beggar's Opera,"* in *Facets of Enlightenment*, 62–68. Bronson develops in detail Gay's ongoing allusions to the "higher" Handelian opera.

8. *The Willoughby Whim* in D'Urfey, *Wit and Mirth*, 1:169.

9. Ian Donaldson, *World Upside-Down*, 172.

10. Allan Ramsay, *Tea-Table Miscellany*, 3 vols. (London: A. Miller, 1733), 2:192. William Stenhouse describes the melody as an "old pipe tune" in *Illustrations of the Lyric Poetry and Music of Scotland* (Edinburgh and London: William Blackwood and Sons, 1853), 62.

11. Doody discusses "the two voices of Augustan poems" in *Daring Muse*, 199–231. Her discussion of Gay focuses on the "disparate and yet related" languages of the scene in the "Cotillon," "Youth's the Season made for Joys" of act 2, scene 4. As she says, "they work in unison and they work counter to each other at the same time. We must be able to hear both. We have here come upon . . . the combination of disparate languages, disparate voices, working simultaneously both with and against each other" (213).

12. For useful summaries, see Langford, *Polite and Commercial People*, 1–57; and Kramnick, *Bolingbroke and His Circle*, esp. 39–83.

13. D'Urfey, *Wit and Mirth*, 4:99-104; reprinted in 5:316–21 of the 1719–20 edition. Simpson discusses the tune in *British Broadside Ballad*, 561–63.

14. *The Roxburghe Ballads*, ed. William Chappell and Joseph Ebsworth, 9 vols. (Hertford: S. Austin and Sons, 1871–99), 8:225–26. Ebsworth notes a variant "Loyal Health" from the following year, 1710. James Hogg publishes a variant of this song, "Over the Seas and far Awa" in *The Jacobite Relics of Scotland*, 2 vols. (Edinburgh: William Blackwood, 1819), 1:51-52. Hogg includes as well, three additional Jacobite texts and a Whig song set to the tune (2:400–402).

15. John J. McAleer, introduction to *Ballads and Songs Loyal to the Hanoverian Succession (1703–1761)*, Augustan Reprint Society publication no. 96 (Los Angeles: William Andrews Clark Memorial Library, 1962), v.

16. *A Pill to Purge State-Melancholy* (London: R. Burleigh, 1716), 141–43.

17. Gay, *Poetry and Prose*, 1:94 (ll. 45–48).

18. Langford, *Walpole and the Robinocracy*, 16.

19. "O'er the Hills" continued to serve as an allusion to the Jacobite/anti-Jacobite conflict well into the eighteenth century, appearing with new ballads about "Bonnie Prince Charlie's" uprising of 1745, the last Stuart threat to the House of Hanover. See Simpson, *British Broadside Ballad*, 562–63.

20. William Donaldson, *Jacobite Song*, 33.

21. See Dianne Dugaw, "'High Change in 'Change-Alley': Popular Ballads and Emergent Capitalism in the Eighteenth Century," *Eighteenth-Century Life* 22 (1998): 1–16.

22. The directors, bankers, and manufacturers of wartime supplies had little knowledge of the commerce between Europe and the Americas by which they, as a trading company, might have raised working assets. Furthermore, in its final form, the treaty severely limited the commercial provisions of the settlement. Moreover, by 1718 hostilities broke out again between England and Spain, halting what little of the slave trade the South Sea Company had begun under the treaty.

23. Nokes, *John Gay*, 288–321. See also Nicholson, *Writing and the Rise of Finance*, 123–38.

24. On the South Sea Bubble, see Dickson, *Financial Revolution in England;* Carswell, *South Sea Bubble;* and Neal, *Rise of Financial Capitalism*, chaps. 4 and 5.

25. Broadside, Harvard, Kress-Goldsmith 5898.25, with tune. A variant of the ballad recasts the preoccupation with Jews, adding "Turks" to the intermingling at the stock trading coffeehouses, suggesting that the new trading poses an even more complex blurring of ancient separations: "Jews, Turks, and Christians, hear my Song." See Simpson, *British Broadside Ballad*, 562.

26. "Italian Songsters" of course is a sexualized reference to the castrati and other "queer" persons (as we would say) associated with the opera.

27. As the editor of *Pills* and a Whig polemicist himself, D'Urfey, of course, knew all the earlier songs mentioned here.

28. The tune is from Simpson, *British Broadside Ballad*, 562.

29. D'Urfey, *Wit and Mirth*, 1:132. The song first appeared in D'Urfey's 1709 play, *The Modern Prophets*.

30. Hogg, *Jacobite Relics*, 1:44.

31. On *Polly* and this paradigmatic heroic dilemma, see Joan H. Owen, "*Polly* and the Choice of Virtue," *Bulletin of the New York Public Library* 77 (1974): 393–406.

32. Critics in recent years have read the play more seriously. For my extended reading of the play's reliance on the ballad Female Warrior, see *Warrior Women*, 191–211. See also Winton, *John Gay and the London Stage*, 128–44. My discussion here is an abbreviated version of my earlier analysis.

33. *The Female Warrior,* from a 1690s London broadside reproduced in *The Bagford Ballads*, ed. Joseph W. Ebsworth, 2 vols. (Hertford: Stephen Austin and Sons, 1878), 1:322. The view of the heroic ideal as gender opposition was especially fashionable in the Restoration era, appearing in work after work. Dryden supplied perhaps the most dazzling emblem of the idea in the masque of Cleopatra as Venus and Antony as Mars which opens the third act of *All for Love*.

34. From an early-nineteenth century Liverpool broadside in Harvard University Collection 54–784, "Miscellaneous Prints," 2:96.

35. For an extended discussion of the streetsong context of authors and publishers, see chapters 1–3 of Dugaw, *Warrior Women*.

36. Thus, Edmond McAdoo Gagey—apparently never imagining that Macheath was not intended as the hero or even the central focus of the play—complains: "Gay was . . . sacrificing the glamour, the charm, and the gallantry of his hero." See *Ballad Opera* (New York: Columbia University Press, 1937), 49. John Fuller also betrays a hint of bafflement at Macheath's debasement: "Polly herself cannot carry the play... Macheath at least retains his self-confidence . . . In context his presumptuousness lacks charm . . . and his death is ignominious." See Gay, *Dramatic Works*, 1:56. For a reconsideration of Polly's virtue and her importance to *The Beggar's Opera* and its sequel, see Toni-Lynn O'Shaughnessy, "A Single Capacity in *The Beggar's Opera*," *Eighteenth-Century Studies* 21 (1987–88): 212–27.

37. Gay, *Dramatic Works*, ed. Fuller, 2:83. My references are to this edition. The im-

agery here also calls to mind the conventional ballad motif of a dead lover, usually an abandoned woman, who pursues her beloved betrayer. See, for example, *The Cruel Ship's Carpenter* (usually titled on broadsides *The Gosport Tragedy*). For versions, see Laws, *American Balladry,* 268–70 (P-36). On the structure of Female Warrior ballads, see chapter 4 of Dugaw, *Warrior Women.*

38.   As Fuller observes (introduction to Gay, *Dramatic Works*, 1:56), "a sexual/political metaphor is substituted [in *Polly*] for the criminal/political metaphor of *The Beggar's Opera.*" That Gay is developing links between racial slavery and gender slavery is apparent in the first act when the slaver Ducat complains of paying the price of "a dozen Negro princesses" for "a handsome Christian" (I.vi.26). Shortly after, Gay weaves into this construction the problem of heroism as Polly, refusing to be Ducat's slave, invokes the unsatisfactory example of Helen of Troy. She declares there "was never yet / So great a wretch as Helen" (I.xi.19–20).

39.   II.i.14–15 in John Dryden, *All for Love*, ed. Maximillian Novak, vol. 13 in *Works of John Dryden*, ed. Swedenberg, Roper, and Dearing. My references are to this edition.

40.   Gay's interest in the distinctions between literal and figurative language parallel Swift's satire in the "School of Languages" of "the Academy of Lagado" in part 3, chapter 5 of *Gulliver's Travels.*

41.   The tune is from "Sawny was tall, and of noble race" from D'Urfey's *The Virtuous Wife* and printed in *Wit and Mirth*, 1:316–17. The original words continue Gay's undercutting of Macheath's heroism and of the pastoral as a heroic form. Cast in the pretend-Scots dialect that D'Urfey made fashionable in the 1680s and 1690s, the song is an abandoned lover's paen to Sawney "tall and of Noble Race" who "will ne'er be [her] love agen." It builds throughout images of the speaker and Sawney as figures in a Caledonian pastoral.

42.   D'Urfey, *Wit and Mirth*, 1:213. The song originally appeared in D'Urfey's play *Wonders in the Sun, or The Kingdom of the Birds* (1706).

43.   Kramnick, *Bolingbroke and His Circle,* 77–78.

44.   For discussion of Gay's portrait of the Indians in *Polly*, see B. H. Bissell, *The American Indian in English Literature of the Eighteenth Century* (New Haven: Yale University Press, 1925), 127–30.

CHAPTER 8. COUNTRY DANCING AND THE SATIRE OF EMPIRE IN *POLLY*

I wish to thank Dorothy Attneave for her help in the analysis and reconstructions of all the dances in this chapter's discussion. Her contributions are indispensable and much appreciated.

1.   For discussion of the play and its suppression, see Dugaw, *Warrior Women,* 191–211.

2.   Thompson, preface to *Whigs and Hunters,* 17.

3.   See Nicholson, *Writing and the Rise of Finance.*

4.   See Swaen, "Airs and Tunes of John Gay's *Polly*": and idem, "Airs and Tunes of John Gay's *Beggar's Opera.*" Comparing the two plays, we find that most of the sixty-nine tunes in *The Beggar's Opera* come from ballads and songs from published broadsides and from Thomas D'Urfey's popular *Wit and Mirth.* Only fifteen tunes from the first ballad opera can be found among Playford's dance tunes. The first edition of John Playford's *The English Dancing Master* was published in 1651 (London: printed by Thomas Harper, and are to be sold by John Playford, 1651). The collection of dance tunes and directions continued to be printed with changes and additions by Playford's descendants and inheritors until

the eighteenth edition of 1728 which was published in three volumes. For discussion of Playford, see *The New Grove Dictionary of Music and Musicians*, ed. Stanley Sadie, 20 vols. (London: Macmillan, 1980). See also Margaret Dean-Smith's introduction to *Playford's English Dancing Master*, ix–xxxi.

5. Keller and Shimer, *Playford Ball*, viii.

6. *New Grove Dictionary*, 4:6–7. Catches were especially popular as a male form, and in the eighteenth century catch clubs—men's fraternities for singing and drinking—became a popular tavern entertainment.

7. Franklin B. Zimmerman in *Henry Purcell, A Guide to Research* (New York and London: Garland, 1989) lists it under "Spurious Ascriptions" (31). The author of the canon was probably Henry Aldrich (1647–1710), dean of Christ-Church of the University of Oxford from 1689 until his death.

8. *The Second Book of the Catch Club, or Merry Companions*, ed. John Walsh (London: John Walsh, 1731).

9. John Playford, *The Dancing Master*, vol. 1, 18th ed. (London: Edward Midwinter and John Young, c. 1728), 104. Further references to vol. 1 are to this edition.

10. Dorothy Attneave has contributed this reconstruction of the dance. The instructions for the last part—"sett down" and jump up"—are ambiguous and unusual. We have presented an interpretation of the directions that can be danced. Our rendering of the "woundy" last part of the dance is based on a figure known in Irish dancing as "Ring the Bells."

11. For references to the tune and its heroine, see Swaen, "Airs and Tunes of John Gay's *Polly*," 408.

12. Playford, *Dancing Master*, 1:57. Both are movements of two people striding in a dance toward each other. The "side" is a shoulder-to-shoulder movement, and the "arm" is the locking of right or left arms and turning. See Keller and Shimer, *Playford Ball*, 116, 114.

13. Iona Opie and Peter Opie, *Children's Games in Street and Playground* (Oxford: Oxford University Press, 1969), 224-25.

14. Cecil Sharp and Herbert Macilwaine, *Morris Dance Tunes* (London: Novello and Co., 1911), 4.

15. From *the Hive*, 4:7, quoted in Swaen, "Airs and Tunes of John Gay's *Polly*," 408.

16. John Gay, *Polly* (London: Printed for the Author, 1729), Air 24.

17. Playford, *Dancing Master*, 1:47. The hey for three used in this dance is an interlocking figure eight in which all three dancers move at once, passing each other until they return to their places.

18. Dorothy Attneave has contributed this reconstruction of the dance.

19. See Leach, *Dictionary of Folklore*, 747–48, 750. See also Rippon, *Discovering English Folk Dance*, 5–50; and Hutton, *Stations of the Sun*, 262–70. Hutton gives good general coverage of the revival of morris dancing at the beginning of the twentieth century spurred by Cecil Sharp and Mary Neal (295–303). The history of morris dancing before the mid-nineteenth century is conjectural because we have no precise records or information. We know that people were dancing "morris" dances much earlier, some with the same names that survive in later tradition. For an early discussion, see the remarks of the antiquarian Francis Douce (1757-1834) in *Illustrations of Shakspeare, and of Ancient Manners: with Dissertations on the Clowns and Fools of Shakspeare; on the Collection of Popular Tales Entitled Gesta Romanorum; and on the English Morris Dance* (1809; reprint, London: T. Tegg, 1839). A theatrical tradition of morris dancing developed for interludes and entr'actes at the Drury Lane Theatre in the first decade of the eighteenth century and lasted into the nineteenth. It signified exactly the evocation of pastoral nostalgia and class consciousness that Gay exploits in *Polly*. See Avery, *London Stage*, 73, 280–81, 325. "The Three Jolly Sheepskins" pub morris as it is now danced was collected from traditional

dancers early in the twentieth century and comes from the "Border morris area" between Wales and England. Some version of a sheepskin hey morris probably dates back to Gay's era (and beyond). Certainly, the tune—identifiably a morris tune by its shape—goes back before the Jacobean era and has a range of traditional associations. I am grateful for informed conjecture on this topic to Dorothy Attneave at the University of Oregon, Michael Heaney of the Bodeleian Library, and Rich Holmes of Flying Bark Morris in Newport News, Virginia. For a survey of scholarship, see Heaney, *Introductory Bibliography on Morris Dancing.* See also Forrest, *Morris and Matachin.*

20. William Dauney, *Ancient Scotish Melodies, from a Manuscript of the reign of King James VI* (Edinburgh: Maitland Club, 1838), 271. For the tune, see 228.

21. Lionel Bacon, *The Morris Ring: A Handbook of Morris Dances* (Winchester: Morris Ring, 1974; London: Morris Ring, 1986), 228–29. Bacon quotes from his early-twentieth-century sources: E. C. Cawte, *Journal of the English Folk Dance and Song Society* (December 1963) and manuscripts; manuscripts of Cecil Sharp and Maude Karpeles; and "The Folk Lore of Herefordshire" by E. M. Leather (1912). Manuscripts are in the Vaughan Williams Library, Cecil Sharp House, London.

22. Playford, *Dancing Master*, 1:357.

23. Dorothy Attneave has contributed this reconstruction of the dance.

CHAPTER 9. SEXUALITY, THE MIDDLING SORT, AND THE INVENTION OF "CAMP"

1. The full title is *Achilles Dissected: Being a Compleat Key of the Political Characters in that New Ballad Opera, Written by the late Mr. Gay. An Account of the Plan upon which it is founded. With Remarks upon the Whole. To which is added, The First Satire of the Second Book of Horace, Imitated in a Dialogue between Mr. Pope and the Ordinary of Newgate* (London: W. Mears, 1733). The title page names the author as Mr Burnet, and the pamphlet, written as a letter, is signed "Alex. Burnet." The identity of this "Burnet" remains unknown. See Noble, "Sex and Gender in Gay's 'Achilles'," 211 n. 16. "Burnet" indicates that he is quoting all but the last sentence of his summary of the play. I have not determined his source.

2. Susan Sontag posits Gay's era as "the soundest starting point" for camp. See "Notes on 'Camp'," in *Against Interpretation*, 275–92. See also Newton, *Mother Camp;* and Bronski, *Culture Clash.*

3. See Leppert, *Music and Image.*

4. See Simpson, *British Broadside Ballad,* 494 for discussion of the tune, which he identifies as "Mr. Lane's Magot" (i.e., "whim," "fancy") in *The Dancing Master,* commencing with the ninth edition, 1695. As he notes, Thomas D'Urfey set words to the tune, which appear, among other places, in *Wit and Mirth,* 2:218.

5. See "Ann Auretti" in Philip Highfill et al., *A Biographical Dictionary of Actors, Actresses, Musicians, Dancers, Managers, and Other Stage Personnel in London, 1600–1800,* 12 vols. (Carbondale: Southern Illinois University Press, 1973), 1:176–77.

6. Joan Wallach Scott, "The Evidence of Experience," *Critical Inquiry* 17 (1991): 789.

7. See John Brewer, "'The most polite age and the most vicious': Attitudes towards Culture as a Commodity, 1660–1800," in Bermingham and Brewer, *Consumption of Culture;* and Brewer, *Pleasures of the Imagination.*

8. The reference here is to the Excise Crisis of 1732, in which the prime minister attempted to reduce land taxation and introduce taxes on wine, salt, and tobacco but received

so much resistance that the taxes were rescinded. The excise controversy eventually built strong opposition to Walpole and checked his power after the elections of 1734. See Langford, *Polite and Commercial People*, 28–33; and idem, *Excise Crisis*.

9. See Leonore Davidoff and Catherine Hall, *Family Fortunes: Men and Women of the English Middle Classes, 1780–1850* (Chicago: University of Chicago, 1987).

10. Sontag, *Against Interpretation*, 281. In "John Gay's 'Achilles': The Burlesque Element," *Ariel* 3 (1972): 17–28, Peter Lewis discusses the irregularities of the parodic strategies in *Achilles* and the problems with identifying them as literary burlesque.

11. Sedgwick, *Epistemology of the Closet*, 71.

12. Sennett, *Fall of Public Man*.

13. Jack Babuscio, "Camp and the Gay Sensibility" in *Gays and Film*, ed. Richard Dyer (London: British Film Institute, 1977), 45.

14. Dollimore, *Sexual Dissidence*, 311.

15. As Peter Lewis observes, commentators have demonstrated perplexity in characterizing the nature of the burlesque in *Achilles*. See Lewis, "John Gay's 'Achilles'," 18–19. Is it farce, classical travesty, or satirical burlesque? Lewis declares that "it is virtually impossible to separate classical travesty from satirical burlesque" and notes Gay's "considerable originality in finding new burlesque weapons" (18). I would go further than Lewis to characterize Gay's innovative strategy as the precursor of modern "camp."

16. Addison and Steele brought this debate before the wide middlebrow readership of the *Tatler* and the *Spectator* from 1708 through 1712. Gay's first burlesque contribution to the discussion came in 1713 with his collaboration with Pope on *Guardian*, no. 40, which ridiculed the "Modern" pastoral style of Ambrose Philips. The following year he continued his burlesquing treatment of the pastoral in these terms with his ambivalent and immensely influential *Shepherd's Week*. See Trowbridge, "Pope, Gay, and *The Shepherd's Week*," 79–88.

17. Case, "Toward a Butch-Femme Aesthetic," 302.

18. Greenberg, *Construction of Homosexuality* 368; John D'Emilio, "Capitalism and Gay Identity," in Abelove, Barale, and Halperin, *Lesbian and Gay Studies Reader*, 467–76; Henry Abelove, "Some Speculations on the History of 'Sexual Intercourse' during the 'Long Eighteenth Century' in England," *Genders* 6 (1989); and Thomas Laqueur, "Sexual Desire and the Market Economy during the Industrial Revolution," in Stanton, *Discourses of Sexuality*, 185–215. For a recent study of masculinity and femininity in Greek myth, see Loraux, *Experience of Tiresias*.

19. Noble, "Sex and Gender in Gay's 'Achilles'," 205–6. As Noble observes, Burnet's discussion suggests that the play was not actually performed as we have it in the published version, but rather various of the scenes took place in a different order. As she observes, "the Lycomedes plot . . . in Burnet's version occupies even more of the play than in the version we read" (212 n. 28).

20. Ovid, *Artis Amatoriae* (Oxford: Oxford University Press, 1989), 1.675–78.

21. *Ovid: The Erotic Poems*, trans. Peter Green (New York: Penguin Books, 1982), 1.675–78.

22. Burnet, *Achilles Dissected*, 13.

23. See Romney Sedgwick, introduction to *John, Lord Hervey, Some Materials towards Memoirs of the Rein of King George II*, 3 vols. (London: Eyre and Spottiswoode, 1931), 1:xxii–xxx; and Robert Halsband, *Lord Hervey: Eighteenth-Century Courtier* (Oxford: Clarendon, 1973), 108–18, 144.

24. Randolph Trumbach, "London's Sapphists: From Three Sexes to Four Genders in the Making of Modern Culture," in Epstein and Straub, *Body Guards*, 116.

25. See Nokes, *John Gay*, 42–50. Nokes's reading of *Achilles* develops this biographical strand of analysis, in which he imagines a problematically "unmanly" and therefore

psychologically hobbled John Gay. Despite some suggestive aspects of his discussion, Nokes's analyses of Gay and of the play are, as previously noted, distorted by an anachronistic projection of Gay's "effeminacy" that is based on an unexamined belief in a modern, gendered psychology for individual identity. Ironically, Nokes's assumptions proceed from just the emerging categories of identity, relationship, and sexuality that are questioned in *Achilles*.

26. See John Gay, prologue to *Shepherd's Week,* in *Poetry and Prose*. See also his *Rural Sports*.

27. On this eighteenth-century feminizing of male homoeroticism, see Greenberg, *Construction of Homosexuality,* 331; Lawrence Senelick, "Mollies or Men of Mode?" in Epstein and Straub, *Body Guards,* 33–67; Trumbach, "London's Sapphists," and "The Birth of the Queen" in *Hidden from History: Reclaiming the Gay and Lesbian Past,* ed. Martin Duberman, Martha Vicinus, and George Chauncey Jr. (New York: Meridian, 1989): 129–40.

28. Noble, "Sex and Gender in John Gay's 'Achilles'," 210 n. 10 for classical sources; pp.185-91 on Gay's familiarity with variant versions of the story.

29. Statius, *Works*, ed. J. H. Mozley, 2 vols., Loeb Classical Library (London and New York: Harvard University Press; W. Heinemann, 1928), 1:161–62. Unless otherwise noted, translations are from this edition.

30. Case, "Toward a Butch-Femme Aesthetic," 304.

31. See Paul M. Clogan, *The Medieval Achilleid of Statius* (Leiden: E. J. Brill, 1968), 7–8.

32. Pierre Vidal-Naquet, "The Black Hunter and the Origin of the Athenian Ephebeia," in *Myth, Religion and Society,* ed. R. L. Gordon (Cambridge: Cambridge University Press, 1981), 158. The *ephebeia* was an institution of the Athenian polis whose dynamics have been traced by scholars in myths that are much older. For general discussion of such rites and myths, see Marie Delcourt, *Hermaphrodite: Mythes et rites de la bisexualité dans l'antiquité classique* (Paris: Presses Universitaires de France, 1958).

33. Nicole Loraux, "Herakles: The Super-Male and the Feminine," in Halperin, Winkler, and Zeitlin, *Before Sexuality,* 34.

34. Winkler, "Laying Down the Law," 176.

35. This rite of passage in the Athenian culture that codified the myths was fundamentally a military one from the *ephebe* training phase of adolescence to the full citizenship of the *hoplite*, who "learned the honorable conventions of phalanx battle," to quote John Winkler, "The Ephebes' Song: *Tragoidia and Polis*," in Winkler and Zeitlin, *Nothing to Do with Dionysos?*, 35.

36. Noble, "Sex and Gender in John Gay's 'Achilles'," 189. In Statius the account of Achilles' response to the armor and recognition by Ulysses is in book 1, ll. 850–85.

37. Gleason, *Making Men,* 159.

38. Winkler, "Laying Down the Law," 182.

39. David Halperin and others discuss the politics of domination and subordination that determine these "insertive" and "receptive" roles. See David Halperin, "Is There a History of Sexuality?" in Abelove, Barale, and Halperin, *Lesbian and Gay Studies Reader,* 418.

40. *The Myrmidons,* a lost play by Aeschylus, refers to intercrural sex between Patroclus and Achilles ("the pleasures of their thighs"). See Bruce Thornton, *Eros: The Myth of Ancient Greek Sexuality* (Boulder, Colo.: Broadview Press, 1997), 205.

41. Clogan, *Medieval Achilleid*, 7. Clogan has surveyed well over seventy medieval schoolbook manuscripts of the text and collates fully the glosses of eleven of these for his edition.

42. Howard, "Statius His Achilles, " 171–282; reissued as *Poems on Several occasions,* 2d ed. (London: Francis Saunders, 1696).

43. On Dryden's relationship to Howard and to the bookseller Herringman, see James Winn, *John Dryden and His World* (New Haven: Yale University Press, 1987), 95–103.

44. *The Works of John Dryden,* ed. Edward N. Hooker and H. T. Swedenberg Jr. (Berkeley and Los Angeles: University of California Press, 1956), 1:17–20. All quotes are from this edition of the poem.

45. Howard, "Statius His Achilles," 238–47.

46. As Noble observes ("Sex and Gender in John Gay's 'Achilles'," 187–88), this "lesbian" framing resembles the similarly cast fragment from (Pseudo-)Bion.

47. On the term, see Dugaw, "'Critical Instants'," 157–81. As "discrete and self-contained 'Instants,' songs in this era functioned in spoken plays to contemplative rather than dramatic ends. Moreover, they typically implicated intertexts which draw into the play other texts, authors, and contexts. The songs stop a play . . . and open it out into a momentary time out of time, a complex and particularly social epiphany" (161).

48. "Phebe. Set by Mr. Gouge," in *The Musical Miscellany,* 6 vols. (London: John Watts, 1729–31), 1:88–91.

49. Noble, "Sex and Gender in John Gay's 'Achilles'," 193.

50. Richard Dyer, *Heavenly Bodies: Film Stars and Society* (London: MacMillan, 1987), 154.

51. Mary Delarivière Manley, *Secret Memoirs . . . from the New Atalantis,* 2 vols. (London: John Morphew and J. Woodward, 1709), 2:43 and such ballads from the age of Queen Anne as "A New Ballad: To the Tune of *Fair Rosamund,"* probably by the Whig balladeer Arthur Mainwaring, which details the "dark Deeds at night" of the "Dirty Chamber-Maid," Abigail Masham who "pierc'd [the] Royal Heart." See *Poems on Affairs of State,* ed. Frank Ellis, vol. 7 (New Haven: Yale University Press, 1975), 306–16.

52. Ruth Perry, "Incest as the Meaning of the Gothic Novel," *Eighteenth-Century: Theory and Interpretation* 39 (1998): 261–78. Perry analyzes this incest dynamic in relation to a shift in kinship relations and values from the clan-based property system of the early modern era to the bourgeois nuclear family of the modern age. See also Ruth Perry, "De-Familiarizing the Family; or, Writing Family History from Literary Sources," *Modern Language Quarterly* 55 (1994): 415–27.

53. M. or R. White, *Catch that Catch Can* (London: W. Godbid for J. Playford, 1667), 77.

54. Enrico Careri, *Francesco Geminiani (1687–1762)* (Oxford: Clarendon Press, 1993). Geminiani was throughout his career an avid and successful art dealer, a business venture that, as Careri notes (46–55), cost his reputation as a musical "artist" in the eyes of such historians as Charles Burney, intent on an aesthetics of music clean in its remove from a vulgar marketplace.

55. See Careri's "Thematic Catalogue" and "Mr. Geminiani's Minuet" in ibid., 287 (1a and 1b) and 292, respectively.

56. On the minuet in relation to European bourgeois music culture, see Wheelock, *Haydn's Ingenious Jesting with Art,* 58-61, 70–75.

57. From John Gay, *Achilles. An Opera* (London: J. Watts, 1733).

CHAPTER 10. LESSONS OF THE "NATURAL" WORLD FROM GAY TO WILLIAM BLAKE

1. Lewis, *English Fable.*

2. Patterson, *Fables of Power.*

3. Nokes, *John Gay,* 379. For a history of many of the editions, see W. H. K. Wright, *The Fables of John Gay with Biographical and Critical Introduction and Bibliographical*

Appendix (London and New York: F. Warne and Co., 1889). A Harvard University copy of Wright's book (shelfmark 15461.4) includes manuscript notes in the hand of Ernest Lewis Gay that cite a number of obscure eighteenth- and nineteenth-century editions, 295–313.

    4.   Irving, *John Gay*, 221–24.

    5.   Ibid., 230–231; Nokes, *John Gay*, 364–98.

    6.   *Fables. By the Late Mr. Gay. Volume the Second* (London: J. and P. Knapton, and T. Cox, 1738), A2.

    7.   [Eliza Haywood], *The Parrot* (London: T. Gardner, 1746), no. 9, 2v.

    8.   Lewis, *English Fable*, 157. The quote is from James Beattie, "On Fables and Romances," in *Dissertations Moral and Critical* (London: W. Strahan, 1783), 507.

    9.   Swift and Pope, *Miscellanies in Prose and Verse*, 2:285–91.

    10.   *The Works of Jonathan Swift*, ed. Walter Scott, 19 vols. (Edinburgh: Archibald Constable and Co., 1824), 13:262. While it is not clear how Scott arrived at this declaration, he showed scrupulous care in such attributions. His information with regard to Swift and his circle came in large part from Lady Louisa Stuart, granddaughter of Lady Mary Wortley Montagu.

    11.   A 1742 edition of the Swift and Pope *Miscellanies*, 13 vols. (London: Charles Bathurst and L. Gilliver, 1742) lists "The Country Post" among works "By Mr. Pope and Mr. Gay" (3:A4r). Vinton Dearing's attribution of the piece to Pope is unconvincing, especially since Pope pointedly claims authorship (with Gay) of "The Memoirs of P.P. Clerk of this Parrish" from this same rural sojourn with no mention of "The Country-Post." See Alexander Pope, *The Art of Sinking in Poetry: A Critical Edition*, ed. Edna L. Steeves (New York: Columbia University Press, 1952), xix.

    12.   For news reports of escalating hostilies on the continent, see editions of *The Weekly-Journal: or, Saturday's Post* from 19 July through August 1718.

    13.   A recently discovered letter reveals Gay writing in a similar vein to his friends the Blount sisters in the persona of their horse. The letter begins: "My two fair and honoured Ladys. Though you may at first be in some Surprise at my Hand, yet your wonder will soon cease when I tell you that I am your Horse of Mapledurham, who had the Misfortune to be sent into Devonshire with a Poet on my Back; I have thought fit as in Duty bound not only to acquaint you with my present Wellfare, but also to give you some Account of my Adventures in this long and perilous Journey." See Nokes, *John Gay*, 545–46, 218. Gay's trip was in the summer of 1716.

    14.   Dearing, introduction to *Fables* in Gay, *Poetry and Prose*, ii.

    15.   Lewis, *English Fable*, 171, 188. In addition to the recent discussion by Lewis, Nokes examines fables from the first set (*John Gay*, 378–91). See also Armens's discussion in *John Gay, Social Critic*, 186–87, which details some of the parallels to other fabulists; and Spacks, *John Gay*, 92–121.

    16.   Gay, *Poetry and Prose*, 2:315. All citations are from this edition.

    17.   Gay may have had in mind the burlesquing remarks of Fainall in Congreve's *Way of the World* who wittily remarks of his own rakish desires: "What a Wretch is he who must survive his hopes! Nothing remains when that Day comes, but to sit down and weep like *Alexander*, when he wanted other Worlds to conquer" (II.i.114–17).

    18.   Finch's poem "The Nocturnal Reverie" was published in Anne Finch, *Miscellany Poems* (London: Printed for J. B. and Sold by Benj. Tooke, 1713), 291, and is often reprinted. See, for example, *Eighteenth-Century Women Poets*, ed. Roger Lonsdale (Oxford: Oxford University Press, 1990), 22–23.

    19.   Thomas Ravenscroft, *Melismata. Musicall Phansies. Fitting the Court, Cittie, and Countrey Humours* (London: W. Stansby for T. Adams, 1611), no. 20.

    20.   Francis James Child, ed., *The English and Scottish Popular Ballads*, 5 vols. (Boston: Houghton, Mifflin, and Co., 1882–98; reprint, New York: Dover, 1965), 5:212.

21. Walter Scott, *Minstrelsy of the Scottish Border*, 3 vols. (Edinburgh: J. Ballantyne, 1803), 3:239. The entire text is:

> As I was walking all alane,
>> I heard twa corbies making a mane;
> The tane unto the t'other say,
>> Where sall we gang and dine to-day?
>
> In behint yon auld fail dyke,
>> I wot there lies a new-slain knight;
> And nae body kens that he lies there,
>> But his hawk, his hound, and lady fair.
>
> His hound is to the hunting gane,
>> His hawk to fetch the wild-fowl hame,
> His lady's ta'en another mate,
>> So we may make our dinner sweet.
>
> Ye'll sit on his white hause bane,
>> And I'll pike out his bonny blue een:
> Wi' ae lock o' his gowden hair,
>> We'll theek our nest when it grows bare.
>
> Mony a one for him makes mane,
>> But nane sall ken whare he is gane:
> O'er his white banes, when they are bare,
>> The wind sall blaw for evermair.

As with other ballads in *Minstrelsy*, it is possible that Scott wrote the "Twa Corbies" or perhaps reworked it from an older version. I have found no evidence that Gay knew this burlesque, though he could have known it, given his own familiarity with Scottish songs as well as his friendship with Allan Ramsay and John Arbuthnot, both musicians.

22. I am grateful to Ian Russell for directing me to the parodic sermon in English folk tradition in general and the vitality of *Two Crows* ballads in that tradition. Of particular importance to me were his "The Parodic Sermon in Oral Tradition," an unpublished paper presented at the American Folklore Society Meeting in October 1989; and "Parody and Performance," in *Everyday Culture: Popular Song and the Vernacular Milieu*, ed. Michael Pickering and Tony Green (Milton Keynes, U.K., and Philadelphia: Open University Press, 1987), 70–104.

23. *Frank Brower's Black Diamond Songster and Ebony Jester &c.* (New York: Dick and Fitzgerald, [c. 1863]), 30–31. The ballad, titled "The Four Vultures. A Burlesque Quartette," is prefaced by the description: "As sung by Frank Brower, Ephe Horn, Nelse Seymour, and Charley Fox. (Always received with shouts of laughter.)"

24. J. La Trobe, *The Music of the Church* (Thames Ditton: R. B. Seeley and W. Burnside, 1831), 198, J. Lightwood, *Hymn-Tunes and their Story* (London: C. H. Kelly, 1905), 80–81; and N. Temperley, *The Music of the English Parish Church* (Cambridge: Cambridge University Press, 1979), 89.

25. Of this genre, Russell observes: "In Medieval Europe, two strands of parodic sermon have been identified . . . the one directed at the highly stylized rhetoric of the monastery, mainly in Latin; the other essentially popular, directed at the practices of village priests and wandering mendicants or friars, usually in the vernacular. . . . Such parodic sermons shared common themes: most were against women, marriage, and chastity, or were in favour

of indulgence, especially gluttony, drink, and sex. Many were in the form of dramatic mono-logues. . . . The mock preacher would often admonish his 'congregation', appeal to them to confess their sins and grant them absolution, and conclude with a request for money. Many of these features are to be found in modern examples of the form." See "Parodic Sermon in Oral Tradition," 1–2.

26. Burke, *Popular Culture,* 122–23. Burke's clarification of the term "mock" in his discussion is important. He says: "Perhaps the adjective 'mock' is misleading. It does not occur in most contemporary descriptions, which refer only to 'trials', 'testaments', and so on. If we decide to use the term, we should at least be aware of its ambiguity. A mock battle may be no more or no less than a battle with blunt weapons . . ." (123). Thus, Burke identi-fies in these popular parodies a suggestive invocation of the form and its institutional con-text quite like what operates in Gay.

27. Such social leveling is the standard theme not only in traditional mock legal argu-ments, but in mock funeral sermons as well. See Gilman, *Parodic Sermon,* 55.

28. Irving, *John Gay,* 312.

29. Already in 1733, B. Creak published *Gay's Fables Epitomiz'd; with Short Poems Applicable to Each Occasion . . . for the Use of Schools* (London: B. Creak, [1733]). By midcentury the fables appeared in a chapbook version published by the Diceys of Bow Churchyard, early publishers of children's books.

30. On the artists and engravers, see Vinton Dearing's introduction to a facsimile edi-tion of *Fables (1727, 1738)* (Los Angeles: William Andrews Clark Memorial Library, 1967), iv–v. For Gay's complaining remarks in letters, see Gay, *Poetry and Prose,* 2:618.

31. Thomas Bewick, *Memoir of Thomas Bewick, Written by Himself* [in 1822–28] (London: Longman, Green & Co., 1862), 41–42.

32. *Fables by John Gay,* 2 vols. (London: John Stockdale, 1793). The engravings by Blake are: "The Shepherd and the Philosopher," and fables 6, 13, 16, 18, 22, 24, 28, 30, and 41 in the first set; and fables 12 and 16 in the second set.

33. *The Egg; or, The Memoirs of Gregory Giddy . . . Conceived by a Celebrated Hen* (London: S. Smith, [1728?]), 14.

34. *Poems by John Gay . . . to Which is Prefixed, A Sketch of the Author's Life* (Manches-ter: G. Nicholson, 1797), 2.

35. [John Lettice], "Letters on Gay's Fables," *European Magazine* 68 (1815): 17–18, 114–15, 213–14, 325–26, 407–8, 505–6; and 69 (1816): 29–30, 119–21, 218, 314–15, 415–16. These letters are identified as being by the "Author of 'Fables for the Fire-Side,'" which is Lettice's collection of rhymed fables.

36. Letter Two, *European Magazine* 68 (1815): 115.

37. Gay, *Selection from Fables,* iii.

38. [Henry] Heath, *Illustrations of Gay's Fables* (London: Published by S. Maunder, 10 Newgate Street, [c. 1830]).

Bibliography

This bibliography presents key primary sources and secondary works of commentary and analysis that have shaped and guided my work for this study. I have not included in the bibliography every text I have consulted and cited in the book. Omitted in this list are the numerous early editions of Gay's works whose commentaries I quote from, especially in chapter 2, as well as many eighteenth-century texts, songs, musical works, and commentaries that supply the contextual grounding for my discussion, especially in chapters 3, 5, and 7. Complete citations for all these references can be found in the notes to each chapter.

Abelove, Henry, Michele Barale, and David Halperin, eds. *The Lesbian and Gay Studies Reader*. New York: Routledge, 1993.

Agnew, Jean-Christophe. *Worlds Apart: The Market and the Theater in Anglo-American Thought, 1550-1750*. Cambridge: Cambridge University Press, 1986.

Armens, Sven. *John Gay, Social Critic*. New York: King's Crown Press, 1954.

Avery, Emmet L., ed. *The London Stage 1660-1800, Part 2: 1700–1729*. Carbondale: Southern Illinois University Press, 1960.

Backsheider, Paula. *Spectacular Politics: Theatrical Politics and Mass Culture in Early Modern England* Baltimore: Johns Hopkins University Press, 1993.

Barley, M. W. "Plough Plays in the East Midlands." *Journal of the English Folk Dance and Song Society* 7 (1953): 68–95.

Barrell, John. *The Dark Side of the Landscape*. Cambridge: Cambridge University Press, 1983.

Bermingham, Ann, and John Brewer, eds. *The Consumption of Culture, 1600-1800*. New York: Routledge, 1995.

Brand, John. *Observations on the Popular Antiquities of Great Britain*, Arranged, revised, and enlarged by Henry Ellis. 3 vols. London: Henry Bohm, 1848–49; reprint, New York: AMS Press, 1970.

Brecht, Bertolt. *Collected Plays*. Edited and translated by Ralph Manheim and John Willett. 5 vols. New York: Random House, 1976.

Brett, Philip, Elizabeth Wood, and Gary C. Thomas, eds. *Queering the Pitch: The New Gay and Lesbian Musicology*. New York: Routledge, 1994.

Brewer, John. *The Pleasures of the Imagination*. New York: Routledge, 1997.

———. *Sinews of Power*. London: Unwin Hyman, 1989.

The British Apollo, or, Curious Amusements for the Ingenious. London: Printed for the Authors by J. Mayo, 1708–11.

Bronski, Michael. *Culture Clash: The Making of Gay Sensibility.* Boston: South End Press, 1984.

Bronson, Bertrand. *Facets of the Enlightenment.* Berkeley and Los Angeles: University of California Press, 1968.

Burke, Peter. *Popular Culture in Early Modern Europe.* London: Temple Smith, 1978.

Carswell, John. *The South Sea Bubble.* Rev. ed. Stroud, U.K.: Alan Sutton, 1993.

Case, Sue-Ellen. "Toward a Butch-Femme Aesthetic." In *The Lesbian and Gay Studies Reader,* edited by Henry Abelove, Michele Barale, and David Halperin. New York: Routledge, 1993.

Cawte, E. C., Alex Helm, and N. Peacock. *English Ritual Drama.* London: Folklore Society, 1967.

Chambers, E. K. *The English Folk-Play.* Oxford: Clarendon Press, 1933.

Clark, J. C. D. *English Society, 1688–1832: Ideology, Social Structure and Political Practice during the Ancient Regime.* Cambridge: Cambridge University Press, 1985.

Clifford, James. *The Predicament of Culture: Twentieth-Century Ethnography, Literature, and Art.* Cambridge: Harvard University Press, 1988.

Clifford, James, and Louis Landa, eds. *Pope and His Contemporaries.* Oxford: Clarendon Press, 1949.

A Complete Key to the Last New Farce The What D'Ye Call It. London: James Roberts, 1715.

Congleton, J. E. *Theories of Pastoral Poetry in England, 1684–1798.* Gainesville: University of Florida Press, 1952.

Cruickshanks, Eveline. *Political Untouchables: The Tories and the '45.* New York: Holmes and Meier, 1979.

———, ed. *Ideology and Conspiracy: Aspects of Jacobitism, 1689–1759.* Edinburgh: J. Donald, 1982.

———, ed. *The Stuart Court in Exile and the Jacobites.* Rio Grande, Ohio: Hambledon Press, 1995.

Dean, Winton. *Handel's Dramatic Oratorios and Masques.* Oxford: Clarendon Press, 1959.

——— *The New Grove Handel.* New York: W. W. Norton, 1983.

Deutsch, Helen. *Resemblance and Disgrace, Alexander Pope and the Deformation of Culture.* Cambridge: Harvard University Press, 1996.

Dickson, P. G. M. *The Financial Revolution in England.* London: Macmillan, 1967.

Dimock, Wai Chee, and Michael T. Gilmore, eds. *Rethinking Class: Literary Studies and Social Formations.* New York: Columbia University Press, 1994.

Dollimore, Jonathan. *Sexual Dissidence.* Oxford: Clarendon Press, 1991.

Donaldson, Ian. *The World Upside Down: Comedy from Jonson to Fielding.* Oxford: Clarendon Press, 1970.

Donaldson, William. *Jacobite Song: Political Myth and National Identity.* Aberdeen: Aberdeen University Press, 1988.

Doody, Margaret. *The Daring Muse: Augustan Poetry Reconsidered.* Cambridge: Cambridge University Press, 1985.

Dryden, John. *The Works of John Dryden.* Edited by H. T. Swedenberg Jr., Alan Roper, and Vinton Dearing. 20 vols. Berkeley and Los Angeles: University of California Press, 1956–2000.

Dugaw, Dianne, "'Critical Instants': Theatre Songs in the Age of Dryden and Purcell." *Eighteenth-Century Studies* 23 (1989–90): 157–75.

————. *Warrior Women and Popular Balladry, 1650–1850*. Cambridge: Cambridge University Press, 1989; reprint, Chicago: University of Chicago Press, 1996.

————, ed. *The Anglo-American Ballad*. New York: Garland, 1995.

D'Urfey, Thomas, ed. *Wit and Mirth: or Pills to Purge Melancholy*. 6 vols. London: W. Pearson for J. Tonson, 1719-20.

Earle, Peter. *The Making of the English Middle Class: Business, Society, and Family Life in London, 1660–1730*. Berkeley: University of California Press, 1989.

Ellis, William D. "Thomas D'Urfey, The Pope-Philips Quarrel, and 'The Shepherd's Week'." *PMLA* 74 (1959): 203–23.

Empson, William. *Some Versions of Pastoral*. London: Chatto and Windus, 1935.

Epstein, Julia, and Kristina Straub, eds. *Body Guards: The Cultural Politics of Gender Ambiguity*. New York: Routledge, 1991.

Epstein, William H., ed. *Contesting the Subject: Essays in the Postmodern Theory and Practice of Biography and Biographical Criticism*. Lafayette, Ind.: Purdue University Press, 1991.

Erskine-Hill, Howard. *Poetry of Opposition and Revolution: Dryden to Wordsworth*. Oxford: Clarendon Press, 1996.

————. *The Social Milieu of Alexander Pope: Lives, Example, and the Poetic Response*. New Haven: Yale University Press, 1975.

Faber, G. C., ed. *The Poetical Works of John Gay*. Oxford: Oxford University Press, 1926.

Fiske, Roger. *English Theatre Music in the Eighteenth Century*. Oxford: Oxford University Press, 1973.

Forrest, John. *Morris and Matachin: A Study in Comparative Choreography*. London: English Folk Dance and Song Society, 1984; Sheffield: Centre for English Cultural Tradition and Language, University of Sheffield, 1984.

Foucault, Michel. *The History of Sexuality*. Translated by Robert Hurley. 3 vols. New York: Vintage Books, 1980.

Friedman, Albert. *The Ballad Revival*. Chicago: University of Chicago Press, 1961.

Gay, John. *Achilles. An Opera*. London: J. Watts, 1733.

————. *The Beggar's Opera*. Edited by Edgar V. Roberts. Lincoln: University of Nebraska Press, 1969.

————. *Dramatic Works*. Edited by John Fuller. 2 vols. Oxford: Clarendon Press, 1983.

————. *The Letters of John Gay*. Edited by C. F. Burgess. Oxford: Clarendon Press, 1966.

————. *Poetry and Prose*. Edited by Vinton Dearing and Charles E. Beckwith. 2 vols. Oxford: Clarendon Press, 1974.

————. *Polly: An Opera, Being the Second Part of the Beggar's Opera*. London: Printed for the Author, 1729.

————. *Rural Sports*. London: J. Tonson, 1713.

Geertz, Clifford. *The Interpretation of Cultures*. New York: Basic Books, 1973; reprint, London: Fontana Press, 1993.

Gilman, Sander. *The Parodic Sermon in European Perspective: Aspects of Liturgical Parody from the Middle Ages to the Twentieth Century*. Wiesbaden: Steiner, 1974.

Gleason, Maud. *Making Men: Sophists and Self-Presentation in Ancient Rome*. Princeton: Princeton University Press, 1995.

Goldgar, Bertrand. *Walpole and the Wits: The Relation of Politics to Literature, 1722–1742*. Lincoln: University of Nebraska Press, 1976.

Green, Thomas, ed. *Folklore*. 2 vols. Santa Barbara: ABC-CLIO, 1997.

Greenberg, David. *The Construction of Homosexuality*. Chicago: University of Chicago Press, 1988.

Gregg, Edward. *The Protestant Succession in International Politics, 1710–16*. New York: Garland, 1986.

Guillory, John. *Cultural Capital: The Problem of Literary Canon Formation*. Chicago: University of Chicago Press, 1993.

Halperin, David, John Winkler, and Froma Zeitlin, eds. *Before Sexuality: The Construction of Erotic Experience in the Ancient Greek World*. Princeton: Princeton University Press, 1990.

Händel, Georg Friedrich. *Acis and Galatea*. Edited by Wolfram Windszus. Basel, London, and New York: Bärenreiter Kassel, 1991.

Harris, Ellen T. *Handel and the Pastoral Tradition*. Oxford: Oxford University Press, 1980.

Heaney, Mike. *An Introductory Bibliography on Morris Dancing*. London: English Folk Dance and Song Society, 1995.

Helm, Alex. *The English Mummers' Play*. Woodbridge, U.K.: Brewer; Totowa, N.J.: Rowman and Littlefield, 1980.

Hinton, Stephen, ed. *Kurt Weill: "The Threepenny Opera."* Cambridge: Cambridge University Press, 1990.

Hollander, John. *The Figure of Echo: A Mode of Allusion in Milton and After*. Berkeley: University of California Press, 1981.

Honan, Park. *Author's Lives: On Literary Biography and the Arts of Language*. New York: St. Martin's Press, 1990.

Howard, Robert. "Statius His Achilles, with Annotations." In *Poems*, 171–282. London: Herringman, 1660.

Hunt, Margaret. *The Middling Sort: Commerce, Gender, and the Family in England, 1680–1780*. Berkeley and Los Angeles: University of California Press, 1996.

Hutcheon, Linda. *Irony's Edge*. New York: Routledge, 1996.

———. *A Theory of Parody*. New York: Methuen, 1985.

Hutton, Ronald. *The Stations of the Sun: A History of the Ritual Year in Britain*. Oxford: Oxford University Press, 1996.

Irving, William. *John Gay, Favorite of the Wits*. Durham, N.C.: Duke University Press, 1940.

Jauss, Hans Robert. *Aesthetic Experience and Literary Hermeneutics*. Translated by Michael Shaw. Minneapolis: University of Minnesota Press, 1982.

———. *Toward an Aesthetic of Reception*. Translated by Timothy Bahti. Minneapolis: University of Minnesota Press, 1982.

Johnson, Samuel. *Lives of the English Poets*. Edited by George Birkbeck Hill. 3 vols. Oxford: Clarendon Press, 1905.

Judge, Roy. *May Day in England: An Introductory Bibliography*. London: Vaughan Williams Memorial Library and Folklore Society Library, 1996.

Keller, Kate Van Winkle, and Genevieve Shimer, eds. *The Playford Ball*. Chicago: A Cappella Books and The Country Dance and Song Society, 1990.

Kightly, Charles. *Customs and Ceremonies of Britain: An Encyclopedia of Living Traditions*. London: Thames and Hudson, 1986.

Klein, Julie. *John Gay: An Annotated Checklist of Criticism.* Troy, N.Y.: Whitson, 1974.

Kramnick, Isaac. *Bolingbroke and His Circle: The Politics of Nostalgia in the Age of Walpole.* Oxford: Oxford University Press, 1968.

Laws, G. Malcolm. *American Balladry from British Broadsides.* Philadelphia: American Folklore Society, 1957.

Langford, Paul. *The Excise Crisis: Society and Politics in the Age of Walpole.* Oxford: Clarendon Press, 1975.

———. *A Polite and Commercial People, England 1727–1783.* Oxford: Oxford University Press, 1989.

———. *Walpole and Robinocracy.* Cambridge: Chadwyck-Healey, 1986.

Leach, Maria, ed. *Funk and Wagnalls Standard Dictionary of Folklore, Mythology, and Legend.* 2 vols. New York: Funk and Wagnalls, 1949–50.

Leppert, Richard. *Music and Image: Domesticity, Ideology and Socio-cultural Formation in Eighteenth-Century England.* Cambridge: Cambridge University Press, 1988.

Lewis, Jayne. *Fables and the Foundations of Literate Culture in England, 1652–1740.* Cambridge: Cambridge University Press, 1996.

Lewis, Peter. "Gay's Burlesque Method in *The What D'Ye Call It*," *Durham University Journal* 59 (1967): 13–25.

———. "John Gay's 'Achilles': The Burlesque Element." *Ariel* 3 (1972): 17–28.

Lewis, Peter, and Nigel Wood, eds. *John Gay and the Scriblerians.* London: Vision Press; New York: St. Martin's Press, 1988.

Loraux, Nicole. *The Experience of Tiresias.* Translated by Paula Wissing. Princeton: Princeton University Press, 1995.

Mack, Maynard. *Alexander Pope, A Life.* New Haven: Yale University Press, 1985.

Maclean, Gerald, Donna Landry, and Joseph Ward, eds. *The Country and the City Revisited: England and the Politics of Culture, 1550–1850.* Cambridge: Cambridge University Press, 1999.

McKendrick, Neil, John Brewer, and J. H. Plumb. *The Birth of a Consumer Society: The Commercialization of Eighteenth-Century England.* London: Hutchinson, 1983.

Melling, Joseph, and Jonathan Barry, eds. *Culture in History: Production, Consumption and Values in Historical Perspective.* Exeter: University of Exeter Press, 1992.

Neal, Larry. *The Rise of Financial Capitalism.* Cambridge: Cambridge University Press, 1990.

Newton, Esther. *Mother Camp: Female Impersonators in America.* Englewood Cliffs, N.J.: Prentice-Hall, 1972.

Nicholson, Colin. *Writing and the Rise of Finance.* Cambridge: Cambridge University Press, 1994.

Noble, Yvonne. "Sex and Gender in Gay's 'Achilles'." In *John Gay and the Scriblerians,* edited by Peter Lewis and Nigel Wood. London: Vision Press; New York: St. Martin's Press, 1988.

———, ed. *Twentieth-Century Interpretations of "The Beggar's Opera."* Englewood Cliffs, N.J.: Prentice-Hall, 1975.

Nokes, David. *John Gay: A Profession of Friendship, A Critical Biography.* Oxford: Oxford University Press, 1995.

Patterson, Annabel. *Fables of Power: Aesopian Writing and Political History.* Durham, N.C.: Duke University Press, 1991.

————. *Pastoral and Ideology*. Berkeley: University of California Press, 1987.

Paulson, Ronald. *Popular and Polite Art in the Age of Hogarth and Fielding*. South Bend, Ind.: University of Notre Dame Press, 1979.

Perry, Ruth, "De-Familiarizing the Family; or, Writing Family History from Literary Sources." *Modern Language Quarterly* 55 (1994): 415–27.

————. "Incest as the Meaning of the Gothic Novel." *The Eighteenth Century: Theory and Interpretation* 39 (1998): 261–78.

Playford, John. *The Dancing Master: Vol. the First.* 18th ed.. London: Printed by W. Pearson and sold by Edward Midwinter, c. 1728.

————. *The Dancing Master: Vol. the Second.* 3d ed.. London: Printed by W. Pearson and sold by John Young, 1719.

————. *The Dancing Master . . . The Third Volume.* London: Printed by W. Pearson and sold by John Young, c. 1728.

Playford's English Dancing Master, 1651: A Facsimile Reprint. London: Schott and Co., 1957.

Pocock, J. G. A. *Virtue, Commerce, and History*. Cambridge: Cambridge University Press, 1985.

Preston, Cathy Lynn, ed. *Folklore, Literature, and Cultural Theory*. New York: Garland, 1995.

Rippon, Hugh. *Discovering English Folk Dance*, 3d ed. Princes Risborough, U.K.: Shire Publications, 1993.

Rogers, Pat. *Grub Street: Studies in a Subculture*. London: Methuen, 1972.

Rose, Margaret. *Parody: Ancient, Modern, and Post-Modern*. Cambridge: Cambridge University Press, 1993.

Rousseau, G. S. "Threshold and Explanation: The Social Anthropologist and the Critic of Eighteenth-Century Literature." *The Eighteenth Century: Theory and Interpretation* 22 (1981): 127–52.

Rousseau, G. S., and Roy Porter, eds. *Sexual Underworlds of the Enlightenment*. Chapel Hill: University of North Carolina Press, 1988.

Russell, Ian. "Parody and Performance." In *Everyday Culture: Popular Song and the Vernacular Milieu*, edited by Michael Pickering and Tony Green. Milton Keynes, U.K.: Open University Press, 1987.

Schultz, William. *Gay's Beggar's Opera: Its Content, History and Influence*. New Haven: Yale University Press, 1923.

Sedgwick, Eve Kosofsky. *Epistemology of the Closet*. Berkeley: University of California Press, 1990.

Senelick, Lawrence. "Mollies or Men of Mode?" *Journal of the History of Sexuality* 1 (1990): 33–67.

Sennett, Richard. *The Fall of Public Man*. New York: Knopf, 1977.

Shepard, Leslie. *The Broadside Ballad*. Hatboro, Pa.: Legacy Books, 1978.

Simpson, Claude. *The British Broadside Ballad and Its Music*. New Brunswick, N.J.: Rutgers University Press, 1966.

Snell, K. D. M. *Annals of the Labouring Poor: Social Change and Agrarian England, 1660–1900*. Cambridge: Cambridge University Press, 1985.

Sontag, Susan. *Against Interpretation*. New York: Farrar, Straus, and Giroux, 1966.

Spacks, Patricia Meyer. *John Gay*. New York: Twayne, 1965.

Stafford, Barbara. *Body Criticism: Imaging the Unseen in Enlightenment Art and Medicine*. Cambridge: MIT Press, 1993.

Stanton, Domna, ed. *Discourses of Sexuality*. Ann Arbor: University of Michigan Press, 1992.

Swaen, A. E. H. "The Airs and Tunes of John Gay's *Beggar's Opera.*" *Anglia* 43 (1919): 152–90.

————. "The Airs and Tunes of John Gay's *Polly.*" *Anglia* 60 (1936): 403–22.

Swift, Jonathan, and Alexander Pope, eds. *Miscellanies in Prose and Verse*. 4 vols. London: Benjamin Motte, 1727–32.

Thompson, E. P. *Customs in Common: Studies in Traditional Popular Culture*. New York: The New Press, 1991.

————. *The Making of the English Working Class*. London: Victor Gollancz, 1963.

————. *The Poverty of Theory and Other Essays*. New York: Monthly Review Press, 1978.

————. *Whigs and Hunters: The Origin of the Black Act*. New York: Pantheon Books, 1975.

Trowbridge, Hoyt. "Pope, Gay, and *The Shepherd's Week.*" *Modern Language Quarterly* 5 (1944): 79–88.

Trowell, Brian. "Acis, Galatea and Polyphemus: a '*serenata a tre voci*'." In *Music and Theatre: Essays in Honour of Winton Dean,* edited by Nigel Fortune. Cambridge: Cambridge University Press, 1987.

Trumbach, Randolph. *The Rise of the Egalitarian Family: Aristocratic Kinship and Domestic Relations in Eighteenth-Century England*. New York: Academic Press, 1978.

Virgil (Publius Vergilius Maro). *Eclogues, Georgics, Aeneid 1-6*. Translated by H. R. Fairclough. Loeb Classical Library. Cambridge: Harvard University Press, 1953.

Weber, William. *The Rise of the Musical Classics in Eighteenth-Century London*. Oxford: Clarendon Press, 1992.

Weinbrot, Howard. *Britannia's Issue: The Rise of British Literature from Dryden to Ossian*. Cambridge: Cambridge University Press, 1993.

Wheelock, Gretchen. *Haydn's Ingenious Jesting with Art*. New York: Schirmer, 1992.

Williams, Raymond. *The Country and the City*. Oxford: Oxford University Press, 1973.

————. *Keywords: A Vocabulary of Culture and Society*. London: Croom Helm, 1976.

Winkler, John. "Laying Down the Law: The Oversight of Men's Sexual Behavior in Classical Athens." In *Before Sexuality: The Construction of Erotic Experience in the Ancient Greek World,* edited by David Halperin, John Winkler, and Froma Zeitlin. Princeton: Princeton University Press, 1990.

Winkler, John, and Froma Zeitlin, eds. *Nothing to Do with Dionysos? Athenian Drama in its Social Context*. Princeton: Princeton University Press, 1990.

Winton Calhoun. *John Gay and the London Stage*. Lexington: University Press of Kentucky, 1993.

Index